842.109 F828
FRANK
MEDIEVAL FRENCH DRAMA

C

6.10

10-31-75

THE MEDIEVAL
FRENCH DRAMA

Oxford University Press, Amen House, London E.C.4

GLASGOW NEW YORK TORONTO MELBOURNE WELLINGTON
BOMBAY CALCUTTA MADRAS KARACHI KUALA LUMPUR
CAPE TOWN IBADAN NAIROBI ACCRA

FIRST PUBLISHED 1954
REPRINTED LITHOGRAPHICALLY IN GREAT BRITAIN
AT THE UNIVERSITY PRESS, OXFORD
FROM CORRECTED SHEETS OF THE FIRST EDITION
1960

THE MEDIEVAL
FRENCH DRAMA

By

GRACE FRANK

OXFORD
AT THE CLARENDON PRESS

For T. F.

PREFACE

THE histories of the medieval French drama that now exist are for the most part pioneering efforts and except for a few books designed for popular consumption none is of recent date. Since their publication further exploration of new and old territory has been undertaken and some discoveries of importance have resulted. Moreover, various parts of the terrain have been subjected to intensive investigations which have proved of value for a study of the whole. The present volume has been written in the hope that the time is now ripe not only for following in the footsteps of the pioneers and the recent explorers but also for further adventuring and a fresh attempt at synthesis.

In considering the liturgical plays I have restricted my discussion almost entirely to those produced in France, cognizant, of course, of the international nature of the church drama, but desiring to stress here not its development everywhere but only its significance for the history of the French theatre.

No attempt to define the limits of the term 'medieval' has been made. In 1548 Parisians were forbidden by Parliament to produce religious mystery plays in public, but these plays continued to be performed in the provinces, and interest in the lay theatre and in the farces, *sotties*, and moralities did not cease until much later. Many a Renaissance and seventeenth-century dramatist witnessed medieval plays and was subsequently influenced by what he had seen.

Actually the prodigious multiplication of plays of all kinds during the fifteenth and sixteenth centuries has rendered the task of analysing all of them impossible. As the Middle Ages waned before the dawning Renaissance, dramatic pieces pullulated and with certain notable exceptions they tended to become stereotyped. In this book, therefore, although many plays of the later Middle Ages are considered, it is the more significant earlier periods that have received most detailed attention.

A word should perhaps be said about the frequent practice, followed here, of separating the serious from the comic theatre. Probably taking their rise in a common source and certainly existing side by side in time, the comedies and religious plays may nevertheless be most conveniently considered apart because in the beginning at least, however much overlapping may have occurred later, their traditions and development, their authors and actors, usually belonged in different categories.

For many years the works of certain authorities like Petit de Julleville, Wilhelm Creizenach, Émile Roy, E. K. Chambers, Gustave Cohen, and Karl Young have been my constant companions. If on occasion I have unconsciously appropriated their opinions without sufficient acknowledgement, I hereby recognize my unrequitable indebtedness to these scholars and to all my other predecessors. Occasionally materials from my own publications have been incorporated and I wish to thank the editors and publishers of *Essays and Studies in Honor of Carleton Brown*, *Modern Language Notes*, the *Modern Language Review*, and *Publications of the Modern Language Association of America* for permission to use them. I should also like to express my gratitude to Professor A. Ewert for his keen criticism of this book, and to Louise Burroughs who, during its preparation, contributed generously of her time and wisdom.

Finally, it should be noted that the abbreviated references in the text to books, articles, and periodicals will be found expanded in the List of Books near the end of the volume, and that when chapters or pages in this volume itself are cited, the words 'above' or 'below' have been added to avoid ambiguity.

G. F.

BALTIMORE, MARYLAND
1953

PREFACE TO THE SECOND IMPRESSION

IN the second impression of this book a few factual and typographical errors have been corrected and some references have been added. The most important changes occur in chapter xii, occasioned by the appearance of the excellent study of the *Miracles de Notre Dame* by Rudolf Glutz.

CONTENTS

I

The Heritage

THAT the formal drama of ancient Rome disappeared and
that Western Europe in the Middle Ages re-created its
drama not from the dead debris of the extinct classical
theatre but from its own living faith, these are facts that usually
awaken surprise when they are encountered for the first time,
and occasionally the initial scepticism persists. Somehow the
posited hiatus between the ancient stage and that of the Middle
Ages seems inexplicable when one remembers the many manuscripts of Terence copied in medieval scriptoria, the copious
citations from these comedies in medieval literature, the Terentian plays of Hrotsvitha, and certain poetical works in Latin
that bear the title of *comoedia*; when one remembers too that
some of the ruins of ancient Roman theatres must have remained
recognizable and not wholly pillaged during the Middle Ages,
and that there are concrete references to both actors and acting
in widely read ancient authors whose allusions could hardly have
escaped the notice of medieval scholars.

Yet the classical Roman theatre had died before the fall of
Rome. The last writer of tragedies whose works are known to
have been produced is the consul, P. Pomponius Secundus, and
he lived in the time of Claudius. Most dramatic works even in
his day were destined for reading.[1] The only Roman comedy
(*togata*) mentioned as having been played during the Empire is
Afranius's *Incendium*, given at a festival sponsored by Nero, and
references to performances of the so-called *palliata*, or new
comedy of the Greeks, which are known to have been popular
in the Empire, are relatively scarce.[2] It may be that some old
plays were revamped, but all the evidence indicates that contributions to the stage in the late Empire took the form of farces
—the Atellan farce and the mime—and pantomimes, types of

---

[1] See Friedländer, *Darstellungen*, ii (1922), 119. The present chapter, now
slightly revised, first appeared in *Essays and Studies in Honor of Carleton Brown*,
pp. 62–78.

[2] Op. cit., pp. 119 n.

B

entertainment that respectively replaced the comedies and tragedies of the Republic.

The Atellan farce, like the modern Punch and Judy show or the Italian *commedia dell' arte*, revolved about certain fixed characters (usually four: Pappus, Dossennus, Bucco, and Maccus), and its development was necessarily limited.[1] The mimes, on the other hand, which long survived,[2] had a broader range of characters and wider interests; in fact, from the testimony of ancient writers, it is apparent that the word *mimus* covered performances of diverse forms, ranging from extemporaneous fooling of the lightest sort to more serious types of comedy that might, at least in part, be committed to writing.[3] The pantomimes consisted essentially of solo dances performed to the accompaniment of singing and musical instruments, and their charm, like that of the modern ballet, depended largely upon the union of dancing, music, and scenic effects. Such texts as formed the basis of the pantomimes have disappeared, although Lucan is said to have written fourteen *fabulae salticae*, and the themes of many others are known to us.[4] In any case no performances of farces, mimes, or pantomimes are heard of in the

[1] These characters appear frequently in art. Cf. the illustrations in Nicoll's *Masks, Mimes and Miracles*. Late references to the Atellan farces are cited there, pp. 138 ff.

[2] Reich, *Mimus*, pp. 778 ff., quotes passages from Salvianus of Marseilles who, in his *De Gubernatione Dei* (dated between 439 and 451), protests that the churches of Marseilles were neglected while the theatres were visited ('nos altaria spernimus et theatra honoramus'; cf. Migne, *PL*, liii. 116). There were performances of some sort in the sixth century at Rome, but, although the words of Isidore of Seville in the seventh century imply that the theatres of Spain were still standing then, he speaks of dramatic performances in the past tense (Reich, pp. 785 ff.). Nicoll, p. 146, thinks that Isidore 'knew of theatres only as disused buildings', but 'was personally acquainted with the activities of the *histriones* and the *mimi*'. That such entertainers performed plays is, however, uncertain. The terms came to be applied loosely during the Middle Ages to various types of entertainers.

[3] Plutarch, *Quaest. Conv.* viii. 8, 4, distinguishes between *paegnion* and *hypothesis* (παίγνιον; ὑπόθεσις). The Oxyrhynchus mime discussed by S. Sudhaus, in *Hermes*, xli (1906), 247 ff., was of course written down, but apparently served merely as the basis for further dialogue and action. Conceivably, a written scenario would be more important to certain types of mimes than to others. At least two mimographs of the second century A.D., Marullus and Lentulus, are referred to in such a way in the fourth and fifth centuries as to indicate that their works had been written down and preserved (Reich, p. 746).

[4] Ancient references to pantomimes and modern discussions of the subject are cited in Friedländer, ii. 125 ff., and by Nicoll, pp. 131 ff.

West after the sixth century, and no texts, so far as we know, survived into the Middle Ages. In fact, despite the Herculean efforts of Reich to establish a continuity of tradition between the ancient mime and medieval dramatic traditions, all records of any sort fail us in the West between the sixth and ninth centuries.[1]

In the East,[2] when the capital of the Empire was transferred to Constantinople, the theatre moved with it. There are records of at least four theatres in Constantinople, and, although no texts of plays performed in them survive, it is evident that the same types of entertainment—mime and pantomime—prevailed there as in the West. It has been suggested that Byzantium created a new drama through the influence of such performances upon the Church, but the suggestion lacks supporting evidence. The curious Greek play, *Christos Paschon*, variously dated from the fourth to the eleventh or twelfth centuries (it is more probably late than early), a mosaic composed of tesserae from the writings of Euripides and other classical Greek dramatists, would be an interesting link between the ancient and medieval theatres, were it not in all probability an example of a literary, closet drama. It seems more likely that in the East as in the West drama latent in the Church emerged independently and eventually created recognizable forms. At Byzantium the sermon appears to have been more potent than the ritual in this process; at any rate dramatic homilies are known there from as early as the fifth century. However, it is uncertain what relation, if any, exists between these and the scenario of a true Greek Passion play preserved in a Vatican manuscript of the thirteenth century.

[1] Reich, pp. 788–93, admits bridging this gap with pure hypothesis. Cf. also Allen, pp. 253 ff., who, however, in the process of destroying some of Reich's theories is apt to cast aside too much of the ancient evidence that has survived. The passages cited by Nicoll from the seventh and eighth centuries (pp. 145–6) are inconclusive for our purposes: Isidore's mention of *histriones* and *mimi* implies no knowledge of stage performances. That the different terms used to designate various types of entertainers (*scenici, histriones, mimi, saltatores*) lived on cannot, of course, be questioned. We are concerned here with the possible survival of the more formal types of dramatic performances, not with the existence of entertainers.

[2] La Piana, *Speculum*, xi (1936), 171–211, gives convenient references to useful, earlier works on the Byzantine theatre by Krumbacher (1897), himself (1912), V. Cottas (1931), and Vogt (1931). Cf. also J. S. Tunison, *Dramatic Traditions of the Dark Ages*, and M. S. De Vito, *Biblioteca della 'Rassegna'* (1938), 69–120.

Attempts to link the Western medieval stage with the Roman through Byzantium have met with little success. That Eastern and Western dramatic forms may have influenced one another in the Middle Ages exists as a possibility, though nothing more. An ultimate Byzantine origin has been suggested for the prophet play; similarities in the dramatic development of certain biblical scenes have been ascribed to direct contacts; the Greek Passion play of the Vatican manuscript is thought by some to have influenced Western plays on this subject, by others to be itself derived from occidental models. Indeed, how far in each of these cases we are dealing with fortuitous analogues, how far resemblances may be due to independent use of the same sources, and how far we are justified in positing direct borrowings remains conjectural.

With the disappearance of the ancient theatre, what became of those who had performed there?[1] We know that during the Empire the old word for actor, 'histrio', was gradually replaced by 'pantomimus', and that the profession itself, which had been amiably regarded in Cicero's day when the drama was in good standing and men like Roscius and Aesopus were highly esteemed, fell upon evil times with the corresponding decline in the quality of the performances.[2] Cicero considered Roscius worthy of being a senator, and Aesopus's son married into the Roman aristocracy, but during the last century of the Republic the censorial stigma of *infamia* rested upon actors who took part in lower-class performances (*ars ludicra*), and later in the Empire all actors were branded with civic disqualifications. As time went on, both *histrio* and *pantomimus* were associated with the *mimus*, and these terms were indiscriminately applied to various types of entertainers who, by the fifth and sixth centuries, included even jugglers, buffoons, dancers, musicians, and bear-tamers.

The Church quite consistently opposed the profession and in various decrees forbade actors and actresses to become Christians or to marry Christians unless they abandoned their calling. The Christian emperors, to be sure, did not suppress the spectacles, merely preventing their performance on Sundays and

---

[1] On the medieval entertainer see Chambers, I, chap. ii; Faral, *Jongleurs*; Allen, chap. xiii. On the mime Vitalis see Faral, *Mimes*, p. xii.

[2] See T. Frank, 'The Status of Actors at Rome', *Class. Phil.* xxvi (1931), 11 ff.

holy days, but the popes were irreconcilable and forbade them at all times.[1]

Did the professional entertainer disappear? Both *mimus* and *pantomimus* must have lost their professions when the theatres fell, and it is possible that those of them who could not turn to some other calling used their talents for a time in performances of an inferior order. The word 'mimus' in any case continues to be used in the general sense of entertainer; up to the ninth century it is the regular term applied to the *jongleur* and thereafter is one of several terms used to denote him.

Chambers believes that the *mimus* somehow merged with the Germanic entertainers—the scops, gleemen, and minstrels—to produce the jongleur, an idea vigorously opposed by P. S. Allen who contends that, although some sort of entertainer survived, he was neither a *mimus*, i.e. a player in mimes, nor a scop, i.e. a creative artist.[2] There seems to be some confusion of definitions involved in this argument, due perhaps to the modern use of the term 'jongleur' to denote both performer and composer and especially to Allen's insistence—plausible in itself, but beside the point here—that the creative impulses of the Middle Ages emanated from monks and churchmen. Whether or not we should speak of 'merging', a none too happy conception, all we need assume, I think, is that there were entertainers of some sort during the Dark Ages: men sang songs, told tales, performed tricks, imitated each other, travestied the world and its ways in various fashions. These men, however, did not preserve the continuity of the formal theatre of ancient Rome or create the formal theatre of the Middle Ages; they merely gave evidence in some of their exhibitions of the perpetuity of the dramatic instinct.

Manuscripts of the Terentian and Plautine comedies, to be sure, remained in existence. Indeed the scriptoria of France, especially those of Corbie, Fleury, Rheims, and Limoges, produced many of our early manuscripts of Terence, and other Terentian manuscripts are localized less specifically as having been written in Touraine and the south of France.[3] Only eight

---

[1] Cf. Henshaw, *Medievalia et Humanistica*, vii (1952), 3–17.

[2] Chambers, p. 25; Allen, pp. 257 ff.

[3] Jones and Morey, *Miniatures of the Manuscripts of Terence*.

of the twenty comedies now ascribed to Plautus were generally known before the fifteenth century (although the other twelve were copied at least three times during the eleventh and twelfth centuries), and references to his works are relatively scarce in France. Yet the Palatine recension of Plautus, according to Traube,[1] goes back to Orléans, and two Frenchmen of the middle of the ninth century, Helperic of Auxerre and Smaragdus of Saint Mihiel, cite him.[2] However, it is evident from the testimony of countless medieval writers[3] that the works of Terence and Plautus were not connected in their minds with any idea of the impersonation of actors speaking upon a stage, that the very meaning of the word 'drama' was misunderstood, and that the terms 'comedy' and 'tragedy' were regularly misapplied throughout the Middle Ages to narrative and even to lyrical forms of literature, 'comedy' being reserved primarily for works ending happily and 'tragedy' for those with an unhappy conclusion.[4]

Servius seems to have been responsible, in part at least, for this misconception. Commenting on Vergil's third Eclogue, he points out its dramatic character, stating that there are three styles of writing, one in which the poet speaks alone; another 'dramaticum, in quo nusquam poeta loquitur, ut est in comoediis et tragoediis; tertium, mixtum'.[5] He says that all three are represented in the Bucolics, and places the first and third eclogues in the second, or 'dramatic' category. Diomedes, another writer of the second half of the fourth century, follows Servius in general, but more definitely classes certain eclogues with tragedies and comedies : 'dramaticon est vel activum in quo

---

[1] *Vorlesungen u. Abhandlungen*, iii. 68.

[2] Manitius, i. 448 and 465.

[3] For medieval references see Manitius's indexes of the three volumes, s.v. *Terenz* and *Plautus*. It must be remembered, however, that many medieval citations of 'Plautus' refer to the *Querolus*, a 'continuation' of the *Aulularia*, which was mistakenly attributed to Plautus in the Middle Ages. Havet in his edition of the *Querolus* (pp. 2–4) assigns it without much evidence to Gaul and dates it *c*. 420–30. Others have placed it in the third or fourth century.

[4] Comedy was further defined as concerned with lowly folk and written in ordinary language, whereas tragedy had to do with the mighty and was written in lofty style. For instance, Placidus defines *comoedia* as 'quae res privatorum et humilium personarum comprehendit, non tam alto ut tragoedia stilo, sed mediocri et dulci'. Cf. Cloetta, *Beiträge*, i. 14 ff.; Creizenach, i. 9 ff.; Chambers, ii. 208 ff.

[5] *Servii Gram. in Virg. Bucolica Com.*, ed. Thilo and Hagen, 1887, iii. 29.

personae agunt solae sine ullius poetae interlocutione, ut se habent tragicae et comicae fabulae; quo genere scripta est prima bucolicon et ea cuius initium est "quo te, Moeri, pedes?"' (that is, *Ec.* ix).[1] Isidore of Seville[2] copies Servius almost literally; Bede[3] follows Diomedes closely, but adds to Diomedes' examples of 'drama' the Song of Songs, saying: 'Quo apud nos genere Cantica canticorum scripta sunt, ubi vox alternans Christi, et ecclesiae, tametsi non hoc interloquente scriptore manifeste reperitur.'

After the conception of drama as allied to the stage had been lost, the terms 'comedy' and 'tragedy' readily became dissociated from the idea of drama. Not only narrative and lyric works containing much dialogue, but others also were thus mislabelled. Boethius, who employed the word 'tragedy' in his *Consolatio* in the general sense of tragic happening, unwittingly led his commentator, Notker, to define *tragoedia* as *luctuosa carmina*,[4] and medieval glossaries regularly define both terms without regard to any dramatic connotations.[5] The non-dramatic works both of antiquity and of contemporaneous writers came to be classified as 'comedies' and 'tragedies' on the basis of their style and contents alone: Horace, Persius, and Juvenal wrote *comoediae*, whereas Lucan's *Pharsalia* and Dracontius's epic *Orestes* (of the end of the fifth century) are called *tragoediae*. Dante speaks of comedy as a kind of poetic narrative ('est comoedia genus quoddam poeticae narrationis'), and, reflecting the tradition of his time, he gives this title to his great work because it begins amid troublesome and bitter things, ends happily in paradise, and is written in the vulgar tongue.

Several factors apparently contributed in some measure to the misconceptions that became current. In the first place it was

---

[1] *Art. Gram.*, Lib. III, ed. H. Keil, *Gram. lat.* i. 482.

[2] *Etymol.* viii. 7 in *PL*, lxxxii. 309.

[3] *De Arte Metrica*, § 25, ed. Giles, vi. 78.

[4] Cf. Isidore, *Etymol.* xviii. 45, De tragoedis (*PL*, lxxxii. 658): 'tragoedi sunt qui antiqua gesta atque facinora sceleratorum regum luctuoso carmine, spectante populo, concinebant.'

[5] In the lexicons of the thirteenth and fourteenth centuries published by Roques, *comedia* is glossed by *chançon de poète*, *comicus* by *poète*, *hystrio* by *glouton vel guglour*, *scenices* by *foles fames*, &c. Cf. pp. 128, 12, 287, 352, 468. On the meanings of *theatrum*, *scena*, *orchestra*, *spectaculum*, and the like see M. H. Marshall, *Symposium*, iv (1950), 1 ff. and 366 ff.

quite generally thought that the plays of Terence had been recited in ancient times by the author himself or by a *recitator*
reading from a pulpit, while pantomimists stood below and
acted out the scenes. Livy's description of the beginnings of the
drama at Rome (vii. 2, followed in part by Valerius Maximus,
ii. 4), with its references to players from Etruria who danced to
the strains of the flute, its mention of actors who used singers
to accompany their gesticulations, and its anecdote about Livius
Andronicus who, after overstraining his voice, was obliged to
call upon a boy to sing the monody while he himself acted his
role in silence, probably had something to do with medieval
ideas about how the classical drama was performed. It may well
be also that writers like Isidore of Seville and vague legends
about the mimes and pantomimes of the Empire played some
part in the formation of the misconceptions. Isidore, for example, says of the ancient orchestra: 'orchestra autem pulpitum
erat scenae, ubi saltator agere posset, aut duo inter se disputare.'[1]
It seems possible, too, that the early confusion of the editor,
Calliopius, whose recension of Terence is now dated in the fifth
century,[2] with a reader or reciter of Terence's works fortified
the erroneous notions current. The Calliopian recension is
usually signed *Ego Calliopius recensui*, and it has been plausibly
suggested that a manuscript abbreviation of *recensui* (rec), resolved as *recitavi*, was originally responsible for the confusion.[3]
In any case, early commentators of Terence[4] and early miniaturists[5] indicate Calliopius in the role of narrator.

---

[1] *PL*, lxxxii. 658.

[2] See J. D. Craig, *Ancient Editions of Terence*, and Jones and Morey,
op. cit.

[3] Creizenach, p. 6; cf. Jahn, *Berichte über d. Ver. d. k. sächsischen Ges. d. Wiss.*
(Leipzig, iii. 1851), 362 f.

[4] Cloetta, *Beiträge*, i, p. 35; Creizenach, p. 6; J. P. Jacobsen, *Essai*, p. 4. According to one recension, Eugraphius (who probably lived in the fifth or sixth
century) in his comment to the ending of Terence's *Andria* wrote: 'verba sunt
Calliopii eius recitatoris, qui dum fabulam terminasset, elevabat auleam scaenae,
et alloquebatur populum "vos valete", "vos plaudite", sive "favete".' Cf.
Donatus, ed. Wessner (Teubner, 1908), iii. 85.

[5] Three early Terence manuscripts from the south and west of France—the
earliest of the tenth century—have miniatures picturing Calliopius; one shows
him enthroned in the centre, reading to the assembled Romans, with Terence at
his right, and the rivals (*adversarii*) of Terence at his left. Cf. Jones and Morey,
i. 165, and plates 10, 166, 329. A later miniature is in P. Lacroix, *Sciences et lettres
au moyen âge* (1877), p. 534.

Yet Terence, however misunderstood, was very much alive throughout the Middle Ages; not Terence the writer of comedies, but Terence the sage who took his place among the philosophers.[1] From Charlemagne's time on his works served as school-books. Few read him as poetry, to be sure—his metres seem to have been ignored or misunderstood—but his neat phrases, which were liked for their compactness and quotability, appear and reappear in countless *florilegia*. Moreover, although his influence upon the medieval drama cannot be posited, it was exercised upon various works of potential dramatic import.

A curious fragment of unknown origin, date, and purpose, which has survived in a unique manuscript of the late tenth or early eleventh century, presents in its scant sixty-four lines a dialogue between Terence and a Persona Delusoris (probably Scoffer here).[2] The Persona Delusoris informs the ancient poet that he has little use for his work; he doesn't know whether it is prose or poetry; and what's the good of it anyway? 'You are old and outworn; I am new and fertile', he boasts. Terence asks him whether he in his vaunted youth has produced anything comparable, upon which the Delusor in a kind of aside admits that the old poet has the best of the argument, but says that he intends to maintain the contrary. The conversation continues in similar vein until presently the fragment breaks off, but it would appear that in the end Terence triumphed. Some have conjectured that this poem served as a prologue to a Terentian recitation, others that it may be merely a clerkly exercise written for the amusement of the author and his friends; Allen believes it a young clerk's jest, the parody of some monastic mind on the tendency to substitute nonsense for art. Is it not rather a defence of Terence penned by a conservative master to warn the young that their desire for innovation is understood, but that the old classics still have their uses? However this may be, the fragment has no parallel and has exerted no traceable influence.

---

[1] References to Terence may be found in J. D. Craig, Jones and Morey, Manitius's indexes, op. cit.

[2] Chambers, ii. 326; the translation in Allen, *Romanesque Lyric*, p. 244, is free and somewhat misleading.

Upon Hrotsvitha,[1] the famous Benedictine nun of Gandersheim who lived in the tenth century, Terence made so fruitful an impression that she wrote what she called a 'dramatica series', i.e. six dramatic pieces in prose, claiming Terence as her model, though carefully explaining that while his subjects too often involve the frailty of women, hers turn on the heroic adherence of saintly women to their vows of chastity. In the various prefaces to her works Hrotsvitha reveals herself as an eager, vivid, original woman, cognizant of her own ability, who, though she realizes the limitations imposed upon her by reason of her sex and her life in a convent, is none the less determined not to waste the gifts that God has bestowed upon her. Perhaps she felt the quickening effects of the revival of culture in the Saxony of her day, for Gerberga, her abbess at Gandersheim, was a niece of that Otto the Great who attempted to re-establish the Empire of Charlemagne and all it symbolized. In any case, Hrotsvitha's dramatic pieces show that she was bound by no precedent, that her imagination was likewise untrammelled, and that her feeling for situation, both material and psychological, could be sensitive and sure.

Whether these pieces, written in dialogue and frequently swift of action, were designed for recitation, representation, or for private reading, we do not know, though the author's introductions to them suggest the last. They turn upon such themes as the conversion of Thais, the courtesan, rescued from her wicked life and led to enter a nunnery by a hermit who approaches her in the guise of a lover (*Pafnutius*), the guilty love of a pagan for a consecrated virgin (*Gallicanus*), or for a holy Christian woman vowed to chastity (*Calimachus*). Medieval in spirit, the product of the cultural environment of a convent, not unrelated in subject-matter to certain saints' lives, these pieces, for all their holiness of purpose, are nevertheless so romantic

---

[1] Hrotsvitha's works have been edited by Winterfeld (1902) and Strecker (2nd ed. 1930). An English translation was made of the plays by Christopher St. John for the Medieval Library (ed. Gollancz) in 1923. Cf. also G. R. Coffman, *MP*, xxii (1925), 239 ff.; Manitius, iii (1931), 1064; Young, i. 543; Zeydel, *MLN*, lix (1944), 382–5. The relative paucity of the manuscripts of Hrotsvitha and the fact that none has come to light outside of Central Europe suggest a restricted public for her works, though Zeydel believes that they may have been better known than is usually assumed.

in the exuberance of their expressions, the erotic overtones in them at times become so insistent, that it is difficult to conceive of their actual performance before a conventual audience even in a day of intellectual renascence. Indeed Hrotsvitha herself refers to her blushes in writing of themes 'not fit for our hearing'.

It has been suggested that the St. Nicholas plays later produced in Germany and elsewhere came out of a similar environment, that perhaps seventy-five years after Hrotsvitha's time an imaginative man reading her dialogues and knowing the liturgical drama of his own day may have been inspired thereby to honour some special saint by writing the first of our miracle plays. However, the step from narrative saints' lives to miracle plays is so short that it hardly seems necessary to assume the interposition of the nun of Gandersheim, and the influence of her remarkable achievement upon the medieval stage, if any, remains entirely conjectural.

Other works that have been assumed by various scholars to have had some formative effect upon the medieval theatre are the so-called 'elegiac comedies'.[1] These are Latin poems written in elegiac verse which, although partly narrative and partly dialogue, sometimes refer to themselves, both in the manuscripts and in the texts, as *comoediae*. Their themes and characters derive in some instances from classical authors, in others from medieval anecdotes. A number of them have been connected with a region bounded by Orléans, Blois, Vendôme, and Chartres—that is, roughly, with a region in which many manuscripts of Terence were copied and in which the liturgical drama flourished—but, since none of them is dated earlier than the twelfth century and some may belong to the thirteenth, the surviving examples at any rate are all posterior to our earliest liturgical plays.

Among the best known of these works are two attributed to

---

[1] On these 'comedies' see Cloetta, *Beiträge*; Chambers, ii. 213; Creizenach, i. 20; Faral, *Rom.* l (1924), 321; Manitius, iii (1931), 1015 ff. They are conveniently printed in Cohen, *'Comédie' latine*, with important individual prefaces (sometimes contradicting the general introduction) to the various poems. Cf. also W. B. Sedgwick, 'Notes, chiefly textual, on Cohen's *La "com." lat.*', in *Bulletin Du Cange*, viii (1933), 164, and H. Hagendahl, 'La "com." lat. au xiie s. et ses modèles antiques', *ΔΡΑΓΜΑ Martino P. Nilsson dedicatum* (Lund, 1939), p. 222.

Vitalis of Blois, the *Geta* and the *Aulularia*, both probably of the twelfth century. The *Geta* must have been immensely popular in its own day, for it was used as a school-book and made the names of Geta and his fellow servant, Birria, proverbial in the Middle Ages. It survives in over forty manuscripts. Its theme (probably acquired indirectly) is that of Plautus's *Amphitruo*, the perennially pungent theme of the attempt of Jupiter and his servant (Geta) to seduce Amphitruo's wife. Some lively satire on the sophistries of pseudo-logicians must have evoked smiles from students of the trivium. (For example, the real Geta upon meeting his double, Archas [i.e. Mercury], remarks : 'All that exists is one, but I who speak am not one. Ergo, Geta is nothing.' And later, to himself : 'Perish dialectic by which I am so completely destroyed! Now I am learned, but learning is harmful. When Geta learned logic, he ceased to exist.') The *Aulularia*, derived not from the Plautine original but from the *Querolus*, tells again of the miser whose story is familiar to modern audiences from Molière's *L'Avare*. Nearly if not quite as famous as the *Geta* was the poem called *Pamphilus* that concerns itself with the manner in which the hero, helped by an old *entremetteuse*, overcomes the none too active resistance of the girl he loves.

The question naturally arises : how were these elegiac comedies performed, if performed at all? Cloetta believes them to have been designed for the half-dramatic recitation of minstrels; Faral regards them as a transitional form between Latin comedy and medieval farce. Chambers calls them school pieces, and Cohen suggests the possibility of recitations in public by one or more persons, or of representations by scholars before their comrades with the assistance of a *meneur de jeu*, perhaps their professor of rhetoric.

A few manuscripts of these pieces seem to show by their rubrics that the poems were intended for representation, and certain passages in the texts would doubtless be enlivened if the full implications of their humorous situations were made manifest by some sort of action. In most of the poems, however, narrative and dialogue are so tightly interwoven (each sharing parts of verses with the other and both needing to be spoken if the metrical scheme is to be observed) that it is difficult to see how such pieces could have been performed as plays. Moreover, in many of them the narrative portions are inordinately developed, the individual speeches are excessively long, and there is nothing to suggest dramatic action. One may reasonably conclude, I think, that these Latin *comoediae* belong to the learned traditions of the Middle Ages, that they were written to be read or studied in schools, and that their vivacious form and content made some few of them adaptable for recitation—perhaps for presentation—by ambitious masters and their pupils. Those few manuscripts (of the *Geta*, *Aulularia*, and *Babio*) in which the names of the suppositious speakers and a few stage-directions have been added—apparently in glosses later than the texts—would seem to preserve versions of the poems that were thus adapted. Most of the manuscripts, however, contain no such rubrics, and one must not be misled by modern editors who frequently supply them.

Similar to the elegiac comedies, closely related to them and products of the same environment, are the so-called 'Horatian comedies'.[1] These are monologues that narrate in the first person the experiences of a single speaker: how he used trickery to gain his love, how he instigated a song contest among three girls and awarded a prize, together with himself, to the fairest, &c. Neither the elegiac nor the Horatian comedies, potential progenitors of the drama though they were, seem to have exercised any influence upon the theatre. Cohen posits likenesses between the *Babio*, the *Garçon et l'Aveugle*, a fifteenth-century Resurrection play, *Pathelin*, and Molière's *Les Fourberies de Scapin*, or again between the *Babio*, the *Baucis et Traso*, and Molière's *L'Étourdi* (op. cit. I. xiii–xiv), but the similarities suggested are too few, too tenuous, and too readily explainable by the universality of their themes to detain us. These Latin pieces are obviously not dramatic in intention, not written to be spoken and acted before an audience by actors suitably equipped to give visible embodiment to their roles. They merely testify to the narrow borderline that separated narrative from dramatic literature in the Middle Ages and to the ease with which, once the impulse had come from elsewhere, narrative poetry could be turned into drama.

[1] As Dain well says (in Cohen, op. cit. ii. 115, n. 1), they form a separate genre only for modern scholars.

It has occasionally been suggested that vestiges of the ancient buildings in which classical plays had been performed must have preserved for posterity some tradition as to the methods of their performance.[1] We hear indeed of 'an extraordinary number of theatres' in Gaul in the second century.[2] Sidonius Apollinaris described the theatre as still flourishing at Narbonne *c*. 460.[3] We also learn of mimes, pantomimes, and acrobats at Narbonne *c*. 470. Among the Roman theatres of Gaul that survived, at least in part, well into the Middle Ages were those of Arles, Autun, Narbonne, Orange, and Paris. But it is clear that the original functions of both theatres and amphitheatres were early lost to memory. The remains of the theatre at Arles came to be known as the *tour de Roland*. Many amphitheatres were used as forts, some passing into the hands of the Arabic invaders. Later these were dismantled (as at Fréjus where, in the tenth century, the stones of the ancient amphitheatre were used in building a church), or were occupied by military orders (as at Nîmes where the amphitheatre was thus occupied till the fourteenth century), or were adopted for tourneys, dwelling-houses, &c. The amphitheatres of Bordeaux and Poitiers both received the name 'Palais Gallienne'.[4]

When plays were no longer performed in the theatre, when the amphitheatres were abandoned, when the Church began linking theatre, circus, and amphitheatre together as works of the devil and suggesting that Christians who desired *spectacula* would find them at hand in the Return of the Lord and the Day of Judgement,[5] when alien invaders introduced new customs and frequent battles obliterated old ones, when the buildings remaining unrazed were devoted to novel functions and received strange names, it is perhaps not so difficult to understand why the ruined remnants of the ancient theatres and amphitheatres failed to enlighten later generations as to their original purposes.

[1] See Friedländer, iv (1921 ed.), 250–3 (cf. also pp. 218 ff. and 223 ff.).

[2] A. Grenier in T. Frank, *An Economic Survey of Ancient Rome*, iii (1937), 540.

[3] *Carmina*, xxiii. 263; cf. S. Dill, *Roman Society in the Last Century of the Western Empire*, p. 117; Friedländer, op. cit. iv. 251, and Chambers, i. 19.

[4] On the interpretation of certain Latin theatrical terms used in the twelfth and thirteenth centuries see R. S. Loomis and G. Cohen, *Speculum*, xx (1945), 92; D. Bigongiari, *RR*, xxxvii (1946), 201; M. H. Marshall, *Symposium*, iv (1950), 374.

[5] Tertullian, *De Spectaculis*, written *c*. A.D. 200. Cf. Loeb Library edition (1931), chs. xxix–xxx.

But what of classical authors who refer in no uncertain terms to the ancient theatres? What of Cicero's *De Oratore* with its references to Roscius (iii. 26, 102), his *Pro Sestio* with its descriptions of acting (lv–lvii), his *De Officiis* which implies that some actors excel in voice, others by their skill in acting, and that they choose their roles accordingly (i. 114)—and so on?[1] Unfortunately, of the many early medieval authors who reveal a knowledge of Cicero, none, so far as I know, happens to mention any of the passages that refer to the theatre. This is true, for instance, of Isidore of Seville. Most of these men, like the West Frank Hadoard,[2] who was the most widely read student of Cicero of the ninth century and who generously excerpted his works, care chiefly for the moral teachings of antiquity. Others, like Lupus of Ferrières[3] (as well as Hadoard), reveal that they possessed only mutilated copies of Cicero, or that, like Alcuin, they cite a number of his works only at second hand.[4] The socalled commentary on Terence, which went by the name of Donatus in the Middle Ages, especially the section attributed to Evanthius,[5] would have proved enlightening, if read intelligently. Unfortunately, that section seems to have been either neglected or misunderstood.

It is evident, however, that here and there students of the classics existed who reconstructed from their reading a fair idea of what the ancient theatre had been like. Thus, John of Salisbury (*c.* 1115–80), who knew Cicero well, betrays such knowledge in his *Polycraticus* when he writes:

And there were actors who by bodily gesture, by the art of words and by modulation of the voice publicly represented tales true and feigned. You find them in Plautus and Menander and by them the art of our Terence became known. After the comic and tragic poets disappeared, when frivolity conquered all, their clients, the comedians and tragedians, were driven away.[6]

[1] See references in T. Frank, 'The Decline of Roman Tragedy', *Class. Journ.* xii (1916), 177–8, and in Merguet's lexicon to Cicero's works, s.v. *histrio, mimus, theatrum*, &c.

[2] Cf. Paul Schwenke's edition of Hadoard in *Philologus, Supplementband*, v (1889), 399 ff., and in general on Cicero's 'Fortlebung' see Manitius, i. 478 ff., and the indexes, s.v. *Cicero*.

[3] Manitius, i. 486; C. H. Beeson, *Lupus of Ferrières* (Cambridge, 1930), esp. p. 7 on defective manuscripts.   [4] Schwenke, pp. 404–6.

[5] Ed. P. Wessner (Teubner, 1902).   [6] Lib. I, cap. viii in *PL*, cxcix. 405.

So, too, Honorius of Autun:[1] 'sciendum quod hi qui tragoedias in theatris recitabant, actus pugnantium gestibus populo repraesentabant.'

But this knowledge seems to have remained sterile so far as any attempt to reproduce the ancient type of theatre was concerned. Nor, except in three instances, have we any evidence that scholars equated the classical theatre with the contemporary liturgical plays (which in the manuscripts are variously called *officium, ordo, processio, ludus, repraesentatio, historia, similitudo, miraculum, misterium*).[2] These three quite different instances are therefore the more significant. One occurs in a commentary on Horace's *Ars Poetica*, a scholium preserved in a manuscript of the eleventh or twelfth century. In explaining Horace's statement that movement on the stage can be accomplished by action or by narration of action, the scholiast says that in the Feast of Herod both action and narration appear. A second instance occurs in a prophet play of 1204 from Riga. This play is surprisingly referred to as a 'ludus prophetarum ordinatissimus, quem Latini Comoediam vocant'. The third appears in a late twelfth-century commentary of Arnulfus of Orléans on Ovid's *Fasti* (i. 47): 'Romani singulis annis conveniebant in Martium Campum et ibi representabant illam interfectionem a Silla [apparently an imaginary slaughter of Marians by Sullans] olim factam, sicut nos modo representamus interfectionem innocentum.'[3]

Sporadic knowledge of the ancient theatre in the Middle Ages can be posited, therefore, but knowledge productive of any continuity of tradition cannot. Before the age of printing, when manuscripts were rare and costly, literary works had to depend largely upon the human voice to gain an audience. Poets recited their verses or others did this for them; the epics and romances of the Middle Ages were chanted, declaimed, or read aloud. In

---

[1] In Young, i. 83. Honorius flourished in the first half of the twelfth century. Others with some understanding of the ancient theatre were Boethius, Gilbert of La Porrée, Hildebert of Le Mans, Gerald of Wales, and Alexander Neckam. On these see Marshall, *Symposium*, iv (1950), 374, and *Speculum*, xxv (1950), 471.

[2] Cf. Young, ii. 407 ff.

[3] The first two instances are cited by Creizenach, i. 7. Cf. Young, ii. 542. For the third, and its interpretation, I am indebted to Jean Holzworth's Bryn Mawr dissertation, *An Unpublished Commentary on Ovid's 'Fasti' by Arnulfus of Orléans*.

many instances attempts at impersonation, with appropriate gestures and voice-changes, must have enhanced the recital of non-dramatic works. But one must distinguish clearly between such non-dramatic works—however dramatically presented—and true drama, written for production by a group of actors who would incarnate their roles, use suitable speech, mimetic action, and vestments, and play their parts to the accompaniment of pertinent scenic effects. Whatever the Middle Ages knew or did not know about the comedies and tragedies of antiquity, they fashioned their own serious drama, not from the ashes of the past, but from the warmth of their faith and the desire to give it a visible, dynamic expression.

II

Liturgical Easter Plays

A T a time when literary works were written to be heard rather than read, potential drama, as has been suggested, resided in various non-dramatic forms. Not only monologues and dialogues, but narrative and even lyrical poems could be made 'dramatic' by clever performers; these works obviously might have developed into true drama, and in some instances they actually did so, but this was only after the initial impulse had emanated from another source.[1]

For drama, with its distinguishing characteristics of dialogue, impersonation, action and scenic effects, was also latent in that nucleus of all medieval life, the Church—in its sermons, in its commemorative ceremonies and processions, in the emotional spirit associated with worship, in the Mass itself.[2] Each of these elements actually made important contributions to the medieval stage, but it is primarily to one of them, the liturgy of the Mass, that we owe the beginnings of the formal drama of the Middle Ages. Strangely enough, the Mass contained within itself almost from the beginning many of the essential elements of those *spectacula* against which the Church thundered. Its singing was antiphonal; its readings of the Gospel narrative frequently introduced voice-changes to indicate changes of speaker; its vestments, music, and decorations shifted from solemn to festive with the seasons; it was performed by special groups before an audience to the accompaniment of chanting, genuflexions, and other gestures; its symbolism and emotional effect were cumulative and climactic. When in the second century Tertullian suggested that Christians who desired *spectacula* should find them in their faith, he doubtless recognized the potent dramatic rivalry of the substitute he proffered.

[1] Cf. Creizenach, i. 383 ff.

[2] Although Young, i. 85, denies that the Mass gave rise directly to the drama, he admits that the dramatic features of the service 'may have contributed suggestions as to the possibility of inventing drama, and may indirectly have encouraged it'.

Beginning in the reign of Charlemagne (768–814) and continuing in the tenth century a new impulse was given to the intellectual, artistic, and religious life of France. The literary renascence furthered by scholars of the Palace School evoked corresponding activity in many of the major and minor arts: manuscripts began to be more brilliantly illuminated; the technique of carving in ivory received a new finish and finesse; churches were redecorated and church services embellished.[1] At this time, too, the liturgy began to be interpreted as symbolically commemorative of the life of Christ, an interpretation that provided a special incentive to dramatic representation and lyrical adornment. From the earliest days of Christianity symbolism had inspired creative exegesis, in the works of the Fathers as on the walls of the catacombs. The desire that the faithful should see, hear, and understand the truths of religion pervades nearly every artistic impulse of the Middle Ages. This desire found one expression in the enrichment of the church service by the practice of troping, a practice destined to provide the fruitful kernel from which issued the earliest text of a liturgical play.[2]

It used to be supposed that the embellishment of the service by an elaborate series of musical notes called *sequelae*, sung upon the final *a* of the *Alleluia* at the end of the Gradual, gave rise in the ninth century at St. Gall to verbal interpolations in the liturgy, written to accompany and help memorize these difficult musical sequences. The story goes that about 860 an unknown monk of Jumièges, driven from his abbey when the Normans devastated it, appeared one day at the abbey of St. Gall. To the surprise of the monks there, his antiphonary showed words attached to the musical flourishes accompanying the final *a* of the *Alleluia*. 'As much as I was delighted by the sight of them', writes Notker Balbulus of St. Gall, 'just as much was I displeased by their taste. Nevertheless I began at once to write in imitation of them.' Notker here admits his indebtedness to French sources, and it is generally held today that sequences

[1] See H. O. Taylor, i, chap. i, Hinks, *Carolingian Art*, and Morey, *Mediaeval Art*, pp. 195 ff. for general background. See also Hildburgh, *Archaeologia*, xciii (1949), 51–101.

[2] See Muller, *ZRP*, xliv (1924), 544 ff.; Young, i. 179 ff. For attempts to explain the apparent discrepancy between the rise of troping and the efforts of the Carolingians to purify the liturgy see Young, i. 181–2.

with words (known as *proses* or simply as *sequences*) originated in the eighth or early ninth century in France, where their composition owed more to religious emotion and the spirit of the age than to the need for a mnemonic device.[1]

Be that as it may, the procedure of decorating the *Alleluia* with independent poems freely detachable from the true liturgy, whether written to pre-existing music or not (and the word *sequence* seems originally to have been a purely musical term), is an innovation associated with the general custom, probably contemporaneous and more important for our purposes, of *troping* various portions of the liturgy, that is, of introducing before, adding to, or interpolating in a portion of the liturgy poems which may be considered as commentaries upon the genuine liturgical text. The *Introit*, the *Kyrie*, and the *Gloria*, for example, were all freely troped. Like the sequences, the tropes probably were first composed in France, but Notker Balbulus, Tutilo, and several other monks of St. Gall extensively cultivated this form of expression and various examples of their work still survive. Early collections have come down to us, however, not only from France, where Limoges was a famous centre, Switzerland, and Germany, but also from England and north Italy, collections that reveal how widely popular the practice became.

Several of the tropes contain dialogue, some were sung antiphonally, and potentially any of these might have developed into true drama by the addition of impersonation. But that role was initially reserved for one of them, a trope destined to have a long, varied, and dramatically significant existence. Sung antiphonally preceding the Introit of the Mass for Easter morning, it reads in its most primitive form (MS. St. Gall 484):

Interrogatio:
> Quem quęritis in sepulchro, Christicolę?

Responsio:
> Iesum Nazarenum crucifixum, o caelicolae.

> Non est hic, surrexit sicut predixerat. Ite, nuntiate quia surrexit de sepulchro.

Resurrexi.

---

[1] *A.H.* liii, *Introd.*; Young, i. 182 ff.; Raby, 210 ff.; Muller, op. cit.

Our earliest manuscript[1] of this trope, in a slightly expanded form, comes from Limoges and is dated between 923 and 934, but its simplest and presumably most primitive version is that just cited from St. Gall which is to be found in a manuscript of almost as early a date. It seems possible indeed that the author of the *Quem quaeritis* was the Tutilo of St. Gall who lived in the second half of the ninth century and was closely associated with Notker Balbulus.[2] Here, made vivid, was the conversation between the angels and the Marys at the tomb of Christ, and although sources for the dialogue were at hand in the Vulgate and the liturgy (potentially, in Matthew xxviii, Mark xvi, John xviii, Luke xxiv, and in the antiphons and responsories of the Easter season derived from the Gospels), this trope must be considered an original creation.

While attached to the Mass the trope remained a lyrical embellishment of the service and nothing more. It did not give rise to any kind of dramatic representation. It was sung antiphonally, to be sure, but in the forty or more manuscripts which preserve it in its original position, there is no evidence that any attempt at impersonation was introduced, no evidence that the trope developed or was expanded. It remained static.[3]

Some time during the tenth century, however, the trope was transferred to the end of the early morning service of Matins where it was interpolated between the conclusion of the third responsory and the final *Te Deum*, and in this new position the *Quem quaeritis* became truly dramatic: its dialogue was sung by half-choirs, by cantors, or by cantors and choir, who impersonated the characters of the Marys and the angels; they played their roles with appropriate gestures and voice-changes in a setting that thereby became for the audience a suitable *mise en*

[1] Bibl. Nat. MS. lat. 1240.

[2] It is because Ekkehart, iv, *Casus S. Galli*, iii. 46, ascribes several other Introit tropes to Tutilo, because two of these are in the same early manuscript, and because his date fits our manuscript that the *Quem quaeritis* is ascribed to him. However, Raby, p. 220, is less inclined to credit Tutilo with its composition than Young, i. 205, or Manitius, iii. 1042, though like the others he attributes the earliest form of the trope to St. Gall.

[3] A seeming exception to this statement is a late and unique version from Brescia in a manuscript dated 1438 which Young is inclined to regard as an imitation of the plays that had been common for centuries before this time at the end of Easter Matins (Young, i. 220–2, 231).

scène. Definite stage-directions in the manuscripts told them how to speak and act, the costumes and properties they were to employ.

What led to the change of position and hence to the dramatization of this particular trope? Fundamentally, there must have been present a desire to make visible and potent to the people the story of the Resurrection and the hope of the Redemption.[1] From earliest times the Roman Church had sanctioned artistic representations of scenes from the Bible; sculptors, painters, and miniaturists in the exaltation of a religious spirit as all-pervading as the world has ever known delighted in giving concrete form for themselves and others to the spirit of their faith. Now, as the Latin language became less and less intelligible to the people, special efforts must have been necessary to strengthen the understanding of the services by the unlearned and to make manifest by ceremonials of various kinds the allegorical content of the liturgy; and the thought that the Church itself might be the theatre for vivifying and elucidating to the *menu peuple de Dieu* the mysteries of Christian doctrine must have occurred to some inspired churchman who himself possessed the soul of an artist. He may have been a poet, a musician, perhaps a man skilled in using colours or modelling in clay; whoever he was, his inspiration contained the quickened seed of a new dramatic life.

It should also be noted that, already established at early morning services, there were three older ceremonies in which there existed the germs of impersonation and dramatization. These were the so-called *Adoratio Crucis*, *Depositio Crucis*, and *Elevatio Crucis*. The Adoration of the Cross on Good Friday was a very old ceremony probably used as early as the fourth century at Jerusalem and certainly known to the Roman liturgy by the eighth; to it were added, apparently in the tenth century, the Deposition and Elevation, ceremonies symbolizing the Burial and Resurrection, which may have come into being as a kind of sequel to the earlier Adoration. The Deposition took place on Good Friday and seems to have begun as a burying of

---

[1] See the *Regularis Concordia* in Young, i. 133, the words of the abbess, Katherine of Sutton, ibid. ii. 410–11, and those of Philippe de Mézières, ibid., pp. 226–7 and 474–5.

the same Cross which had previously been adored, but in some versions a Host, and in others both a Host and a Cross, were laid away. The Elevation of the object or objects buried occurred very early on Easter morning, before Matins, and commemorated by the time of its performance, as well as by its content, the mystery of the Resurrection.[1]

Transferred to Matins the *Quem quaeritis* trope constituted a fitting climax to these lyrical and potentially dramatic ceremonies, and its transference to its new position doubtless owes much to the appropriateness of picturing the visit of the Marys to the tomb after the *Elevatio*. Moreover, the responsories of Easter Matins provided a suitable introduction to the trope, and the hour of Matins was the hour of the Visit. Since in some versions the Marys carry thuribles as well as, or instead of, spices, it is possible that the traditional use of incense at the end of Matins had some influence upon the introduction of the trope at this point. In certain churches, too, the doors, which had been closed during the *Depositio* and *Elevatio*, were thrown open to the laity just before the end of Matins. This then was a time when any ceremony, dramatically presented, could be used to impress its theme upon the people.

Our trope, dialogued, sung antiphonally, and bearing within itself the rudiments of mimetic action, must have appeared particularly well designed for this purpose. Its theme was both human and divine. The transition from the sad questioning of the Marys to the jubilant *surrexit* of the angel suitably reflected the seasonal contrast between the mourning of Lent and the joy of Easter. From every point of view, then, a dramatic office representing the Visit to the Tomb—the *Visitatio Sepulchri*, as it may now be called—would appropriately serve as an introduction to the services of Easter Day.[2]

We find the trope connected with the Sepulchre ceremonies as early as the tenth century. The testimony comes from England, but the usage there seems to come from Fleury.[3] In this

[1] Young, i. 114 ff., believes that the reservation of the Host consecrated on Thursday for the Missa Praesanctificatorum of Good Friday may have influenced these ceremonies in some way.

[2] See Brinkmann, pp. 106–43, and Young, i. 232 ff.

[3] For an edition of this part of the *Regularis Concordia* see Chambers, ii. 307 ff. (on p. 308 occur the words 'ad fidem indocti vulgi ac neofitorum

document, the *Regularis Concordia*, a set of rules drawn up for
the use of the English clergy between 965 and 975 by Ethelwold,
Bishop of Winchester, it is expressly stated that all these ceremonies are for the strengthening of the faith of the vulgar and
unlearned. That this purpose widely obtained is evident from
the fact that of the *Visitatio Sepulchri* in its new position at the
end of Matins over 400 manuscripts survive, manuscripts which
span the years from the tenth to the sixteenth centuries (sporadi-
cally even later) and which are found in Europe from northern
England to southern Italy, from Spain to Poland, thus bearing
witness to the immense popularity of this dramatic office.

Once detached from the Mass, i.e. from the most important
and essentially stable observance of the day, and placed in a
position where it formed the conclusion of vividly symbolical
ceremonies, the trope lent itself admirably to expansion and
development. Additions and variations designed to make the
dialogue more attractive or impressive were introduced almost
at once. To the original scene between the angels and the Marys
(known as the first stage) an apostle scene was appended showing Peter and John hurrying to the tomb, each eager to surpass
the other. This second stage is primarily associated with the
Empire from which most of the surviving manuscripts emanate
(none of the manuscripts is earlier than the twelfth century,
though the scene may be older), and its inception may well have
taken place in some German church. Yet France undoubtedly
knew it very early: Belethus writing his *Rationale Divinorum
Officiorum* in the twelfth century describes the apostle scene as
part of the regular usage in France; Durandus in a work of the
thirteenth century also mentions it, though he may be describing an Italian use[1]; and it occurs in later French plays of the
more developed sort, i.e. in the Fleury *Visitatio Sepulchri* and
in the *Ludus Paschalis* of Origny.[2] With the incorporation of
the apostle scene, the action of the little drama became more
spirited; the sedate and almost static ceremonial at the tomb

corroborandam'); for bibliography see Young, i. 582; on its indebtedness to
Fleury see E. Wright, p. 146, and Symons, especially pp. 279 and 287. Realism in
the medieval drama and its role in the teaching of religious tenets is discussed by
Auerbach, *Mimesis*, chap. vii.

[1] Cf. E. Wright, p. 151.
[2] See Schüttpelz, p. 21. For Belethus see *PL*, ccii. 119.

took on animation and movement. Some of the stage-directions almost suggest a 'race', as John with quickened pace seeks to outstrip Peter: 'veniant denique in persona Ioannis et Petri Apostolorum duo alij celeri gressu'; or again, 'Petrus et Ioannes currant, precurratque Ioannes, sequente Petro'; or again, 'pervenit unus citius alio, sicut Ioannis cucurrit citius Petro.'[1] For many churches the office reached its logical conclusion at this point.

Some churches, however, added still another scene, the appearance of the Risen Christ to Mary Magdalen (a third stage), thus making the action still more dramatic and, by the innovation of presenting the Risen Christ in person, paving the way for future departures from precedent. It seems possible that this scene was not included before the latter part of the twelfth century and that it originated in France, where its simplest forms are found and where it became very popular.[2] The presence of the Dominica Persona bearing His Cross, the weeping Magdalen's approach to her Lord whom at first she mistakes for a gardener, her sudden recognition that it is He, her prostration at His feet with the loud cry *Rabboni*, His injunction *Noli me tangere*, all these details from the Gospels, visualized and set to music, give the scene a mounting human poignancy that adds a new note of tragedy and emotional intensity to the simpler, earlier plays concerned only with the angels, the Marys, and the apostles.

At each of these three stages interpolations and variations, some simple, some elaborate, could be introduced, and these might be taken from the liturgy or they might be non-liturgical in origin. One of the favourite liturgical texts associated with the *Visitatio* was the *Victimae Paschali*, originally an Easter sequence written in the eleventh century and especially appropriate in subject-matter since it concerned the questioning of the Marys as to what they had seen:

> Dic nobis, Maria, quid vidisti in via?
> Sepulchrum Christi viventis, et gloriam vidi resurgentis.

---

[1] Young, i. 324; 321; 341.

[2] See Manitius, iii. 1042. Among the texts of the third stage from France are those from Rôuen, Mont-S.-Michel, Fleury, Coutances, as well as the longer *ludi* from Origny and the Tours MS. Testimony to knowledge of the scene in England as early as 1196 is discussed by F. Lecoy in *Rom.* lxxiii (1952), 502–6.

Angelicos testes, sudarium et vestes.
Surrexit Christus, spes mea; praecedet vos in Galilaeam.

Obviously this sequence was well adapted to dramatic presentation because of its dialogued form and because it had been sung
antiphonally before its connexion with the *Visitatio*. Indeed the
Victimae Paschali sequence so thoroughly attached itself to the
scene at the tomb that most of our later vernacular Passion
plays retain it in translation. Other tropes and metrical hymns
also served to expand and enrich the original text which thus
might vary considerably from church to church.

Of the non-liturgical additions none is more important than
the introduction of the spice-merchant (*unguentarius*) who made
his appearance, probably in the twelfth century, selling spices
to the Marys with which to anoint their Lord. This lay figure,
destined to reappear in the vernacular drama and give ample
scope to dramatic ingenuity, may in the beginning have been
the contribution of some young clerk or goliard: the spice-
merchant's stanzas first occur in a verse-form characteristic of
so-called goliardic poetry. Even in the liturgical drama the role
inspired originality: the merchant is accompanied by his wife
in the Benediktbeuern text and there is a *mercator juvenis* in the
Tours manuscript.[1]

Other new characters who enter the liturgical plays are the
bragging Roman soldiers sent to guard the tomb. They are
found in manuscripts dating no earlier than the thirteenth
century, three of which are French (from the Sainte Chapelle,
Coutances, and the manuscript now in Tours), two German,
and one from Sulmona that may represent French usage where
their role is greatly expanded.[2] It is probable that they did not
appear upon the liturgical stage until the plays had become
quite elaborate. To be sure, they figure in a *Visitatio Sepulchri* of
the first stage from the Sainte Chapelle where their presence is
optional and their actions merely mimetic, but the manuscript
is of the fifteenth century, and the Coutances text, where no

----

[1] On the spice-merchant see Dürre, *Mercatorszene*. On the versification of these
stanzas and others like them see Young, i. 677, and Wm. Meyer, *Frag. Bur.*,
pp. 106 ff.
[2] See E. Wright, p. 180. Eight versified lines are exactly alike in the Sulmona
and Tours texts.

words are assigned to them—they merely *dicant personagia sua*— is of the same late date. Reminiscent of their classical ancestors, the *milites gloriosi*, and of their farcical descendants in the vernacular plays, the *fanfarons*, they boldly declare they will allow no one to steal Christ's body and to pretend He has risen, but then after the angel's appearance they become frightened, and in the Tours and Sulmona manuscripts they insist on the truth of the Resurrection, unlike their behaviour in the German texts where they accept bribes to spread false reports.

It must be remembered, however, that although the primitive text of the *Quem quaeritis* was thus capable of being diversely expanded and elaborated, not all churches adopted such forms. Many continued to use the original version or a simple adaptation differing only slightly from it. The simplicity or elaboration of the text adopted depended upon the individual needs and resources of the churches, some indeed preserving in their service-books both simple and elaborate versions of the same office for use on varying occasions. Nor did the process of growth discontinue after the office had reached its so-called third stage. Scenes suitable for performance before and after the *Visitatio* were added and the texts became so expanded by the intrusion of profane elements, metrical embellishments, and elaborated stage-settings that some modern authorities would now call them *ludi* rather than dramatic offices.[1]

The fully developed Easter play, or *Ludus Paschalis*, is represented in France by two texts, one from a Norman church, though preserved in a thirteenth-century manuscript of Tours and generally called the Tours *Ludus Paschalis*,[2] the other copied in the convent of Origny-Ste-Benoîte near St. Quentin. In the Norman play, which is fragmentary, the action begins with an event that took place on the day before Easter, i.e. the setting of the soldiers' watch at the tomb; it includes an expanded spice-merchant scene with two merchants, a young *mercator* as well as a presumably older one; the scenes involving the three Marys at the tomb are ornamented with original lyrical lamenta-

---

[1] See Young, i. 411–12. Authorities are not agreed, however, about when an office becomes a *ludus*: Young considers four texts as Easter *ludi*, but Wm. Meyer would add some six others to these. I am not inclined to distinguish between offices and *ludi*.

[2] See E. Wright, pp. 179 ff. Printed by Young, i. 438.

tions; Christ's Resurrection is reported to Pilate; and His Appearances to Mary Magdalen and the disciples together with the Doubting of Thomas and the *Victimae Paschali* conclude a text that thus dramatizes certain events following the Resurrection as well as some of those preceding it.

The Origny play is remarkable for the introduction of both French verses and French stage-directions. While less inclusive than the Norman text, it contains original material not found elsewhere and is notable for an unusual and highly dramatic version—partly in the vernacular—of the Appearance of the Risen Christ to Mary Magdalen, in which, amid her versified laments and the angels' attempts to console her, she unexpectedly exclaims: 'Je cuit de duel me tuerai.' The fact that the play was probably destined for a community of nuns and the fact that it seems to have been written in the thirteenth or fourteenth century may account for the introduction of the vernacular and the emotional quality of some of the language. To be sure, French is used timidly for the most part, chiefly in the translation of well-known Latin stanzas (the music of which it employs) and as an embellishment or aid to understanding, but its possibilities for creating additions to a strictly liturgical text are here evident.[1]

Another play of Easter week, that of the *Peregrini* or Pilgrims to Emmaus, is clearly an extension forward of the *Visitatio*.[2] This play, based on Luke xxiv, dramatizing the Appearances of Christ to His disciples and sometimes including the Doubting of Thomas, comprises several scenes and according to the rubrics might be performed on either Easter Monday or Tuesday. Versions survive in France from Saintes, Rouen, Fleury, Beauvais, and also form part of the so-called *Ludus Paschalis* of the Tours MS. as well as of a Sicilian text that probably represents Norman liturgical use.

Our earliest liturgical Passion plays carry the action still further back than the developed Easter plays we have consi-

[1] On the Origny text see E. Wright, pp. 86 ff. and 184 ff. It is printed by Young, i. 413. On its music see Liuzzi, *SM*, N.S., ii (1929), 74 ff. Marichal, p. 45, is not certain whether the play was actually performed at Origny, but only that it was copied there after 1317. On the use of the vernacular by Hilarius and the *Sponsus* see below, Chaps. V and VI.

[2] See Young, i. 451 ff.

dered above, namely to the events of Good Friday or before. Some scholars regard the Passion play as an independent growth, evolving either from the *Planctus Mariae*, a lamentation of Mary at the foot of the Cross sung in some churches on Good Friday, or from the dramatic reading of the *lectiones* of Good Friday with suitable voice-changes.[1] However, the various *Planctus*, though potentially dramatic, remained lyrical and static, so far as we know, and though adopted ready-made into the later plays seem in no instance to have been the starting-point of any surviving text. As for the readings of Good Friday, these are taken from John and Matthew, whereas our early Passion plays do not depend on these Gospels more than on the words of Mark and Luke. Moreover, there are few records of Passion plays performed on Good Friday: almost all were played on Easter Day, a fact that awakens no surprise when one remembers that the services of Good Friday are the most solemn of the year and would not readily lend themselves to dramatic embellishment. Finally, our earliest example of a Passion play shows the scenes antecedent to the *Visitatio* closely linked to it. The Passion play, therefore, seems best regarded as an extension backward of the Resurrection scenes. Although no example of the play exists in a French manuscript, a fragment from Sulmona suggests the type of text probably known there, for Sulmona had belonged to the Norman kingdom of Sicily and may well have followed Norman usage.[2] So far as the testimony of our surviving texts is concerned, however, the Easter drama reached its culmination in French churches in some such form as the *Ludus Paschalis* of the Tours manuscript.[3]

Additional material available for performance during Easter week was also at hand, for instance a dramatization of Christ's visit to the lower world and the freeing of the souls from Limbo. The so-called *Descensus ad Inferos*, or Harrowing of Hell, was fully described in the apocryphal Gospel of Nicodemus; and the twenty-fourth Psalm, which supplies much of the dialogue

---

[1] See Young, i. 537 ff.

[2] See E. Wright, p. 180; Young, i. 701. Except for the Sulmona fragment, only two liturgical Passion plays survive, both in the *Carmina Burana*. They are printed by Young, i. 514 ff.

[3] A play on the Ascension is known from Moosburg (see Young, i. 484), but none has survived from France.

of the scene, was early used in Palm Sunday processions and at
the dedication of churches, later in connexion with the *Elevatio*.
This material was ready for adoption when needed, and though
our surviving liturgical texts that embody it are, with one
thirteenth-century exception, of ceremonies, not true plays, and
happen to be later than the vernacular plays using the same
theme, it is possible that this chronology does not represent
the original order of development.

In any case the growth of the fully developed liturgical
Easter plays proceeded upon the same principle: one scene was
added to another, each evolving in accordance with the needs,
resources, and ability of the sponsors. Nevertheless, despite the
exaltation of the announcement 'He is risen', and the sudden
climax of the resurrected Christ's appearance to Mary Magdalen,
despite too such opportunities for action or comedy as the
hurrying of the Apostles to the tomb, the bargaining with the
spice-merchant, and the fanfaronade of the soldiers, the Easter
play provided less scope for dramatic contrasts than the Christmas play. The stellar roles demanded liturgical restraint; the
minor characters were essentially of little importance; with the
tomb as *mise en scène* and simple vestments serving as costumes
differences in accessories remained limited. Solemnity and
reverence, stylized speech and gesture, characterize practically
all of the Easter plays.

III

Liturgical Christmas Plays. *The Procession of Prophets. The Feast of Fools*

DERIVED from the Easter play and paralleling its growth in many ways was the Christmas play.[1] More appealing to humble piety and to simple human emotions than the drama of the Resurrection, the scenes associated with the birth of the Christ-child were essentially more picturesque. And, just as the services of the Christmas season were more adaptable and plastic than those of Easter, so the plays of the Birth, though fewer in number than the Easter plays, show greater textual diversity and a wider variation in arrangement.

The nucleus of the earliest Christmas play, the *Officium Pastorum*, is a trope closely modelled on the Easter trope in which the shepherds at the crib take the place of the Marys at the tomb:

> Quem queritis in praesepe, pastores, dicite?
> Salvatorem Christum Dominum, infantem pannis involutum . . .
> Adest hic parvulus cum Maria matre sua . . . nunc euntes dicite quia natus est. . . .

Originally sung as a trope to the Introit of the High Mass on Christmas Day and rendered simply by half-choirs, or by the choir and a selected member or members of it (in one case by deacons and cantors), the dialogue was later transferred to the service of Matins. There the latent possibilities of dramatic impersonation, action, and *mise en scène* emerged: the questioners were identified with the apocryphal midwives who supposedly assisted at the Birth, the shepherds approached the crib equipped

---

[1] Some have assumed that the cult of the actual *praesepe* at Bethlehem and of relics from it transferred to Rome had something to do with the origin of the shepherd play, but Young, ii. 24 ff., finds no evidence for this view. It may be remarked that the Rouen *Pastores* of the thirteenth century was sung to the same melody as the Tours Easter play of the twelfth. For other resemblances between the tropes for Christmas and Easter see Brinkmann, pp. 108–9, 130–3, and Böhme, pp. 33–36.

with staffs, and the crib itself, at first represented merely by the altar or by figures upon the altar table, came to be a special structure, standing behind or near the altar, which might at times be large enough to be entered.

What influenced the transfer to Matins we do not know: Böhme suggested the presence there of earlier crib ceremonies, but Young considers this theory highly speculative and himself believes the change was due either to the influence of the Easter custom or to the appropriateness of the time, since the visit of the shepherds, according to Luke ii. 8, took place while the shepherds were keeping watch over their flock by night. In any case, except in one instance, the trope was loosely attached to Matins, occurring after the *Te Deum*, not before, and serving as an introduction to the first Mass of Christmas rather than as a conclusion of the earlier service of Matins. The characters of the office might rule the choir of the first Mass following, re-appear at Lauds, and continue to extend their activities into the Magna Missa itself. As Young points out (ii. 20), the characters of no other play took so active a part in the official liturgy of the Church.

Although authorship of the trope may be safely attributed to Limoges, where it is found in the eleventh century, the drama-tized form occurs in few French churches as a separate play. We have a text from Clermont-Ferrand and several versions from Rouen, but in France as elsewhere, the pure shepherd play was seemingly absorbed by the Epiphany play of the Magi to which it early became attached.

The use of Rouen, as described by Young, ii. 19, will give some indication of how the *Officium Pastorum* was performed:

The *praesepe*, it appears, was behind the main altar, and contained artificial figures of the Virgin Mary and the Child, behind a curtain. As the five shepherds, suitably costumed, enter the west door of the choir, a boy up under the vaulting, representing an angel, announces the Nativity. After seven other angels have sung *Gloria in excelsis*, the shepherds begin their march to the *praesepe*, singing, as they traverse the choir, first a responsorial poem *Pax in terris*, and then, as they round the altar, the verse *Transeamus*. At the manger they find two priests in dalmatics, who represent midwives, and with whom they carry on the familiar dialogue. At the words *Adest hic parvulus*, the *obstetrices* draw aside the curtain, and point first to the Child, and then, at the words *Ecce virgo*, to the Mother. The shepherds kneel before the figure of the Virgin, singing the verses *Salve, virgo singularis*, and after obeisance to the Child, they turn to the chorus, singing the usual sentence *Iam vere scimus*. This leads directly into the Mass, during which the *pastores* rule the choir, and read or sing considerable parts of the liturgical text.

But, as has been said, the shepherd play, originally destined for Christmas Day, soon became merged with the Epiphany play of the Magi performed on 6 January.

This Magi play, also called the *Officium Stellae*,[1] offered richer possibilities for drama than the *Officium Pastorum*, more opportunity for action, characterization and costume, and its widely differing texts, many of which include scenes involving the shepherds, are sometimes distinguished by considerable originality and literary skill. The dramatization of the visit of the Three Kings to Jerusalem and Bethlehem (Matthew ii. 1–16) seems to have formed a sequel to a much older oblation ceremony.[2] In the simplest form of this play from the use of Limoges,[3] the Magi slowly enter the choir singing the prose *O quam dignis celebranda dies ista laudibus*. They announce their gifts of gold, frankincense, and myrrh, and then one of them, singing *Hoc signum magni Regis*, points to a moving star which they proceed to follow from the middle of the choir to the high altar. There they deposit their gifts, whereupon from behind the altar a boy, representing an angel, announces the birth of Christ. Surprised (*attoniti et admirantes*), the kings return to the sacristy, singing the antiphon *In Bethlehem natus est Rex coelorum*.

This version is attached to the offertory. Another more elaborate office from Besançon is connected with the intoning of the gospel, and there the Magi are accompanied by attendants who carry the gifts in gold vessels and who are appropriately dressed, two to represent Persians, one blackened to represent a Moor.

[1] For other designations see Young, ii. 432.

[2] The Three Kings were early identified with those of Psalm lxxi.10:'Reges Tharsis et insulae munera offerent; reges Arabum et Saba dona adducent.' This verse was used in the offertory of the Mass of Epiphany. On the older ceremonies and the Magi plays see Young, ii. 29 ff.; on traditions connected with them see Sturdevant.

[3] This text is undated, but other texts and records point to the eleventh century as the date of origin. See Anz, pp. 122–4; Young, ii. 101.

The procession moves from the choir to the pulpit, where the gospel is recited, and then, as the star seemingly appears, to the main altar symbolizing the manger, where the offering is made.

The two versions just considered, intimately enmeshed in the Mass, were obviously restricted in their development by this position. But others, less closely associated with the Eucharistic service, show that the action might be much extended. Several texts, to be performed after Terce, survive from Rouen, and in these plays the kings, accompanied by their servants, proceed from the eastern, northern, and southern parts of the church, follow the star, meet before the altar, and there exchange kisses. Then they sing together *Eamus ergo et inquiramus* and continue in procession from the choir into the nave where they see a circle of lights over the altar. On their arrival at the altar they are asked their errand by two clerics in dalmatics who, when the kings disclose it, draw aside a curtain permitting them to see Mother and Child. (This crib scene recalls the *Officium Pastorum* and the two clerics, identified in other similar texts, obviously represent the midwives, whereas the *praesepe* here, as in the shepherd plays, is symbolized by the altar.) The Magi worship and present their gifts, while the people and priests bring additional offerings. Then, as the Magi pray, an angel behind the altar warns them to return another way and they depart, re-entering the choir by a side door.[1]

The angelic warning of the Rouen texts had, of course, implied the danger involved in a meeting between the Magi and King Herod, but the king was not represented in person. As soon as Herod himself appeared in the plays further opportunities for dramatic development became obvious and liturgical authors soon made effective use of his presence. They could now introduce not only a more complicated plot, with an element of suspense, but also portray a villain whose speech and actions, costume and accessories might be used to suggest his vicious character. The Three Kings had been slightly individualized in dress, perhaps in deportment, but Herod's was the first role capable of giving us a real person and not a type.

---

[1] The kings and their attendants play a role in the following Mass, and at the regular offertory they make a second oblation.

The contrast between the cruel, powerful, worldly monarch on his richly decorated throne, surrounded by ornately costumed courtiers, and the innocent child in the manger, as well as Herod's angry action in brandishing his sword and his fierce words uttered in loud tones, all contained new emotional possibilities, so that the incidents concerned with Herod regularly came to be added to the simpler Magi plays.

Two eleventh-century texts from Nevers show the King alone, without followers, and his behaviour in them is calm and sedate enough. But even in that same century, in a version from Compiègne, scenes between Herod and his scribes, his *legati*, *nuntius*, and *armiger* were included, and these followers, some of whom served as messengers between the King and the Magi, made the action more spirited.[1] Since, too, such messengers— a necessity in the simultaneous stage-setting of the Middle Ages, as in the ancient theatre—were, like the midwives, non-biblical additions, they paved the way for the appearance of other apocryphal characters and incidents. At first the Herod scene had merely been inserted between the scene in which the star appeared and the succeeding worship of the Magi at the *praesepe*. However, in the more developed versions the Magi are warned not to return to Herod, and this gives the King a fine opportunity to display his anger and motivates his vengeance in ordering the slaughter of the innocents.

The remarkably original, artistic, and dramatic text from Compiègne, just mentioned, presents innovations of literary form by introducing hexameters and rhymed lines. It also introduces innovations of arrangement. In this play the Magi come from various directions and meet; then Herod's *legati* address them while a *nuntius* hurries to advise Herod of their approach; presently the King greets his visitors with a kiss, learns their errand, consults his scribes regarding it, and hears from them the prophecy of the birth of his rival in Bethlehem. He bids the Magi search for the boy and report back to him. They proceed on their way, are interrogated by the midwives, discover the newly born child whom they seek, and present their gifts. However, an angel counsels them to depart by another route,

---

[1] The Nevers texts are in Young, ii. 50–51 and ii. 439 ff.; the Compiègne text is in Young, ii. 53–56.

which they do; whereupon a messenger tells the King he has been deceived, that the Magi will not come back, and a personage invented by the liturgical playwrights, *Armiger*, advises killing all young children so that the boy of whom they have learned may be put to death. Herod gives the order while an angel sings the antiphon, *Sinite parvulos venire ad me, talium est enim regnum caelorum.*

The Compiègne text, like the earlier plays in which Herod did not make a personal appearance, shows the influence of the Christmas shepherd play in the presence of the midwives and the wording of the scene at the *praesepe*. It remained, however, to introduce the shepherds themselves, and this combination of *pastores*, Magi, and Herod occurred in a large number of texts in which the shepherds, returning from Bethlehem, are portrayed as meeting the Magi. These fully developed Epiphany plays gave scope to the imagination of their authors and almost every version delights in some original contribution: Herod becomes more and more the bombastic character known to Shakespeare;[1] sometimes he replies to Armiger with a passage from Sallust (*incendium meum ruina extinguam*), sometimes he throws down the book of prophecies in great anger and menacingly brandishes his sword; his son, Archelaus, appears in various texts and, like his father, threatens the Magi and the Innocents. In one play, preserved in a Montpellier manuscript, the Magi speak a pseudo-Hebraic gibberish that reminds one of the invocation of Salatin in Rutebeuf's *Miracle de Théophile* or of the 'Turkish' in Molière's *Bourgeois Gentilhomme*. In another play, from Bilsen, the Magi are thrown into prison, while in a Fleury text, Herod's son has an extended role and attempts at one point to pacify his father who is *furore accessus*. In arrangement and versification these plays also show their independence. One indeed, that of the Fleury collection, imitates a few Vergilian lines from the *Aeneid*, whereas the Bilsen play versifies not only its text but even its rubrics.

In four texts, three of them from France, the Slaughter of the Innocents is actually dramatized.[2] A text from Laon, entitled

---

[1] *Hamlet*, III, sc. 2. The importance of this role in the liturgical plays is indicated by such titles as *Versus ad Herodem faciendum*, and the like.

[2] On these texts see Young, chap. xx.

Ordo Stelle, represents this scene directly after Herod has ordered the killing of the children: a procession of children with a lamb enters; soldiers slay them as they ask *Quare non defendis sanguinem nostrum?*; an angel answers and admonishes them; then Rachel, personification of a sorrowing mother, appears weeping and is comforted in a long colloquy with a *Consolatrix*. This dialogue has a lyrical quality and is developed in leonine hexameters. In three other versions of the Slaughter—one of which (from Freising) is entitled *Ordo Rachelis* and another (from Fleury) *Ad interfectionem puerorum*—the scene constitutes an independent play. The simplest and earliest of these Innocents plays comes from Limoges and consists of little more than a dramatized trope indicating a dialogue between Rachel and a consoling angel. In the much longer and more artistic text from Fleury, after the entrance of the children and the lamb, Joseph with Mary bearing the Child is warned by an angel to flee into Egypt, while Armiger tells Herod of the disappearance of the Magi. Herod, beside himself (*quasi corruptus*), seizes a sword and seems about to kill himself (*arrepto gladio, paret seipsum occidere*). He is saved from suicide by his followers, but presently, as the Innocents who follow the lamb are singing, he gives the order at the suggestion of Armiger to slay them. The children are slaughtered despite their own appeals and the prayers of their mothers. Then Rachel appears, weeping and at times fainting, while two *Consolatrices* try to comfort her. The play ends with the resurrection of the children and the deposition of Herod in favour of his son, Archelaus, as an angel advises Joseph to return from Egypt, and Joseph, together with Mary and the Child, departs for Galilee singing *Gaude, gaude, gaude, Maria virgo*. Original lyrical compositions of considerable intricacy and music that is very elaborate[1] characterize this Fleury play which, well motivated and arranged, is appealing and effective.

The connexion of these three texts with a fourth, that from Freising, need not long detain us, nor the related question whether some ceremony on Holy Innocents' Day preceded the incorporation of the scene into the Magi play. Young believes (ii. 123–4): 'We can be sure only of a French tradition which includes the compositions from Limoges and Laon, of a German

[1] On the music see Gérold, p. 62.

tradition represented by the play from Freising, and of a union of the two traditions, in some manner, in the play from Fleury.' E. Wright posits (156–7) 'an early [lost] Fleury play which served as source of the present Laon text and which was itself modified by contact with a German play from Freising or some church connected with Freising' to give us our extant version. Too few texts survive for certainty and all except that of Limoges are late, whereas even the Limoges version shows a sophisticated artistry in its ten- and twelve-syllabled verses. It seems possible that some trope, like that elaborated at Limoges, was in existence fairly early, ready for adoption to complete those Magi plays which, as we have seen, ended with threats by Herod and his followers to slaughter the innocents, and that, as Young infers (ii. 124), 'the use of the trope in a concluding scene of the Magi play preceded its use in an independent dramatic composition'. It is unnecessary, therefore, to attribute the origin of the scene to some unknown ceremony of Innocents' Day, and it is best regarded as an extension of the Magi play.

There can be no doubt that the Epiphany play of the Magi, like the plays of Easter and Christmas, arose in France at Limoges, probably in the eleventh century. Its growth can be traced from a simple visit of the Magi to the *praesepe*, through a version or versions incorporating their appearance before Herod and Herod's consultation with his scribes, through more elaborate types of texts in which messengers rush back and forth between the Magi and the King, to still more highly developed plays which include one or more scenes involving the shepherds or the slaughter of the innocents.

Artistry in form, the use of hexameters and rhymed verse, corresponding no doubt to intricacies of musical structure, indicate the concern of the playwrights for their work. But more important from our point of view are the dramatic potentialities of these plays. The shepherds, the midwives, and the Magi, King Herod, his messengers, scribes, and courtiers, do not have the reverend religious associations of the Marys and the Apostles who figure in the Easter plays, and their roles naturally lent themselves to a more dynamic treatment. Moreover, action and contrast inhered in these characters: the messengers sped to and fro; Herod and his son visibly raged; the

Magi came in procession from the far corners of the church; the splendid costumes of oriental potentates must have glowed brilliantly beside the tunics of the shepherds and the white robes of the angels; Herod's pride and arrogance would be accentuated by the humility of the worshippers before the *praesepe* of the Holy Child, his rage and vindictiveness by the pathos of the killing of the young children and the lamentation of their mothers.

THE PROCESSION OF PROPHETS

Once the impetus toward dramatization had appeared in the Church, first at Easter time and then at Christmas, not only extensions of these representations became possible—one scene being added to another—but new plays suitable to other occasions might arise. From a sermon once attributed to St. Augustine, entitled *Contra Judaeos, Paganos et Arianos Sermo de Symbolo*, perhaps by way of a *lectio* based on part of this sermon, came the *Procession of Prophets* known to us in its dramatized liturgical form from three French texts, those of Limoges, Laon, and Rouen.[1] The *lectio* was used in many churches at Matins on Christmas Day or at other services of the Christmas season, and its subject, the summoning of the Jews and pagans to bear witness in their own words to the coming of Christ, readily lent itself to dramatic recitation.

It seems possible that the transition from a monologued recitation, perhaps with voice-changes, to dialogue and impersonation took place in the monastery of St. Martial of Limoges, though a late manuscript of 1594, from the cathedral of Salerno, shows a more primitive version of the dramatized *lectio*. In any case at Limoges the narrative and expository elements of the *lectio* were eliminated, the prophecies were versified and set to music, the prophets appeared in a more nearly chronological order than in the sermon or *lectio*, the figure of Israel was added and that of Zacharias dropped (though Zacharias was represented by his wife, Elizabeth), so that the whole betrays an untrammelled author, using liturgical material with a free hand to

---

[1] On the *Ordo Prophetarum* cf. Young, chap. xxi. On its use in the *Mystère d'Adam* see below, Chap. VIII.

produce a dramatic effect. At which service his play was performed we do not know.

His successors at Laon and Rouen evidently wrote for the Feast of the Circumcision on 1 January (Young, ii. 153, 168), and their versions, far more elaborate than that of Limoges, introduce new characters, new scenes, original verses, and many suggestions concerning impersonation, action, costume, and stage properties. The play of Laon is noteworthy for a short scene in which Balaam appears, mounted upon an ass: in dumb show an angel halts the beast and Balaam strikes it, asking, *Quid moraris, asina, obstinata bestia?*—to which a boy, hidden *sub asina*, answers for it, explaining that the presence of an angel with a sword prevents it from proceeding.

At Rouen the play, preserved in several manuscripts, is frankly entitled *Ordo Processionis Asinorum*, although Balaam is only one of the more than twenty-eight characters involved. Fourteen of these persons appear for the first time in the Rouen text, which, while borrowing or adapting some of the original portions of the Laon version, also adds much to it that is entirely new. For example, although Balaam utters the same prophecy in both plays, the scene develops differently in each and at Rouen the angel has a speaking role. So too the various prophets sometimes utter the same, sometimes dissimilar, versified prophecies. The most striking innovations of the Rouen text, however, derive from the additional characters and action that it introduces. The *lectio* had named Isaiah, Jeremiah, Daniel, Moses, David, Habbakuk, Simeon, Zacharias, Elizabeth, John the Baptist, Vergil, Nebuchadnezzar, and the Sibyl. The Limoges version omitted Zacharias, adding Israel. Laon omitted both Zacharias and Israel, but contributed the important figure of Balaam with his ass. Rouen introduces two groups of six Jews and six Gentiles, omits Israel, keeps the thirteen characters of the *lectio*, though changing the order of their appearance, and adds Amos, Aaron, Balaam, Samuel, Hosea, Joel, Obadiah, Jonah, Micah, Nahum, Zephaniah, Haggai, Zechariah, Ezekiel, and Malachi. Moreover, subsidiary figures take part in several little scenes. After antiphonal interchanges between two singers and the chorus, and after the long procession reaches the middle of the church, six Jews stand on one side, six Gentiles on the other, and the *Vocatores* challenge each group and each replies. Then the prophets are summoned in turn, give their prophecies, and are led off by the *Vocatores* who repeat after each one: 'Iste cetus | psallat leus; | ⟨error vetus | condemnetur⟩', while the chorus similarly reiterates: 'Quod Iudea | ⟨perit rea, | haec chorea | gratulatur⟩.' When Balaam's turn is reached, he is summoned, not by the usual *Vocatores* who challenge the others, but by two messengers sent by King Balak to fetch him; then the little scene already mentioned, between him, his ass, and the angel, takes place.

More important and longer, however, is a wholly new scene near the end of the play derived from Daniel iii. 12 ff., which centres about Nebuchadnezzar and the furnace described in the opening rubric of the play: 'Tercia cantata, paratis Prophetis iuxta suum ordinem, fornace in medio navis ecclesie lintheo et stupis constituta.'[1] Nebuchadnezzar, apparelled as a king, points to an idol, orders two soldiers to come forward, and then they in turn command three youths (i.e. Shadrach, Meshach, and Abednego) to worship the image. The youths refuse, the soldiers bring them to the King, and he, learning of their disobedience, angrily orders them to be punished, whereupon the soldiers cast them into the furnace and light the fire. But the youths, *facti liberi*, sing *Benedictus es, Domine Deus*, and the King, hearing this, asks the soldiers what is being sung. The soldiers reply that the youths are praising God. Now the *Vocatores* come forward and demand of Nebuchadnezzar what he said when he saw the three in the fiery furnace and he answers with his 'prophecy': 'Tres in igne positi pueri ⟨quarto gaudent comite liberi⟩.'

THE FEAST OF FOOLS

Since the Rouen service-books call the *Ordo Prophetarum* a *processio asinorum* and since it was performed at the feast of the Circumcision, it is natural to ask whether the prophet plays are in any way related to the liturgical revels of the lower clergy known as the Feast of Fools and also as *asinaria festa*.[2] Such

---

[1] The furnace is also mentioned when Moses, the first of the prophets to be summoned, is led away *ultra fornacem* after prophesying.

[2] Various other names are used, *festum stultorum, fatuorum*, &c. On this and other details see Young, i. 104 ff., 551, ii. 169 ff.; Chambers, i. 274 ff., ii. 280–2.

revels, which originally may have been a Christian adaptation
of the pagan festivities of the Kalends, when great licence was
permitted the lower classes, were widespread in France during
the Christmas season and especially at the festivities of the subdeacons on 1 January. Though the observances varied in different churches, they usually included burlesqued services,
censing with unseemly objects, more or less riotous behaviour,
and in many places the presence of an ass. At Beauvais, Sens,
Autun, and elsewhere a humorous Prose of the Ass was recited
and at Beauvais there was mock braying by the participants.
The Prose of the Ass began: 'Orientis partibus | Adventavit
asinus', and each stanza had as refrain some variant of 'Hez,
Sire Asne, hez!' The ass itself was not necessarily a comic
figure; it served as the mount of the Virgin for the Flight into
Egypt and of Christ for the Entry into Jerusalem; moreover it
was associated with the ox in *praesepe* observances and at all
times has been regarded as a faithful, patient beast of burden.
But at the feast of the subdeacons the ass undoubtedly became
an object of fun, a fact apparent from later church decrees forbidding its presence there.

Quite probably the appearance of Balaam and his *obstinata
bestia* in the prophet play owes something to the revels of the
Feast of Fools: though the *Ordo Prophetarum* is the older ceremony, it seems likely that the use of the ass there was introduced
late, perhaps as a kind of counter-attraction to the merrymaking
of the subdeacons, 'an attempt to turn the established presence
of the ass in the church to purposes of edification, rather than
ribaldry' (Chambers, ii. 57). In any case the curious title of the
Rouen play must be due to the conspicuous figure of Balaam
and his *asina*, a beast that seems to have wandered into the
prophet play from the Feast of Fools.

No liturgical Christmas play survives from France which
combines the *Prophetae* with scenes involving the shepherds,
Magi, Herod and the Innocents, but the Benediktbeuern manuscript from Germany provides an elaborate version of this
combination that also includes Augustine in person, a Boy
Bishop, a humorous Archisynagogus, the figure of Diabolus,
as well as scenes showing the Annunciation and the visit to

Elizabeth.[1] Notwithstanding its highly developed and ornately versified form, this text, like those from Fleury and indeed like all the vernacular plays on the same religious subjects, still betrays the liturgical seeds from which it sprang. Thus in the midst of the many new dramatic effects of the Benediktbeuern Christmas play we find the old question, *pastores, dicite quidnam vidistis* . . .? and the old reply, *infantem vidimus pannis involutum*. . . . Those who have attempted to deny the liturgical origins of the medieval drama forget how completely visible its germs remain from beginning to end and how readily its development from those germs can be traced.[2]

[1] On the Christmas play from Benediktbeuern see Young, chap. xxii. On the Boy Bishop here and elsewhere cf. Chambers, i. 336 ff. and ii. 72.

[2] Stumpfl attempted to prove that Germanic folkways underlie the liturgical drama, but the pagan survivals mentioned by him—e.g. the *unguentarius* representing a tribal witch doctor, the three Marys a *matres* cult, the race to the tomb a spring folk contest, &c.—seem less directly connected with the origins of the drama than the established ritual of the Church. Pascal, *MLR*, xxxvi (1941), 369–87, considers some of Stumpfl's pagan survivals to be later intrusions grafted upon earlier Christian practices in a period of religious and social transformation; in any case he believes that the liturgical drama began as an ecclesiastical, not a popular ceremony. Despite Chambers's plausible and exhaustive investigations of folk customs with their negative results for the origin of the medieval drama, Cargill attempted to show that its beginnings were popular; all competent authorities, however, have rejected his thesis. On Cargill see Young, i. 542–3. On the dramatic tradition established by the liturgical drama see Marshall, *PMLA*, lvi (1941), 962–91.

IV

The Fleury Play-Book

WE come now to French liturgical plays that reveal what sophisticated writers could do to adapt and extend traditional material, how they could devise new scenes and wholly new plays, inject more pageantry and realism into old ones. From a manuscript now preserved in Orléans, but presumably written in the monastery of Fleury, also called S.-Benoît-sur-Loire, comes a collection of ten plays, some of which—the *Visitatio Sepulchri, Ordo Stellae, Ordo Rachelis,* and *Peregrini*—have already been mentioned.[1] These plays on biblical subjects are among the most finished of their respective types, each retaining some prose passages, but most adding thereto verses of varied structure admirably adapted to the sentiments and characters involved. Indeed the collection as a whole, by its diversity, originality, and the artistry of its individual plays, is a fitting memorial to a place where the principles of versification were extensively taught and practised, a place very near

[1] For earlier bibliography, contents, &c., see Young, i. 665–6 and Index. Cf. also E. Wright, pp. 137 ff., and Albrecht, chap. i and *passim*. Young prints all the texts. He and others follow the old catalogues in dating the MS. Orléans 201 (formerly 178) in the thirteenth century, but Albrecht, pp. 3–4, believes from the form of the musical notation that it must be of the twelfth. The attempt of S. Corbin, *Rom.* lxxiv (1953), 1–43, to prove that the plays do not come from Fleury but from the relatively obscure Saint-Lomer-de-Blois rests primarily on the presence of a sequence dedicated to S. Lomer in the same volume as the plays, on the unusual number of plays concerned with S. Nicolas, on the form of the musical notation in the manuscript, and on a denial of Fleury's presumed dramatic activity as indicated by the *Regularis Concordia*. But MS. Orléans 201 is a composite manuscript and the fourteenth-century sequence has no connexion with the earlier plays; Fleury's library reveals a sympathy for S. Nicolas which in any case would be natural in a medieval school; the evidence of the musical notation depends upon comparison with a single manuscript, unsupported by other palaeographical data; and Fleury's influence upon the *Regularis Concordia* is incontrovertible (see above, Chap. II, p. 23, n. 3). Outweighing Corbin's arguments are the traditional provenience of the manuscript and the certainty that it was at Fleury by the sixteenth century (see Cuissard, pp. iii, xxxiii, and Corbin, p. 3), as well as the variety of the plays in form and content and their relation to other texts, indications that they originated in a centre where literary and musical activity flourished over a considerable period and where associations with France, England, and the Empire were extensive. Cf. Chap. VII below.

Orléans, which Faral considers the 'capitale poétique de la France pendant tout le XIIᵉ siècle'.[1] Although the widespread connexions and influence of this centre of the liberal arts would suggest that Fleury once possessed more primitive forms of the liturgical drama than those preserved in its famous play-book, the versions that survive are all of a relatively complicated nature, perhaps representing revisions of earlier texts now lost.[2]

Besides the elaborate Easter and Christmas plays discussed above, the Orléans manuscript contains two New Testament plays on other subjects, a *Raising of Lazarus* and a *Conversion of St. Paul*, as well as four plays concerned with various miracles performed by St. Nicholas, the so-called *Tres Filiae*, *Tres Clerici*, *Iconia Sancti Nicolai*, and *Filius Getronis*. Two of these six plays, the *Conversio Sancti Pauli* and the *Filius Getronis*, are unique in subject among liturgical texts, whereas the *Raising of Lazarus* and the three other St. Nicholas plays may well have originated at Fleury and given rise, though in an earlier and simpler form, to the few liturgical texts on the same subjects found elsewhere.

The *Raising of Lazarus* faithfully reproduces the Gospel account and, unlike the Easter and Christmas plays, is entirely in verse. It begins with a sequence, then continues with original verses independent of the liturgy. Much of the action takes place in the house of Simon at Bethany, but there are also *loci* representing Galilee, Jerusalem, and the tomb of Lazarus, with every movement to and from them across the *platea* carefully indicated in the rubrics. The stanzaic uniformity (six-lined stanzas composed of decasyllabic couplets followed by a single verse of four syllables: aa^{10} b^4 cc^{10} b^4) is only slightly relieved by the occasional division of a single stanza between two speakers or by the attribution of two stanzas to a single speaker. Despite its monotonous structure, however, and despite the fact that there is no attempt to adapt verse forms to individual characters, the play as a whole achieves a stately, stylized effect consonant with its general subject. The exact day for which it may have been destined is unknown. Although the events dramatized suggest the period before Easter, the feast of St. Lazarus on 17 Decem-

---

[1] Faral, *Littérature latine*, p. 23.
[2] This is the plausible deduction of E. Wright from a study of all of them in their relation to other texts, pp. 148 ff.

ber seems equally possible; perhaps, since this play is not necessarily bound to any given service, it may have been written to be used on more than one occasion.[1]

The *Conversion of St. Paul*, like the Lazarus play, follows the biblical narrative quite closely, and is versified throughout. Its author's originality consists in his production and staging of a play on a subject treated nowhere else, so far as we know. Written in decasyllabic couplets arranged in quatrains, it gains some solemnity from this fact, as well as a certain monotony, and though considerable opportunity for action is provided by the story, the tempo of the play itself is slow and its poetical quality somewhat pedestrian. Yet the rubrics betray a playwright capable of visualizing a somewhat complicated *mise en scène* : Jerusalem is represented on one side of the playing-space, where the high priest and the young Saul occupy separate *sedes*, Damascus on the other side, where Judas and the chief of the synagogue have their places; between the two sets of *sedes* a bed is placed on which Ananias is to lie. Moreover, when Saul has to leave Damascus because of the anger of the high priest, he is lowered in a basket from a high place representing a wall ('Saulus cum discipulis suis in sporta ab aliquo alto loco, quasi a muro, ad terram demittatur'). Whatever the literary defects of the play, its scenic elements are imaginatively exploited.[2]

It is convenient to consider the four St. Nicholas plays together, although there are significant differences between them. All concern a saint unknown to the Gospels and are properly classified as miracle plays (cf. the rubrics at the beginning and end of *Iconia* : 'Aliud miraculum de sancto Nicholao . . .' and 'Finitur miraculum'). All seem to have been prepared for use on the feast-day of the saint, 6 December, and to have been composed at Fleury where the saint was much honoured. Three of the plays end with liturgical pieces in prose and one with a liturgical antiphon.

However, there are important dissimilarities between the four plays which suggest differences of authorship, date, and

---

[1] This seems to have been the case in the *Filius Getronis* where there is provision for *omnes vel primus, omnes vel secundus*, &c., showing that more than a single performance was contemplated.

[2] Young believes, ii. 224, that the play was destined for the feast of the Conversion of St. Paul, 25 Jan.

possibly of purpose. The first two, *Tres Filiae* and *Tres Clerici*, are simpler than the others; they have almost no stage directions and few complexities of rhythm. To be sure, *Tres Filiae* varies its monorhymed stanzas of two, three, and four decasyllables with refrains of four syllables and its few monorhymed stanzas of fifteen-syllabled lines with refrains of seven syllables, but *Tres Clerici* is content with four-lined stanzas of decasyllabic couplets throughout and has no refrains. *Filius Getronis* also uses decasyllables throughout (iambs instead of the trochees of *Tres Clerici*) and likewise arranges them in four-lined stanzas, but its more extensive stage directions, dramatic action, and its involved musical pattern distinguish it from the first two plays. As for *Iconia*, it is technically the most elaborate of the four.[1] Its complicated rhythms include quantitative hexameters with various types of rhyme as well as verses of seven, eight, ten, twelve, and fifteen syllables,[2] many arranged in monorhymed stanzas of different lengths, and it also uses refrains of four and five syllables. In action and *mise en scène* it is more highly developed than *Tres Filiae* and *Tres Clerici*, though less complicated than *Filius Getronis*. Musically *Iconia* is also more ambitious than any of the others: it employs 46 melodic units compared with the 23 of the longer *Filius Getronis* and with the 6 each in the two simpler plays. Moreover, both *Iconia* and *Filius Getronis* seek to adapt their musical themes to the characters portrayed, giving to each an appropriate melody and differentiating somewhat between the emotions exhibited in various scenes.[3]

Tres Filiae concerns the dowerless daughters of an impoverished father, each of whom in turn seeks a way in which she may help the family fortunes, each of whom is miraculously dowered by St. Nicholas and provided with a suitable husband. A curious symmetry characterizes the play; not only are the same refrains constantly repeated (*me miserum* and *me beatum* by

---

[1] *Filius Getronis*, however, is longer (175 lines against *Iconia*'s 113 in Albrecht's edition or 157 in Young's) and its stage directions, resembling in some ways those of the *Conversion of St. Paul*, are much fuller. Textually it is the most ambitious of the four, though not from the point of view of versification and music.

[2] Young, ii. 350–1, refers to these as fifteen-syllable units, but on pp. 344 ff. prints each unit as three lines. Cf. Albrecht, pp. 129 ff.

[3] Reese, p. 196, says that *Tres Filiae* employs two different strophes and *Tres Clerici* only one. The strophes, however, use six different melodic units. See Albrecht, pp. 118–29 (A B C D E F, with additional variations of E and F).

the father, *care pater* by the daughters), but the scenes involving
the first two daughters proceed in much the same way and
for the most part in the same words: the father laments, the
daughter begs him to desist and offers her counsel (the first
daughter agrees to become a prostitute, the second argues against
this in favour of a virtuous life, the third advises fear and love of
God), the gold appears, the father rejoices, a prospective son-
in-law presents himself, the father asks his daughter whether the
man is acceptable, the girl consents, the father blesses the union
and the happy pair depart. In the case of the third daughter, after
the girl's commendable suggestion and the miraculous appearance of the bag of gold, the father sees and detains St. Nicholas,
thanks him and is told by the saint to thank God, not him, for
the gift; then father and daughter rejoice and the scenes with
the third son-in-law proceed exactly as in the case of the other
two. If one remembers that all these verses were sung and that
realism had no part in the author's purpose, it becomes obvious
that the effect must have been not inept and humorous, as it
might seem to the modern reader, but formal and dignified, a
kind of oratorio accompanied by stately action, played with
appropriate costume and scenery.

Tres Clerici recounts the tale of three scholars who seek
lodging, and of an old man and his wife who offer it but subsequently rob and murder the boys. Forthwith St. Nicholas
appears as a pilgrim and requests food, not that which is placed
before him, but fresh meat: *carnem vellem recentem edere*. When
the old couple deny that they can furnish this the saint, aware
of the murders, insists that they lie. Then the host and hostess
recognize their guest and admit their crime, pleading for mercy.
St. Nicholas prays God that the scholars be restored to life and
that He hear the pleas of the sinners, and the play ends with the
choir singing *Te Deum laudamus*. Though the literary form of
the play exhibits little variety, the action is swift, and individual
touches, such as the energetic behaviour of the host's wife and
his subservience to her, give it more interest than its scant
length of seventy-five lines might lead one to expect.

The *Iconia Sancti Nicolai* dramatizes a legend well known to
many from Jean Bodel's famous version. A pagan—in this
instance he is particularized as a Jew instead of the source's

barbarus—somewhat hesitatingly entrusts his treasure to the guardianship of an image of St. Nicholas because the Christians ascribe to this saint miraculous powers. Robbers steal the contents of his coffer and thereupon the pagan loses all faith in the image. But St. Nicholas in person forces the thieves to return the treasure, and forthwith the Jew recovers full belief in the saint's potency. The remarkable variety of rhythms and melodic themes in the play gives it greater vivacity than this bare outline reveals. The two long monologues of the Jew, one at the opening of the play, when he expresses scepticism and derides Christian trustfulness, and the other, when he bewails his loss, denounces the Christians, and promises the image a beating, are effectively contrasted in versification and musical pattern, yet remain characteristic in both cases of the person portrayed. The thieves, too, are individualized both rhythmically and musically, and after the third thief has referred to the Jew as a man likely to guard his possessions carefully, there is some by-play between the three of them, the first finding it impossible to lift the coffer, the second advising that they break it open, and the third rejoicing to find it unlocked; they also react characteristically to the saint's harsh command to return the booty, the first suggesting that they divide it instead, the second that they take further counsel, and the third prudently advising restitution, since this would be better than losing one's life.[1] The contents of the chest—silver, vestments, and gold—are mentioned both by the Jew and the saint. Yet the properties and *mise en scène* of this play are relatively simple; nor does the action make heavy demands on the imagination of producers or audience. The remarkable diversity of rhythms and melodies and the careful delineation of the five persons involved constitute the play's chief claims to distinction.

Filius Getronis, the only extant play on this subject and a more ambitious and spectacular piece than *Iconia* in its plot, relates the story of the boy, Adeodatus, stolen from his Christian parents, Getron and Eufrosina, by the armed forces of the

---

[1] Young, ii. 350, writes, 'it is, indeed, surprising that the play-book which shows such ineptitude in managing the three *generi* in the dowry play should show so much flexibility in the treatment of the *fures* here'. I suspect the plays were written by different authors.

pagan king, Marmorinus, and miraculously returned to them
after a year through the good offices of St. Nicholas, in whom
his father and mother have kept their faith. The play seems to
have been designed for performance on St. Nicholas's day and
may have been attached directly to the liturgy.[1] The action
moves dramatically from the oriental splendour of the King's
court, where Marmorinus orders his soldiers to slay any who
resist him, to a simple scene enacted in dumb show, depicting
Getron, Eufrosina, and their son worshipping in the church of
St. Nicholas. To this church come the soldiers who capture the
boy and bring him before the King. When Marmorinus interrogates his captive and learns of the boy's religion, there is a
spirited debate between them, the King defending his own god,
Apollo, the boy reviling him:

> Deus tuus mendax et malus est;
> stultus, cecus, surdus et mutus est.

Meanwhile Eufrosina returns to St. Nicholas's church and in
lyric stanzas of great poignancy laments for her son as *Consolatrices* seek to comfort her. After the lapse of a year Getron
and his wife again visit the church of the saint, and the mother
prays for the return of her child. She then goes home and prepares bread and wine for the clergy and the poor. While these
are eating, the scene shifts to the court of Marmorinus and we
see the King dining in splendour with servants offering him
food and washing his hands. Among them, Getron's son, now
the King's cup-bearer, is heard bewailing his lot and longing
for home and kindred. As the cruel Marmorinus forbids his
departure, the saint appears, snatches up Adeodatus, goblet in
hand, and brings him before the gates of his native city. There
one of the citizens meets him, asks who he is and who gave him
the cup. When the boy replies, identifying himself and praising
St. Nicholas, the citizen hurries to Getron with the news.
Eufrosina runs to meet her son, embraces him, and thanks God
and the saint for his safety.

Although the play follows the traditional legend quite closely,
and the influence of other liturgical plays is obvious (Marmorinus is Herod transmogrified; Eufrosina sings one of Rachel's

---

[1] Cf. Albrecht, p. 110, with Young, ii. 360.

laments and the *Consolatrices* have a similar liturgical origin;
Getron repeats the words of *Pater* in the *Tres Filiae*; and many
connexions with the *Conversio S. Pauli* might be indicated),[1] yet
the characterizations, the creative details in the development of
the story, and the visualization of certain scenes, as well as the
whole dramatic movement, suggest a playwright of unusual
originality and competence. Moreover, notwithstanding a lack
of variety in the versification, there is no sense of monotony;
indeed the handling of the simple poetic structure, whether in
pure dialogue or in lyric stanzas, shows considerable subtlety in
producing exactly the desired impression. This was doubtless
aided by the music of the play, for the themes of each person
differ and in addition adapt themselves to the specific emotions
of the varying characters and circumstances. The soldiers'
abduction of Adeodatus, the boy's defiance of the King, his
homesickness, Eufrosina's grief and prayers, the realism of the
two feasts and of the citizen's behaviour, all give a sense of
concreteness and naturalness unusual in the liturgical drama.
On the other hand, as the action swiftly speeds back and forth,
as the persons of the play sing their characteristic melodies,
and as the contrasts between pagans and Christians—between
splendour and simplicity, arrogance and humility—are given
substance, the audience must have felt a mounting dramatic
tension strongly tinged with religious emotion.

The Fleury play-book contains the repertory of a famous
monastery and suggests the resources available in such a place
for dramatizing a large variety of subjects and making them
piquant to the faithful. However didactic the purpose or familiar the content, competent singing and acting, accompanied by
a skilful use of properties and costume, would turn any of these
pieces into highly dramatic entertainment.

[1] Cf. Albrecht, pp. 47–49. On the legend see Mombritius, ii. 307–9, and Young,
ii. 358 and 492–5.

V

Old Testament Plays. Hilarius.
The Beauvais *Daniel*

I N the Church, Old Testament plays never achieved the popularity of scenes derived from the New Testament or from
the life of St. Nicholas. The *Procession of Prophets*, though
characterizing the prophets and occasionally expanding their
words into little scenes, nevertheless derived most of its interest
from predictions of the coming of Christ. Of the many dramatic
stories in the Old Testament which were later to be exploited
by vernacular dramatists two alone seem to have appealed to
French liturgical playwrights : the stories of Joseph and Daniel.[1]

Amiens and Laon, both in the same ecclesiastical province of
Rheims, once possessed plays about Joseph, but only that from
the Cathedral of Laon now survives. Its end is lacking, yet
within its 245 lines it all too swiftly covers the sequence of
events from Jacob's dispatch of Joseph to inspect the flocks of
his brothers, through their sale of him into Egypt, the attempted
seduction by Potiphar's wife, Joseph's subsequent imprison-
ment, his interpretation of dreams, his restoration to power,
and the appearance of his brothers in Egypt seeking food, to
his false accusations and demand for Benjamin. Despite some
variety of versification, the metrical pattern seems monotonous :
predominantly written in short rhymed lines with no attempt
at adapting verse to speaker and no literary distinction of vocabulary, the total effect is pedestrian. The events recorded in
Genesis xxxvii–xlv have been condensed without imagination
or dramatic emphasis. The scene with Potiphar's wife is de-

---

[1] For the *Isaac and Rebecca* from Vorau see Young, ii. 258 ff. The semi-liturgical
Mystère d'Adam as well as the possible relations between the Old Testament plays
and the *Ordo Prophetarum* are discussed below in Chap. VIII. Young prints the
Old Testament plays, chap. xxv. On Hilarius see Fuller, Spanke in *ZFSL*, lvi
(1932), 249 ff., and Young, index, s.v. 'Hilarius'. It is not known on which side
of the Channel Hilarius was born. He addresses some poems to English persons,
others to persons connected with Angers. The references to Angers, his association with Abelard, his use of French and the fact that the only surviving manuscript of his works seems always to have been in France are inconclusive as
evidence of nationality, but it is evident that he at least resided in France.

scribed in the rubrics and apparently action here took the place
of speech. It is of course remarkable that such a scene should
have been enacted at all in a church, but the dramatist made no
attempt to highlight it in his play, though he reveals its importance to him in the second stanza of his prologue (a prologue
that reminds one of the introductions so ubiquitous in the later
vernacular theatre):

> Sequantur homines
> Joseph consilium;
> vitent mulieres
> nature vitium.

HILARIUS

It is a pleasure to turn from this dull play to the works of
Hilarius, a wandering scholar of the twelfth century, sometime
pupil of Abelard, and one of the few liturgical playwrights
known to us by name. Hilarius's three *ludi*, a *Raising of Lazarus*,
an *Iconia Sancti Nicolai*, and a *Daniel*, appear in a manuscript
containing miscellaneous verses and various poems addressed
by him to nuns, boys, and his teacher. Each *ludus* is preceded by
a statement as to how many *dramatis personae* are necessary, and
at the end of the *Lazarus* and the *Daniel* provision is made for
the singing of the *Te Deum laudamus*, if the play is to be performed at Matins, of the *Magnificat anima mea dominum*, if the
play is to be given at Vespers. It is apparent from these directions that although these plays are truly liturgical, their position
in the service was not fixed. As in the case of the Fleury texts,
a step toward freedom had been taken.

The *Lazarus*, similar in outline to that in the Fleury play-
book, is nevertheless more diversified, more original in verse-
structure, and livelier in action. Especially notable are the lyrical
laments of Mary and Martha written in lines of four, six, seven,
and eight syllables arranged in stanzas of varying lengths. At
the end of some of these the author has added short but poi-
gnant French refrains which must have given them a potent
immediacy for his audience. For example:

> hor ai dolor,
> hor est mis frere morz,
> por que gei plor.

Or again,

> Lase, chative!
> Des que mis frere est morz,
>   porque sui vive?

The lyrical laments themselves recall analogous passages in the
Latin *planctus* and in the later French Passion plays,[1] but here
the introduction of vernacular refrains in a liturgical text both
heightens its emotional power and represents another advance
on the road toward laicization of the drama.

No certain connexion can be established between Hilarius's
play and that of Fleury, but since he wrote another *ludus* on a
subject treated there (his St. Nicholas play), some relationship
may be plausibly posited. While Hilarius's *Lazarus* seems
fresher and more flexible than Fleury's, his *St. Nicholas* is closer
to the Latin source, contains only two speaking roles (those of
Barbarus and the Saint: the *IIII^{or} vel sex Latrones* play a silent
though not inactive part), and in general reveals less originality.
Again, however, as in his *Lazarus*, French refrains decorate
and enliven the speeches; in this case they appear only in the
speeches of Barbarus where the macaronic effect is perhaps in-
tentionally humorous. It seems possible that Hilarius may have
known earlier, simpler versions of the Fleury plays which have
since disappeared and that it was these which influenced his
compositions.

In any case his third and most elaborate play, the *Daniel*,
has no counterpart at Fleury, but apparently served to inspire
an even more remarkable play on the same subject written
at Beauvais. Hilarius's play dramatizes the events described in
Daniel v and vi. We see the feasting of King Belshazzar and his
followers; then the words *Mane*, *Thecel*, and *Phares* mysteriously
appear above the King's head and the prophet is summoned on
the advice of the Queen to interpret them. This leads to the
honouring of Daniel and his investiture by the King *pulcher-
rimis indumentis*. A second act[2] brings Darius with his army into
the action. He kills Belshazzar, assumes the crown, and invites

---

[1] On the *planctus* see Wechssler, Lindner, and Young, i. 496 ff.

[2] In the cast of characters we read *in cuius prima parte he persone sunt necessarie*;
and then *in secunda vero parte* the first person mentioned is *Rex unus sub persona
Darii*.

Daniel to sit beside him. But certain *Invidi*, jealous of the King's friendship, persuade Darius of the prophet's disloyalty and upon their advice Daniel is cast into the lions' den. While he is there an angel appears, sword in hand, and shuts the lions' mouths. As in an apocryphal addition to our Old Testament version, a second angel also appears, this time to Habakkuk, who thereupon brings food to Daniel. When the King visits the prophet and learns from him how his life has been saved by his God, he orders that the jealous accusers be cast to the lions and leads Daniel to his throne. There Daniel prophesies the coming of Christ and the play ends with an angel singing the Christmas hymn, *Nuncium vobis fero*.

The court scenes with their pomp, ceremonies, and ornamental trappings, their processions of kings, and the appearance of the Queen accompanied by her various attendants, contrast sharply with the simplicity of the prophet, the terrible nature of his punishment, and the gentleness of the angels. The audience must have stared in amazement as the handwriting appeared on the wall, as the lions' mouths were closed by the angel. Moreover, the variety of action and character in this play is reflected in its vocabulary and versification. Tone, rhythm, and rhyme change with the speakers and their moods. The text proceeds from long and stately verses with rich rhymes to short, staccato stanzas, from lines with many liturgical overtones to lines reminiscent of the goliards. Indeed the whole play reminds one of those medieval tapestries in which the combined wealth of colour, pattern, and movement creates a jewel-like impression.

Because the names Jordanus (four times), Simon (twice), and Hugo (once) have been added in the margin of our manuscript, it has been plausibly conjectured that fellow students aided Hilarius (whose own name appears five times) in writing his play.[1]

THE BEAUVAIS *DANIEL*

Joint authorship must in any case be attributed to the *Daniel* of Beauvais which begins:

> Ad honorem tui, Christe,
> Danielis ludus iste

[1] See Young, ii. 288–9, for arguments against considering these the names of actors.

in Belvaco est inventus,
et invenit hunc juventus.

This play like that of Hilarius seems to date from about the
middle of the twelfth century and to have been intended for
performance during the Christmas season. Both depart from
the canonical story of the Vulgate in the same way and both
follow the same dramatic pattern. Actually, there are so many
likenesses between them of structure, phrase, and metre that
the assumption of direct relationship is inevitable.[1]

Coffman[2] has called the Beauvais *Daniel* 'the most finished and
beautiful product of mediaeval religious drama', and it obviously
surpasses the work of Hilarius in various ways. Additional dialogues improve the motivation in certain scenes; the character
of Darius emerges as more consistent and that of Daniel as more
human; above all the choral pieces of the Beauvais students reveal a brilliance and fertility of invention unmatched in any of
the plays by Hilarius. Because of this superiority of the Beauvais
Daniel in literary and dramatic values, most critics consider it
the later of the two texts, reasoning that if Hilarius had known
it he would not have overlooked the chances it afforded to make
his own work more effective.

Such critics are inclined to assume that a teacher in the cathedral school of Beauvais, perhaps a certain Raoul, who, like
Hilarius, studied with Abelard, gave his pupils the task of
adapting Hilarius's play: the students were not asked to re-
dramatize the story, but merely to follow the pattern of the
other work, improve upon it where possible, rephrase its
speeches, and turn them into different metres. As E. Wright
says, pp. 106–7: 'This explanation would account for both the
likenesses and the differences of the plays, the similar order and
length of most of the speeches and the constant, half-hidden
resemblances between them in vocabulary and sentence-
structure.'

Curiously enough, although Hilarius had used French passages in his *Lazarus* and *St. Nicholas*, none appears in his *Daniel*.
They do occur, however, in the *Daniel* of Beauvais, indicating

---

[1] See Young, ii. 301 ff., and E. Wright, pp. 102 ff., for a detailed comparison
of the plays.
[2] In *Speculum*, ix (1934), 115.

perhaps a knowledge there of Hilarius's other works. In all these plays where bits of the vernacular are found they seem designed as decorative touches, extrinsic rather than intrinsic, probably intended to sharpen the attention of the audience.

With the Old Testament plays, with Hilarius and the Beauvais *Daniel*, the drama has moved forward. New possibilities in subject-matter, versification, and scenic effects have been discovered; liturgical bonds have been somewhat relaxed; the vernacular has been introduced into plays performed in connexion with church services.

VI

The *Sponsus*. The *Presentation of the Virgin Mary in the Temple*

THAT the vernacular might be more extensively and purposefully used than in the plays considered up to now is evident from the text of the *Sponsus*, a dramatization of the parable of the Wise and Foolish Virgins, written in the Benedictine abbey of S. Martial of Limoges.

Limoges, at the confluence of roads from Sens, Saintes, Périgueux, and Clermont-Ferrand, on the route both to the Orient and to the pilgrimage shrines of St. Martial and St. James of Compostella, early became a political, ecclesiastical, commercial, and literary centre. Here were held fairs visited by travellers of all sorts, pilgrims, crusaders, merchants from the East, clergy from far and near; and here arose the great abbey of S. Martial of Limoges, an institution that was to become famous for its school of music, its fine library, and the intellectual pre-eminence of its clergy, that was destined also to become the first exponent of the liturgical drama in France and largely responsible for its dissemination.[1]

During the period of its greatest power and influence there were written at S. Martial not only numerous examples of the dramatic *Quem quaeritis* tropes, but also an *Ordo Stellae*, *Ordo Rachelis*, *Ordo Prophetarum*, and, most ambitious of all, the earliest surviving text of a play that contains any considerable number of French verses, the *Sponsus*.[2] This text, clearly neumed for singing, is preserved in the oldest portion of a S. Martial manuscript now in the Bibliothèque Nationale of Paris.[3] It was copied by a southern scribe at the end of the eleventh or

[1] Cf. E. Wright, pp. 24 ff.

[2] On the *Sponsus* see Young, ii. 361 ff., 495–6; Rauhut, *Rom. Forsch.* l (1936), 21–50; Liuzzi, *SM*, N.S., iii (1930), 82–109; L.-P. Thomas, *Rom.* liii (1927), 43–81, lv (1929), 45–112; his ed., 1951; Cloetta, *Rom.* xxii (1893), 177–229. Facsimiles of the manuscript are in Monaci and in Coussemaker, *Histoire*. Cf. also Spanke, *ZFSL*, liv (1931), 282 ff. and 385 ff., lvi (1932), 450 ff.

[3] MS. lat. 1139.

beginning of the twelfth century and is immediately preceded
by one of the dramatic Easter tropes mentioned above and
immediately followed by the *Ordo Prophetarum*.

A performance of this play about the Wise and Foolish Virgins is even today remarkably impressive. The Virgins all take
their places, probably five on each side, as in plastic representations of the parable,[1] and all fall asleep. At the introductory
exhortation to be vigilant for the Bridegroom is coming, the
Wise (Prudentes) awake and trim their lamps, while the Foolish
(Fatuae) sleep on, their lamps reversed, the oil escaping. Only
after a second warning do the Fatuae awake and perceive their
sinful carelessness. They desperately attempt to obtain oil, first
from their wiser sisters, then from obdurate merchants, chanting their laments and their haunting refrain, *Dolentas, chaitivas,
trop i avem dormit*, with increasing poignancy after each refusal.
The urgency of their need to be supplied before His coming and
their mounting grief and terror at every failure reach a climax
when the Bridegroom appears. Once more and for the last time
they seek a remedy for their sins and admittance to His feast.
When He too repulses them, when the Wise are admitted and
the gates are everlastingly closed against the Foolish, when
these unworthy ones, beating in vain against the barriers, are
led off to eternal damnation by the demons, no medieval audience, identifying, as it did, the Wise Virgins with the blessed
and the Foolish with the damned, could fail to be stirred by the
pathos and horror of what they had seen and heard.

The play is, of course, based directly upon Matthew xxv.
1–13 (perhaps slightly influenced by xxiv. 42 and 44), and the
few differences between play and Gospel are attributable to the
requirements of dramatization or to the need and desire for
exegesis. Modifications include the explicit identification of
the Bridegroom with Christ and the second Adam, warnings
and refusals that are repeated, and the fact that the Foolish
Virgins spill their oil instead of failing to provide themselves
with this necessity. The variations in every case clarify and
make vivid. It is possible, though unprovable, that a reading
of the biblical parable preceded the performance.

In any case, the play as we have it opens with the announce-

[1] See Mâle, *xiie siècle*, pp. 148 ff.

ment in Latin by an unnamed speaker of the imminent approach of the Bridegroom, who is Christ, the second Adam who expiated the sin of the first and suffered for us on the Cross, and the Virgins are exhorted to be vigilant for His coming. Editors usually attribute this introduction to a Chorus, to Gabriel, or to some unknown angel. There are five stanzas of four lines each, and the metre is that so frequently used in medieval hymns and metrical sequences, the trochaic septenarius catalectic. Their melody we may designate as A.

These lines are followed by four French decasyllabic stanzas with refrains, which are addressed by the archangel Gabriel to the Wise Virgins. They are much like the preceding verses in content: the Virgins are again told to await the coming of the Bridegroom, whose name is Jesus, who suffered and died, but who is risen (*resors es*), and they are cautioned not to sleep. The melody differs from that of the introductory verses and may be called B.

The Foolish Virgins now approach the Wise, admitting that they have slept and carelessly spilled their oil; they beg the Wise to share the light of their lamps with their unfortunate sisters so that these may not be cast without the gates when the Bridegroom calls. (The melody of these verses of the Foolish Virgins is known as C.) The Wise Virgins refuse, directing the Foolish to buy oil of the merchants (melody D). Five of these stanzas of the Wise and Foolish Virgins—of four lines each— are in Latin hexameters, and a sixth, displaced in the manuscript but attributed to the Wise and probably destined to follow the others sung by them, is in decasyllabic French lines with the same refrain and melody (D).

The Fatuae, lamenting, proceed to ask the merchants for oil (two Latin stanzas with vernacular refrains in the same metre and with the same melody, C, as those sung before), but the merchants reply that the *domnas gentils* should return quickly to their five sisters and ask aid of them since the Bridegroom is approaching. The merchants employ French stanzas of four decasyllabic lines each and melody C of the Foolish Virgins.

Now the Fatuae complain that they cannot find what they seek and will never be allowed to go in to the marriage. At this point the Bridegroom apparently appears and closes the gates; the Foolish Virgins address Him, imploring Him to open the gates to them (in two Latin decasyllabic stanzas with vernacular refrains, the second lacking a final line and refrain and being without neumes, but probably like the first sung originally to melody C).

The play concludes with the refusal of Christus ('I know you not; go, unhappy ones, you shall be consigned to everlasting punishment in Hell'), and with the stage direction that demons shall lead the Foolish Virgins away and cast them into the lower world. Christ's speech, for which neumes are lacking, is partly in Latin, partly in French: the first four lines in Latin are in the same metre as the Introduction and may have been sung to the same melody (A); the last three lines in the vernacular are decasyllabic and it has been conjectured that they were sung to melody B, or possibly to D, or perhaps to some melody that has not survived. It also seems possible to me that they might have been effectively declaimed.[1]

For which liturgical service the *Sponsus* was destined we do not know. Since in the manuscript the preceding trope belongs to Easter and the merchants of our text often appear in Easter plays, since the words *resors es* occur in Gabriel's speech and the music of the *Sponsus* has been connected with that of Holy Week, some authorities believe its performance took place at this season. Others suggest that the theme makes it more appropriate to Advent or Christmas and that other considerations likewise indicate such a time: the allusions to the Coming of the Bridegroom, here identified as Christ and the second Adam; the presence of the *Ordo Prophetarum*, based on a Christmas *lectio*, which follows in the manuscript; and the fact that an antiphon, *Tamquam sponsus*, is sung during the *officia* of Christmas week. According to a third view—a compromise between the other two—the original Latin play which may underlie our fused Latin and French text was designed for Advent but the French redactor (responsible *inter alia* for the merchant scene and the words *resors es*) adapted the earlier text for Easter.

However, to the Middle Ages the parable of the Wise and

---

[1] Since these lines appear in the midst of passages above and below that all bear neumes, the absence of musical notation has the appearance of being deliberate rather than inadvertent.

Foolish Virgins dramatized by our play represented a prefigura-
tion of the Last Judgement: at the Second Coming of Christ
the unworthy would be consigned to hell, the wise enthroned
in paradise; the sleep of the Virgins symbolized mankind's long
sleep in death, the cry that awakened them was the trumpet call
of the archangel. So in plastic representations of the Last Judgement the Wise and Foolish Virgins are shown respectively among
the blessed and the damned. Now, although certain services
in Advent and Christmas week hint at the Second Coming—
together with the First—the parable itself is not definitely incorporated in them. It figures in the common of Virgins and
was therefore read on the feast of any saint who was a virgin,
but it could also be used at various other times in different communities: morning prayer, the fourteenth Sunday after Trinity,
&c. All this shows, of course, that its place in the liturgy was
not fixed. Since the only surviving record of a performance of
a *Ludus de decem virginibus* indicates that the *ludus* was played on
4 May 1321,[1] it seems best to believe that our *Sponsus*, though
doubtless written for some specific occasion, of itself required
no fixed time for its performance.

The suggestion has been made that a wholly Latin play preceded our version, and the suggestion seems plausible. The
Latin portions of the text form a fairly complete play by themselves and the vernacular verses reveal themselves on analysis
as merely translations of, or additions to, this hypothetical substructure. Thus the speech of Gabriel is a kind of paraphrase of
the introductory Latin exhortation and the single French stanza
given to the Wise Virgins seems a free translation of their two
Latin stanzas, whereas the merchants' two stanzas, the vernacular refrains, and the last three lines spoken by Christus may be
regarded either as translations—the first two of verses later
eliminated—or as additions designed to expand the original
Latin text. Similar conclusions have been reached by Rauhut[2]
in his study of the music: the music of the Latin portions seems
complete in itself and the French verses either adopt it (cf. their
use of melodies C and D) or add to it (melody B) or, as in the
case of the vernacular refrains to Latin stanzas, introduce a

---

[1] Rauhut, p. 24.
[2] Rauhut, p. 38. On the music see also Liuzzi.

superfluous and incongruous addition to a melody already concluded. Accordingly, although a single author—like Hilarius,
for example—might have been quite capable of writing a play
in which Latin and French verses succeeded one another, it
seems more likely that in the case of the *Sponsus*, as in that of
the Origny play,[1] a dramatic office written in Latin preceded
our present version. Our fused text, therefore, may be reasonably attributed to some redactor who paraphrased and added
to a Latin original so that lay audiences might understand the
action they were witnessing, an action implied, though not
described, in the biblical parable.

The language of the vernacular part of this play, a language
on the borderline between French and Provençal, suggests that
its author came from the region between Angoulême and
Limoges, and that the text was copied by a scribe who spoke
Provençal. The few Latin words incorporated in the French
portions (*virgines* [twice], *scriptura, oleo*) may reflect the posited
Latin original or may have been deliberately introduced because
of their holy or liturgical connotations.

An attempt has been made to prove that more of these emo-
tive Latin words than are now present were originally introduced into the vernacular portions of the text and that certain
corrupt or difficult verses may be reasonably corrected by the
incorporation of at least one such word in each stanza.[2] But this
attempt involves resort to a hypothetical type of caesura and to
several questionable emendations, and on the whole raises more
problems than it solves. Something has also been written to
show that an intentional symbolism underlies the number and
arrangement of the stanzas (the five strophes of the Latin prologue signifying the five Virgins or the five senses, the ten
strophes attributed to the Virgins signifying their number, &c.),
but there is little tangible evidence to support this suggestion,
and the numbers proposed have been questioned.[3]

It is perhaps enough to say that the structural symmetry and
the varied metres of the play, as it has come down to us, reveal
considerable conscious artistry and that the music likewise,

[1] See Chap. II above.
[2] Thomas, *Rom.* liii (1927), 43 ff.; lv (1929), 45 ff.
[3] Thomas, *Rom.* lv (1929), 109–11. Cf. Rauhut, p. 49.

with its four melodies carefully adapted to the different speakers as leitmotifs—the hymn-like prologue, the repetitious melody of Gabriel, the plaintive, agitated cadences of the Foolish Virgins and the richer, more developed notes of the Wise Virgins —suggest the studied musicianship of some master of the famous school of S. Martial of Limoges. Whether or not this man, like some medieval Wagner, was both musician and playwright, the music and the action of the piece complement each other, creating the melodramatic effects of opera rather than the religious calm of oratorio.

THE *PRESENTATION OF THE VIRGIN MARY IN THE TEMPLE*

The possibilities of liturgical representations were not exhausted even by such elaborate plays as the two Daniel *ludi* and the *Sponsus*. Liturgical material unused in earlier texts might at any time provide creative writers with new opportunities to write plays in which colourful persons and actions, suspense and tension could profoundly stir religious emotions, in which stately processions and magnificent costumes might delight the eye and beautiful music serve as an exciting background. Once the impulse had been given, subjects of every sort proved available.[1]

Philippe de Mézières, for example, brought to Avignon, perhaps in 1372, surely in 1385, a dramatic performance of the *Presentation of the Virgin Mary in the Temple* that contains every element necessary for a supremely moving spectacle. His characters number twenty-two persons and include the little Mary, her father and mother, two maidens, Gabriel, Raphael, Michael and nine angels, Ecclesia and the villains of the piece, Synagoga and Lucifer. Detailed directions for staging this magnificent pageant describe the organization of its two great processions, the two stages required for its performance, which had to be set up at the eastern end of the church, and all the sumptuous costumes and properties needed. Provision is even made for the chains and howling of Lucifer and for the laughter certain to arise when Synagoga is pushed down the west steps of the

[1] The great Tegernsee *Antichrist* of the twelfth century indicates how early and how far such original plays might develop. Cf. Young, ii. 369 ff.

stage by Gabriel and Raphael, loses her banner as well as the tables of the Old Law, and flees weeping from the church.[1]

Plays as late as this may well have been influenced by the contemporary vernacular theatre. Indeed, just as the performances without the church drew their initial inspiration from the liturgical drama, so the later performances given within the sacred precincts must have found suggestions for new life in the secular plays.

[1] On this play see also Chap. VII below, and for this and other plays about the Virgin see Young, chap. xxiv. Philippe de Mézières and his possible authorship of the French Griseldis play are discussed below, Chap. XV.

VII

Distribution, Dissemination, and Production
of the Liturgical Drama

IT seems probable, as we have seen, that both the Easter and
Christmas plays arose in France, the former in the tenth,
the latter in the eleventh century. Thence they spread over
the Continent, England and Ireland, finding a home even in
the Church of the Holy Sepulchre in Jerusalem where they were
introduced by the predominantly French clergy who accompanied the Crusaders.[1]

The Abbey of S. Martial in Limoges apparently was the earliest exponent of the liturgical drama and created in embryonic
form most of the important plays adopted elsewhere. But
while it was an innovator, its plays, with the exception of the
unique *Sponsus*, remained essentially simple and the task of de-
veloping them fell upon other churches. Those of Normandy
expanded the more primitive versions of S. Martial, and texts
displaying typical Norman contributions found their way, as
might be expected, to England, Ireland, and Sicily. Perhaps the
greatest number of texts and the most ambitious plays that survive are associated with the ecclesiastical provinces of Rheims
and Sens. In the province of Rheims the cathedral of Beauvais
produced a *Peregrini* and a *Daniel* of superior literary quality,
whereas the convent of Origny-Ste-Benoîte provided an unusually moving and original *Ludus Paschalis*. The monastery of
Fleury in the province of Sens not only created plays reaching
the highest degree of perfection and bequeathed to posterity
the richest collection in any single manuscript, but also seems
to have been a potent influence in spreading the liturgical drama
elsewhere in France as well as in England and perhaps in Germany and Spain. This monastery, like the Abbey of S. Martial
in Limoges, was famous in the Middle Ages for its school of
music, its relics, intellectual accomplishments, and the wise

[1] See Young, i. 262; ii. 508.

management of its properties. Both churches attracted pilgrims and officials of other foundations who came to study their customs. Their monks were in demand elsewhere as teachers; their participation in associations of friendship and hospitality was widely sought. It is evident how and why their plays were carried abroad as well as why it happens that our very earliest reference to the Easter ceremonies comes from an English document, the famous *Regularis Concordia*, which mentions its indebtedness to the custom of Fleury.[1]

Plays survive from cathedrals, monasteries, and convents. Naturally, the longer, more highly developed texts belong in general to the larger, more prosperous institutions. Cathedrals sponsoring plays include those of Beauvais, Laon, Rouen, Coutances, Nevers, and Paris. Among the monastic orders the Benedictines were almost the only ones to produce plays; it was their monasteries that inspired the notable texts of S. Martial of Limoges and Fleury, as well as those of Compiègne, Mont-S.-Michel, Fécamp, and S.-Ouen. Three Benedictine convents for women, Origny-Ste-Benoîte, Notre-Dame of Troyes, and Ste-Croix of Poitiers, also produced excellent plays that not unexpectedly reveal some sort of relationship with one another.[2] Many churches were content with a fairly simple Easter or Christmas play, or both, and with them alone. But others owned more ambitious texts. Amiens seems to have had an *Ordo Joseph* and a *Purification of the Virgin*; Bayeux had a *Peregrini*; Beauvais sponsored a Daniel play and a *Peregrini*; Fleury could claim a *Conversio Sancti Pauli*, an *Ordo Rachelis*, a *Peregrini*, a *Resuscitatio Lazari*, and four plays about St. Nicholas; Laon had an *Ordo Joseph* and *Prophetae*, as well as the Rachel scenes in its Christmas play; Limoges possessed an *Ordo Rachelis*, *Prophetae*, and the unique *Sponsus*; Rouen fathered a *Peregrini* and *Prophetae*, both of which survive in a number of manuscripts; Saintes had a simple *Peregrini*; Tours provided a *Prophetae*—and most of these texts are in addition to one or more versions of the Easter and Christmas plays.

[1] On the *Regularis Concordia* see Chap. II above. On Fleury see Young, i. 665; Albrecht, pp. 4-5; E. Wright, pp. 137 ff. In the present chapter I am greatly indebted to E. Wright's valuable monograph.

[2] For the preponderant role of the Benedictines in the vernacular productions of the English cloisters see Legge, pp. 3-4.

In the texts themselves many similarities occur that can only be the result of direct borrowings. Within each ecclesiastical province it was natural that the same play, perhaps with a few individual changes, might be taken by one church from another. But the plays made their way farther afield, and here such influences as have been posited in the case of Fleury and S. Martial of Limoges may be assumed. Occasionally we can detect some individual, perhaps a bishop, abbot, cantor, or simple clerk, in the act of taking a play from one community to another. Thus Hilarius, the talented wandering scholar, probably borrowed some of the lines of his *Raising of Lazarus* from the early playwrights of Fleury, whereas he himself, in his *Daniel*, seems to have inspired the liturgical dramatists of Beauvais, perhaps by way of Raoul, a fellow student under Abelard. Similarly, we learn that the scribe of the Easter play of the convent of Notre-Dame of Troyes apparently brought that play there from Origny-Ste-Benoîte. It is also possible that Hugues III, who studied at Laon in his youth, may have introduced at Rouen, when he became archbishop there, a *Prophetae* which he had seen at Laon as a student.[1]

For the most part, however, the anonymity of the plays is complete; liturgical influences and the use of the same liturgical proses, hymns, &c., tended to keep texts conservative and to reduce innovations; and though great creative talent is often apparent, we can only credit it to some nameless master in S. Martial of Limoges, in the monastery of Fleury, or in one of the other famous medieval centres of art and learning. Who first versified the prophecies, who conceived initially of using the dramatic *Noli me tangere* scene, who introduced the *mercator* or the bragging soldiers at the tomb, who made the momentous leap from plays of the Easter and Christmas seasons to plays appropriate to other occasions, we shall probably never know. Nor are we likely to learn who created the aesthetic innovations that produced the elaborate versification and musical accompaniments of some of these plays. During the early Middle Ages anonymity was the rule, not the exception, and throughout the period the names of authors of dramatic compositions and of the music accompanying their performance have only infre-

[1] On all these conclusions see E. Wright, pp. 166 ff.

quently survived. The liturgical dramatists seem to have created for the glory of God alone.

The actors who presented the plays in the churches might be selected from almost any rank, ranging from the higher clergy, who would usually be entrusted with the more important and dignified roles, down to the *clerici* and *pueri* who normally sang the smaller parts and women's roles.[1] Similarly in the cloister schools and convents, any of the competent inmates might participate. The words were sung or chanted, frequently with books open before the singers, and occasionally the congregation might join in a hymn at the end, although the regular conclusion of the liturgical plays was the *Te Deum laudamus* sung by the players alone.

Church vestments supplied most of the costumes. Surplices, copes, chasubles, dalmatics, stoles, albs, &c., are mentioned repeatedly in our texts. No strain would be put upon the sacristies in furnishing these or the simple properties required, the scrolls, chests, banners, tablets of the law, the staffs for pointing out the star or for indicating pilgrims, the seats for the prophets, the crowns for the kings, and the like. But for the more elaborate plays, for example the Rouen *Prophetae* requiring an ass and a fiery furnace, for all the plays involving armed soldiers and for such *ludi* as the Beauvais *Daniel* where men in skins and masks probably represented the lions, recourse to the laity must have been necessary.

The *mise en scène* of the Easter play was the Easter sepulchre.[2] The nature and position of the sepulchre varied, however. Sometimes the altar itself served as tomb, sometimes a vessel or small structure on the altar might be used, but, more realistically, the tomb might be represented by a chapel or separate structures of different sorts, of stone or wood, temporary or permanent, some of which could be entered for heightened effect. In France the action of the *Visitatio* usually took place in the chancel, either around an altar serving as sepulchre or a

[1] We read of the apostles being represented by *antiquiores et honorabiliores canonici* (Schüttpelz, p. 25), of *tres clerici de maiori sede* impersonating the Magi at Rouen (Young, ii. 436), and we find among the texts of the *Visitatio* that those who played the roles of the Marys and the angels are *cantores, custodes chori, fratres, pueri, capellani, diacones, sacerdotes, presbiteri, scolares*, &c.

[2] See Bonnell, *PMLA*, xxxi (1916), 664 ff., and Brooks, *The Sepulchre of Christ*.

specially prepared structure, and in general for the earlier plays of Easter and Christmas the eastern part of the church served as stage. Many texts expressly mention the choir. Processions might start in cloisters or in adjacent sacristies or chapter-houses which served as dressing-rooms, and they might then enter the church either through the nave or a transept. The three Magi often proceeded from different directions and met before the high altar.

However, the more complex representations soon found the choir inadequate for their expanded action. It is evident that in Germany such performances as those of the Benediktbeuern Christmas play[1] and the Tegernsee *Antichristus* made use of the nave, and in France the directions for the great performance of the *Presentation of the Virgin* at Avignon in the fourteenth century call for the erection of special stages between the great west portal and the choir-stalls.

For most liturgical plays the so-called 'simultaneous staging' was the rule. Thus in the Fleury *Conversion of St. Paul*, Jerusalem is on one side of the playing-space, Damascus on the other; in the Daniel plays, the *domus* of the hero to which he retires, the lions' den, and the throne occupied successively by Belshazzar and Darius, all are in view from the opening of the plays. Similarly the various St. Nicholas plays move the chief characters from one part of the playing-space to another, but always to stations visible to the audience from the beginning to the end of the performance. Only in such a highly organized spectacle as the *Presentation of the Virgin* do we find some provision for a distinct change of locale: in that *ordo* the two stages have a symbolical value, the second connoting Mary's reception into the church after her presentation. Processions were, of course, introduced at times to suggest journeys and therefore scene-shifts, but once the actors had arrived at the playing-space, the stage-setting, however far-flung the action, remained fixed.

Although the *Presentation of the Virgin* adapted by Philippe de Mézières can hardly be used as typical of the earlier plays, its copious directions will show to what lengths the more elaborate

---

[1] I agree with Young (ii. 196) that *in fronte ecclesiae* in the Benediktbeuern text probably refers to the front part of the church or west end of the nave.

ceremonies might go.[1] The costumes and properties are described minutely and they must have been superb. Silks and satins in gleaming white or rich shades of blue, green, and other colours vied with costumes all of gold and there were countless gold and jewelled crowns, crosses, brooches, &c. Ecclesia, for example, 'induetur totum de auro in habitu diaconi, capillis pulcerrimis mulieris extensis super humeros; et super capud portabit quandam coronam auream cum liliis et lapidibus preciosis'. She bore a golden cross in one hand, a golden apple in the other, and a gilded *calix* was attached to her breast. The colours of the vestments described have symbolical values: Mary's tunic is *albissima* without superfluous artifice, though it is pleated; her mantle too is white, of sendal or silk. She wears only white and gold, according to the text, indicating her purity and virginity and the splendour of her love. Even the villainous Synagoga, though darkly garbed, carried a ruby-red banner with S.P.Q.R. inscribed upon it; and Lucifer, with horns, menacing teeth, and a horrible expression, rattled the bright iron chain by which he was bound to the archangel Michael who, according to the directions, was armed in a most fair fashion and brandished aloft a flashing sword.

Perhaps more important than the directions for the costumes are those for the construction of the two stages required by this *repraesentatio figurata*. One stage (*edificium de lignis, seu stacio*; also called *solarium*) was to be erected in the middle of the church between the great west portal and the entrance to the choir, though a little nearer the choir, located so that it might be clearly visible from all parts of the church. It was to stand 6 feet high,[2] to be 10 feet from north to south, and 8 feet from east to west; it was to be reached by stairways on the west and east, and these stairways, 3 feet wide, were to be closed by wooden boards so that none but the actors could use them. A railing 2 feet high surrounded the platform in order that it would appear more suitable for the performance and also to prevent

[1] See Young, ii. 225 ff. These directions are even more explicit than the famous rubrics of the *Mystère d'Adam* with which they can profitably be compared.

[2] One would like to know the exact value of these *pedes* in Avignon in 1372-85, but twelve inches should be approximately correct, since the late Roman and late French medieval foot varied only slightly from this norm. For the date see Chap. VI above.

the performers from falling off. The floors of the *solarium* as well as the bench and the seats upon it were all to be covered with cloths or tapestries, and the entire structure was to be built as strongly as possible to resist the pressure of the populace.

A bench (*scampnum*)[1] for Joachim, Mary, and Anna was placed on the northern side of the platform and this bench extended from west to east. So that the little Mary, who sat between her parents, might be visible to the audience, her seat in the middle of the bench was to be raised. Between the bench and the northern extremity of the stage there must be space at the two corners for Gabriel and Raphael to stand behind Mary. Across, on the southern side of the stage, two seats of the same height as the bench, one toward the east and the other toward the west, were provided for Ecclesia and Synagoga respectively. These balanced the bench, and, balancing the angels Gabriel and Raphael, were two young *pulsatores* (musicians) who stood in the corners of the southern side.

Another smaller and higher stage was also to be erected, this one between the choir-stalls and the great altar on the northern side of the church. This served for the end of the play when, after the principal characters had proceeded from the larger stage through the choir and had assisted at Mary's presentation to the bishop at the high altar, she ascended the smaller stage, accompanied only by two virgins and the angels Gabriel and Raphael, there released her dove, and there remained throughout the following Mass.

This second stage was to be placed against a wall or pillar *in loco eminenti* (cf. the location of terrestrial paradise in the *Mystère d'Adam*) at a height of 7 or 8 feet. It was to be 6 feet square, surrounded by a light wooden railing a foot high. It, like the other *solarium*, was to be carpeted *de tapetis*, and a footstool and two cushions, one smaller than the other, both covered with silk, were to be placed in the centre for Mary to kneel and sit upon.

In the remarkable document preserving our text nothing is left to chance. Arrangements have been made for an appro-

---

[1] On the *scamnum* used by the prophets of the *Mystère d'Adam* see *PMLA*, lix (1944), 15, note 18.

priate curtained dressing-place, for the proper marshalling and ordering of the processions, for the behaviour at every point of those concerned in the performance, and for the music, both vocal and instrumental, *ad excitandum populum ad devotionem*. Not only are the costumes and gestures described in detail, but also the exact position of the actors and the manner of their entrances and exits. We learn, for example, that the procession must start early because at the time of the celebration, 21 November, *dies tunc breves sunt* and the *misterium representationis prolixum est et devotissimum*. Obviously the author did not want his pageant spoiled by haste. The path had to be cleared for Mary and her retinue and their persons protected by strong young men (*juvenes et robusti*) armed with spears. Mary ascends the stage *hylari facie*; all heads bow reverently before her throughout the piece; hands are raised toward heaven at appropriate moments; Michael *cum pedibus verberabit* a bound and howling (*ululantem*) Lucifer, and shall drive him from the church where he shall appear no more; chanting, singing, the playing of instruments or their cessation, all are indicated by such directions as *alta voce quasi cantando incipit dicere*, or *voce grossa mulieris vidue et provecte dicet*, or *quasi flendo cantabit*, or *instrumenta pulsabuntur modicum*, or *instrumenta amplius non pulsabunt*.

From all this it is obvious that the medieval drama of the Church must have been more stimulating emotionally than any modern opera. To the colour, stirring action, and musical evocation of our contemporary stage were added 'plots' and persons associated with the deepest experiences of a medieval audience and a sense of religious participation that made attendance at these liturgical plays an act of worship as well as a source of exciting entertainment.

VIII

Transitional Plays.
Le Mystère d'Adam

THE gap between liturgical and non-liturgical plays has
been conveniently bridged by the use of the term 'semi-
liturgical'. But actually no exact line of demarcation can
be drawn. While still performed within the church, the medieval
drama had expanded to absorb themes taken from every aspect
of sacred history, including material not only from the New and
Old Testaments but from a sermon, the apocrypha, eschato-
logy, and saints' lives. Although many plays continued to be
attached to the church service, some were so loosely connected
that they need not be given at any specified office. And while
liturgical or biblical passages were freely incorporated in the
simpler, earlier texts, the more elaborate, later plays came to be
characterized by an increasing use of original compositions.
Even the vernacular, as we have seen, was sanctioned in plays
performed within the churches.

From one point of view or another, therefore, some of the
plays already considered might be regarded as transitional. The
various St. Nicholas plays, the Daniel *ludi*, the Fleury *Conversion
of St. Paul*, the *Sponsus*, and the *Procession of Prophets* exploited
lay characters or lay scenic effects to a remarkable extent. The
Ordo Prophetarum was readily detachable from the liturgy and
two of the plays by Hilarius might be performed either at
Matins or at Vespers. There are French passages in Hilarius's
Lazarus and *St. Nicholas*, in the Beauvais *Daniel*, and in the
Origny-Ste-Benoîte *Ludus Paschalis*, whereas the *Sponsus* relies
for its effects upon an even more abundant use of the vernacular.
Most of these texts exhibit independence in manner as well as
matter, and some achieve poetry of rare distinction.

Besides an ever-expanding range of subjects, a more flexible
connexion with the liturgy, original verse forms, and the introduction of the vernacular, other changes mark the evolution of
the drama from its beginnings in the simple Easter trope to its

emergence from the church. The tone of the plays, stately and impersonal at first, gradually became coloured with the heightened emotions of a Magdalen, a Herod, a Rachel, or those Foolish Virgins who were damned for all eternity. And this change was reflected in more elaborate costumes and stage-effects. Whereas church vestments and an unadorned ecclesiastical setting had sufficed for the earlier offices, in the case of the later Christmas plays, the Daniel *ludi*, and the Fleury *Filius Getronis*, for example, it must have been necessary to resort to lay properties. A tendency toward realism and even comedy appeared: soldiers guarding the tomb who boasted of their prowess but exhibited cowardice when put to the test; spice-merchants with an eye for a bargain; irate and bombastic Herods; a howling Lucifer; a Synagoga pushed amid laughter down the steps of the stage. With the introduction of more varied metres and rhymed stanzas, musical accompaniments became more original and ornate. It is also possible that in some of the later plays chanting and singing were replaced by recitation.

Above all, the tendency toward expansion, toward the introduction of longer plays with many *loci* and characters, perhaps, too, of characters not quite consonant with religious worship, eventually put something of a strain upon the churches. It must have been tempting, especially in fine weather, to move the spectacles out of doors. Precedent was at hand, for quite early we hear of performances given in refectories, schools, and cemeteries.[1] Outside the church a larger audience might be attracted and accommodated, more stations could be provided, freedom from the constrictions of time as well as space would be achieved. Lay actors could also more readily be pressed into service. The desire to make the teachings of religion visible, potent, and palatable to the common folk, reflected in the use of the vernacular and the introduction of realism, found new allies when the plays were performed outside the sacred edifices.

---

[1] Gerhoh von Reichersberg speaks of plays in the refectory of Augsburg in 1122–3 (Young, ii. 411). On miracle plays in the schools see Chap. X below. Our earliest records of plays in Limoges mention that they took place near the stone cross in the cemetery of S. Martial in 1290 and 1302 (Petit de Julleville, *Mystères*, ii. 2). On secularization of the plays see Chambers, ii, chap. xx, Creizenach, i. 94 ff., Young, ii. 397 ff.

Now recitation might in large measure replace singing, now diversion could be openly acknowledged.

LE MYSTÈRE D'ADAM

The *Mystère d'Adam*, which is roughly contemporaneous with some of the more ambitious liturgical plays, though actually earlier than others, embodies to a marked degree most of the changes we have signalled. It is the first surviving French play that is wholly in the vernacular except for its Latin stage-directions, its use of Latin versified prophecies, and its occasional introduction of liturgical readings and responsories. It is destined for recitation, rather than singing, although during the performance certain responsories were to be sung by the choir. Above all it indicates by its humour and realistic treatment of sacred themes that its object was to entertain as well as instruct.

This play may properly be called semi-liturgical in that it is still attached to the church by its use of the outside of the building as a stage and the inside as dressing-room and backstage. It also relies on the church choir for readings and responsories that belong to the offices of Septuagesima. And finally it adapts and versifies, sometimes in the vernacular, sometimes in Latin, a liturgical prophet play.

The *Mystère d'Adam* is usually dated in the third quarter of the twelfth century (between 1146 and 1174) and the author, according to most authorities, was an Anglo-Norman.[1] The work is one of the most delightful and original compositions of the Middle Ages and it has been of special interest to historians of the theatre because of its remarkable text, its transitional character—partly lay, partly liturgical—and because

---

[1] Editions by Grass and Studer. Cf. Breuer, *ZRP*, li (1931), 625–64 and lii (1932), 1–66; G. Frank, *PMLA*, lix (1944), 7–17. For an English translation of the play see E. N. Stone, *Washington Univ. Pub. in Language and Literature*, iv (1926), 159–93. Breuer suggests that the author, though Anglo-Norman, may have written for spectators on the Continent. Creizenach, i. 127, believes that the use of the Anglo-Norman dialect would have restricted the audience to the Norman conquerors and finds it remarkable that the play was not destined for the *Volk*. But, according to Walberg, *Quelques aspects*, p. 22, all classes in England understood French by the second half of the twelfth century, and it seems to me that the spirit of the play as well as the devils' sallies among the people who sit outside the church (cf. *per populum, per plateas*) indicate a popular rather than a limited public.

of its comprehensive stage-directions which show the poet's professional concern for its correct performance in matters of diction, *mise en scène*, and costume, and which also give us much information about medieval dramatic techniques.

Unfortunately, the text is incomplete at the end, and all that remains are three sections which may conveniently be termed 'acts'. The first treats the story of Adam and Eve; the second that of Cain and Abel; the third is a prophet play in which individual figures from the Old Testament predict the coming of Christ. Curtailed as it is, however, the originality of the characterizations and the liveliness of action and dialogue make the play an outstanding achievement.

Particularly adroit is the scene in which Diabolus tempts Eve, coaxing and flattering her, appealing to her pride, vanity, and ambition. He approaches her by insinuating that he wants to help her and advance her interests. Next he begins to arouse her curiosity: he will tell her a wonderful secret, if she will promise not to reveal it. After she promises, he says cunningly that he will trust her and put himself completely in her power. Then he proceeds to contrast her wisdom and exquisite tenderness with Adam's stupidity and obstinancy. She admits that Adam is a little hard and proud. 'He'll soon be soft', says the devil, 'and as for his pride, why, Adam is nothing but a slave. He can't even take care of himself. You at least must look out for your own future. You're a dainty, weak little thing—whiter than a snow-flake, more delicate than a rose. The Creator made an ill-assorted couple in you two: you are too soft and Adam's too hard. Nevertheless, you are the wiser one, you have a good head and an understanding mind.'[1] 'And yet', he continues, 'God tricked you. The fruits of the garden that you are permitted to eat have no virtue; only the one He has forbidden can make you strong and give you power; in it is the grace of life and the knowledge of Good and Evil.' Eve asks what this fruit tastes like. 'Ah', says the devil, 'it has a celestial flavour', and if she will only eat of it she will be queen of the whole world, of heaven and hell,

---

[1] Cf. lines 205 ff. Note especially the subtlety of Diabolus's language, for example, his use of the diminutive *fieblette* (227) in the charming lines: 'Tu es fieblette e tendre chose, / E es plus fresche que n'est rose; / Tu es plus blanche que cristal, / Que neif que chiet sor glace en val.'

master of all knowledge, in short, he slyly promises, she will at last occupy a position befitting her lovely face and figure.

Adam is obviously made of sterner stuff than Eve. Early in the play he twice rebuffs Satan, saying he is content with his lot, that he loves and fears his Creator, that he has no desire to disobey God's commands. After Eve's colloquy with the devil, Adam scolds her for listening to so evil a counsellor. But even as Adam and Eve are speaking, an artificially constructed serpent arises near the forbidden tree. Eve leans close and pretends to listen to its advice. Then she takes the apple and offers it to Adam, alternately enticing and taunting him. Its flavour, she says, is delicious; he can't imagine how good it is unless he tastes it. He's a coward to hesitate. Such sweetness no man ever knew before. Why delay? What's he afraid of? . . . And so, between Satan and Eve, Adam's downfall is accomplished.

The second act, the story of Cain and Abel, while somewhat less subtle and entertaining than the first, nevertheless betrays again an artist who has the power of re-creating and visualizing for himself. And here, as in the first act, the dialogue is deftly managed; couplets and even single lines are divided between the speakers, so that an effect of great swiftness and vivacity is achieved. Moreover, the brothers are carefully differentiated. Abel, a simple man, is always pious, gentle, and affectionate. Cain, cynical and sophisticated, accuses Abel of being a weakling, of sermonizing and trying to gain God's favour at his brother's expense, and at one point he crossly exclaims: 'You're a fine preacher! If anyone cared to listen to you, he'd soon have little to offer. As for me, I don't like giving tithes. Do as you will with your own possessions, and I'll do as I like with mine. You won't be damned for my sins.'[1] By considerably expanding Genesis iv the author emphasizes the enmity between the brothers and supplies additional reasons for God's rejection of Cain's offering. Thus the murder, which is finally perpetrated after considerable suspense, comes as a well-motivated climax.

The third act, the prophet scene, is usually dismissed as a translation of some lost liturgical *Ordo Prophetarum*, but it can be shown that the author used a good deal of latitude and originality even in this part of the text. The underlying source

[1] Lines 611 ff.

of all our prophet plays, as we have seen in Chapter III, is a pseudo-Augustinian sermon against Jews, Pagans, and Arians, but although the author of the *Adam* sometimes uses this sermon directly, he also turns to the Scriptures at times and gives his wise men prophecies to recite that are not found in the sermon; in two cases he seems to have used a Greek homily, probably known in the West in a Latin translation, and at other times he apparently translates from a versified Latin play similar to those that have survived. Clearly the author, like the liturgical playwright of Rouen, had a definite picture in mind of each of his prophets and they are carefully described in the accompanying Latin rubrics. In short, throughout this whole remarkable composition we are in the presence of an inventive genius and even in the most conventional part there is original and creative eclecticism.

The versification of the entire play has been artfully adapted to the effects desired. Sprightliness and animation are achieved by octosyllabic couplets, each line of which may be spoken by a single speaker or even be broken up and shared by two speakers. On the other hand for the more solemn moments of the play, such as the installation in terrestrial paradise, the lamentations of Adam and Eve, &c., longer and more stately measures have been adopted. Rhymes are usually grouped in couplets, a few times in quatrains, and once in a twelve-line tirade, but there is no attempt at linking speeches together by so-called mnemonic rhymes. Whether because of faulty transmission or because of the dialectal idiosyncrasies of the author or scribe, many verses seem incorrect by continental standards. If the author of the *Adam* was an Anglo-Norman, his native speech may in part be held responsible.[1] In any case the spontaneity and flexibility of his lines, their verve and swing, more than compensate for any syllabic irregularities. And the vocabulary, like the versification,

---

[1] See Legge, pp. 137 ff., and *La Seinte Resureccion* (*ANTS* edition), pp. lxxii ff., for wise conclusions about Anglo-Norman versification. Studer probably emends his edition unnecessarily by assuming too many arbitrary rhythmic rules, but it is obvious that our dramatist was himself a perfectionist since in his very first stage-direction he insists that all persons should be instructed to speak in good order and to make gestures fitting to the thing of which they speak and that they should neither add nor subtract a syllable from their lines ('in rithmis nec sillabam addant nec demant').

subtly furthers plot, motives, and characterization by being in turn colloquial and sedate.

Of course many of the admirable qualities of the *Adam* have long been recognized: the acumen displayed in its characterization and motivation; the realism[1] and lively freshness of its dialogues; the skill with which the verse forms have been manipulated. Yet its author has seldom been given sufficient credit for the originality of his whole conception. Here is a play, still attached to the church, through its use of the church itself and of church properties, through its incorporation of liturgical readings and responsories, and through its adaptation of a liturgical *Ordo Prophetarum*. Nevertheless, as we have seen, the author has dramatized and observed for himself the stories of Adam and Eve, Cain and Abel, and he has done this with more spirit, delicacy, and imagination than any of his medieval successors. Moreover, so far as we know, he had no predecessors in dramatizing these stories. Surely a man capable of such creative and untrammelled writing needed few 'sources' and may be presumed, when proof to the contrary is lacking, to have drawn largely upon his own inspiration.[2]

Sepet's suggestion[3] that the first two acts of the *Adam* in some fashion 'budded off' from a liturgical prophet play is no longer accepted. Rather it would seem that the liturgy itself may be held ultimately responsible, since, as Émile Mâle has pointed out for the arts and Hardin Craig and A. Jenney for the origins of the medieval Old Testament plays, nearly all the scenes and legends pictured in medieval painting, sculpture, and the drama represent the same selections that appear in the liturgy of the church. And, of course, in our *Mystère d'Adam* the *lectiones* and *responsoria* have been directly incorporated.

It may well be that in this play we have an early attempt at cycle-making. Just as the scene of the *Quem quaeritis in sepulchro?* expanded to include events preceding and following the Resurrection, even as the Christmas plays came to embrace more and more of the scenes preceding and following that of the shep-

---

[1] For an analysis of this realism see Auerbach, chap. vii.

[2] See G. Frank, *PMLA*, lix (1944), pp. 7 ff., for a fuller exposition.

[3] Sepet, *Prophètes, passim.* On his views see W. Meyer, *Frag. Bur.*, pp. 53–56; H. Craig, *MP*, x (1913), 473 ff.; A. Jenney, *MP*, xiii (1915), 59 ff.; Young, ii. 171. Mâle's suggestions are in his *xiiie siècle*, p. 182. Cf. also G. Frank, loc. cit.

herds, so the author of the *Mystère d'Adam* may have been inspired to enlarge his canvas and extend the action of his play back as far as the Creation and forward into the New Testament. Indeed his prophets may have served merely as a link between scenes from the Old and New Testaments. To be sure, others may have had this idea before him, but, if so, their plays do not survive, and there seems no reason for not crediting him with a conception that might have occurred independently to many a medieval artist. We find it at any rate about his time on a twelfth-century façade of Notre-Dame-la-Grande at Poitiers, which pictures the prophets flanked by Adam and Eve on one side and by the Annunciation on the other. It occurs again in an account from Regensburg dated 1194 where it is recorded that an *ordo* was celebrated concerned with the angels and the fall of Lucifer, with the creation and fall of man, and with the prophets. We find it, of course, in later plays like the Ste Geneviève *Nativité*, which begins with the Creation and Fall, shows Adam and Eve encountering Isaiah and Daniel in hell, and proceeds to the marriage of Joseph and Mary; and it may be observed in the great English cycles where a play about the prophets regularly serves to form a transition between scenes from the Old and New Testaments.

That our author possessed a sense of unity and had his first two acts in mind while writing his third is evident from the fact that five of his eleven prophets, unlike their biblical prototypes and unlike those of any known *Prophetae*, expressly mention Adam by name, ending their prophecies by predicting that Christ will deliver Adam from his sufferings and save the sons of Eve. Our play is, of course, incomplete, so that whatever further unity it may have possessed must be a matter of conjecture. Some authorities have suggested that the prophets here, as in the Benediktbeuern Christmas play, introduced a scene associated with the Nativity, and this would be consonant with their role in the English cycles. Craig, however, believes they may have introduced scenes from the Easter series, as in the St. Gall play and the *Frankfurter Dirigierrolle*. If so, or if our author contemplated a still more ambitious scheme, including the Nativity, Passion, and Resurrection in his work, a fitting end to the whole would have been a Harrowing of Hell in which Adam, Eve, Abel, and the prophets would have been shown emerging from torment, saved by the *Adam novus*.

Some slight support for connecting this play with Easter—or later—rather than with Christmas is provided by practical considerations involved in the time of its performance. Because of its liturgical lessons and responsories (for Septuagesima Sunday and the following Monday) and because the *Ordo Prophetarum* was associated with the Christmas season, most authorities have held that the play was written for performance 'any time during the Christmas and New Year festivities'.[1] If, however, as is universally recognized, the *Mystère d'Adam* was to be played outside a church, whether in England or Normandy, the most inclement and coldest time of winter would hardly seem like a propitious season. Northern snows and rains, coupled with the play's incomplete state and the likelihood that it may have contained scenes from the drama of the redemption, make the period of Easter a more plausible time for its performance, unless, like so many cyclical plays, it was produced in midsummer.

Elaborate stage-directions give a remarkably clear picture of the playwright's concern for the performance of his drama. Not only are the costumes and movements of the actors described, but even their facial expressions and manner of speaking. Paradise (i.e. terrestrial paradise) is to be placed in a conspicuous, or higher, position; it is to be surrounded with silken hangings disposed in such a way that people within may be seen from the shoulders up; sweet-smelling flowers and boughs of trees are to be there. God is to wear a dalmatic, Adam a red tunic, and Eve vestments of white silk. Adam is to stand near God, his countenance serious and composed; Eve is to look a little humbler. There follow the directions so often likened to Hamlet's words to the players: Adam is to be well taught when to reply, and in this he should be neither too quick nor too slow. And not only he, but all the other persons, should be properly instructed so that they speak in good order and make suitable gestures and preserve the rhythm of their lines, neither adding nor omitting syllables. . . . After Adam has eaten the forbidden fruit he is directed to show the greatest measure of grief, and

[1] Studer, p. xxi.

a little later he and Eve are directed to be sad and bowed down as if in shame for their sins.

It seems possible that a side entrance to a church, perhaps the entrance to one of the transepts, was used in the performance of the play. The church itself served as God's heavenly dwelling, from which He and the prophets made their entrance. The top step or platform leading into the church represented terrestrial paradise where Adam and Eve remained until they were driven from the Garden of Eden. By using a large enough space on this higher level Adam and Eve could be represented as strolling about, later as hiding, and adequate room could be provided for the trees, flowers, and other decorations needed to portray the delights of terrestrial paradise. Around this space would be hung the silken draperies which concealed the lower parts of those within. Here would come the prophets of the third act when they uttered their prophecies.[1]

To the lower level went Adam and Eve after the fall, and there the scenes involving Cain and Abel took place. It was from this lower level that the audience viewed the play, the devil and his demons making sorties among them *per plateas*, apparently at the front of the church steps. The *infernus* of this play—more properly limbo than hell—seems to have occupied a separate structure, whether portrayed as a prison or by the jaws of a dragon we are not told. (Precedents exist for both means of picturing limbo.) To judge from later plays this *infernus* was at the right of the spectators and jutted out diagonally from the church steps in such a way that its gates would be visible to the audience. The gates are specifically mentioned as well as the fact that smoke arises from the structure, and the rubrics provide that the demons, clamorously rejoicing within and beating on kettles and cauldrons, should do so loudly enough to be heard outside. Hither the devils dragged Adam and Eve in chains, hither they led Cain, repeatedly beating him as well as Abel, though the latter was to be treated more gently than his brother (*Abel vero ducent micius*).

It would seem then that in the staging of the *Mystère d'Adam*,

---

[1] On the *scamnum*, probably an ecclesiastical property, used by the prophets, see above, Chap. VII, p. 72, n. 1, and on the staging, as well as the genesis, of the *Adam* cf. Frank, loc. cit., pp. 11 ff.

as in its composition, our author had few precedents. He knew
liturgical texts and performances, but in departing from them
he presumably used the same skill and creative imagination that
pervade his lively, realistic dialogues, his clever characterizations, and his facile verse forms. His play—midway between the
church drama and the laicized mysteries—exhibits restraint
even in its humour: it never descends to horseplay, but preserves a kind of ecclesiastical stateliness in its lighter as well as
its graver scenes. Indeed no more entertaining and delightful
example has survived of how the early medieval theatre might
achieve its purpose of making vivid to the laity the doctrines
of the Church.

IX

Les Trois Maries. La Seinte Resureccion

THOUGH the late twelfth and thirteenth centuries have left us French miracle plays and various French comedies by such competent writers as Jean Bodel, Rutebeuf, and Adam le Bossu, there survive of the French plays on biblical subjects from this period only a short fragment of forty lines known as *Les Trois Maries*, the much longer but still fragmentary *Seinte Resureccion* written in England, and a dramatization of the parable of the Prodigal Son called *Courtois d'Arras*. The two fragments deviate only slightly from their biblical prototypes in matter and spirit. *Courtois d'Arras*, on the contrary, transposes the parable to its own time and introduces purely imaginary scenes that belong to the domain of comedy.

Obviously the distinction between serious and non-serious plays cannot be too sharply drawn at this time. Even the *Mystère d'Adam*, as we have seen, is at times not without humour. Bodel's *Jeu de S. Nicolas* was written to honour the saint and harks back in origin to the liturgical plays on the same theme, yet its thieves, tipplers, gamblers, and other realistic characters were designed to arouse laughter. So too, although *Courtois d'Arras* dramatizes a biblical parable, the piece spices its teachings with lusty scenes of low life that border on farce. We shall reserve the treatment of miracle plays and plays with comic episodes for later pages. It should be remembered, however, that chronologically their place is beside that of the two fragments to be considered below.

LES TROIS MARIES

Les Trois Maries is essentially little more than a French translation of some liturgical *Quem quaeritis* which included the *Victimae Paschali* sequence.[1] Mary Magdalen laments and begs God for a sign; an angel appears and asks whom she seeks and,

---

[1] Ed. by P. Meyer in *Rom.* xxxiii (1904), 239–45. The final lines are attributed by the manuscripts and editor to 'Duo Angeli' but seem more appropriate to the two Marys.

upon hearing that it is Jesus, tells her that He is risen and that she should urge the Apostles to go into Galilee. At this point it is possible that a scene with the Risen Christ may be lost. The fragment continues with the other two Marys asking what news she has heard (this echoes the sequence's *Dic nobis, Maria, quid vidisti in via?*); she replies that she has seen the tomb, the body, the angel, vestments, and sudary (cf. the sequence: *angelicos testes, sudarium et vestes*); and the scene breaks off after six lines of jubilation over the resurrection and the consequent discomfiture of the Jews.

This poor little text was copied about the middle of the thirteenth century, probably at Rheims. The date of the original cannot be determined, but both in style and matter it seems archaic. Determination of date and dialect is difficult because our copy is by a scribe of such inferior accomplishments that P. Meyer thought him *quelque écolier malhabile* little acquainted with French who wrote from memory. It seems possible that, like the French lines in the Origny *Ludus Paschalis*, the plays of Hilarius, and the *Sponsus*, the vernacular here may have supplemented a liturgical text now lost. If so, the absence of the *Noli me tangere* might be explained by the fact that this scene was played in its original Latin form. In any case the French verses limp, though they reflect a lyric intention. The uneven lines have four, six, seven, and eight syllables, roughly arranged in stanzaic patterns, and, while no neumes appear in the manuscript, may well have been designed for singing. The chief value of this fragment is that it furnishes yet another link between the liturgical and vernacular drama. The French dialect suggests a lay performance, but the relationship to purely liturgical texts is so close that the piece could have been used in some none too exigent church to supplement and illuminate its Easter service.

LA SEINTE RESURECCION

La Seinte Resureccion, often referred to as *La Resurrection du Sauveur* or the *Anglo-Norman Resurrection*,[1] is much more ambitious than *Les Trois Maries*, though less imaginative and skilful than the *Mystère d'Adam*. It reveals considerable freedom from its obvious biblical, apocryphal, and legendary sources. It also

[1] Ed. by J. Wright in *CFMA* and by Jenkins *et al.* in *ANTS*.

combines its materials and motivates its scenes with an ingenuity that heightens their dramatic value. Although the play lacks the realism and subtlety of the *Adam*, it compensates to some extent for their absence by its stylized dignity. The characters are in general differentiated as types rather than as persons; they frequently address each other in balanced phrases built on similar verbal and rhythmic patterns; and because of this and of the very infrequent use of run-over or broken lines, a formalism results which produces a more archaic effect than one finds in the freedom and raciness of the *Mystère d'Adam*.

The piece begins with a prologue that explains how it is to be staged. Then Joseph of Arimathea appears before Pilate and asks permission to bury the body of Jesus. But Pilate cannot agree until he has ascertained that Jesus is indeed dead and so he dispatches his soldiers to find out. They encounter the blind beggar Longinus who is glad to earn a few pennies by striking and testing the Crucified. As the blood flows over his hands and he laves his face, Longinus's sight is restored and the soldiers hurry back to Pilate to report the miracle as well as to affirm the truth of Jesus's death. Pilate urges them to be silent and does not allow them to recount the details of what they have seen, but, turning to Joseph, requites him for past services by granting him the body of the Crucified. Not until Joseph has departed does Pilate hear the full story of the miracle and he then has Longinus thrown into prison.[1]

Joseph seeks Nicodemus and tells him they must bury Jesus, but the timid Nicodemus demurs until he shall have heard from Pilate himself that permission has been given. They both go before the procurator who reassures them. Then they proceed to the Cross, take Jesus down, and, after anointing the body, place it in the tomb. (Here, in one manuscript,[2] Joseph relates his vision of angels unfolding a pall above the stone destined to become the sepulchre.) Now Caiaphas appears before Pilate to warn him that, according to the Jews, the Crucified predicted He would rise on the third day, and advises placing guards at the tomb to see that His disciples do not steal the body and

---

[1] On the originality of arrangement and conception in these and the following scenes, cf. the *ANTS* edition, pp. xcvi ff.

[2] *C*, lines 313 ff., and cf. pp. cii ff. of the *ANTS* edition.

claim that Jesus has risen. Pilate agrees, and Caiaphas goes off
with four boastful soldiers who have been duly sworn in by the
priest Levi to keep faithful watch over the tomb. One manuscript (P) breaks off at this point, but the other (C) proceeds
with scenes that describe Joseph's arrival at the tomb and his
wrapping of the body of Jesus in a cloak, only to be apprehended
by the guards and brought before Caiaphas.

Both manuscripts of this late twelfth-century play are incomplete. The references in their prologues to its staging indicate
characters and scenes which do not appear in either fragment.[1]
The Paris manuscript (P) preserves an older version of the play,
though it dates from the late thirteenth or early fourteenth century. The other manuscript (C), long unknown, was copied at
Canterbury about 1275 and paradoxically contains a more re-
dacted version than P. This Canterbury text rearranges some
incidents, adds or corrects a few others, but though it has 522
lines and P only 371, it does not carry the action much beyond
that in P. One of its editors believes C shows the work of two
revisers, a man interested in making the play more lively and
another who on the contrary was especially concerned with
doctrinal and didactic matters. Another editor is less certain of
this.[2] In any case we may observe in these two manuscripts how
a single dramatic text might be changed by time and circumstance, and how little regard for their 'original' might be felt
by those charged with the production of medieval plays.

The dialect of both versions is Anglo-Norman; apparently
all concerned with producing the play lived in England and
used the French of their time and locality, so that it is obvious
why not only the versification but the treatment of certain incidents reflect English rather than continental usage.[3] It is also
obvious that this play was designed for popular consumption.
Anglo-Norman was widely understood in England by 1275,
and there is no need to assume that our piece would appeal only
to the aristocracy.[4]

[1] References to stations for the disciples and the three Marys, to a hell where
the chained patriarchs appeared, to structures representing Galilee and Emmaus,
all suggest that the Visit to the Tomb, the Appearances and a Harrowing of Hell
must have figured in the original play.

[2] See p. cxxiv of *ANTS* edition for both views.

[3] See *ANTS* edition, pp. xcvi ff.   [4] Cf. Chap. VIII, p. 76, n. 1, above.

Both manuscripts contain narrative lines unsuited to a true play, and it has been much debated whether these are merely versified stage-directions, lines to be spoken by a *meneur de jeu*, or phrases introduced to make a dramatic text easier to visualize when read. Since in the early Middle Ages composition in verse was an entirely normal and natural procedure, the fact that these narrative lines scan need not rule out stage-directions. In fact those at the beginning which concern the staging of the piece seem to be such directions for they are couched in the present (mostly subjunctive), the future or imperative forms of the verb. Conceivably they could be spoken by a Prologue or suppressed altogether. But in the body of the play the narrative lines regularly describe actions in the past tense and give the impression of an attempt to adapt a text which was primarily dramatic for reading or recitation. The fact that most of them appear in both manuscripts makes it likely that they formed part of the author's own conception.[1]

The prologue begins as follows in the two manuscripts:

> P. En ceste manere recitom
> La seinte resureccion.
> Primerement apareillons
> Tus les lius e les mansions. . . .

> C. Si vuz avez devociun
> De la sainte resurrectiun
> En l'onur Deu representer
> E devant le puple reciter,
> Purveez ke il eit espace
> Pur fere asez large place,
> E si devez bien purver
> Cum les lius devez aser. . . .

The prologue of *P* seems designed for a single, first performance of the play: 'In this fashion let us recite the holy resurrection. Let us first prepare all the places and mansions. . . .' By the time

---

[1] M. K. Pope, *ANTS* edition, p. cxxiv, believes these lines were spoken during the performance and that the use of the past tense was intended to show the audience that the events they were witnessing took place in the past. But the different procedure in the prologue, the testimony of other dramatic texts, and the sacrifice of dramatic immediacy that would be involved, if this hypothesis were true, argue against its acceptance.

the Canterbury revision had been made the play was apparently in general circulation and the text addresses anyone concerned with its performance: 'If you have the devout desire to represent the holy resurrection in the honour of God and to recite it before the people, provide that there be scope for a sufficiently wide playing-space, and you must also arrange for the way in which the stations (*lius*) are to be located. . . .'

It is obvious from the directions in both manuscripts that the author had in mind the simultaneous staging used by the liturgical drama, the *Mystère d'Adam*, and most succeeding medieval plays.[1] Heaven was to be on one side, hell on the other. In the centre was the tomb. Between it and heaven stood the crucifix; between it and hell, the gaol. Raised platforms with representational structures upon them (called variously *estals*, *estages*, and *mansions*) accommodated Pilate and his soldiers, Caiaphas and the Jews, Joseph (*C* adds Longinus here), Nicodemus, the disciples, and the three Marys. In the middle of the playing-space Galilee and Emmaus were to be portrayed.[2]

Obviously all staging depends on the imagination of the audience. Elizabethans needed only a few meagre properties to project battle-fields, storm-tossed seas, or the dwellings of kings. The French stage of the seventeenth century, more realistic in its representation of details, nevertheless, like that of the Middle Ages, introduced cheek by jowl throne-rooms, jungles, ships in full sail, and so on.[3] Actually the simultaneous stage had many advantages. It made possible a splendid and highly diversified spectacle. It allowed the action of a play to move from station to station without scene-shifting so that the sequence of events could proceed without breaking the illusion no matter where the action occurred. At need action could even go forward in different places simultaneously. Above all, in the

---

[1] Cf. above, Chaps. VII and VIII.

[2] There are slight differences between the prologues of the two manuscripts which need not detain us. The Marys have a station in *P* but seem, though mentioned, to have none in *C*. On the contrary, Longinus is provided with a *liu* in *C* but not in *P*. The tower of David and the name of Bartholomew occur in *C* alone which also mentions angels, devils, patriarchs, and pilgrims not specifically referred to in *P*. In general, as the editors recognize, the reviser of *C* is more interested in describing and visualizing the actors in their roles than in listing their exact positions on the stage. See *ANTS* edition, pp. cxiv ff. and cxxi.

[3] See H. C. Lancaster, *Mémoire de Mahelot, passim*.

religious plays, such staging kept a synthesis of the play's meaning constantly before the audience. In our *Resureccion*, for example, heaven and hell, the crucifix, the tomb, the mansions of
Pilate and the high priests, Emmaus and the Sea of Galilee were
continuously in sight, each with its overtones of significance,
each thus contributing to the momentous solemnity of the
drama of the redemption.

The literary value of this Anglo-Norman play lies in its
formalized dignity and in its original and effective combinations
of traditional materials within a limited sphere. Reminiscent of
some of the liturgical plays is the stylized effect achieved, for
example, when Joseph greets Pilate by invoking his God who
saved Moses and Aaron from the hands of Pharaoh (four lines)
and Pilate replies by greeting Joseph and invoking *his* God,
Hercules, who slew the dragon and destroyed Gerion (four
lines) and when the dialogue continues with Joseph and Pilate
exchanging amenities first in a pair of six-lined stanzas and then
in a pair of eight-lined stanzas. Similar balance and symmetry
frequently occur elsewhere, notably among the soldiers who
guard the tomb : each in turn and in similarly cadenced verses
boasts that if anyone tries to steal the body he will destroy the
thief. (Incidentally, these swaggering soldiers greatly resemble
their liturgical ancestors, and, of course, their descendants decorate many a later Passion play.) Despite the play's dignity, however, due in part to the story itself and in part to its treatment
here, some unexpected details serve at times to enliven and per-
sonalize the roles. Pilate is both timid and tricky : he fears to
anger Rome lest he lose his life, and he exercises craft in sup-
pressing news of the miraculous healing of the blind Longinus.
Nicodemus, too, possesses individuality. He likewise is a timor-
ous man, though a good one. He longs to help Joseph bury
Jesus, yet refuses to do so unless he first receives promises of
safety from Pilate's own lips. He is content to stand at Jesus's
feet during the entombment—his traditional position—but
adds a human touch to the scene by telling Joseph to stand at
the head since he is the elder.

For the history of the theatre, both in France and England,
the play has significance because it contrasts so strikingly with
the slightly earlier but more dexterous *Mystère d'Adam*. It is

also important because its two divergent manuscripts reveal the casual treatment accorded dramatic texts in the Middle Ages, because its prologue adds to our knowledge of the simultaneous stage-setting, and because its embedded narrative lines suggest. how an essentially dramatic text might be adapted for reading or recitation. The play reflects English rather than continental traditions in its language, versification, and handling of certain incidents. But in its close relation to the liturgical drama it represents the universal evolution from its source of the theatre in both France and England. And when one remembers the political connexions between the two lands at this time, the continuous crossings of the Channel in both directions by kings, nobles, and their retainers, it is easy to understand why the *Mystère d'Adam* and the Anglo-Norman *Resureccion*, for all their insular traits, may well have been witnessed in England not only by the natives and their conquerors, but also by the continental Poitevins, Angevins, Normans, and even Francs de France who, for one reason or another, frequented the land occupied by the Normans and ruled over by kings who were dukes of Normandy and Aquitaine, counts of Anjou.[1]

[1] Cf. Chap. VIII, p. 76, n. 1, above. On the relations between the two lands at this time, see among others Sidney Painter, *William Marshal* and *The Reign of King John*; Amy Kelly, *Eleanor of Aquitaine and the Four Kings*.

X

The Beginnings of the Miracle Play in France. *Le Jeu de S. Nicolas* by Jean Bodel

MANLY'S definition of a miracle play—a miracle play 'is the dramatization of a legend setting forth the life, or the martyrdom, or the miracles of a saint'—was approved by Coffman and Young, Young adding that it is, of course, non-biblical legends of saints that are intended, the legends that accumulated about the names of hallowed and canonized men and women, not about such biblical persons as the Virgin Mary, Mary Magdalen, Lazarus, or Paul. According to Manly, there was no gradual transition from undramatized legend to dramatized legend, but at the moment when legend was first cast into dramatic form, a miracle play was born. As Young has shown, however, the model was present in the widely known liturgical plays of the Easter and Christmas season; various legends were versified and sung as unofficial embellishments of the liturgy; and it needed only 'the application of metrical, musical and dramatic form directly to the traditional legends' for the creation of a miracle play.[1]

Coffman pushed Manly's theory of sudden birth further, seeking to explain the rise of the miracle play in 'the complex factors of the eleventh century', showing that saints' lives flourished then in monasteries and cathedral schools and that these were to churchmen what secular romances were to the laity, an escape from commonplace routines. He pointed out also that monasteries were being brought into close relations with the laity at the time, that they had become commercial, industrial, and educational as well as religious centres, that they fostered experiments in poetry and music, and he concluded

---

[1] See Manly in *MP*, iv (1907), 577–95, esp. p. 585; Coffman, *New Theory*, p. 7, also *Nomenclature* in *PMLA*, xxxi (1916), 448–65, *New Approach* in *MP*, xxii (1925), 239–71, and *Miracle Play*, pp. 205–11. See also Young, ii. 307–11, 503, and *Origin*, p. 268.

that 'secular intrusions' are in some measure responsible for the creation of a St. Nicholas play by its first author.

How far secular intrusions may be held responsible, it is difficult to say. All the plays in the Fleury play-book connect with the liturgy, and Hilarius's *St. Nicholas*, like his *Lazarus* and *Daniel*, was probably to be performed at some point in the Canonical Office.[1] Geoffrey of Maine, on the other hand, doubtless produced his St. Catherine play at Dunstable for the instruction and edification of the laity (see note 2, below). It would seem that once dramatic principles had become established and were understood, the short step from the dramatization of one kind of story, the biblical, to another, the saint's legend, might have been taken by an innovator at any time for some pertinent occasion. Indeed the idea might conceivably have occurred to more than one original mind. The available evidence would indicate therefore that the dramatized saint's legend is merely a logical extension of the Church's desire to enliven its teachings by embellishing its liturgical services, a desire that had already manifested itself in the process of troping and in the development of the Easter and Christmas plays.

The Latin miracle play, as we have seen, became established in France quite early. In the twelfth century the texts of the Fleury play-book and those by Hilarius were written and there are indications that miracle plays were performed in the schools and monasteries even earlier.[2] With such precedents at hand as

[1] See Young, ii. 343.

[2] The Fleury plays, as we saw above, Chap. IV, seem to have had predecessors, now lost. We also know that Geoffrey of Maine, later of St. Albans, a secular clerk who had lived in Normandy, organized his production of a play about St. Catherine at Dunstable. This may have been in the eleventh century. The tale goes that, needing costumes for the play, he borrowed some copes from St. Alban's Abbey. These were destroyed by fire, and, unable to reimburse the Abbey, he 'offered himself as a holocaust to God', and became a novice there. In the year 1119 he was chosen Abbot. Now the time between Geoffrey's arrival in Dunstable and his becoming Abbot may have been considerable. The St. Alban records refer to the play only incidentally and with no indication that it was an innovation (cf. *quem 'Miracula' vulgariter appellamus*); it seems unlikely, therefore, that Geoffrey himself invented the play but more probable that he introduced at Dunstable a play which he had known in Normandy. Hence the beginnings of the miracle play may well date from the eleventh century. See H. T. Riley, ed. *Gesta Abbatum Monasterii S. Albani*, i. 72–73 (Rolls Series, London, 1867). Cf. also C. B. C. Thomas, *MLN*, xxxii (1917), 337 ff.; C. Brown, *SP*, xxviii (1931), 594 ff.; Fawtier-Jones, *Rom.* lvi (1930), 80 ff.

the liturgical plays about St. Nicholas and with the availability
of numerous Latin and vernacular narratives about him, it is
not surprising to find that our earliest vernacular miracle play
concerns this well-loved patron of students, children, merchants, travellers, sailors, and young girls eager to marry. Nor
should it be forgotten that St. Nicholas has always ranked high
among the great miracle-working saints and, as an intercessor
for erring mortals, has been considered second only to the
Virgin Mary herself.

LE JEU DE S. NICOLAS

Jean Bodel's *Jeu de S. Nicolas*, though the earliest surviving
play of its type in French, is perhaps the most remarkable of
all.[1] With great skill our author combines a serious, even a religious theme with realistic scenes of low life that are often
comic. In deftness of characterization and motivation, in swiftness of action and inventive detail, the play surpasses any considered so far. The Latin liturgical plays about St. Nicholas (two
treat the same legend underlying Bodel's,[2] six are concerned
with other legends about the saint) are all comparatively simple
and little developed. The parallels between our French *jeu* and
its potential sources—the Latin plays, a Latin life by John the
Deacon in its various recensions and the vernacular derivative
of this life by Wace—are few and seem more or less fortuitous.
They merely serve to underscore Bodel's ingenuity.[3]

His originality springs, of course, from his own artistic
endowment, but its flowering may also owe something to the

---

[1] Ed. Jeanroy, *CFMA*, 1925; F. J. Warne, 1951. On Bodel see Rohnstroem,
Étude. On sources see Albrecht, Ronsjö, Warne, and Foulon in *Mélanges Cohen*,
pp. 55–66. On the games and tavern bills see Cousins, G. Frank, Knudson, Gill,
Foulet and Foulon. Cf. also the bibliography in Warne's edition. The significance
of the play for French comedy is discussed above and below in Chaps. IX and XX.
Fragments of the prologue of a fifteenth-century play on the same subject as
Bodel's are printed by Samaran in *Rom*. li (1925), 191–7, and liii (1927), 297–9.

[2] One is by Hilarius, the second is in the Fleury play-book. Three other plays
from Fleury, two from Hildesheim, and one from Einsiedeln dramatize different
stories involving St. Nicholas.

[3] The part played by the Easter and Christmas plays in our *jeu* has been little
stressed. Yet the Pagan King recalls Herod, the Emirs owe much to the Magi,
their boasts echo those of the soldiers sent to guard Christ's tomb, and the angelic
announcements are reminiscent of many in the liturgical texts. See G. Frank,
RR, xlii (1951), 283.

time and place of his professional life. He lived in Arras when that town had become a centre of literature, commerce, and industry, when its rich, luxury-loving nobility and citizenry consciously cultivated the arts and freely indulged in festivities designed to foster them, when its literary societies or *puys* supported poetry of every sort, lyric, narrative, and dramatic. An anonymous writer says of it:

> Arras est escole de tous biens entendre;
> Quand on veut d'Arras le plus caitif prendre,
> En autre pais se puet por boin vendre.
> On voit les honors d'Arras si estendre,
> Je vi l'autre jor le ciel là sus fendre:
> Dex voloit d'Arras les motés aprendre.[1]

Significantly enough, though so many of our early medieval writers are anonymous, those of Arras have left us their names and we still prize and possess the works, among others, of Gautier d'Arras who wrote the romances *Eracle* and *Ille et Galeron*, of Conon de Béthune, a trouvère and statesman who composed at least ten poems, and of Adam le Bossu, a craftsman of many skills, author of comedies (the *Jeu de la Feuillée* and *Robin et Marion*), various lyrical pieces, and an unfinished epic. Bodel's contribution to the poetry of Arras, distinguished as it is by its diversity and professional competence, its gaiety and pathos, seems characteristic of the best Artois traditions.

Our knowledge of the poet, who died in the winter of 1209–10, derives for the most part from his works and from the *Nécrologe artésien* or *Registre de la Confrérie de la Ste Chandelle* which indicates his calling and records the date of his death.[2] Besides our play, Bodel wrote four or five *pastourelles*, an epic *Chanson des Saisnes*—a poem about the Saxons which a later poet, Girard d'Amiens, praises in his *Roman de Charlemagne* for its *langue polie*, its *bel savoir*, and *science aguisie*—and the famous *Congé* in which he bade farewell to his friends and fellow townsmen after leprosy had cut short his career and prevented a contemplated journey to the Holy Land. His lyrics reflect a

---

[1] See Monmerqué et Michel, pp. 22–23.
[2] On this *Nécrologe* or *Registre* see G. P[aris] in *Rom.* xxix (1900), 145, and Langlois's edition of Adam le Bossu's *Jeu de la Feuillée*, CFMA, 1923, p. iv.

personal note, especially the pathetic *Congé*, and his epic indicates a desire to renew and refine that form of poetry. From all these and the later references to him, we can picture the man and his life. Bodel was a native of Arras who held some post in the town, for in the *Congé* he addresses its municipal officers and mentions being in their service; he also refers familiarly to many of its citizens. His membership in the Confrérie de la Ste Chandelle suggests that he was a trouvère by profession. This was a 'société des jongleurs et des bourgeois d'Arras' that acted as custodian of a candle which had miraculously appeared to one of its members by placing itself on his *vielle* while he knelt at the altar, and in Bodel's *Congé* (lines 505 ff.) the poet expressly takes leave of the candle which Notre Dame gave to the jongleurs and of the *menestrel, douch compaignon*, who have been kinder than brothers to him. Bodel's popularity among his contemporaries and successors is attested by the references to him that survive; it also emerges indirectly from the gentle spirit of his *Congé*, its absence of rancour, and the way in which he addresses his friends and colleagues there.[1]

Unfortunately, at the end of his life this talented poet had to submit to the terrible scourge of leprosy. In his *Congé* resignation mingles with self-pity; to his regrets at leaving his friends and especially at having to forgo an expedition to the Holy Land—the Fourth Crusade of 1202—are added his horror at the ravages of the disease upon his body and his impending sense of isolation and separation from the world. At one point (line 72) he asks God to consider his shame as penance, 'quar trop aroie en deus enfers'. He begs the *maieur d'Aras* and the *eskevins* to provide him with the means to enter an institution for lepers, preferably at *Miaulens* or *Biaurain* (i.e. Meulan or Beaurains) near Arras, and presumably his plea was heeded.

Nothing directly concerned with his illness is discernible in our play, but its Oriental scenes and the conflict between Saracens and Christians seem to echo Bodel's enthusiasm for the crusades. Since the *Congé* must date before 1202 and since Bodel

---

[1] Bodel's *Congé* is printed in *Rom.* ix (1880), 216, by Raynaud, who there expresses some doubt about Bodel's authorship of the *Chanson des Saisnes*, a doubt dispelled, however, by Rohnstroem's *Étude*. Rohnstroem, p. 100, prints the words of Girard d'Amiens.

probably wrote little between his retirement from the world and his death in 1209–10, it has always seemed probable that the *Jeu de S. Nicolas*, with its crusading fervour, must have been written shortly before the *Congé*, perhaps between 1199 and 1201. Warne plausibly proposes 5 December 1200 as the time of the first performance, on an occasion when the sacred candle of the Confrérie to which Bodel belonged seems to have been transferred from the Chapel of St. Nicholas to a new position in the Petite Place. In any case the text twice refers to its performance *anuit* (lines 4 and 105) and once makes clear that this *nuit* was St..Nicholas's Eve. As the saint's feast-day occurs in winter, 6 December, a performance not only at night but indoors is indicated; the use made of candles in the text would then have special pertinence.

In the earlier versions of the legend an infidel—sometimes called Judeus, sometimes Barbarus, variously described as a toll-gatherer or money-changer—hears of the miracles performed by St. Nicholas and determines to entrust his treasure to the saint for safe-keeping. Robbers steal the treasure, however, and the infidel, on discovering the theft, threatens to take vengeance on the saint. But St. Nicholas appears to the thieves in person, forces them to make restitution, and straightway the infidel decides to embrace Christianity. In a few versions the infidel is a member of an invading pagan army and hears of the saint's powers from a captive Christian.

From such meagre materials Bodel fashioned his lively play. Of the lowly Judeus-Barbarus he made a pagan king, surrounding him with an obsequious Seneschal, a harsh gaoler, and four mighty Emirs from the East. These pagans in superior numbers war against Christians who meet them and die like crusaders, calling upon the Holy Sepulchre for aid and welcoming death in the firm conviction that by dying nobly in a great cause they will merit paradise. It is the only survivor among the Christians, called merely Preudom, who affirms his faith in God and St. Nicholas, who is comforted by an angelic messenger, and who eventually effects the conversion, via the miracle-working saint, of the wicked pagans. Bodel happily contrasts this simple Preudom with the mighty pagan King; he also contrasts the holy image of the saint, worshipped by the Christian, with the tricky, unpropitious statue of Tervagan in whom the pagans place their faith.

Furthermore, Bodel added to the bare bones of the legend meaty scenes of low life and new characters created in the spirit of his day. The three thieves drink, gamble, and quarrel in a tavern kept by a grasping host and his rascally servant-boy. Here come criers of town and King and a messenger who joins in the drinking, gambling, and quarrelling. All these people are pure Artois; indeed there is no desire to hide the fact; they observe the contemporary division of Arras into *cité* and *vile*, they mention such nearby towns as Hénin, Fresnes-lès-Mont-auban, Gavrelle.

But Bodel's additions to the narrative go beyond the 'plot' and the transformation of scenes and persons. Though he may have been hampered to some extent by the conventions of the tradition he was interpreting, nevertheless even his most tradi-tional characters have contemporaneity. For example, his saint can call the thieves *fil a putain* when he orders them to restore the treasure, his angelic messenger embodies the Christian philosophy of the crusades, and his symbolic Preudom, despite great faith, humanly trembles before his gaoler, exclaiming pitifully:

Sire, con vo machue est grosse!

As for the newly knighted young warrior, anonymous though he is, his proud words as he dies (lines 408–9) have been likened to those of Corneille's Rodrigue in the *Cid*, Act II, scene 2: cf. 'Segneur, se je sui jones, ne m'aiés en despit! / On a veü souvent grant cuer en cors petit' with 'Je suis jeune, il est vrai; mais aux âmes bien nées / La valeur n'attend pas le nombre des années'.

It is, of course, in connexion with the more original charac-ters created by Bodel that his stagecraft becomes most evident. The pagan King out-Herods Herod in rage and tyranny, he terrifies his Seneschal, curses his own god Tervagan and later has him thrown from the temple. The Seneschal is a wily cour-tier, afraid to commit himself without assurance of immunity, who flatters and fears but serves his master well. Durand, the gaoler, menaces vehemently and delights in the prospect of torturing the poor Preudom. Of the four Emirs, one, unlike his

companions, refuses at the end to become a Christian and has
to be forcibly vanquished; even then he affirms that his conversion is of the word and not the faith: St. Nicholas will have
only the husk (*escorche*), *li creanche est en Mahom*.

The three thieves with their picturesque names—Cliquet, the
jabberer, Pincedé, the dice-pincher, and Rasoir, the razor
(sharper, filcher)—are carefully distinguished. The talkative
Cliquet is a hard drinker and a bad loser. After he has quarrelled
with Pincedé, he is rebuked by the tavern-boy for using bad
language. Later he tries to welsh on his commitments, but in the
end he loses his cloak to pay not only his own debts but those
of his companions. Finally he counsels flight and then, like the
others, is off—but with plans for a new robbery, that of the
maire of Fresnes.

Pincedé, the ringleader of the group, is also a heavy drinker
and even more pugnacious than his fellows. He quarrels with
both of them and, when he comes to blows with Cliquet, he
nearly tears off his cloak. Pincedé, as an expert, is delegated to
spy out the land, and, after the robbery, when the others complain about the weight of the booty, he shoulders the heavy
sack himself. He is the first to see St. Nicholas, the only one to
talk to him, and later it is he who addresses the tavern-keeper
and accuses him of being an accessory to the crime. The other
thieves elect Pincedé to carry back the treasure and as he does
so, bolder than they, he invites each of them to filch a handful
of coins. With a warning to Cliquet to beware of the *mairesse*,
he takes to his heels, announcing that he intends to 'rinse' (i.e.
steal) some laundry that he has spied near by.

The third thief, Rasoir, is a swaggerer, but a weak fellow.
He is the one who has first heard of the King's unguarded treasure, and before announcing this discovery to the others he
orders extra wine and brags of coming wealth. But later he
finds the booty too heavy for him and proposes, since they are
all weary from their hard night's work, that they go to sleep.
After the appearance of the saint, he is anxious to have the
treasure returned and the statue replaced in its former position.
Finally he departs and, unregenerate like the others, makes off
to steal a bride's trousseau.

The two criers, as well as the thieves, have distinct personalities. Connart, an old man, is employed by the city magistrates and has lived by his calling for over sixty years. Raoulet, obviously younger and more mettlesome, is in the service of the townsmen and temptingly advertises the virtues of the tavern-keeper's wine. Auberon, too, the King's messenger, is a real person. He boasts of his speed, then dallies at the tavern for a drink and a little game, shaking dice with Cliquet to see who will pay for the wine, bargaining with the host to try to reduce its price. The audience may well have recognized the originals of these three portraits.

The most engaging of Bodel's rogues is the sly young Caignet (little cur) who acts as servant-boy at the tavern. He is crafty and grasping and no doubt rightfully accused of mischarging and giving short measure. In the lad his master's traits reappear magnified and with additions. The inn-keeper, who has an eye for gain and his own interests, fawns upon the thieves when they seem likely to prove good customers, is willing to participate in the fruits of their robbery before the appearance of the saint, but repudiates them and has them thrown out after the saint has spoken. In all these matters the boy ably seconds his master. Caignet warns the host to make Cliquet pay his old scot before he runs up a new bill, and disgustedly estimates that there will be no gain in either Cliquet or Pincedé. When ordered to bring a candle he demands payment at once, and when his set of dice is borrowed and he is promised a stake in the game in return for the loan, he knowingly answers that he will get his share. He later provides extra candles without invitation and, since payment is not immediately forthcoming, reaches over the players and purloins coins from the pot. As the thieves come to blows Caignet tells his master that they are destroying their pledges and soon there will be no clothes worth having. In the end it is he who despoils Cliquet of his coat and, to the charge that he has no equal at collecting pledges and giving short measure, impudently replies—his last words in the play—'Now you can go to the devil!'

It has been suggested that 'Bodel's power of observation . . . is superior to his power of invention' and that the latter failed him when he localized his tavern scenes in Arras.[1] But it was

[1] Warne, p. xxi.

precisely because of this localization that the dramatist produced his happiest effects. Just as the religious spirit of the crusades evoked by the King, his Emirs, and the battle between Christians and pagans gave immediacy to the miracle performed by the saint, so the realism and comedy that pervade the scenes involving the thieves—their drinking, games, and quarrels in an Artois tavern—produced contemporaneity and verisimilitude. Nor does the transition from the realm of the African king to the town of Arras prove difficult. Auberon, the King's messenger, travels from one to the other 'swifter than a camel' and Connart serves as crier not only to the Oriental potentate but to the magistrates of Arras. These phenomena troubled no medieval audience, nor need they bother us.

The theme of St. Nicholas and the robbers probably was dictated to Bodel by local circumstance: a desire to honour the saint on the eve of his day. Bodel at this time—when enthusiasm for the Fourth Crusade prevailed over a wide territory—was himself contemplating a journey to the Holy Land. In his play he was concerned with picturing the faith, exaltation, and courage of the crusaders in the face of death and their unwavering belief that participation in a crusade assured them eternal life. But, a professional trouvère, he shared in the gaiety of Arras, knew its customs and characters, and, in order to entertain, to spice his material and give it zest, he added those tavern scenes which form about half of his play, no doubt the more popular half.

His inventiveness is revealed not only in the encompassing of his tripartite material and in his effective mingling of religious and chivalric ideals with low comedy, but in the wit of his humorous realism, in the local colour he introduces throughout, and in the skill with which he motivates scenes and contrives transitions.

Modern authorities may not be agreed about the proper interpretation of the quarrels and misunderstandings in the dice-games, the reckonings and misreckonings of the scots, the befuddling and cheating of the thieves, but all recognize that these must have amused medieval audiences. Other comic or realistic details are too numerous to list, indeed they are so numerous that this play in a sense must be considered in the categories of both humorous and serious plays. Such details include the King's summary treatment of Tervagan and his regrets at having covered the god's ugly face and body with gold to no purpose; Auberon's objection that the host's wine-cup is too shallow, fit only for sampling; one Emir's reproach to the other 'sir killers' that they are disposing of all the Christians and leaving none for him; Connart's reference to the statue of St. Nicholas as a 'horned Mohammed, quite dead since he does not move'; Raoulet's puff of the tavern's wine as leaping like a squirrel, sparkling like a sinner's tear; Caignet's distress when the pledged garments are being torn to pieces and his slyness in outwitting the thieves; the penitent robbers who unexpectedly revert to type and plan new escapades; the recalcitrant Emir who refuses to be converted and claims to be deaf 'in that ear' when he is urged to become an apostate and who has to be forcibly subdued; the final booting out of the temple of the false god Tervagan, with the statement that he is free to mis-count the steps as he hurtles down them.

Bodel has given his pagans an Oriental colour by references to their supposed gods, Apollo, Mohammed, and Tervagan, to their curious type of oath and ritual, and to various fantastic practices in their putative homelands. His Artesians, of course, could hardly be of purer dye, and the contrast between the scenes laid in far-off, exotic countries and those in the familiar pub around the corner must have captivated the audience.

From palace to tavern, from tavern to the lands of the Emirs and on to the battlefield, from battlefield to prison and again to the tavern, the action swings back and forth with diverting variety and constant dramatic effectiveness. But the motivation never falters, the transitions are always justified. For example, the battle between pagans and Christians leaves the lone survivor in a position to proclaim the virtues of St. Nicholas which thus precipitates the robbery and eventually the conversion of the King. The scenes in palace and tavern are united by having the King's messenger stop at the tavern and by having the King's crier quarrel with the tavern's crier. Nothing could be more natural than the way the thieves enter the tavern one by one or than the boastful secretiveness of Rasoir, the last to

appear, who alone has heard of the unguarded treasure.[1] With
artistic symmetry the play begins and ends in the King's palace,
and the pagan god, consulted in fear at the start, is cast out of
the 'synagoge' at the conclusion. Thus the triumph of Christianity is effectively symbolized not only by the conversion of
the pagans but also by the contrast between the King's adoration of the wonder-working St. Nicholas and his deposition
of the false Tervagant.

Despite the variety of movement in the play, few properties
and little in the way of scenery would have been needed for its
staging. At the far left there may have been placed a paradise to
house the angelic messenger and St. Nicholas. Some indication
of the King's dwelling at one side and of the tavern at the other
would have been needed. The exotic lands of the Emirs might
or might not have been suggested by *mansions* of some sort;
probably one of these little structures housed the Christians,
whereas in another, representing a prison, Durand the gaoler
took his stand. The great battle must have occurred in the
playing-space in front, and there messenger and criers could
also have their say. The well-differentiated likenesses of pagan
god and Christian saint would be necessary properties, and,
of course, so would be the wine-cups, candles, coins, and dice
of the tavern scenes, as well as a chest for the King's treasure,
some items to represent its contents, and a sack in which to
carry them off.

Bodel handles his versification with more artistry and technical skill than any of his dramatic predecessors. The accomplished trouvère is evident in his writing. His octosyllables and
sixains have lightness and vivacity, his decasyllables and alexandrines possess weight and stateliness. He varies his usual octosyllabic couplets with stanzas of different structures that, as in

---

[1] The King's alacrity in leaving his treasure exposed on such seemingly flimsy
evidence as the Preudom's faith in the saint is better justified in the Prologue than
in the play. There, in a summary of the plot, the Christian promises that wealth
entrusted to the saint will be multiplied (l. 38) and this, of course, happens in the
play (1398–9 in Warne's edition, 1400–1 in Jeanroy's). It has appeared to some
critics that the host's repudiation of the thieves and their booty (1312 ff. in
Warne, 1314 ff. in Jeanroy) is too precipitous, but this would probably not have
been true for an audience: to them it would have been evident that the host, like
the thieves, saw the saint (cf. the implication of line 1283 in Warne, 1285 in
Jeanroy).

Courtois d'Arras, pay little heed to individual speeches and changes of scene; this shifting pattern must have given pleasure and satisfaction to the poet, but only a finely attuned ear in his audience could fully have appreciated it, though to such an ear it would have been music indeed. None, however, could fail to delight in his rhymes, which embrace many that are leonine or rich, many that contain puns or are used with playful effect. Apparently Bodel wrote with ease and pleasure. He seems not only to have mastered the swing of the best epics and the intricacies of the troubadour lyric, but to have been able to incorporate them appropriately in a play largely dependent for its success upon swift, natural, and realistic dialogue.

If French drama had continued along similar lines, France need not have waited until 1830 for the 'romantic play'. The *Jeu de S. Nicolas* with its original and fresh mingling of comedy and tragedy—to use ill-fitting terms—has possibilities not fully exploited until later times. The serious parts give the impression of sincerity and high purpose, the humorous scenes add happy realism and gay entertainment to an essentially religious theme. The whole has the freedom, vigour, and simplicity of young, exuberant talent, something the great Passion plays could not hope to recapture, something the other miracle plays failed to achieve.

XI

Le Miracle de Théophile and *Le Dit de l'herberie* by Rutebeuf

No direct influence of Bodel's *Jeu de S. Nicolas* on the second surviving French miracle play can be posited. Whether Rutebeuf, writing his *Miracle de Théophile*[1] in Paris around 1261, had ever heard of his Artois predecessor's work, whether other plays of this sort were written between these two and have been lost, we do not know. Conceivably more than one talented writer might independently arrive at the notion of dramatizing the miraculous rescue of penitent sinners by divine mediation.

In the case of Bodel's play there were, of course, precedents in the liturgical drama. No liturgical play concerning Theophilus survives, however, although his legend early became a popular *exemplum* used in sermons honouring the Virgin Mary, and in the eleventh century received the honour of being incorporated in the liturgy. Among the many instances of the power of Notre Dame this miracle alone was thus adopted by the Church, and thereafter representations of it in art and literature became frequent.[2] The liturgical stage, to be sure, knew the Mother of Christ in the Christmas and Easter plays and in such scenes as the Annunciation, Presentation in the Temple, Purification, and Assumption. And the miracles of Our Lady had been famous in Latin and vernacular narratives long before Rutebeuf's day and were destined to be loved for many centuries afterward on the stages of many lands. But in Rutebeuf's piece the Virgin Mary appears for the first time in the theatre,

---

[1] Editions by Jubinal, Kressner, Frank. On Rutebeuf see also Clédat, Leo, Lucas, Bastin et Faral, Cohen, *Miracle*, Faral in *Rom.* lxxii (1951), 182–201, Frank in *RR*, xliii (1952), 161–5.

[2] See Mâle, *xiii*e *siècle*, pp. 261–2 and Chevalier, p. 134. From the eleventh century on, one of the proses sung at Mass on feasts of the Virgin included the words:

> Tu mater es misericordiae
> De lacu faecis et miseriae
> Theophilum reformans gratiae.

so far as we know, fulfilling her extraordinarily potent role of intercessor for erring mortals, the *advocata nostra* in otherwise desperate cases.

Rutebeuf, like Bodel, was a professional. Though apparently of lower station, with no fixed post, he seems to have been a man of wide interests and diverse talents. Many sorts of poems, besides our play, are associated with his name: personal lyrics, satirical and polemical verses about events of the day, poems written to order for prominent persons, religious poems, a number of *fabliaux*, and, especially important for our purposes, several lives of saints and a monologue, the *Dit de l'herberie*.

Rutebeuf's poems about the crusades, the mendicant orders, and the quarrels of the University of Paris show him to have been bravely outspoken for a man who, according to his personal lyrics, suffered from poverty and from dependence upon the charity and goodwill of others. Self-pity and a begging note occur frequently. He resented the subservience of the king, Louis IX, to the mendicant orders, especially when the ruler's fasting and interruption of festivities deprived him and other poets of an opportunity to exercise their calling. But his attitude toward the issues of his time reveals something more than self-interest. A truly religious man, he was obviously a convinced advocate of the expeditions to the Holy Land. In his passionate devotion to the cause of his friend, Guillaume de Saint-Amour, and in his attacks on the mendicants for their part in Guillaume's banishment, he seems to have feared that not only the welfare of the University of Paris and the independence of the Church were involved, but also, because in this matter the king had yielded to the pope, the very freedom of the state itself.[1] Something of the poet's own resentment against those in control of his destiny seems echoed in his play.

According to the legend underlying the piece, Theophilus, who lived in the sixth century, was a pious and charitable ecclesiastic, administrator of a bishopric in Asia Minor. When his bishop died Theophilus was elected to succeed him, but declined the honour, and another man was chosen. The new bishop deprived poor Theophilus of even the humbler position he had formerly occupied and, to regain it, Theophilus made

---

[1] See Bastin et Faral, pp. 4–6, and Lucas, *Poèmes*, pp. 28–29.

a pact with the devil swearing allegiance to the forces of evil.
Some time later, however, despite his reinstatement in his old
post, Theophilus became truly penitent, appealed to the Virgin
Mary whom he had served faithfully in the past, and she, after
recovering his pact from Satan, restored him to her favour and
that of the Church.

Our play begins after Théophile has lost his post and is
lamenting the results of his downfall. He says he has so loved
God in the past that he has given away all his possessions to the
poor and now nothing is left him, indeed he fears that he and
his household will soon die of hunger. Since God has turned
from him, he will turn from God. He is ready to do anything
to regain his former estate and seeks out Salatin, an infidel who
is able to conjure up the devil. The sympathetic Salatin says he
quite understands how anyone accustomed to easy living must
feel at being dependent on others for food and drink, and in
addition at having to listen to *gros mots*. With the infidel's help
Théophile makes his agreement with the devil: he promises to
abandon the poor and sick, to renounce charity and eschew humility, to cease loving God, doing penance and living chastely,
on condition that he regain his former status. All this comes to
pass, and we see Théophile restored to his old position. But he
is no longer a good man; he behaves arrogantly toward those
around him, including the penitent bishop and the priest whose
place Théophile has now assumed. Yet all the time we are
aware of some contrition in the sinner, and at long last we find
Théophile prostrating himself before the Virgin Mary. In
moving words he repents his sins, repudiates Satan and his
ways, and implores forgiveness. Notre Dame sternly rebukes
him, but, because of his former devotion to her, she finally re-
lents and undertakes to wrest from Satan the contract Théophile
has signed.

Of this ancient Faust-like legend, Rutebeuf fashions a remarkably effective play. He has so identified himself with the
sufferings of his hero that one feels at times as if Rutebeuf and
Théophile were one. Indeed the dramatic pathos of his protagonist's role is echoed in the poet's more personal lyrics. Both
hero and poet suffer from the misery of poverty, dependence
upon others, temptations of the flesh, fear of damnation. Both

seek help from the all-powerful Virgin Mary, and in each case their lamentations and prayers evoke our pity because of their obvious sincerity.

Rutebeuf in this play seems to have combined a Latin derivative of Paul the Deacon's version of the legend, perhaps by Fulbert, with a French narrative adaptation of the same work by Gautier de Coincy,[1] but his own imaginative touches are apparent in his departures from his sources. His play gains dramatic impact by beginning *in medias res* at a climactic point in the story, and Théophile's opening exposition of his plight not only orients the spectators about the past but wins their sympathy from the start. Moreover it is couched in vivid, colloquial language: The Bishop has checkmated me in a corner; I'll die of hunger unless I pawn my clothes for bread; God turns a deaf ear upon my troubles; He has placed Himself in so high a place to escape His enemies that no one can reach Him; now my fiddle is broken and everyone will say I am done for; people will point at me and I won't dare go out or sit among them; God has played me a scurvy trick. These are hardly the words of an ecclesiastic, but they are the words of a suffering man whom a medieval audience could understand. They prepare the way for Théophile's desperate appeal to Salatin and his terrible hesitation before the enormity of risking hell by coming to terms with Satan.

Rutebeuf has admirably indicated the slyness of Salatin and his readiness to conjure up the devil. The spectators must have held their breath in horror as Salatin spoke his formula of abracadabra and the devil appeared, proclaiming his annoyance at thus being summoned and disturbed. Satan's subsequent instructions to the renegade on how to become a disciple of wickedness may well reflect Rutebeuf's own conception of the evil-doer: Théophile is never to offer alms to any poor wretch, but to turn away in pride, for, says the devil, gentleness, humility, pity, and charity all give him a pain in the stomach and make him feel as if serpents were gnawing his vitals. Our playwright must have been in a quandary as to how to show his apostate hero returned to power. He solved the problem by

---

[1] In the case of another saint's life, that of St. Mary the Egyptian, Rutebeuf eclectically used Latin and French sources in the same way. See Bujila, pp. 1-27.

letting us see Théophile arrogantly talking to the Bishop and his messenger, quarrelling with two priests, and rejecting all their efforts to apologize, to placate, and make restitution. Again the language is contemporaneous and colloquial: I don't give a fig for the Bishop's hatred; I commend the canons to the devils; when peasants come to pay me homage, I'll make them sweat; a man is worth nothing who is not feared. Even the Virgin Mary in some measure partakes of Rutebeuf's spirited and original visualization of his story. After she has regained the pact from Satan, she expresses her scorn for him in the words: 'Et je te foulerai la pance.'

Flaws in the play can, of course, be detected. Both motivation and characterization might have been improved. Théophile's repentance is inadequately prepared for and comes as a shock, though a break in the performance may perhaps have mitigated its suddenness. The characters are but lightly sketched. Yet the desperate and later sincerely penitent Théophile, the crafty Salatin, the irascible, wicked Satan, and the humanly angry Notre Dame are sufficiently individualized to carry conviction. At any rate in a performance of the play its flaws disappear. The utterly pitiful plight of the hero, the terrible implications of his pact with the devil, the contemporaneity of language and ideas, and the swift transitions of the plot, all make a potent and immediate impression on an audience.

The true artistry of the play, however, resides in its poetry, and the finest poetical effects occur in the pathetic lamentations and contrite prayers of the protagonist: into these Rutebeuf poured not only his religious fervour, his own despair and remorse, but also his best technical skill. The fashion of his day applauded certain verbal flourishes that modern taste rejects, and Rutebeuf was adept at playing with words, turning and twisting their meanings, punning and quibbling. He used his ingenuity all too profusely in the show-pieces of our play. But when one disregards such excesses and looks beyond them, one finds in the *Repentance* and *Prière* of Théophile phrases filled with devout music, lovely images, and a graceful beauty that reflect authentic feelings. Throughout the play it is evident that a master's hand has been at work. The octosyllabic couplet is used comparatively seldom, but one of Rutebeuf's favourite

rhythms, $aa(a)^8b^4$ (the couplet or tercet of eight syllables followed by a short verse of four syllables which introduces the
next rhyme), occurs frequently and is employed in dialogue
with an excellent effect of lightness. For certain solemn moments
in the play monorhymed quatrains of twelve syllables set the
tone; in the *Prière* remarkable twelve-lined stanzas use six-
syllabled lines, rhyming *aabaabbbabba*, to play a full-toned
melody about the delicate language they enhance. In sum,
varied rhythms, intricately patterned stanzas, and rich rhymes
all reveal a professional poet at his best.

When the *Miracle* was written and performed is unknown,
but its resemblance in vocabulary and emotional colouring to
the poems by Rutebeuf which can be confidently dated *c.* 1261
suggest that it was composed about this time, and Faral has
plausibly conjectured that it was destined for performance on
the occasion of some feast of the Virgin, probably the Nativity
or the Conception.

That the playwright used the simultaneous stage-setting of
his time can be assumed. In that case he doubtless followed
tradition in placing heaven and the abode of Notre Dame at
the far left of the spectator, the devil's lair at the far right.
The Bishop and his clerks would probably have their *mansions*
next Notre Dame's, Salatin's would be beside Satan's, thus
leaving Théophile the centre of the stage and producing an
aesthetic and figurative balance of good and evil around the
protagonist's important position.[1] Such a disposition of the
players would be consonant with the theme of the play which,
considered from a general point of view, visualizes the struggle
between good and evil for the possession of a man's soul.

The prevalence in the text of mnemonic rhymes—rhymes
shared between two speakers—and the presence at the end of
the *Te Deum laudamus* mark it as a true *pièce de théâtre*. However,
the shortness of the play (663 lines), the few characters involved
in it, the way in which never more than two characters appear in
any single scene, the disproportionately long role of Théophile
(242 lines out of 663), and the fact that Rutebeuf wrote a dra-

---

[1] It is difficult to understand why Faral would place Notre Dame 'vers le fond
de la scène' (*Rom.* lxxii [1951], 189) and why Cohen, in his performance of the
piece, added God and his angels to the *dramatis personae*.

matic monologue which he probably recited himself all make it
seem possible that our play might also have served on occasion
as a vehicle for recitation by its author, perhaps assisted by a
companion.

LE DIT DE L'HERBERIE

Rutebeuf's dramatic monologue, the *Dit de l'herberie*, need
not detain us long, but it serves to emphasize once more the
close relations existing between narrative and dramatic literature in the Middle Ages. In this recitation the performer—
probably the author himself—impersonates a charlatan who
claims to have gathered herbs, precious stones, and medical
recipes from all over the world. His wares, he promises, will
cure or prevent every sort of bodily ill, rejuvenate the old and
even resuscitate the dead. A clever jongleur using a few ordinary
properties could make this harangue entertaining: it is full of
wit and broad comedy and obviously satirizes a kind of quackery
that actually prevailed. In fact the prose portion—it is half in
verse, half in prose—begins by denying that the vendor is one
of those poor ragged herb-sellers who spread their wares on
carpets in front of churches. Those fellows, he says, sell pepper,
cumin, and other useless spices under false pretences.

We know of at least two other *Dits de l'herberie*, besides
Rutebeuf's, and this theme seems to have provided a well-
established type of recitation.[1] It may even have influenced the
spice-merchants' harangues in the later Passion plays. In any
case we find a similar parody incorporated in the *Palatine Passion*
where the spice-merchant, like Rutebeuf's charlatan, claims to

---

[1] See Faral, *Mimes*, pp. 55 ff., for these and other dramatic monologues and
dialogues of the thirteenth century. It is evident from the narrative *Du Vilain au
buffet*, lines 142 ff. (Faral, op. cit., p. 59), that the repertoire of the jongleurs included various recitations and impersonations of this sort:

> L'uns fait l'ivre, l'autre le sot,
> Lis uns chante, li autres note,
> Et li autres dit la *Riote*,
> Et li autres la *Jonglerie* . . .
> Aucuns i a qui fabliaus conte,
> Ou il ot mainte gaberie,
> Et li autre dit l'*Erberie*
> La ou il ot mainte risée.

On the dramatic monologues of the fifteenth century see Chap. XXIV below,
and Picot, *Le Monologue dramatique*.

come from the medieval medical centre of Salerno and offers to the three Marys on their way to the tomb various herbs with the same properties as those ascribed to his merchandise by the quack of the *Dit de l'herberie*.[1]

Monologues and dialogues of this sort, sometimes called mimes, are not true plays, but they contain dramatic elements, and in this instance it is clear how readily they might be made to serve the purposes of drama.

[1] See P. Abrahams,'Mercator-Scenes in French Passion-Plays', *MedÆ* iii (1934), 112–23.

XII

Les Miracles de Notre Dame

FROM the fourteenth century a large and varied collection of *Miracles de Notre Dame* has come down to us.[1] No less than forty of them are preserved in two small folio manuscripts of the late fourteenth or early fifteenth century in the Bibliothèque Nationale, fonds français 819 and 820, often called the Cangé MSS. from the name of their eighteenth-century owner. Each play is preceded by a beautifully executed miniature depicting a scene from the following miracle. The plays themselves have been dated between *c.* 1339 and 1382 and have been assigned to the Parisian guild of goldsmiths.[2]

The miracles as a whole give a curious impression of both similarity and diversity. In each of them[3] a grievous sinner is rescued by the Virgin Mary and she appears in person, usually accompanied by the archangels Gabriel and Michael who regu-

[1] Ed. by G. Paris and U. Robert in *SATF*. On these plays see Magnin, Petit de Julleville, *Mystères*, i. 115 ff., ii. 226 ff., Schnell, Jensen, Forkert, Roy, *Études*, Hélène Meyer, Stadler-Honegger, D. Penn, and especially Rudolf Glutz, *Miracles de Nostre Dame par personnages*, Deutsche Akademie der Wissenschaften zu Berlin, Veröffentlichungen des Instituts f. Rom. Sp. ix, 1954.

[2] Unlike anyone before him Glutz (op. cit.) succeeded in deciphering certain erasures in the manuscripts and in reading more than half the rubrics that originally occurred after the *Incipit* of each play. He discovered that whenever these rubrics can be deciphered they form part or all of the phrase *joue au pui des orfeures a paris*. In seven instances the date of the performance had been indicated before the erasure, and from the distribution of these dates it is clear that the plays were given annually—possibly with a few negligible lapses—over a period of about forty-three years and that their appearance in the manuscripts is chronological. Two miracles not in this collection, though sometimes associated with it, *Le Chevalier qui donna sa femme au diable* and *Une Jeune Fille laquelle se voulut abandonner a peché*, were ascribed to the fourteenth century by Petit de Julleville, *Mystères*, ii. 335 ff. and 340 ff., but Roy, op. cit., pp. cxlix ff. and clii ff., shows they are probably later, the second surely after 1413.

[3] The *Nativité*, play V, used to be regarded as outside the general pattern, and of course the Virgin here rescues no sinner. But divine intervention takes the place of the usual intercession of the Virgin and in other respects the play conforms to type: the sermon at the beginning, the versification, and the interpolated lyrics are all typical. Notre Dame does not appear in XXXVIII, but the end of that play is lacking and in its general scheme it too resembles the others.

larly sing interpolated *rondeaux* in her honour.[1] The versification of the dialogue—octosyllabic couplets, each speech ending with a cue-line of four syllables that rhymes with the first line of the next speech—is the same in all the plays with one negligible exception[2] and the interpolated *rondeaux*, though more diversified in rhythm than the dialogue, nevertheless adopt conventional formulae in metre and vocabulary. In twenty-seven of the plays a prose sermon in the vernacular appears either at the beginning as a prologue or within the framework of the action— and evidence exists that other plays once contained such sermons. Yet despite this similarity of treatment and pattern, there are important variations of detail in the miracles and, above all, the greatest diversity of plots obtains. Themes have been taken from such disparate sources as Gregory of Tours and Gautier de Coincy, from *chansons de geste*, romances, chronicles, saints' lives, and folk legends. The range of characters in them is enormous and the wealth of subjects embraces such heterogeneous material as the stories of Robert the Devil, the nun who left her abbey, the baptism of Clovis, the Nativity, Amis et Amile, and Berthe au grand pied, so that together these plays offer a treasure-house of medieval lore which gives them an exciting variety within their relatively uniform framework.

Because of their similarity in construction and diction it used to be thought that all the *Miracles* were by a single author, but it seems more likely that they are the work of a number of different writers, and that their uniformity derives from their purpose. They were obviously designed for a guild devoted to the Virgin and were perhaps to be performed on one or another of her holy days—the Conception, Birth, Purification, Annunciation, or Assumption, especially the last three. Since only a single play was performed each year, the plays represent a considerable lapse of time and probably involved a varied authorship even though a fairly consistent tradition regarding them was followed. D. Penn suggests fifteen or twenty different

[1] The role played by Notre Dame and by her Son differs somewhat in the plays and occasionally various saints or unnamed angels appear. In some plays it is the angels and saints, as well as the archangels, who sing *rondeaux*. But these minor variations do not impair the general impression of uniformity.

[2] The first play has no four-syllabled cue-lines, but the octosyllabic speeches are bound together by mnemonic rhymes.

writers; Schnell finds twenty-seven; Stadler-Honegger merely shows that some of the plays—e.g. XXIX, XXXI, XXXII—may be by the same person. In any case the twenty-three lyrical pieces (*serventoys*) in praise of the Virgin which appear between certain plays point to a kind of poetical contest fostered by the religious and literary members of the *puy* that sponsored the *Miracles*: these pieces refer to the *prince du puy* at times and once to a *serventoys couronné au dit puy*,[1] although the name of the *dit puy* has since been erased. The universal adoration of the Virgin in the plays and in the sermons incorporated in them confirms the impression that our plays constituted the repertory of a society probably similar in some respects to the Confrérie de Notre Dame de Liesse, founded in Paris in 1413 and of which we have records, a society that gave banquets accompanied by dramatic performances *au siège de la Confrairie*.[2] The statutes of another *puy*, that of Amiens, fill in the picture. This society held an annual banquet at Candlemas 'et durant iceluy disner fera le maistre jouer ung jeu de mistère', and the master was also to give a silver crown to the man who should compose the most successful *chant royal* on that occasion. Among the master's other duties during the year was having *ballades* made to honour the Virgin on her five holy days and rewarding the best.

The exact relation of the *serventoys* to the miracles remains uncertain. Between some plays there is one, between others two of these lyrical pieces. Sometimes they are qualified as *couronnés*, sometimes as *estrivés* (i.e. admitted to the contest but not crowned), sometimes they bear no other title than *serventoys*. Many of these poems are beautiful, others seem contrived and artificial; all resemble the courtly lyrics of the trouvères and troubadours in form and diction. They comprise five stanzas and an envoi (usually addressed to the prince or the *prince du puy* or to the Virgin herself), the stanzas vary from ten to twelve lines which are mostly decasyllabic, and the same rhymes in the

---

[1] Vol. i, p. 244. In *Romance Philology*, xii (1959), pp. 240–3, I have tried to show that the erasures probably occurred after meetings of the goldsmiths were banned and their plays passed into the hands of the Confrérie de la Passion.

[2] On this society, for which Jean Louvet wrote twelve *Miracles* very similar to ours performed between 1536 and 1550, see Roy, *Études*, pp. cxlv ff. Louvet seems to have belonged both to this society and to the famous Confrérie de la Passion. On the Puy d'Amiens see Faral, *Jongleurs*, pp. 139 ff.

same order are repeated in each stanza (in Provençal termino-
logy, *coblas unissonans*). Magnin called these pieces a mixture of
mysticism and gallantry; both components occur though in
differing proportions. The more religious and simpler *serventoys*
give an impression of sincere devotion; the more elaborately
amorous with their involved erotic metaphors (one is actually
addressed to the *prince d'amours*) hardly appeal to modern taste.
Gröber[1] suggested that these poems were taken from song-
collections, but it seems more likely that they are the result of
contests instituted by the puy and that on those occasions when
Notre Dame was honoured by the members, whether by the
performance of one of her miracles or otherwise, *serventoys* were
recited—perhaps the winner of the contest recited his own
serventoys couronné—which were then duly copied into the manuscripts that preserve our plays. Since the *serventoys* almost unani-
mously honour the Annunciation and the plays may have been
given on other holy days as well, the connexion between poems
and plays may sometimes be fortuitous.

The order of the plays in our two manuscripts has been
shown to be chronological although the manuscripts themselves
seem designed for readers or possibly as an official *registrum* like
that which, for example, preserves the English guild plays of
York. D. Penn believes that succeeding plays took cognizance
of their predecessors, imitating successful scenes and devices,
and that in general the later plays are more complex in their
staging than the earlier ones. In any case it is true that we find
longer plays, involving more and more complicated *mise en
scène*, toward the end of the series, simpler and shorter plays at
the beginning, and that the longer plays reflect more sophistica-
tion and a less naïve faith than the shorter ones. But it is also
obvious that the practical requirements of the guild on specific
occasions—the importance of the celebration, the availability
of actors and playwrights, financial considerations, &c.—might
influence the choice of a simple or elaborate performance at a
given time.[2]

---

[1] *Grundriss*, ii. 1, p. 1215.
[2] Roy, who dated XII after 1364 and probably after 1380, XV before 1358,
XIX before 1363, and XXXIII before 1360, naturally reached the conclusion
that the order of the plays in the manuscripts is not chronological (see p. clxxxix).

The language of these texts is remarkably free from dialectal traces and this, as well as certain references to Paris, supports the other evidence that the miracles were written for a guild in the capital. There are significant local allusions in plays XII, XV, XIX, XXVI, XXXIII. For instance, in XIX a convent, located elsewhere in the source of the play, is transferred to Paris and the Parisian Hôtel de Sens appears; in XXVI the prisons called 'la Gourdaine' and 'Paradis', which were in the Châtelet, are familiarly mentioned (690, 692); in XXXVI a beggar goes from the church of St. Eustache through the Halles to the well-known tavern of the Grand Godet and on to the vicinity of the 'port Nostre Dame' (the Port de Grève today). It is probable indeed that, as Roy conjectured, the site of the guild sponsoring our plays was in the neighbourhood of the Halles, especially since the Rue des Orfèvres is in the vicinity.[1]

Although the great variety of subjects and wealth of plots in the *Miracles* embrace people of all classes of society and can be used—with caution[2]—to interpret certain contemporary customs and manners, it must be remembered that the stories involved are not of the fourteenth century and that, despite potent

But his dates do not accord with Glutz's. Stadler-Honegger, who believes the plays may have been written over a period of some forty years, is not sure that they are now in their original order, but finds in general a gradual evolution in them despite the possibility of some displacement. She detects in the longer, presumably later plays a tendency to escape from religious dogmatism towards a freer choice of subject and mode of treatment. On the staging see Penn, who shows that a relatively small indoor stage could be used for all of them.

[1] See Roy, *Études*, pp. cxxvii ff. Paris and the Louvre are directly mentioned in plays XXIII and XXXIX, but the city fulfils its natural role of capital of France in these. Penn's suggestion that the guild may have been in Boulogne seems untenable. The eight references to Boulogne involve Notre Dame de Boulogne, a well-known place of pilgrimage, seven of them may have been induced by the rhyme, and in two cases the characters definitely leave their own localities to go on a pilgrimage to this famous shrine (I, 782; X, 830 ff.—here Miss Penn misinterprets *par my vostre chappelle* which means 'by way of your chapel'). On the Rue des Orfèvres see Glutz, op. cit., p. 200,

[2] Forkert, pp. 122 ff., is aware of the important role of hermits in the plays and the less honourable part played by monks and nuns, but fails to equate these facts with fourteenth-century conditions which they undoubtedly reproduce. On the other hand, Otto Patzer in *MLN*, xx (1905), 44–48 attempted to find reflections of the life of the fourteenth century in the plays, but most of the details mentioned by him can be duplicated in earlier and later times: the description of an invasion, the exercise of certain feudal rights, trial by single combat, the use of ecclesiastical courts by the clergy, the poverty of the peasants, the military importance of the bourgeoisie, &c.

possibilities for being otherwise, these are essentially religious plays. Written during the Hundred Years War, few allusions to it occur.[1] To be sure, it has been suggested that heaven's easy appeasement in the plays reflects the cynicism of the time, the lack of faith in spiritual and temporal powers, and that a profound disgust prevails in these texts since both monarchs and clergy are helpless without divine intervention. But one must beware of transposing modern attitudes into the Middle Ages. Actually, changing social and historical conditions have made the plays differ little in spirit from their sources, predecessors, and successors: the same naïve reverence and faith in heaven's omnipotence occurs in the thirteenth-century miracles of Gautier de Coincy and Rutebeuf, in the sixteenth-century miracles of Jean Louvet.[2]

Interest centres in the Virgin's intercession, her aid to sinners, however wicked, who have repented. This moral may be tucked away in various exciting tales intended to keep a restive medieval audience entertained, yet it is always there. Modern taste may be offended by the way in which the worst of criminals have only to offer opportune prayers to be forgiven.[3] But the spectators who first witnessed these miracles performed were concerned in paying homage to their tutelary saint, and the greater the crime the greater the power of the Mother of God. Worship and adoration of her pervade not only the plays but the sermons incorporated in them and the *serventoys* preserved with them in our manuscripts. As the Prescheur says in play XIX[4]: '. . . les festes de la glorieuse vierge mère Marie, pour qui amour et reverence nous sommes cy assemblez, devons nous garder . . . pour elle magnifier.' The sermons,[5] though spoken by members

---

[1] See, however, in XIX, 736, *les Anglois m'ont tout tolu.*

[2] On this question compare Petit de Julleville, *Mystères,* i. 135, Lanson, *Histoire,* p. 193, and Roy, *Études,* pp. cxxiii ff.

[3] The Abbé Poquet, who edited the narrative miracles of Gautier de Coincy which furnished our playwrights with many of their plots, objected so much to three of them that for various reasons they are omitted from his edition. Ulrich, *ZRP,* vi (1882), 325–46, prints all three.   [4] Vol. iii, p. 138.

[5] On the sermons see Hélène Meyer. The relation of the sermons to the plays is close since, although in prose, they are bound to the preceding or following dialogue by rhyme. These sermons conform to a type used outside the regular church services and known, from the readings at meals in monasteries, as *collaciones* (Fr. *collacions*). Meyer believes them to be taken from a common source, some medieval collection of homilies now lost. Apparently individual playwrights

of the guild, are as reverent in tone as if delivered in church, and the *serventoys*, whatever their function in the celebrations of the guild, are permeated with the passionate devotion reserved by the courtly poets for their mistresses. It is with the spirit of these prose sermons and these poetic transports in mind that one should approach the *Miracles de Notre Dame*.

And yet the value of the plays as entertainment must never be forgotten. In the fourteenth century, when many of the plots were unfamiliar and numerous details fresh and unexpected, the spectators must have enjoyed the worldly aspects of the performances as much as the religious experiences accompanying them. Even in our own day, when one knows that the Virgin Mary as *dea ex machina* will eventually rescue the most abominable of these sinners, when one has heard their stories before and can anticipate the conclusions, the impact of the plays is still forceful. The *Nun who Left her Abbey* (VII) and the *Woman Saved from Burning* (XXVI) have been played in modern times to sympathetic and deeply moved audiences.

It is obvious that the miracle plays, to a far greater extent than the biblical mysteries, could depend for success upon the elements of surprise and suspense. Many of our *Miracles de Notre Dame* make full use of this advantage; free from any of the conventions of the 'unities' or the 'well-made' play, they introduce new characters and new developments at will, often toward the end of the piece, in order to sustain interest and arouse further curiosity. Unlike the biblical plays—except in their unbiblical additions—they could also benefit from a piquant immediacy. The characters of the *Miracles* are for the most part neither hallowed persons nor remote heroes of antiquity but men and women like the spectators, and even when of more elevated station they respond to familiar motives and emotions. Fleshly temptations and guilty passions, faithless spouses and over-zealous gossips, misunderstandings and false accusations, these are of all times.[1] A cardinal reduces a mer-

were free to introduce the preaching where they chose: at the beginning as a prologue or within the drama as part of the action. Twenty-four plays contain complete sermons and seven others show signs of once possessing them; in only nine are all indications lacking.

[1] On the falsely accused woman in these plays see Micha in *Mélanges Cohen*, pp. 85–92.

chant's price from 1,000 *livres parisis* to 1,000 *livres tournois*
(VIII, 1098); business men make off to Flanders, one of them
'assez sage . . . scet parler maint langage' (XI, 165–6); women
writhe and cry out in the agony of child-birth and have heavy
books placed upon their bodies to hasten delivery (XV, 384 ff.).
Such realism is timeless. Universal too is the appeal to emotions
of horror, pity, and terror and to the titillation emanating from
the sight of the degradation of the powerful. Malefactors about
to be burned alive, children who meet violent deaths, women
on the point of being raped, nuns and monks yielding to worldly
lures, an abbess who becomes pregnant, all are certain to produce fascinated shudders in an audience.

And the characters in the plays are as diverse and potentially
appealing as the plots. The hierarchy of both church and state
is represented, from popes and cardinals to humble priests,
clerks, and hermits, from emperors, empresses, kings, and
queens to heralds, bailiffs, sergeants, and executioners. Included
also, among others, are knights, citizens of both sexes, students,
children, minstrels, fools, harvesters, beggars, pilgrims, secretaries, messengers, huntsmen, midwives, inn-keepers, chamber-
maids, and other servants. Mingling with these mortals on the
easiest of terms are God, the Virgin Mary, archangels, angels,
saints, and devils. An earthy familiarity exists between all of
them. Petit de Julleville says cogently: 'Rien ne paraît plus
naturel dans ces drames que le surnaturel.'[1]

Musical interludes must also have contributed in no small
measure to the pleasure and emotional stimulation of the spectators. Songs constitute an invariable element of every play: they
are introduced more or less deftly (as in modern musical plays),
but introduced they must be. Usually they are sung by the
archangels accompanying the Virgin, sometimes by angels or
saints.[2] Notre Dame's instruction in XXXVII, 3007 is typical:

---

[1] *Mystères*, i. 133.
[2] The *rondeaux* are all sung in honour and praise of the Virgin. (So, too, the
chanson of XXX, 1607.) The form of the *rondel* varies in length and number of
lines, but the element of repetition is essential: usually the first lines (*aab*) are
repeated as a whole by way of refrain at the end and in part in the middle (*a* or *ab*).
And in most plays part of the *rondel* is sung again after its first performance. Some
plays have several of these songs. Characteristic is their sophisticated seven-
syllabled line with masculine or feminine rhymes, sometimes interspersed with

'Chantez tellement c'on vous oye, / Par quoy toutes ces gens en joye / Soient meuz', to which an angel replies, 'Nous n'en serons pas recreuz. / Avant: disons a haulte alaine.' In an early miracle (III, 652) three minstrels seek their instruments in order to play at the festivities inaugurating a new bishop, but no mention of the actual performing is made. Several late miracles, however, end with music, either songs or instrumental music, which accompanies the actors as they leave (cf. XXXII: 'Icy jeuent les menesterez, et s'en va le jeu.' See also the end of plays XXXI, XXXVII). It is apparent that at times specially trained clerks or choirboys assisted in the final singing: les clercs are sent for in XXVIII to sing at dinner 'un motet qui soit deduisant, / Plaisant et bel' (2076), and in XXX, 1577 ff., 'deux clerjons', who presently arrive with their master, 'chanteront a haulte alaine'. It would seem that once the device had been discovered of getting the actors off the stage in a procession to the happy strains of songs or instruments, succeeding plays adopted it whenever they liked. The early plays in our collection sometimes used religious music for this purpose—not only the *Te Deum laudamus* but such church hymns as the *Veni creator spiritus*. These were probably sung by the whole assembly, whereas the more elaborate later miracles introduced special singers or instrumentalists for the purpose.

Despite obvious defects, the artistic values in certain of these plays and in many passages of others should not be minimized. For example, although the sudden determination to kill and the abrupt discovery of the murder in XXVI (the *Woman Saved from Burning*) seem insufficiently motivated, the slow awakening of suspicion in this same play has been capably handled. Moreover, comparison with its source—a miracle narrated by Gautier de Coincy[1]—reveals how much the playwright has tightened his action both in time and place and how some of his original additions contribute to the development of the plot. Similarly in XXVII (the *Emperor of Rome*) nothing adequately prepares the audience for the unjust accusation and condemnation of an innocent woman, and yet the soliloquy of a guilty lover in-

lines of five syllables. In both form and matter these *rondeaux*, like the *serventoys* between the plays, resemble the courtly lyric of the troubadours and trouvères.

[1] Cf. Väänänen, *D'Une Fame de Laon*.

flamed by passion for his brother's wife competently analyses
a state of mind and makes good use of that medieval equivalent
of modern psychology, the allegorical abstraction. This play
also illustrates the powerful appeal of so many of these miracles
to the emotional responses of an audience: in this case to pity
for a chaste wife unfairly calumniated.

If the opportunities for character-portrayal, psychological
analysis, and for giving significance and universality to these
widely differing tales had been fully exploited, the development
of a secular theatre in France might well have been hastened.
Here are themes dear to the Elizabethans—the Cymbeline motive (XXVIII), the young girl disguised as a youth (XXXVII),
the unswerving loyalties of friendship (XXIII)—but they remain
sterile of import. When Amile learns that he can heal his friend
Amis by killing his sons, he does so almost without scruple or
debate, although in the romance from which this play derives,
the natural sorrow and hesitancy of a father in such circumstances are appealingly suggested.[1] In the same way great crimes
are insufficiently motivated, e.g. Guibour's determination to
slay her son-in-law in XXVI, the brother's unjust accusation of
the Empress of Rome and her husband's determination that she
must die a shameful death for her supposed adultery (XXVII).
In the play concerning the nun who left her abbey (VII), the
nun, though supposedly of high reputation, yields too easily to
the knight, her reasons for doing so are barely indicated and
seem out of character (she desires to be a *chevalresse* and complains of being too long in the convent), and, both when she is
prevented from leaving the convent by Notre Dame and when
she eventually succeeds, the emphasis is on the technicalities of
religious observance, not on any mental or spiritual state. So
too her repentance, like that of most of the sinners in these
plays, comes with unexpected abruptness. (In some of the narrative versions of this story, notably Adgar's, the nun regrets her
sin at length.)

Many other ineptitudes and unrealized possibilities in the
plays might be pointed out. Undramatic are the recitals that
repeat what the audience has already witnessed, the way in

---

[1] Cf. lines 2917 ff. of the romance, edited by Konrad Hofmann, Erlangen 1882,
with lines 1686 ff. of play XXIII.

which characters unnecessarily announce what they are doing
or have just done, the clumsy means used to effect transitions
or indicate lapses of time.[1] In some cases the narrative sources of
our plays have been followed too slavishly; in general most of
the faults can be traced to technical deficiencies of medieval
stagecraft and to an imperfect realization of the potentialities of
dramatic representation. The purposes and occasions for which
the plays were destined must also have shackled their authors,
serving to confine them within traditional limitations. Men of
genius could, of course, have surmounted all these handicaps,
but none of our writers possessed genius. They were at best
good craftsmen of a rather pedestrian order. That some of the
plays nevertheless continue to move and excite an audience is
a tribute to their sincerity, to the faith that permeates them, and
to the perennially absorbing stories they have to tell.

[1] For example in XXVI the playwright, following the narrative of Gautier de
Coincy, recapitulates at length the details of a murder with which the audience is
thoroughly familiar. Such typical expressions as 'vez me cy lez vous assis' take
the place of stage-directions, which are sparingly used, especially in the earlier
miracles. Programme notes and modern scenery—not to mention more subtlety
—would enable a contemporary dramatist to dispense with such an awkward
indication of the passage of time as 'Doulce amie, espousé avons / Et esté si lonc
temps ensemble / Que deux enfans, si com me semble, / Avez de moy qui sont ja
grans' (VII, 652).

XIII

The Development of the Passion Play

La Passion du Palatinus. La Passion d'Autun.
Le Jour du Jugement

A<small>T</small> the end of the twelfth or beginning of the thirteenth century a very popular poem about the Passion was widely circulated by the jongleurs in France and England. It obviously attempted to rival the contemporary epic tales, for at least two of the manuscripts have a prologue scolding audiences that prefer to hear about Roland and Oliver rather than about our Lord's Passion:

> Plus volentiers oroit conter
> coment Rolan[s] ala jostei
> a Olivier, son compaignon,
> k'il ne feroit la passion
> ke Dex soufri o grant enhan
> por le pechié ke fist Adan. (ll. 23–28)

This so-called *Passion des Jongleurs* occurs not only as a separate poem but incorporated in longer works, e.g. in Geoffroi de Paris's *Bible des sept états du monde*; résumés of it appear in the versified *Romanz de S. Fanuel* and in the prose *Chronique* by Jean d'Outremeuse; and it was early translated into English. The poem stresses scenes made familiar by the liturgy, scenes early popularized by sculpture and painting as well as literature, and it also adds to these many picturesque legends that in turn made their way later into art and the drama. In its varying forms this narrative poem was of course available to medieval authors desiring to fashion a play about the Passion.[1]

---

[1] On the *Passion des Jongleurs* see Theben, Pfuhl, F. A. Foster. On its relation to art see *Le Livre de la Passion*, p. iv, and to the drama, G. Frank in *MLN*, xxxv (1920), 257–69, in *PMLA*, xxxv (1920), 464–83, and *Passion du Palatinus* (*CFMA* edition), v–vii. The prologue cited above also appears as an introduction to the *Quinze Signes du Jugement* on which cf. Foster, p. 51, Studer, p. xxxi, and Roy, *Mystère*, p. 27*. For Latin sermons expressing the same idea see B. Hauréau, *Notices et extraits de quelques manuscrits latins de la Bibliothèque Nationale*, iv (1892), 24–25.

At hand, too, for the dramatists were the ultimate sources of
the poem—the Bible, the Gospel Harmonies, the liturgy—and
various popular theological works. Few books were commonly
read in the Middle Ages, but those, such as the works of the
Church Fathers and certain commentaries, were read over and
over again and must have formed part of the learning of any
competent medieval dramatist.[1] He would also have been familiar with the liturgical plays of the Church and the widely circulated lyrical *planctus Mariae*.[2]

It is obvious that the substructure of one early group of
the Passion plays which survive is the old narrative poem circulated by the jongleurs. Its direct discourse and entertaining
apocryphal matter made it easily adaptable to dramatic presentation, and upon such a base additions of various kinds, both
lyrical and narrative, borrowed and original, could easily be
superimposed.

LA PASSION DU PALATINUS

The earliest French Passion play that we possess, the *Passion
du Palatinus*, belongs to this group. It dates in its present form
from the fourteenth century, but its relation to a fragment of
87 lines known as the *Fragment de Sion* and to two later texts,
the *Passion de Biard* and the *Passion de Roman* (named from their
copyists and known collectively as the *Passion d'Autun*), points
to a lost play or several lost plays on the same subject that must
have preceded it. It is not only the earliest of the French Passion
plays, but, before Greban's great masterpiece, in many respects
the most original.[3]

La Passion du Palatinus opens, after a monorhymed, dodeca-
syllabic quatrain that serves as prologue, with the Entry into
Jerusalem—lines taken almost literally from the jongleurs'
poem—but soon shows its originality by inserting a dialogue
between the welcoming children of the city and a song sung by
them. In most of the following scenes—the Host's reception
of Jesus, Mary Magdalen's anointing of her Lord, Judas's

---

[1] Cf. Duriez, *Théologie*, pp. 21 ff.

[2] On the plays cf. Chap. II above; on the *planctus* see Chap. V, p. 54, n. 1.

[3] Edited by G. Frank in *CFMA*. On the *Fragment de Sion* see Bédier, *Rom.* xxiv
(1895), 87. The *Passion d'Autun* is edited by G. Frank in *SATF*. All these texts
seem to be associated with Burgundy.

reproaches to his Master, the Last Supper, the Agony in the
Garden, the appearances before Pilate and Herod, &c.—the
Passion des Jongleurs reappears, almost line for line. Our dramatist, however, uses his ingenuity even in some of these, and
especially upon certain minor characters seemingly of his own
invention.

Thus he enlivens his play by showing Judas with the Jews
counting out his thirty pieces of silver and protesting that there
are only twenty-eight; he introduces realistic scenes with the
torturers, Cayn and Huitacelin, who beat their victim until they
are tired out, and with the executioners, Haquin and Mosse,
who rejoice volubly in their ugly calling. He brings upon the
stage, probably for the first time (though the narrative poem
included it), the forging of the nails for the crucifixion by the
smith's wife, who, when her miraculously stricken husband refuses to perform the task, undertakes it gratuitously and no
doubt clumsily, cursing Jesus the while. The playwright gives
us an amusing and vivacious Harrowing of Hell in which Satan
and Enfer quarrel as to how best to defend themselves against
the coming Christ, Satan boastful and mock-heroic, Enfer fearful, both calling each other names and indulging in picturesque
curses. Although the knights who guard the tomb in this play
resemble those of some of the later liturgical texts, men who are
braggarts first and cowards later, they give an impression of
reality in their bravado, their cupidity, and their terror at having
lost the body. The spice-merchant, too, has contemporaneity,
indeed he proclaims himself a physician of Salerno, the great
medieval school of medicine, and offers to the three Marys a
variety of herbs with magical properties, some of which are
well known to medieval herbalists and supposedly confer on the
purchaser miraculous powers to prophesy, become young again,
assume invisibility, achieve immortality, and the like.[1]

The narrative poem of the jongleurs was written in monotonous octosyllabic couplets, but our playwright frequently
varies his rhythms, adapting them to his special requirements,
long lines for the more solemn parts and shorter ones for the
more spirited scenes. He also introduces stanzaic structure at

[1] Cf. Chap. XI above for a comparison with the charlatan of Rutebeuf's *Dit
de l'herberie*.

times and with excellent effect in some of the *planctus* and in the *diablerie*. But whether he writes stanzas of the popular form aaa^8b^4, bbb^8c^4, &c., or monorhymed quatrains of eight or twelve syllables, whether he interlaces his rhymes or uses simple couplets, one feels that his measures have a purpose consonant with his themes and with their lyric or dramatic treatment. A few narrative lines have made their way into the play, but these seem to be versified stage-directions contributed by the copyist. They obviously form no part of the author's original intention and there can be no doubt that, as in the case of the Anglo-Norman *Resureccion*, we are dealing with a truly dramatic text.[1]

Where suspense is ruled out by an audience's knowledge of a theme, the effectiveness of a medieval play depended necessarily upon original conceptions of well-known characters, small additions to the plot, apocryphal incidents, and technical virtuosity. In the *Palatine Passion* the biblical characters retain their traditional traits and yet the playwright's tenderness and sympathy for those who must suffer, his hatred of those who inflict hurt, are everywhere manifest. His Pilate and Longinus deviate from the typical and betray a personal conception of these roles. Realistic scenes and light touches of humour are especially frequent in the play, and the audience would surely have been diverted by the quarrel between Satan and Hell and the coarseness of their language, by the sadism of the torturers and executioners, by the charlatanry of the spice-merchant's harangue. Nevertheless the dignity and seriousness of the great story of the Passion emerge with poignancy, and the original elements of the piece, designed to enliven the action and hold the attention of restless spectators, served the dual purpose of such performances, to entertain and instruct.

It is obvious that this play must have been represented upon a stage capable of suggesting many different localities simultaneously. The action takes place on the road to Jerusalem, in the home of Simon the Leper, on the Mount of Olives, before Caiaphas, Pilate, and Herod, in the house of the smith, at Gol-

---

[1] For example, St. Peter's use of his sword after line 258 and the tearing of St. John's cloak after 506 would have had to be visibly represented to make the following lines intelligible. On the narrative lines in the *Resureccion* see Chap. IX above, and on those in the Palatine text see the *CFMA* edition, pp. iv–v.

gotha, &c., and the characters wander to and fro from one site
to another as the various episodes demand. The manuscript
gives no indication of the staging, seldom even mentions the
names of the speakers involved, and, except for our knowledge
of the Bible, of how similar plays were staged, and of contemporary representations in art, we should be left without clues.[1]
From these, however, we may deduce that small structures suggested the dwellings of Simon, of the high priest, the governor,
the smith, and others, that a cross connoted Golgotha, a tomb
of some sort served for the burial and the visit of the Marys,
that heaven and hell occupied their usual positions at the far
left and right of the spectator, respectively, and that a considerable part of the action took place in a neutral foreground.
How many 'mansions' would be required must have depended
on the resources of the director and upon the imaginative responses to be expected of the audience.

LA PASSION D'AUTUN

Related to the *Palatine Passion*, as has been indicated, is a fragmentary text of only 87 lines found at Sion and two fifteenth-
century manuscripts known collectively as the *Passion d'Autun*.
There are striking similarities of phrase between all of them
which make it clear that they must ultimately derive from
some lost play or plays strongly influenced by the narrative
Passion des Jongleurs. Each author adapted the material at hand
in his own fashion and to suit his own purposes. The fragment
is too short to make accurate judgement possible, but the two
texts of the *Passion d'Autun* apparently give a better idea of the
lost original than the Palatine text, for both of them are singu-
larly dull and unimaginative by comparison with the Palatine
play and it is difficult to conceive of any writer who had that
text to work upon leaving out its more original and vivid
scenes.

Of the two manuscripts of the Autun version, the one copied
by Biard contains many narrative lines so interwoven with the
text that they could hardly have been suppressed at a performance. They seem to have been added to a text originally dramatic

---

[1] On the iconography of the Passion see Cohen, *Théâtre*, i, plates; Mâle, *Fin*,
chap. ii; and G. Frank in *PMLA*, xlvi (1931), 333 ff.

to adapt it for reading or recitation. Also added by the Biard copy are a number of lyrical laments and a reworking of lines found in the related texts. Unfortunately, the results of all these efforts mount up to a relatively insipid work.

The same must be said of the much shorter Autun version called the *Passion de Roman*. This version greatly abridges the material found in the related texts and includes none of the narrative lines of the Biard copy. But it contains scenes and persons not in the others, notably the Veronica incident and characters named Lot and Bot, as well as an unnamed hand-maiden of Pilate's wife and an unnamed companion of Longinus. It ends abruptly just before the Deposition and appears to be incomplete.

The versification of both these texts is pedestrian and frequently faulty. Some of the imperfections may be attributed to the two execrable scribes, Biard and Roman, responsible for our fifteenth-century manuscripts and to the linguistic habits of that period. But not all. It is obvious that we have to do here with poor craftsmen, with the conditions underlying popular representations, and with simple, unambitious redactors.

Consideration of our most primitive Passion plays leads to the conclusion that the first writer faced with the problem of staging the last days of Christ in the French language builded upon liturgical precedents, studied his Bible, his Gospel harmonies, and his patristic commentaries, but also found at hand, in the vernacular, narrative material that was easily dramatized and lyrical poems ready to serve as embellishments. From these the first Passion play was fashioned. However, not all communities could provide talented playwrights, even though many desired to have as their own a performance of our Lord's Passion. Accordingly, less exigent groups contented themselves with local writers, often men of little education, who adapted the work of others. These men merely cut and patched and added to suit the conditions obtaining around them—the equipment and number of actors available, the length of time allotted to performances, the predilections of the audience, &c.—and they could always count upon oral presentation to cover up lapses in style and poverty of invention. Dull, unpretentious plays might result. On the other hand primitive material in the hands of the better dramatists—a simple man like the author of the Palatine version or a great poet and musician like his most famous 'descendant', Arnoul Greban—readily became the basis of both moving and beautiful productions.

To the same family of plays as those just considered belong not only the *Passion* of Greban, but the *Passion de Semur* and various other plays of the fifteenth and sixteenth centuries. These made use of earlier members of the family, pruning, embellishing, transposing, and substituting. In all of them faint echoes of the old narrative *Passion des Jongleurs* persist. It is obvious therefore that this primitive poem and the early plays which built upon it furnished many a community with the basic materials from which subsequent Passion plays could be constructed.[1]

LE JOUR DU JUGEMENT

Another play of the fourteenth century, *Le Jour du Jugement*,[2] in some ways resembles the *Palatine Passion*. Here again we find councils of devils in hell, summoning angels who sing, a blind man reminiscent of Longinus, Jews named Mosse and Haquin, boasting knights, a list of the damned, and a vocabulary which often recalls that of both the *Palatine Passion* and its source, the *Passion des Jongleurs*. However, despite the fact that the story of Antichrist and the Last Judgement offered many more possibilities for inventiveness than the biblical account of the Passion, the author of *Le Jour du Jugement* was not quite equal to his opportunities. Some of them, to be sure, he seized, but he lacked the verve of the Palatine playwright—his multifarious characters are little differentiated and exhibit neither realism nor humour—and he failed to vary the monotony of his octosyllabic couplets except in a single speech and by an unrestrained use of leonine rhymes.

Yet the play as a whole is exciting to read and must have been impressive to see. The author, a truly religious and learned man, seems to have been acquainted with the works of many

[1] Cf. Chap. XVII below, *Passion du Palatinus* (*CFMA* edition), p. vii, and *Passion d'Autun*, pp. 22–23.
[2] Edited by Émile Roy, Paris, 1902.

Latin authors, to have known the dramatic traditions of his day (among others, the use of mnemonic rhymes), and to have exhibited such talents as he possessed in the selection and arrangement of his diverse materials for representation. One has only to compare his play with the twelfth-century liturgical *Ludus de Antichristo* from Tegernsee—and both of these with their most important ultimate source, the so-called *Libellus de Antichristo* written by Adso about the middle of the tenth century—to discover how much the French dramatist has skilfully added to make a traditional legend stage-worthy.[1]

After an introductory sermon by Le Prescheur we find Satan and his devils preparing to send one of them, disguised as an elegant youth, to seduce a woman of the tribe of Dan in Babylon. This devil, Angignars, speedily accomplishes his purpose and Antichrist is born of the union. The devils now begin instructing Antichrist in all their arts, and presently he is able to make the blind see, to cure the leprous, revive the dead, and heap riches upon the poor. He readily wins over the Jews and grows so powerful that even kings and cardinals pay him homage. Only the Pope himself and Enoch and Elijah who have been sent by God to wage war against the enemy are able to resist the magic of Antichrist.

Since the time of the coming of Antichrist was fixed by tradition at three and a half years before the Last Judgement, our play is able to end with the triumph of good over evil. Antichrist is overthrown, Enoch and Elijah who have been killed by his orders are resurrected, and the damned, as in so many poems concerned with the Harrowing of Hell or the Dance of Death, pass in review before us.[2] Here they include an abbess and bishop who have sinned together, a king, bailiff, provost, lawyer, adulterous queen, erring prioress, a usurer, his wife, his servant, and even his small child. Although eight pages of the manuscript are missing, it is obvious that the God of our author was especially condemnatory of all who lived on the fruits of usury and was especially concerned with those who were kind or unkind to the poor (cf. lines 2030, 2343,

---

[1] For the *Ludus* and Adso's version see Young, *Drama*, ii. 369 and 496. Young also discusses the origins of the legend.

[2] Cf. *Jour du Jugement*, 1938 ff., with *Palatine Passion*, 1314 ff.

2360, &c.). In the final reckoning angels pour out vials of
wrath, apostles and saints aid in the task of separating saved
from damned, and eventually the just are duly rewarded and
the wicked driven to hell by menacing devils. The play ends
with a few unique lines of seven syllables spoken by St. Paul,
who says that the damned have been taken to hell for eternal
torment

> Et nous joie avrons.
> *Te Deum* or chantons
> A hautes allenées.

The manuscript of this piece comes from Besançon[1] and has
been dated by diverse scholars as of the fourteenth or beginning
of the fifteenth century.[2] In any case there is no reason to
doubt that the text itself is of the fourteenth century. The hypothesis of Émile Roy, who connected the play with *le grand
schisme* and the year 1398 when the emperor and the kings of
France and England opposed the Avignon pope, Benedict XIII,
was so effectively disproved by Noël Valois that Roy himself
admitted his error.[3] Valois in turn suggested that the play might
vaguely reflect the conflict between Louis the Bavarian and the
much respected French pope, John XXII, but he did not press
the point and wisely concluded that *Le Jour du Jugement* 'n'est
point un drame politique'. He plausibly dated the text from the
first part of the reign of Philip VI, perhaps *c.* 1330.

The number of characters listed by the manuscript as taking
part—more than ninety-four in all—indicates how ambitious
a spectacle this must have been. The theatrical effect of the
movements, costumes, and contrasts of every sort could hardly
fail to be imposing. Included in the *dramatis personae* are Antichrist, his mother and her servant, large numbers of colourfully
named devils, Jews and kings, besides the heavenly hosts: God,
the Blessed Virgin, many saints, and various members of the

---

[1] Bibliothèque de la Ville, MS. 579.

[2] Cf. *Rom.* xxxii (1903), 636, where the manuscript is dated from the fifteenth
century, though it is conceded that the play may be older, with Noël Valois's
statements in *JS* (1903), pp. 677–86. Both scholars support their differing opinions
by referring to the script, but Valois believes that the costumes of the miniatures
are surely of the fourteenth century.

[3] Cf. Valois, op. cit., with whom Creizenach, *Geschichte*, i. 136, agrees, and
Émile Roy's handsome retraction in his *Mystère*, p. 67*.

celestial hierarchy. There are also a prophet and a patriarch, a pope, two cardinals, several knights, groups of poor and sick, and the diverse persons mentioned above as doomed to eternal hell-fire. Suspense and surprise must have accompanied the unexpected shifts of scenes and characters, with the spectator's interest constantly mounting as one exciting episode succeeded another. Moreover, the playwright adroitly speeded the movement of his drama (as, for example, in the performance of Antichrist's miracles) by choosing only the more significant incidents and arranging them climactically. He was also capable on occasion of translating character into action, so that the haughtiness of Antichrist becomes apparent and inevitably contrasts with the humility of Christ in such similar circumstances as the giving of alms to the poor, the curing of the sick, and the raising of the dead.

For the most part, however, he depends for success not on characterization—of which there is all too little—but on the sublimity of his themes, on action, plot, and antitheses of various kinds. Within the brief span of 2,438 lines (and the original contained only some 300 lines more than those that remain) we meet an endless variety of scenes and persons, we move back and forth between heaven, hell, and earth, and at the end we witness the awe-inspiring drama of the Last Judgement, the terrible plight of the damned, the jubilation of the saved. Moreover, the songs bear neumes and the angels sing to such lovely melodies as the *Aeterne Rex Altissime*, *Veni Creator Spiritus*, and *Urbs Jerusalem Beata*. It is certain that music must have contributed vastly to the solemnity and emotional impact of the piece.

Plays about Antichrist and the Last Judgement seem not to have been as common in France as in Germany. No other complete text has survived from France and there are records of only two late performances of plays concerned with the Last Judgement, one at Orléans in 1550, the other at Modane in 1580, neither of which can be connected with our text.[1] *Le Jour*

---

[1] Cf. Petit de Julleville, *Mystères*, ii. 157, 169, 460–1. The fragment of a fifteenth-century text and the sixteenth-century manuscript, both described on pp. 460–1, include various allegorical figures that suggest a morality play. The sixteenth-century play seems to be the one performed at Modane.

du Jugement therefore occupies a unique place in the history of the French stage. Moreover, it is unusual not only in its theme but in the way the dramatist has conceived of his task. The length and technical treatment of the play are clearly of its epoch, the fourteenth century. In range of characters and emphasis on plot, the piece recalls the miracle plays of the time. Its eschatological subject relates it to the earlier biblical mysteries. However, its ambitious design, the number of roles involved, and the scale of the performance demanded all set it apart from other plays of the period. In these respects the playwright seems an innovator, a precursor of the authors of the grandiose and more pretentious spectacles of the following centuries.

XIV

Collections: Plays from the Bibliothèque Ste Geneviève; The Chantilly Collection

WHEN viewed as a whole the plays of MS. 1131 of the Bibliothèque Ste Geneviève seem heavy and didactic.[1] Indeed some of the longer speeches expounding doctrines of the faith and answering objections of doubters appear to have strayed into the theatre from the pulpit. Yet, mitigating the ubiquitous moralistic tone, there are realistic or comic interludes obviously designed to entertain the attending public of *lais* and *clercs*.[2] Low characters who administer cruel tortures, who make indecent jokes and satirize their betters in argotic locutions, mingle with saints who enter upon lengthy scholastic and theological discussions of such questions as the virtues of baptism, the sins of laggard or false confessions, and the nature of the Trinity. From a literary point of view, these plays must be judged individually, but taken together they exhale a strange mixture of religious fervour, dialectic, dogmatism, coarse humour, and savage brutality.

The plays fall roughly into two groups, one on biblical subjects, the other concerned with the lives, martyrdoms, and miracles of various saints. But the order and arrangement in the manuscript, obscured in our only complete edition, indicate that this classification was not followed by the scribe. At the beginning three biblical plays—the *Nativité*, *Geu des Trois Roys*, and *Resurrection*—precede a *Vie Monseigneur S. Fiacre* which is itself interrupted about one-third from the end by a farce. After the *Vie* and a partially blank page, the manuscript continues

---

[1] First published as a whole by Jubinal in 1837 with the awkward title *Mystères inédits du quinzième siècle*. Three of the series have received modern editions: *Les Miracles de Sainte Geneviève* by Sennewaldt, the *Nativité* and *Geu des Trois Roys* by Whittredge, in both of which useful bibliographies and studies of details will be found.

[2] See Jubinal, i. 99. *Gens d'église* are also mentioned in one of the *Miracles de Ste Geneviève* (Sennewaldt, p. 126).

with an independent Passion play. This is succeeded by some non-dramatic material (including prayers and a prose life of St. Genevieve) after which come the closely related *Martyrdom of St. Stephen, Conversion of St. Paul, Conversion of St. Denis, Martyrdom of St. Peter and St. Paul*, and the *Martyrdom of St. Denis*. Two blank pages follow and then appear fourteen short scenes concerned with the life and miracles of St. Genevieve.

A summary of the varied contents of these plays may be useful. The first play, the *Nativité*, after the customary sermon, begins with the Creation of Man and the Fall, followed at once by a conversation between the Prophets referring to the coming of the Redeemer, an arrangement which recalls that of the *Mystère d'Adam*. Seth then goes to Paradise for the oil of mercy, the Prophets again converse, and an angel persuades the High Priest to sanction the betrothal of Joseph and Mary. Conventional scenes follow chronicling the Annunciation, Birth, Coming of the Shepherds, &c., and the play ends, like the others in the manuscript, with the *Te Deum laudamus*. But this *Nativité* is much more inclusive than any surviving predecessor and, like the *Mystère d'Adam* and various English cycles, it connects the Old and New Testaments by way of the prophets. Many of its unusual details derive from a narrative source sometimes known as the *Histoire de Marie et de Jésus*,[1] and some of its apocryphal scenes, such as the Marriage of the Virgin, the Fall of the Idols, the Doubting of Joseph, and the Miraculous Coals that become roses in Joseph's tunic, endow it with variety and excitement. It is also brightened by comedy. Devils and remarkably realistic shepherds enliven the action at times, and many short scenes that take place in various parts of the stage almost simultaneously, together with the constant coming and going of messengers, give the play colour and a sense of movement.

The *Trois Roys*, a shorter, less elaborate, and more sober piece than the preceding *Nativité*, uses the same narrative source and in other ways indicates that it is probably the work of the same author. Also, provision is made for joining the two plays. The principal scenes of the *Trois Roys* include the Adoration of the

---

[1] The Provençal *Esposalizi de Nostra Dona* and the Spanish *Misterio del Rey Herodes* use this same source. Cf. Whittredge ed., pp. 57 ff., and on the Provençal play see Kravtchenko-Dobelmann in *Rom.* lxviii (1944-5), 273.

Magi, the Slaughter of the Innocents, and the Flight into Egypt. But to these are added certain unusual details and especially the apocryphal legend of the Sower. The Sower in our play meets Joseph on his journey to Egypt and promises not to reveal the fact. When queried almost at once by Herod's soldiers, he truthfully answers that he has seen no one since sowing his wheat: actually his wheat has miraculously sprouted and become ready for harvest after Joseph's departure. The various scenes in this play, like those in the *Nativité*, are cut up, presented in small sections, and so interlaced that the spectators' interest moves back and forth with increasing suspense: in successive short scenes the Sower prepares his ground; Herod rages and sends out his guards to find the Three Kings; the Sower plants his seed; the guards vainly seek the Kings and return to tell Herod of their escape; Herod orders the slaughter of the Innocents; God sends Raphael to warn Joseph; the devils lament in hell, foreseeing its eventual harrowing; Joseph and Mary depart for Egypt; the Mothers of the Innocents proudly rejoice in their children; Joseph addresses the Sower; the slaughter occurs and after the slaying the Sower tells the soldiers he has seen no one since planting his wheat. All this takes place in less than 400 lines. The author of these two plays reveals a sure sense of character, individualizing his Joseph, Sower, soldiers, and mothers, but he is especially happy in exploiting the simultaneous stage for the dramatization of action.

The *Resurrection* which follows has a number of lines in common with the *Nativité* and *Trois Roys*. The prologues and epilogues of these three plays definitely indicate direct verbal borrowing. More important, similar doctrines and similar scenes, some of them not found elsewhere, occur in the *Resurrection* and *Nativité*.[1] Either a single author wrote all three plays, borrowing from himself at times, or revisers have transplanted words, scenes, and even doctrines from one play to another. The plays are in no sense a cycle, however, and it is obvious that the *Resurrection* was designed for independent performance. After a sermon, it begins, like the *Nativité*, with the Creation

---

[1] See Whittredge, pp. 18 ff. and 199. Whittredge thinks the *Trois Roys* borrowed something from the *Resurrection* and that the *Resurrection* at times borrowed from the *Nativité*.

and Fall. Then there is a sudden transition to the Setting of
the Watch and the boasting of the soldiers sent to guard the
tomb. Next we find the souls in hell praying for release with
devils in attendance bewailing Lucifer's fall and the prospective
Redemption. Soon Christ appears and liberates the imprisoned
souls to the discomfiture of the devils. Now we hear the Virgin,
the three Marys, and St. John lamenting at great length, and
eventually the three Marys proceed to buy ointment from a
spice-merchant, go to the tomb, discover it is empty, and are
told of the Resurrection by Gabriel. The terrified guards also
discover the empty tomb and, suspecting each other of planning
to inform the Jews, they fall to blows.[1] The play concludes with
the Appearances to Mary Magdalen and the other Marys. A
certain soberness in this play no doubt derives from its themes
and traditions, and except for lighter touches here and there—
in the *diableries* and guard scenes—the author has for the most
part restricted himself to well-established usage. The apocryphal
Gospel of Nicodemus, the *Victimae Paschali* sequence, even the
guard scenes and other matter familiar to the liturgical plays
have been embellished without much essential change. But the
general arrangement of the play, its transition from the Fall to
the Setting of the Watch, is unusual and so is the emphasis on
the doctrine of the Redemption and on the belief that man was
created to replace Lucifer and the fallen angels in heaven.[2]
Since the *Nativité* and *Resurrection* similarly stress this theme,
the same author or redactor may well have introduced it into
all three plays.

The fourth play in the manuscript is *La Vie de S. Fiacre*, a
play unlike any of the others in the collection. It was clearly
designed for independent performance, possibly at Meaux,
where most of the action occurs and with which its chief characters, SS. Fiacre and Faro, were associated.[3] It is unusual both
in its versification, for it regularly uses the four-syllabled cue-
line, and in its contents, which include not only the life of the

[1] On this scene see J. Wright, *Study*, p. 75.

[2] See J. Wright, *Study*, pp. 110, 142, and Whittredge, p. 19. Wright finds in the
arguments of the fallen angels and a few other details the probable influence of
the *Roman de l'Estoire dou Graal*.

[3] Note too the importance of SS. Sentin and Antonin of Meaux in the *Martyrdom of St. Denis* and of St. Céline of Meaux in the *Miracles de Ste Geneviève*.

saint and the miracles performed at his tomb after his death but also an interposed farce. The farce, though totally unrelated to the *Vie* in matter, is technically part of it because the first and last lines of the farce rhyme with parent-lines in the play. St. Fiacre's life closely parallels in many ways that of the better-known St. Alexius. It too personifies the virtues of chastity and devotion to the work of God. Our play opens with young Fiacre refusing marriage to an estimable damsel chosen for him by his parents and fleeing from home to escape the girl's own importunities. He takes ship for France, makes his way towards 'Meaulx en Brie', meets St. Faro (an early bishop of Meaux), and establishes himself as a hermit near that town. The maid he spurned follows him overseas but he successfully evades recognition by prayer and, it must be confessed, a bit of sophistry. At various times God and His Mother with the aid of the angels Gabriel and Michael protect the chaste saint from temptations and misfortunes, and in the end they see that he receives the last rites of the Church from Bishop Faro. The angels bear his soul to glory and St. Faro buries him.

Here the farce is inserted, a rather feeble thing with little action and less wit.[1] The *dramatis personae* are a peasant, a sergeant, their wives, a brigand, and a tavern-keeper. The brigand asks the way to St. Omer of a fearful peasant who seems wilfully to misunderstand him. Angered, the brigand robs him of a fat capon, whereupon a sergeant appears, and during the ensuing fracas the brigand breaks the sergeant's arm. In a new scene the peasant's wife tells the sergeant's lady of her husband's misfortune and invites her to have a drink. The latter accepts, since, because of his broken arm, she need fear no beating from her cruel and faithless mate. The peasant's wife asserts that she is not a bit afraid of her man, and so they both have a good carouse at the tavern. However, the two husbands come in and are furious at the potations of their spouses, both of whom now receive blows. The sergeant's wife blames the peasant's wife for leading her astray and they threaten to maul each other. Peace is soon restored, however, and the farce ends.

The *Vie de S. Fiacre* now continues with Bishop Faro, at God's direction, translating the body of St. Fiacre to a new

[1] Cf. Harvey, p. 113, however, who thinks well of it.

tomb where the sick may visit it. At once a leper appears, sounding his bell. He is cured and then, in turn, blind and lame men, a 'bourgoise de Langny' (Lagny is about eleven miles from Meaux and about seventeen and a half miles from Paris), a *chevalresse* and another woman visit the tomb and all are healed. Only the last woman's husband and a thieving canon declare their lack of faith in the saint, and both of them are at once stricken with illness. They repent just in time to be forgiven and the play ends with the usual *Te Deum laudamus*.

The next play in the manuscript, the long, independent *Passion*, includes scenes from the Resurrection which are in no way related to those in the Resurrection play of the same manuscript and which, indeed, often follow a divergent tradition. The two plays obviously were designed for different exigencies of occasion and circumstance. There is reason to believe that, in its present form, the *Passion* is a revision of a much earlier text. Its popularity is attested by fragments from it in another copy and by Greban's use of it later.[1] In length it stands midway between the Palatine and Semur *Passions*. It adds to the material incorporated in the earlier piece and also expands some scenes found there. Lazarus gives an account of hell and its punishments, describing the nine torments of the damned. Pilate's son and daughter join their mother in pleading that Jesus be spared. The short scene in which the smith's wife forges nails for the Crucifixion gives us her name—Maragonde—and shows her using one of the executioners to light her fire and blow upon the forge. The legend of Veronica and the debate between Church and Synagogue, both so popular in medieval art and literature, here appear, and there are revealing inventories of the wares of cloth and spice merchants.[2] On the whole, however, this *Passion* is a rather dull affair. In the Harrowing of Hell it closely follows its ultimate source—the second part of the apocryphal *Gospel of Nicodemus* known as the *Descensus Christi ad Inferos*[3]—but the scenes between Satan and Beelzebub

---

[1] See J. Wright, *Study*, p. 144 and *passim*; Whittredge, pp. 24–25.

[2] The likeness of the spice-merchant's wares here (Jubinal, ii. 299) to those in the *Passion de Semur* misled Roy, *Mystère*, 69* and 87*. Cf. Whittredge, p. 25, n. 3. Similar lists occur in a poem by Robert de Blois, ed. *Rom.* xxxv (1906), 370, in Chrétien's *Perceval*, ed. Hilka, lines 3325 ff., and elsewhere.

[3] See Wright, *Study*, p. 87.

are shorter and much less lively than the *diableries* of the Palatine text. Some attempt at characterization invests the guarding of the sepulchre with realism; the three knights receive names—Pinceguerre, Baudis, and Mossé—and their fright is indicated by references to trembling limbs and to hair that stands on end. The play concludes with the appearance to Mary Magdalen and with a short, somewhat unexpected sermon by Centurion who invites those present to sing the *Te Deum laudamus* and then the *Benedicamus*.

Following the *Passion* are the six saint plays which could be joined or separated in various combinations at the desire of the director. After an initial sermon that might cover the whole series or could be curtailed to refer to only a part, comes the very short *Martyrdom of St. Stephen*. The saint preaches, testifies, is challenged by Annas and Caiaphas, and then suffers protracted indignities and tortures at the hands of Jews who include the as yet unconverted Saul. A concluding *Te Deum* is provided.

In the next play, the *Conversion of St. Paul*, which could be connected with the preceding by omitting the *Te Deum*, Saul receives baptism, regains his sight, and becomes Paul. He preaches to the Jews in Damascus, meets other apostles, and is congratulated on his change of faith. The play, if joined to the St. Stephen play, could end with his kissing of the disciples and the inevitable *Te Deum* or it could continue and be attached either to the following *Conversion of St. Denis* or to the *Martyrdom of St. Peter and St. Paul*.

The *Conversion of St. Denis* contains incidents readily accessible in the *Legenda Aurea*. Our plays about this saint show the frequent medieval confusion between Denis the Areopagite, Denis the Apostle of Paris, and a Denis who wrote theological works. In our version Denis, *le tiers philosophe*, queries St. Paul about his God and shows him the altars to his own gods, Jove, Mercury, Priapus, Mars, Venus, and Hercules, admitting, however, that one altar is for an unknown god of whom he learned in Egypt. Paul says the unknown is his God, the one and only true God; there is a long scholastic argument between them (St. Paul addresses St. Denis as *maistre*) and St. Denis, practically convinced, goes home to think over the discussion. Then St. Paul proceeds to perform a miracle, healing a man blind from birth, and at this point not only St. Denis but his wife, Demaris, his two children, the blind man, and an unnamed philosopher are ready for baptism. Afterwards St. Paul sends St. Denis out to preach the faith, Demaris becomes a *béguine*, and the scene ends with St. Denis sitting down to write a book. This scene does not conclude the play, however, for there is no *Te Deum*, and, on the other hand, there are directions for continuing either with the following *Martyrdom of St. Peter and St. Paul* or with the next following *Martyrdom of St. Denis*.[1]

All the legends introduced into the *Martyrdom of St. Peter and St. Paul* can be found in the *Legenda Aurea*, but the lively development of certain scenes betrays a practised dramatist. The play opens with St. Peter preaching to the doubting Romans. They argue with him, and Simon the Magician challenges his powers, proposing that each of them try to revive a dead man. Although Simon makes the corpse shake its head, Peter maintains that it has not actually moved. But the Romans taunt Peter, promising him death unless he succeeds where Simon has failed. When Peter asks: 'What will you give me if I make the dead move? You promise me only grief if I do not', the citizens reply that, if he performs the miracle, they will believe his doctrine and punish Simon. St. Peter then prays and the corpse revives. Now Simon, to show his prowess, calls upon devils to fly him to heaven and, as he mounts on their shoulders, the Romans marvel. Peter, however, prays to Jesus to defeat the devils and, as he makes the sign of the Cross, they fall prostrate. He then cries, 'Now fly, Simon, fly', but Simon, confessing that Jesus is too strong for him, dies and shrieking devils carry him off to hell. St. Peter continues preaching, explaining the virtues of baptism and baptizing St. Clement among many others. Next we are at Nero's court where death for the saints is being prepared. Peter's friends urge him to flee and, though hesitating at first, he consents. But on his way he meets Jesus and asks the famous *Quo vadis?*, receives the answer: 'I go to Rome to die again on the Cross', and, understanding the significance of the words, returns to Rome. Both St. Peter and St. Paul are now tortured by brutes who taunt them the while with coarse witticisms. Nero condemns Paul, the noble Roman,

[1] See Jubinal, i. 100: 'Le Geu Saint Denis continue ainssy.'

to be beheaded and Peter, the poor fisherman, to die on the cross. St. Peter says he is unworthy to die in the posture of Jesus and begs to be crucified upside down. After the death of the saints the citizens rise up against Nero who eventually kills himself and is borne off to torment by devils. Domitian succeeds him as emperor and St. Clement is made the new pope. An ending, complete with the *Te Deum*, is provided, but provision is also made for joining this play to the next.

Near the beginning of the following long *Martyrdom of St. Denis* we find St. Denis dispatching various disciples to France —incidentally, two of them, Sentin and Antonin, are sent to Meaux[1]—and himself departing for Paris with two companions. Once there he proceeds to preach, argue, and use the Socratic methods of the schools to convince. He is accused by the citizens of indulging in bad logic and sophistries, but soon his explanations of the unique yet triune nature of God convert many doubters. Now in a series of bloody scenes, interspersed with gentle sermons on the true faith by St. Denis, the Parisians and the Roman emperor attempt to kill him. He survives repeated and terribly cruel tortures but is finally decapitated and, with his head in his hands, is led off to glory by singing angels. Some of his converts, among them Lisbie and Lisbie's wife, Larcie, receive similar inhuman treatment and are at last put to death. The sergeants responsible for the orgies of torture and killing, appalled at all they have heard and seen (including the headless saint making off to the accompaniment of song), decide to accept the invitation of a good woman to eat and drink in her home before they throw the bodies of 'the fools decapitated on Montmartre' into the Seine. They drink themselves into a stupor, giving Catulle, their kind hostess, a chance to have the bodies properly buried. Quite unexpectedly, the two disciples sent to Meaux—Sentin and Antonin—now appear seeking lodging at an inn. St. Denis had asked them to record his martyrdom and they are on their way to give their account to the pope. Antonin, who is very ill, soon dies and the wretched inn-keeper steals the money entrusted to him for Antonin's care and throws the body into a repulsively filthy ditch. When Sentin learns of this ignominy from the angel Michael, who has

[1] Cf. Jubinal, i. 104, 364.

been sent to him by Jesus, he resuscitates his companion, and reads the inn-keeper a lesson on his duties as a host and on the sins of avarice and ingratitude. Provision for an ending with the usual *Te Deum* is made, if desired, and it is only later that we discover this play could perhaps on occasion be joined to one or two of the *Miracles de Ste Geneviève*.[1]

The contents of the fourteen short scenes, each concerned with an episode in the life of St. Genevieve, are summarized in Sennewaldt's edition, pp. 16–20. For the most part they derive from a narrative account, but the playwright, in adapting them for the stage, has made each scene usable independently. At two points (after lines 2486 and 2590) we find indications for definite endings, if desired,[2] so that it is evident that the individual short miracles could be performed as a whole or with omissions. The episodes include the saint's birth, childhood, the healing of her mother who had suddenly become blind because she had cuffed her daughter, the saint's arrival in Paris, cure of the maid accompanying her friend St. Céline of Meaux, protection of Paris from the onslaught of the Huns, serious illness and miraculous recovery, encounter with an unchaste and unregenerate nun whom she reclaims, resuscitation of a child drowned by devils, intercession for an unjustly treated boy, building of the church where St. Denis and his companions lay buried, and finally her healing of the leprous, lame, dropsical, blind, &c. Some of these scenes are more dramatic and diverting than others, but throughout there is an obvious effort to lighten the long didactic passages by humorous or realistic episodes and to diversify the action by the introduction of numerous characters, brief incidents, and spirited dialogue.

That the entire collection was designed to serve as a repertory may be deduced from the many directions offered for the joining or omitting of plays and scenes at the discretion of the producer.[3] Was it the repertory of the Confrérie de la Passion?

[1] The miracles concerning the tomb of St. Denis. Cf. Jubinal, i. 167 with ed. Sennewaldt, line 2591.

[2] Cf. lines 2489–90: 'Chantons, tant becus que camus, / Bien hault: Te Deum laudamus' with the similar conclusions of the *Nativité* and *Trois Roys*: 'Sy chantons, (tant) becus que (et) camus, / Chascun: Te Deum laudamus.' The rhyme for *laudamus* in all the other plays is different.

[3] Cf. Sennewaldt, p. 3, and Whittredge, pp. 16–17.

This seems likely. The fact that the manuscript belonged, as far back as it can be traced, to the Abbaye Ste Geneviève and the nature of its contents—biblical plays, a farce and saint plays, with emphasis on such saints as Genevieve and Denis—together with the many local allusions to Paris and the absence of dialectal traits in the text, have always suggested that our collection originated in or near the capital.[1] To be sure, the early history of the Confrérie is by no means clear. We know that by 1380 the performance of the *Passion* was an annual event in Paris, that on 3 June 1398 the Provost of Paris forbade performances without express authorization of farces, lives of saints, *ne autrement*, in Paris, Saint-Maur, and other nearby towns, and that this prohibition was flouted by a performance of the *Passion* in Saint-Maur. We also know that the famous letters patent of 1402 of Charles VI gave the Confrérie the right to 'jouer quelque Misterre que ce soit, soit de la dicte Passion, et Résurreccion, ou autre quelconque tant de saincts comme de sainctes'.[2] But the exact relation of the Confrérie to the earlier groups of 1380 and 1398 is unknown. The Confrérie is represented in the document of 1402 as having been founded in the church of the Trinité in Paris, as having played before the king in the past, and as petitioning him at this time merely for official permission to perform in public for their own profit as well as in the royal presence. Had they given public as well as court performances at an earlier date? Their full name, the Confrérie de la Passion et Résurrection, may relate them to the group which even before 1380 had annually appeared in a Passion

---

[1] Långfors, *Rom.* lxv (1939), 263, mentions Picardisms of the copyist, but does not deny a Parisian origin. The deliberate use of dialect for a realistic effect may also point in the same direction (see Jubinal, i. 157 ff.). Another argument for Parisian origin is the fact that Greban's *Passion*, written at the instigation of the Parisians, knows the Ste Geneviève *Passion* and borrows freely from it (see J. Wright, *Study*, p. 144). For further discussion of the question of Parisian origin see Roy, *Études*, pp. cxc ff. and cciv ff., Whittredge, pp. 26 ff., and Sennewaldt, p. 5. On the other hand, one of Roy's suggestions for connecting our collection with the capital, i.e. that the *Passion de Semur* has used it and that a provincial text would be likely to borrow from the capital, rests on insufficient evidence. Cf. p. 141, n. 2, above.

[2] See Antoine Thomas, *Rom.* xxi (1892), 606 ff., and Petit de Julleville, *Mystères*, i. 414 ff. See the latter also for the later history of the Confrérie de la Passion. On a performance of the *Passion* at Chelles, near Paris, in 1395, see Cohen, *Rom.* xxxviii (1909), 587 ff.

play. Their repertory and the fact that they were granted permission to play in the suburbs as well as in Paris suggests a possible connexion with the group mentioned at Saint-Maur in 1398. In any case, from 1402 on they were allowed to perform mystery and miracle plays whenever and wherever they wished without obtaining further permission.[1] Our collection with its audience addressed as *lais* and *clercs* and its long didactic speeches interspersed with scenes of crude humour and violent realism seems to have been destined for a general rather than a royal audience, but the repertory conforms so closely to that ascribed to the Confrérie and the connexion of these texts with Paris is so close that we are probably safe in assuming that we have here the plays used in their public performances by the first theatrical company established on a permanent basis in the capital.

The plays in their present form seem to date from different times and appear in some cases to be by different authors. It is generally agreed that those of biblical derivation are earlier than the saint plays and it is probable that some of the former go back to the mid-fourteenth century whereas the most recent of the latter date from *c.* 1420. Those plays that could be merged may well have been written by a single author, but this is not wholly certain since variations in tone and versification can be detected even in them. For example, the *Nativité* has a number of comic incidents and in general is far less serious than the *Trois Roys* to which it could be joined; it also employs a short four-syllabled cue-line and a long line divided between two speakers, both of which are absent from the *Trois Roys*. Yet these two plays make use of the same apocryphal narrative source and in other respects seem closely related. Interpolations

---

[1] The letters patent of 1402 expressly gave the Confrérie permission to play in 'Paris, comme en la Prévosté, Viconté ou Banlieue d'icelle' or wherever they pleased, and to proceed unmolested in their costumes (Petit de Julleville, *Mystères*, i. 417). The large number of allusions in our text to Meaux, the capital of Brie in the Middle Ages, with which SS. Fiacre, Faro, Sentin, Antonin, and Céline were connected and whose cathedral is dedicated to St. Stephen, suggest the possibility that our company may have travelled as far as that town. Sennewaldt's objection to the Confrérie as sponsors of our plays (p. 7) because she sees a reproach to the king in one of the *Miracles de Ste Geneviève* and concludes that Charles VI would therefore not have granted permission for its performance is of little weight: the scene is laid in the time of St. Genevieve and the terms are general. See also Whittredge, p. 30, and in *RR*, xxx (1939), 195–6.

and redactions may account for their dissimilarities. In any case they differ widely from the *Passion* which, in its present form, gives evidence of being the revision of a much earlier play, and it in turn is quite independent of the preceding *Resurrection*. Similarly, *La Vie de S. Fiacre*, with its interposed farce, in no way resembles the other saint plays in the collection. It would appear that our present manuscript, like the register of the English plays from York, represents a transcript of the repertory at a given moment in its history but that the component parts were written and revised at different times to serve varying purposes.[1]

The authors of these plays content themselves for the most part with octosyllabic couplets; infrequently they use alternating rhymes or a simple stanzaic structure.[2] In two instances —part of the *Nativité* and all the *Vie de S. Fiacre*—the short four-syllabled cue-line appears. All the plays make use of the mnemonic device whereby the last line of one speech rhymes with the first line of its successor. The division of a single line between two speakers occurs only once in the biblical plays, in the shepherd scene of the *Nativité* which is probably interpolated, but it appears in several of the lighter passages of the *Miracles de Ste Geneviève* where it produces a vivacious effect and speeds the action.

Directions for the staging of these plays are unusually detailed and revealing. An indoor stage seems to have been employed and few *mansions* were needed, but it is obvious that these had floors raised above the level of the *champ* or playing-field. Directions for characters to pass beneath paradise, to mount *un pou hault*, to descend from paradise or from other stations *d'en hault*, or to occupy the *plus hault ciège* indicate a relatively high

[1] For example in the Ste Geneviève collection we seem to have a 'modernized' *Nativité* which could still be used in connexion with an older *Trois Roys*, and the man responsible for the (probably interpolated) shepherd scenes in the former seems to have had a hand in certain of the *Miracles de Ste Geneviève*. Variant versions of our plays have also been discovered in other manuscripts. See Andresen in *ZRP*, xxvi (1902), 76, O. Erler, and P. Pietresson de Saint-Aubin. On revisions in the English mystery plays see G. Frank in *MP*, xv (1918), 565 ff.

[2] For example, the long sermon introducing the saint plays and the short scene at the beginning of the *Miracles de Ste Geneviève* are written in octosyllabic, eight-lined stanzas with interlaced rhymes. On the versification in general see Whittredge, pp. 79 ff., and Sennewaldt, pp. 48 ff.

plane for some of the action. On the other hand, the *champ* in front of these stations was extensively used and actors are repeatedly directed to leave it or sit there when not needed.[1] Paradise was at the spectator's left, hell at the right. God, Notre Dame, and various saints had their stations in paradise and in one play we learn that Damascus was beside it. Devils are directed to carry victims *bellement sur leurs espaules*, to run off the field howling, to throw Nero into a 'chaudiere assise un pou haut enmy le champ'. The properties to be provided in connexion with the various tortures include whips, lashes, timber mares, a grill, a furnace, and wild beasts. The decapitated St. Denis was to take his head in his hands by some sort of *truc*. After St. Antonin had been thrown into a ditch, he was to pretend to smear his face with mud. When Raphael took the soul of St. Genevieve from her body, we learn that this soul was represented by *une ymagete*. Similarly devils snatched *une ymagete* from the child who died unbaptized and angels struggled violently with these devils for its recovery. At one point St. Denis and his companions are thrown into prison and the rubrics state: 'En la chartre soient vestemens pour prestre, pour dyacre et soudiacre, autel et calice et du pain.' These costumes and accessories are to serve for the later celebration of Mass by the prisoners. Although music is introduced less deliberately than in the *Miracles de Notre Dame*, the songs to be sung are regularly indicated, and apparently singing was so usual an accompaniment to the appearance of the angels that, when absent, the fact is expressly noted and they are told to go or come *sans chanter*. All the directions—and they are more frequent in the saint plays than in those of biblical origin—point to playwrights experienced in visualizing their productions. Even when directions are few, evidence exists of skill in the art of dramatic representation: often short scenes are enacted in quick succession in various parts of the stage, exciting or humorous scenes follow dull or serious ones, messengers coming

[1] Cf. 'Cy voisent hors du champs sans plus faire, puis reveignent quant Néron sera tué . . .' (Jubinal, i. 92); 'Cy se départent et voisent où ilz vourront' (p. 104); 'Lors se assiéent à terre' (p. 113). Other directions cited in this paragraph occur in Jubinal, i. 27, 28, 72, 94, 112, 117, 128, 130, 133, 138, 147, 161. For the staging of the *Nativité* and *Trois Roys* see Whittredge, pp. 63–78; for that of the *Miracles de Ste Geneviève*, see Sennewaldt, pp. 34–39.

or going simulate action, and apocryphal material is introduced for suspense where interest might lag.

The religious, moral, and didactic purposes of the plays need not be stressed. They emerge from almost every page. The whole history of Christ and the Redemption, the lives and acts of many of His disciples, pass in review before the spectator, vivid and real. The punishment of mortal and venial sins, the rewards of those who practise the tenets of the faith, lengthy explanations of various doctrines of the Church and frequent attempts to confute sceptics and atheists, all these are amply illustrated.

But, as has been indicated, realism and humour are deliberately introduced to leaven the teachings and sermons. The protracted beatings and tortures of the martyrs appealed to the same human emotions aroused today by the horrors of the cinema. In the *Martyrdom of St. Denis* the saint and his companions are in turn scourged, put on a rack, roasted on a grill, exposed to wild beasts, plunged in a fiery furnace, crucified, and beheaded. Their tormentors are directed to break their bones and make their bowels spring from their bellies. Apparently comic to the Middle Ages were the *farsses* inserted in one of the *Miracles de Ste Geneviève* 'afin que le jeu soit meins fade et plus plaisans'. The leprous, blind, lame, dropsical, and other afflicted persons here detail their physical symptoms and their complaints supposedly furnish the fun. Modern taste hardly finds these pathetic creatures amusing.[1] As for the farce in the *Vie de S. Fiacre* it is an early example of a type later destined for great popularity, an example exhibiting little finesse or subtlety, to be sure, though it does achieve its purpose of introducing levity into a serious play.

Usually both comedy and realism are to be found in the speeches of the commoners of these plays, the shepherds and swineherds, the sergeants and torturers, messengers and fools. Colloquialisms, proverbs, argot, puns, and inconsequential maunderings sometimes veil parody and satire from which even the lower clergy is not exempt.[2] A priest intersperses his devo-

[1] Among them appears a short and dull version of the scene between the blind man and his boy which is found elsewhere in the medieval theatre. See *Le Garçon et l'Aveugle*, Chap. XXI below.

[2] Cf. Långfors, *Rom.* lxv (1939), 262, and Lozinski, *Rom.* lxvi (1940–1), 538.

tions with irrelevancies and is scolded at length by another for his *janglerie*.[1] The language is sometimes crude and coarse. When SS. Peter and Paul sit on the ground, one of their torturers jeers: 'See how they crouch. They are hatching eggs', and after Paul is decapitated another remarks: 'Alons-ly querre un orinal; / Il pisse trop malement rouge.' Before the crucifixion of St. Denis, Menjumatin proposes: 'Or ly coupons doncques le v . . .'[2] Incidentally, the torturers bear such humorous names as Masquebignet, Hapelopin, Humebrouet, Menjumatin, Maubué, and the messengers are ironically called Trotemenu, Legier, Gratemauvez.

One of the *Miracles de Ste Geneviève*—that concerned with the building of the church of St. Denis 'a Lectree'—is almost wholly humorous, brightened in quick succession by conversations between two priests, two swineherds, and three thirsty workmen. It also contains one of the three drinking scenes in the repertory.[3] The wine, amusingly enough, is provided by the prayers of St. Genevieve, who wants to content the artisans building the church of St. Denis, but with paradoxically unforeseen results. A priest, a carpenter, and two masons cannot get their fill of this miraculously excellent beverage. The goblet goes round and round, the men become quarrelsome and so sleepy that, though they promise wonders for the next day, they finally quit work.[4]

Most scenes involving devils introduce an element of humour and in one of the *Miracles de Ste Geneviève* there is an exceptionally animated struggle between the forces of good and evil (lines 1709 ff.). The devils use every argument to keep for themselves the soul of a child who died unbaptized, insisting, among other things, that God in trying to take the soul from them does not keep His own laws. Presently the dispute becomes not only

[1] See *Miracles de Ste Geneviève*, lines 2066 ff. The scene bears two revealing rubrics, one indicating it might be omitted, but the other counselling that it be read 'car el est bien notable pour gens d'eglise'. See the rubrics after lines 2060 and 2063.

[2] Jubinal, i. 78, 86, 134.

[3] One is in the farce of the *Vie de S. Fiacre* and the other is that in the *Martyrdom of St. Denis* where the sergeants quarrel, eat and drink until they fall asleep and the Host (as well as his guest, St. Sentin) sometimes speaks a southern dialect.

[4] Six fools appear in this play, two of them singing a parody of the *Sanctus* of the Requiem Mass. See Solange Corbin, *Rom.* lxxiii (1952), 240.

philosophically but physically strenuous, as Gabriel curses Satan and a violent tug-of-war follows before the angels, repeatedly striking the devils, forcibly wrest *l'ymagete* (i.e. the child's soul) from the fiends. Elsewhere, too, the modern reader may be amused where the medieval spectator was supposed to find more edification than diversion. After a description of the torments of hell there is a comprehensive list of sinners due to burn there which includes not only the more usual thieves, murderers, pagans, Jews, false witnesses, usurers, &c., but also women who paint or use rouge (lines 988 ff.). One of St. Genevieve's more discerning miracles concerns a nun who visits her and pretends to be chaste. The saint is not deceived but says explicitly: 'In April on the third day, in the garden of Gautier de Chantelou, you suffered his shepherd to deflower you beneath a peach-tree' (lines 1209 ff.). The nun at first tries to excuse herself with various sophisms. 'I'm sorry but such was my fate, God knew I should sin, He must have made me to be damned', &c., all of which the saint spiritedly refutes. Of course in the end—and at great length—the nun becomes truly penitent.

This collection of plays occupies a unique place in the history of the French theatre. Its character as a repertory of mysteries and miracles, with a farce for good measure, gives an indication of the kind of plays performed by the early Parisian *confréries*. The elaborate stage-directions make vivid the way in which such performances were handled, and the many allusions to Paris and the environs give the collection an added fillip. The biblical mysteries in this manuscript represent a transitional stage between the short early plays of this kind and the longer, more pretentious cycles. Although the *Nativité* and *Trois Roys* could be merged, they might also, like the *Passion* and *Resurrection*, be performed independently. The saint plays, like the *Miracles de Notre Dame*, make use of divine intervention, but the role of the Virgin and her Son is little stressed, and the emphasis in many instances falls upon the lives and martyrdoms of the saints rather than upon their miracles. Even in the case of the *Vie de S. Fiacre* and the *Miracles de Ste Geneviève*, which introduce a number of wonders performed by these saints, it is their lives in human terms, not their miraculous powers, which receive most attention. Especially interesting for the history of the drama are the attempts at humour and realism. Designed to alleviate the many moral and doctrinal lessons in the texts, they introduce themes and characters of pure comedy and demonstrate once again how difficult it is to establish modern concepts of comedy and tragedy for the drama of the Middle Ages. The fact that the plays address *lais* and *clercs*, including *gens d'église*, indicates a wide public for them, and the universality of their appeal is further evidenced by the diversity of their subject-matter and the relative lack of subtlety in its treatment. These are essentially religious plays, but with mundane admixtures that would make them palatable to a general public.

THE CHANTILLY COLLECTION

Of minor interest, uncertain date, and provincial origin is a collection of *Mystères et Moralités* found in MS. 617 of the Musée Condé in Chantilly.[1] The collection contains charming Nativity scenes and three moralities. It seems to have been copied in the second half of the fifteenth century by nuns living in the convent of S. Michel at Huy near Liège and the *Nativité* scenes may have been played there by the sisters.

In general these *Nativité* scenes conform quite closely to liturgical plays on the same theme, but the addition of shepherdesses—an interpolation, as its script and position in the manuscript indicate, and one which may well be due to the feminine nature of both performers and audience—gives them an original touch and a special appeal. Undistinguished from a literary point of view, the scenes nevertheless are effective because of their simplicity and *naïveté*. The historical importance

[1] Ed. Cohen. Hoepffner in *Rom.* xlviii (1922), 62–92, suggests that the so-called fragment of a second *Nativité* in the collection is really part of the first, but Delbouille thinks fragments of two plays by the same author are involved which were never performed. In any case he and Hoepffner agree that the texts are of the fifteenth century, much later than Cohen thought. Hoepffner plausibly proposes that the irregularities in the verses are due to an ignorant Walloon author working from a Latin original, whereas the more regular pieces in the same manuscript are based directly on French models. Cf. also Lângfors in *Rom.* xlvii (1921), 511; Hoepffner, ibid., p. 607, and in *Rom.* l (1924), 14; Salverda de Grave in *Neo.* vi (1921), 274; Delbouille in *Mélanges Haust*, pp. 97–125, and *Mélanges Cohen*, pp. 75–84. In both the sixteenth and seventeenth centuries this Walloon *Nativité* found its way into French.

of the text resides in its intimate connexion with the liturgical drama and its revelation of how the vernacular plays evolved from it. Though written in a Walloon dialect, it not only follows the pattern of various Latin Christmas plays but makes direct use of their antiphons and tropes, sometimes in the original Latin, more often in translation. Like the Easter play copied in the convent of Origny-Ste-Benoîte (see Chap. II above), it demonstrates how short the step was from strictly liturgical texts to those suitable for independent performance and wider dissemination. The introduction of two shepherdesses, Eylison and Mahay, who accompany the shepherds adds a homely note: the shepherds bring their flutes to comfort the *petit enfan*, the shepherdesses bear a lamb, two lamps, and a basket with nuts and apples.[1] An outspoken *Sot* in the court of Herod is an even more original and unexpected development. These two short scenes indicate a desire to heighten interest in a text that otherwise has progressed no very great distance from the earlier Christmas *officia*. Relatively full stage-directions and the frequent use of liturgical pieces for the singing give an excellent idea of how not only these Nativity scenes but the church plays from which they derive were performed.

The *Nativité* scenes use the same epilogue as another play in the Chantilly collection, the pastoral morality (perhaps dating from the fourteenth century) entitled *Moralité de l' Alliance de Foy et Loyalté*, and a few other details in the two texts also show some similarity. But these do not necessarily imply common authorship. The adoption of the same conclusion by different dramatic pieces in a repertory is a practical consideration readily understandable and the other similarities seem quite fortuitous, reflecting a general resemblance between the rustic habits and implements of all literary shepherds in the Middle Ages.[2] Our morality represents its allegorical characters as *bergers* and *bergères* and chronicles the marriage of Faith and Loyalty with

---

[1] Reasons for considering the shepherdesses a later addition to an earlier text are given in *MLN*, xxxvii (1922), 106–10, and *Rom.* xlviii (1922), 83. See also Delbouille in *Mélanges Cohen*, p. 81. For the scene in art see Cohen's edition, pp. cxxiv ff.

[2] Cf. the shepherds in Adam le Bossu's *Robin et Marion*, the lyric *pastourelles*, *Aucassin et Nicolette*, the Ste Geneviève collection, the various English Nativities, the *Estoire de Griseldis*, &c. See also Hulubei, *L'Églogue en France*, chap. v.

the aid of Love, Prudence, Honour, and Peace. Insistence that Peace dwell with the pair and obscure references to Loyalty's and Faith's abandonment of the *Trois Estas* because of the presence there of Covetousness, Ambition, Presumption, Avarice, and Pride give the play political overtones which have not as yet been satisfactorily explained. This play, like the two other moralities, seems more sophisticated than the *Nativité* scenes and in all essentials derives from a very different tradition.

The two other moralities follow narrative sources that have been identified: the *Moralité des Sept Pechés Mortels et des Sept Vertus* is an adaptation of *Le Miroir de vie et de mort* written in 1266 by Robert de l'Omme;[1] the *Moralité du Pèlerinage de la vie humaine* is a version of the well-known poem by Guillaume de Deguilleville. The first of these adds a considerable amount of material to its source in order to make it more dramatic, but also introduces prayers and moral and theological discussions which counteract such efforts. The so-called Psychomachia theme of the conflict between the vices and virtues served widely as the basis for morality plays in France and England, and though our Walloon text is probably the earliest surviving example, it can hardly be characterized as successful. The dramatization of Deguilleville's poem is clumsy and unoriginal.

The *Nativité* scenes and their revealing connexions with the liturgical *officia*, the Walloon provenience of the collection and its probable origin in a convent of nuns, the curious combination in the same manuscript of very simple Christmas scenes with early examples of the artificial morality play, these are some of the factors that give extrinsic interest to the Chantilly texts.[2]

---

[1] See Långfors in *Rom.* xlvii (1921), 511, and l (1924), 14. Långfors would date the play from the first half of the fourteenth century, Hoepffner from the end of the fifteenth. Långfors in *Rom.* l, pp. 40 ff., analyses the play, compares it with its source, and corrects Cohen's edition. *Les Gieux des sept vertuz et des sept pechiez mortelz* were given in Tours in 1390. See Petit de Julleville, *Répertoire*, p. 324.

[2] Cf. also Chap. XXIV below.

XV

L'Estoire de Griseldis

I N the *Estoire de Griseldis* we possess the first example of a
French play that is serious yet non-religious. Although it
recalls in some ways the *Miracles de Notre Dame*, the *mystères*
and the *moralités*, it differs from all of them in its worldly atmosphere and subject-matter. At a time when the serious theatre
still betrayed its ecclesiastical origins in its themes and when its
direction still remained in the hands of religious organizations,
our play departs from precedent by dramatizing—for the first
time, so far as we know—a secular tale made famous by
Boccaccio and Petrarch.[1]

It may perhaps be compared with those *Miracles de Notre
Dame* in which the Virgin is not essential to the plot, for instance, with *Amis et Amiles* or *Robert le Diable*, but its motivation is mundane and moral, rather than religious, it makes no
use of the supernatural, contains no sermon, and introduces
no devotional lyrics. Like the *mystères* and Bodel's *Jeu de S.
Nicolas*, it opens with a summarizing prologue, and, like the
Christmas plays, it presents us with birth scenes and shepherds.
However, these have no hagiologic or biblical implications and
even when the subject-matter is similar the treatment differs.
Because the play dramatizes the virtues of wifely patience and
submission, it has sometimes been equated with the moralities,
but here again to mention a likeness is only to emphasize a
difference: the characters of this play are real persons, not
allegorical symbols or humanized abstractions.

The *Estoire* retells the story contained in Boccaccio's last
novella somewhat as it appears in Petrarch's mellower Latin
translation. This Latin translation, however, was turned into
French prose by Philippe de Mézières between 1384 and 1389,
and the French prose version is the direct source of our play
which merely versifies and dramatizes it. Many passages are

---

[1] Editions by Groeneveld, Glomeau, and B. Craig. On the French prose
versions see Golenistcheff-Koutouzoff and on Philippe de Mézières see N. Jorga.
The legend is discussed by D. D. Griffiths and J. B. Severs.

almost exactly alike, the derivation of others is equally certain, and together these 'borrowings' account for over two-thirds of the piece. Since Philippe de Mézières, a distinguished diplomat, traveller, and crusader, the intimate adviser of the pope and counsellor of the royal family, is known to have had an interest in dramatic performances—he personally prepared a Latin liturgical play for performance on the Feast of the Presentation of the Virgin and probably helped the king's brother, Louis, duc d'Orléans, to plan *une mommerie et danses* designed to provide an *esbatement pour complaire et resjoïr les dames*—it seems probable that he adapted his own translation of Petrarch for the stage and is himself the author.[1] We know at any rate that our only manuscript of the play[2] dates from 1395, a time when Philippe de Mézières was urging a marriage between the young princess, Isabelle of France, and King Richard II of England and when in a letter to the latter, written between May and July of that year, he mentioned Petrarch's story and wished the monarch a wife like Griseldis.

In the prologue of his play the author, conscious of his purpose and technique, says that his *estoire* will be *fait par personnaiges* because the heart of man is more moved by seeing than by reading. The play itself then begins with a group of noblemen trying to persuade the Marquis de Saluce to take a wife, and the similarity between their arguments and those advanced by Mézières in his letter to Richard is striking. Indeed one of the knights, *le quint chevalier*, a creation of the dramatist, closely resembles Philippe himself: he is described by another character in the play as a wise old courtier, a good Catholic, one devoted to public welfare, who had seen more of the world than other men of his country.[3]

After a series of hunting scenes during which the Marquis is

[1] On the Latin play see Chap. VI above. For the unfortunate *mommerie* that ended in a holocaust see Froissart's *Chroniques*, ed. Kervyn de Lettenhove, vol. xv, pp. 84–92 and especially 367–9. In the accounts of the duc d'Orléans for 1392 and 1393 four *joueurs de personnages* are mentioned by name and the amounts paid them recorded (see *Hist. litt.* xxiv. 200). For Mézières's authorship of the play see Frank, *MLN*, li (1936), 217–22 and Craig's edition.

[2] Bib. Nat. MS. fonds fr. 2203.

[3] One may also see allusions to the marriage in the words of Le Faulconnier, a title used to describe Philippe as the preceptor of Charles VI. See Jorga, pp. 409, 421, 429.

persuaded to marry, he suddenly encounters the poor shepherdess, Griseldis, dutifully devoting herself to her aged father,
Janicola. To the surprise of his knights the Marquis presently
announces his intention of marrying the humble maiden and
the wedding takes place. On all sides we hear of the charms and
goodness of the new Marquise and the first 'act' ends with two
shepherds rejoicing at her elevation, but also, after a debate
between them on the relative merits of the courtly and the
pastoral life, deciding that it is best to be content with one's
own station.

The second part of the play reveals the trials and eventual
triumph of the Marquise. Her husband, for all that he finds her
a paragon of virtue, nevertheless determines to test her, giving
as an excuse that his courtiers despise her humble origin and
that he must yield to their wishes. One after the other he has
her two small children taken from her, and though he has
secretly conveyed them to his sister's care Griseldis does not
know this. Each time she displays her superhuman docility,
pathetically praying that her son and daughter may not become
the prey of wild beasts unless, of course, this be the will of her
lord. Testing her even further, the Marquis professes to have
had their marriage annulled and to be about to take another
wife. Griseldis, after laying aside her fine raiment, goes back
to her father's home, only to be summoned presently by the
Marquis to do honour to his new fiancée, to clean and arrange
her quarters and to train her in her future responsibilities. The
fiancée turns out, of course, to be Griseldis's own daughter. All
is explained, and the Marquis, certain that what he has done for
the best can only result in good, orders minstrels summoned so
that every one may be of good cheer. The play concludes with
the two shepherds, after playfully misunderstanding each other,
rejoicing in Griseldis's return to her high estate and in the great
honour conferred thereby on *bergerie*, and expressing their joy
by singing an 'amoureuse chançonnette'.

The dramatist faithfully follows his source, as this outline
will have revealed. Only in the manner in which he has prepared the tale for the stage and in his original additions to it
does he reveal his ingenuity—and limitations. The scenes at the
beginning which show two hunts in progress and the various

nobles discussing the desirability of their young lord's marriage, together with his reactions to their arguments, expand and dramatize bare statements of the French prose narrative. Here our author seems to be writing from personal experience. The hunt for herons introduces a realistic falconer, that for deer is made amusing by the claims of rival *veneurs* and their cries to packs of fancifully named hounds. The discussion of the Marquis's marriage may have served an ulterior motive, as suggested above; in any case it helps characterize the hero and motivate somewhat his subsequent inhuman behaviour. The emphasis on the hero's aversion to marriage, his desire for independence, and on his wife's lowly station may have been designed to mitigate what Boccaccio called *matta bestialità* and what Petrarch considered a kind of aberration.

The shepherd scenes are also original additions of our playwright. They add a note of comedy and, though reflecting material used elsewhere in the drama, as well as in lyric and narrative poetry (cf. Chap. XIV, p. 154, n. 2, above), they are artfully connected here with Griseldis's relation to *bergerie* and serve as a comment on her fate. They may also reflect the author's own attitude toward the advantages of a simple life.

The scenes involving the birth of the heroine's two children and her forced separation from them, which lose dramatic value by repetition, nevertheless betray originality in details that heighten the pathos of the story. Griseldis's devotion to her son and daughter and her frequently expressed desire to have her children near her make their loss the more tragic. So, too, her relations with her old father illustrate her goodness and prepare us for her later miraculous patience. Throughout, the dramatist neglects no chance to make his play pictorially effective. The poor hut of Janicola, the humble occupations of his daughter, and the lowly condition of the shepherds are contrasted with the pageantry of the hunts, the processions and festivities of the court, and the magnificent costumes and jewellery of the nobility.

But in the somewhat slavish following of his source and in the creation of those minor roles necessitated by transforming narrative into action the dramatist seems to falter. Servants, messengers, secretaries, nurses, sergeants, a bishop, and a pope, though doubtless carefully distinguished on the stage in speech, make-up, and dress, all emerge from similar moulds. Of these only *le quint chevalier*, mentioned above, is adequately character-ized and carries conviction. Nor does our playwright depart from precedent in versification. He uses the pedestrian octo-syllabic couplet and the traditional mnemonic device of couplets divided between speakers.

When, where, and by whom was the play first performed? The *explicit* of our only manuscript is dated 1395, and this seems to be the year when the play was both written and copied.[1] The manuscript is charmingly illustrated and, though not luxurious, may possibly, as the unreliable Chevalier de Mouhy reports, have been presented to the king. In any case, the marriage con-tract of Isabelle, second daughter of Charles VI, who became the second queen of Richard II, was signed 9 March 1396, and, as Glomeau says, pp. xv–xvi: 'Les réjouissances nuptiales, qui dominent la pièce, faisaient écho aux événements de l'époque.' It is tempting to see in the piece one of those *esbatements* pro-duced in the *salle de l'ostel* of the duc d'Orléans, the king's brother, or even in the Louvre itself. If Philippe de Mézières had a role in producing as well as writing it, he might have used court retainers—so many of whom appear in person in the play—as actors and their magnificent possessions as properties. The production would offer no difficulties, require few mansions or *trucs*, and could readily have been made on a small indoor stage. The theme, its splendid trappings, and the emphasis on con-trasts of social status would be certain to appeal to an aristo-cratic audience.

The play represents a departure in subject-matter that, had it given rise to others of the sort, might have hastened the coming of the later tragi-comedy.[2] In its exemplification of the virtues of obedience and patience it stresses themes related to those of the religious theatre, but in its wholly secular development of the plot it approaches the drama of a much later time.

---

[1] An early print of the play (Bib. Nat. YF Réserve 124) is plausibly dated *c.* 1550. See Brunet, *Manuel*, iii. 1968–9.

[2] See H. C. Lancaster, *The French Tragi-Comedy*, pp. 1–15.

XVI

The Fifteenth Century and Later

Survivals. Staging and Organization. Authors and Directors. Manuscripts and editions. Influence of the plays on art

WITH the fifteenth century the various types of plays already considered expanded and developed. Guilds, both religious and lay, favoured performances for the benefit of their own members and the general public. *Mommeries* and *esbatements* in the halls of the nobility continued to entertain hosts and guests. Texts often became so complex and long that they were necessarily played out of doors, many days were required for their performance, and a large part of the populace might be engaged in producing them.

But the evolution from the liturgical drama left its mark.[1] The liturgical texts had borne titles of various sorts, liturgical terms like *ordo*, *officium*, *processio*, and even *festum* (*asinorum*), designations by subject like *Visitatio Sepulchri*, *De Peregrino*, *Suscitatio Lazari*, and descriptive captions such as *historia*, *miraculum*, *misterium*, *ludus*, *repraesentatio*, *similitudo*, and exceptionally even *comoedia*. Our vernacular plays have similar titles: the Anglo-Norman *Mystère d'Adam* is liturgically and descriptively defined as *Ordo representacionis Ade*; the word *feste* occurs in numerous texts and documents; and of course subject titles abound. *Griseldis* is an *estoire*; Rutebeuf's *Théophile* and many of the plays showing the intervention of Notre Dame are termed *miracles*; the vernacular *mystère* appears in 1374 (linked with

---

[1] Cf. Young, ii. 407 ff.; Chambers, ii. 103 ff. *Miraculum* appears in the Fleury play-book; the origins of *misterium* and the confusion between *ministerium* and *mysterium* are discussed by Young, ii. 409–10, 501. In England the guilds were frequently called 'mysteries' (see among others Edith Rickert, *Chaucer's World*, *passim*). For *feste* see a document of 1395 published by Cohen, *Rom.* xxxviii (1909), 587 ff., the Sion fragment where pardon is granted to 'vos qui estes ci venu, / Qui nostre feste avez veü', the prologue of the *Passion d'Autun*, MS. *R* (*la feste vulunt comancer*), and note that the narrative version of the *Passion d'Autun*, MS. *B*, replaces the word *feste* by *ystoyre* and *traictier*.

miracle) when a confrérie of Rouen is recorded as obliged to
play each year *aucun vrai mistere ou miracle*, in 1400 when a *Mystère de la Passion* is recorded from Orléans, and, of course, in
1402 in the letters patent granting permission to the Confrérie
de la Passion of Paris to play 'misterres, tant de saincts, comme
de sainctes, et mesmement de la Passion'.[1] It is obvious that the
modern distinction between the words 'miracle' and 'mystery'—
the first now usually applied to miracles of the Virgin and to
miracles or lives of the saints, the second to plays with biblical
themes—did not obtain in the Middle Ages. In England 'miracle
play' came to be the generic term for all religious plays, in
France *mystère* could refer to saint plays, dumb shows, and
later even to non-religious texts (in 1548 we hear of *mystères
profanes*).

Of the terms used for vernacular plays only *jeu* (*jocus*) seems
never to have been applied to liturgical texts. However, the
parallel term *ludus* was employed for both popular revels and
ecclesiastical performances (cf. *Ludus breviter de Passione*, *Danielis
ludus*, &c.) and perhaps *jeu* merely translated it in the vernacular.
The close relations between *joculator*, *jocare*, and *jocus* would
make the word available for any sort of lay performance, and it
may be significant that this is the designation of Bodel's humorous *Jeu de S. Nicolas* and the light comedies of Adam le Bossu.
In any case *jeu* very early comes to be a generic term in our
documents, where it characterizes serious as well as not so
serious entertainment.[2]

One of the most persistent vestiges left by the liturgy on the
lay theatre was the convention by which almost all plays concluded with the hymn of Matins, the *Te Deum laudamus*.[3] This

[1] See Roy, *Mystère*, p. 11*, and Petit de Julleville, *Mystères*, i. 187 ff., 417.

[2] See Chambers, ii. 104, and Faral, *Jongleurs*, pp. 3 and 12. Faral says that the entertainment of the ancient *mimus* was known as both *ludus* and *jocus* and that the
medieval French terms, *jogler* and *jogleor*, cannot date earlier than the end of the
eighth century. The word *jeu* appears with serious connotations in a document
of 1380, printed by A. Thomas in *Rom.* xxi (1892), 606 ff., which speaks of 'jeux
. . . en l'onneur et remembrance de la Passion Nostre Seigneur' performed, it
should be noted, 'par aucuns des bourgois et autres bonnes genz' of Paris. A
Miracle de Théophile performed at Aunay-lès-Bondy in 1384 is referred to as a *jeu*.
We hear of *jeux de personnages*, including both farces and saints' lives, in 1398, and
the letters patent of the Confrérie de la Passion of 1402 similarly equate *jeux* with
misterres. (See Petit de Julleville, *Mystères*, i. 414 ff.)

[3] See Young, i. 63–64. During the Middle Ages the hymn which marked the

might be sung by the performers, but often the audience was invited to participate. Occasionally a procession of the actors, to the accompaniment of vocal or instrumental music, conveniently and festively terminated a performance, but even then the *Te Deum* might be introduced.

Another continuing reminder of liturgical performances was the so-called simultaneous staging of the vernacular plays. The convention whereby all localities represented in the action appeared side by side in full view of the audience can be directly related to the origins of the lay drama in the church. The full stage-directions of such texts as the *Mystère d'Adam*, the Anglo-Norman *Resureccion*, the plays of the Bibliothèque Ste Geneviève, the *Estoire de Griseldis*, and the directors' copies, or *Abregiés*, used for the *Mystère de la Passion* performed at Mons in 1501, together with various illustrations in our medieval manuscripts, give an excellent idea of how our plays were staged.[1]

All places where the actors were to be stationed—variously called *lieux*, *mansions*, *maisons*, *estals*, *estages*, *logeis*—were prepared in advance. They consisted of little structures, usually raised, capable of supporting simple furniture—a throne, chair, table, altar, &c.—and they could be curtained off at need. Much of the action, however, took place *enmi la place*, that is, in the playing-space situated in front of the structures, and this space might also be used to represent some special locality at the discretion of the playwright or director. It might even contain a few installations of its own (for instance, the sea of Galilee and the *petit chastel* of Emmaus in the *Resureccion*). Players not needed for the action might be directed to sit down until again required or, if not wanted later, to go off where they liked. An informal relationship between actors and

---

end of Matins was sung antiphonally, usually by semi-choruses. It regularly appears at the end of the church plays. In the lay theatre it remains even in certain sixteenth-century plays, especially in the moralities. On the persistence of the Easter sequence, *Victimae Paschali*, see above, Chap. II.

[1] See the chapters above devoted to these plays, Cohen, *Mise en scène* and *Livre de conduite* (where the *Abregiés* are printed), Stuart, *Stage Decoration*, Penn, *Staging*, and Frank, *Iconography*. The simultaneous stage-settings inherited by such later playwrights as Hardy and Rotrou are pictured in Lancaster's *Mémoire de Mahelot*, where a cavern or a ship in full sail may be found abutting directly on the throne-room of a palace.

audience obtained; very early we hear of devils making sorties among the spectators, and it is likely enough, given the non-professional status of actors during the Middle Ages, that between turns on the stage performers often sat with their friends in the audience. The separate structures could be fashioned to represent churches, palaces, hermits' cells, hovels, or any other place by conventional devices or even placards; actors wearing mitres, crowns, or some similar identifying properties helped in their recognition; and often the texts are so explicitly worded that no further indication of locality would be required. For example, in the seventh *Miracle de Notre Dame*[1] the text itself points out in succession a house, its entrance, a table, the seating arrangements to be observed by the characters, the services performed by two servants, and throughout our plays such expressions occur as *Voy la en son throsne seoir, De France approchons, Sus ceste pierre me tenray*, statements making the locale clear to the spectators and serving also as stage-directions to the actors.

Certain structures had a traditional position and design. Thus heaven regularly appeared at the left and hell at the right side of the stage.[2] Heaven, like the terrestrial paradise of the *Mystère d'Adam*, was adorned with flowers, foliage, and silken hangings and often had an upper level from which the Virgin and angelic messengers visibly descended to converse with erring mortals below. The entrance to hell was through gates or through the steaming jaws of a monstrous beast, and within the infernal regions cauldrons not only created smoke and flame but, when beaten by devils, produced a horrible din. In the late plays the jaws of hell might open and close at need and hell itself, like heaven, might embrace more than one level. Sometimes indeed the pit of hell seems to have occupied a lower level than the other installations.[3]

---

[1] Ed. *SATF*, i. 338, lines 698 ff.

[2] See Stuart, pp. 116, 118, 170, 175. Hell was still at the spectator's right in the seventeenth century. See Lebègue in *Mélanges Cohen*, p. 221.

[3] Scaffolds are mentioned in France as early as 1395. See Cohen, *Rom.* xxxviii (1909), 587. References to scaffolds and to higher and lower levels are also frequent in the comic theatre. On scaffolds in the English plays see Chambers, ii. 136, and J. J. Jusserand in *An English Miscellany presented to Dr. Furnivall* (Oxford, 1901), p. 183.

Upon the stage the actors moved about freely from and to their fixed positions, long journeys could be simulated by roaming around the playing-space, and the use of messengers realistically brought widely separated persons into close relationship. The illusion of excitement and suspense within a fairly static play could be furthered by short scenes played swiftly in succession, now in one part of the stage, now in another, the spectator's eye and mind travelling rapidly through space and time.

The simultaneous, stationary stage just described was the normal type in France, although there, as in England, the wheeled or chariot stage, drawn from place to place before an audience that remained at fixed points along the line of march, was also known. Processional performances of this sort have been noted from Béthune, Abbeville, and Lille, but in France such performances were more usual for dumb shows than for true plays. Of dumb shows, *mystères mimés*, there are many records. An early example of 1313 from Paris is typical. This was a spectacle given by the citizens of the capital under Philippe IV in honour of the visit of Edward II of England and his wife, Isabelle of France. From the different chroniclers who describe the occasion we learn that the whole history of Jesus Christ from birth to resurrection was presented, that at least ninety angels and more than one hundred devils took part, and that, together with diverse spectacles showing the glory of the blessed and the pains of the damned, there were many different scenes involving Renard the Fox and other animals. Godefroi de Paris suggests the odd mingling of themes when he says one saw

> Herod et Cayphas en mitre
> Et renard chanter une espitre.

Such *mystères mimés* were usually given at great festivals or on the occasion of the visits of royalty. The carts or floats, like the English *pageants*, proceeded from point to point and at intervals along the way scaffolds might be erected for the spectators, or the various carts could be stationed at fixed places and the spectators might wander from one place to another to view them. Usually the actors of these tableaux were mute and indicated the small amount of action involved by pantomime, but sometimes a few words were spoken.[1]

A favourite time for these and other outdoor spectacles was Corpus Christi or Whit Sunday, though plays might be performed at any time of year. Originally performances were on days appropriate to the subject—the Resurrection at Eastertide, the Nativity plays during the Christmas season, the saint plays on their holy days—but later market-days and the long periods of fair weather in summer became especially popular. Outdoor festivities conveniently adopted public squares for their purposes, and we also hear of cemeteries and old Roman amphitheatres serving in this connexion.

Some medieval plays were acted indoors, however. The feast days of particular saints and especially the holy days of the Virgin were often celebrated by plays in their honour, and many of these plays were sponsored by guilds and performed within their assembly or banquet halls. In its early as well as later days the Confrérie de la Passion of Paris gave indoor performances, and many references survive not only to plays enacted in the palaces of the nobility but to students' theatricals that took place inside school buildings.[2] Naturally the productions in relatively small halls were more restricted by considerations of space than those in the open air. The dimensions of the average medieval indoor stage have been calculated to have been about 40 by 20 feet; both the stage of the Hôpital de la Trinité in Paris and that required for the *Miracles de Notre Dame* seem to have been approximately of this size.[3]

It is obvious that performances of medieval plays must have varied greatly according to time, subject, occasion, audience, and other circumstances. In general the earlier plays, whether sacred or profane, used few and simple settings. So did the later farces. But the magnificent outdoor spectacles contemporaneous with the farces were often splendid affairs requiring

---

[1] On *mystères mimés* see Petit de Julleville, *Mystères*, ii. 186 ff., and Stuart, chaps. iii and ix.

[2] See *Hist. litt.* xxiv. 187, 200, 452–3; Faral, *Jongleurs*, p. 247. Cf. also P. Sadron in *Mélanges Cohen*, pp. 205–18.

[3] For these calculations see Stuart, pp. 190–1, Penn, p. 13, Cohen, *Mise en scène*, p. 87. On the other hand, an outdoor stage at Rouen measured over 195 feet in length (Cohen, loc. cit.).

huge stages, elaborate *mansions*, and ingenious mechanical contrivances. Differences between Paris, the provincial towns, and the rural villages also obtained. Moreover, the great spectacles were given in the provinces long after they were forbidden in Paris. Sometimes, as at Lyons, *c.* 1520, we hear of outdoor mystery plays being replaced by shorter ones performed indoors, and the first permanent theatre established at Lyons (1538–41) played both mysteries and farces, presumably on the same stage.[1]

The quality and equipment of the performers also varied greatly. With the rise of the towns, control of the plays sometimes passed out of ecclesiastical hands, though we long hear of *clercs* and *gens d'eglise* as participants and audience, and some of the associations giving plays were certainly religious in origin. Such *puys* and *confréries* as those *des Douze Apôtres, du Saint Sacrement, de Notre Dame* and *de la Passion*, like the Pater Noster guild of York, bear revealing titles.[2] Many of these associations must have long continued to be partly clerical, partly lay. Eventually, however, the laity in many cases succeeded the churchmen in financing and directing performances. We actually hear of rivalry between them in England in 1378 when the choristers of St. Paul's in London petitioned King Richard II 'to prohibit some inexpert people from presenting the history of the Old and New Testament, to the great prejudice of the clergy, who had been at great expense, in order to represent it publicly at Christmas'.[3]

The *puys* and *confréries* of France, whatever their different purposes—religious or lay, charitable, literary, or purely recreational—probably recruited their actors from their own members, many of whom must have been 'inexpert people'. The *confrères* of Paris were derisively referred to by their enemies as *gens ignares, artisans mécaniques* who tried to give themselves airs.[4]

[1] See V.-L. Saulnier in *Mélanges Cohen*, pp. 147 ff.

[2] The word *puy* (from *podium*) has been connected with the meaning of platform, railing, &c., but Margarete Rösler in *ZRP*, xlvi (1926), 687–93, suggested a connexion with the idea of support, aid (cf. *appuyer*), which may mean that these societies were, like ancient and modern benevolent societies, devoted to mutual assistance in times of need.

[3] See Robert Davies, *Extracts from the Municipal Records of York*, p. 231.

[4] Petit de Julleville, *Mystères*, i. 423.

As in England, the craftsmen banded together in guilds liked to give plays appropriate to their callings and patron saints; for example, the shoemakers presented the story of SS. Crépin and Crépinien in 1443 and 1458, the masons and carpenters ordered a play about St. Louis from Gringore, *c.* 1512.[1] All these actors were non-professionals and it is generally thought that no troupes of professional actors appeared in France before the sixteenth century. However, accomplished individuals capable of expert performances could be recruited from among the jongleurs. It is likely that in the late twelfth and thirteenth centuries authors like Bodel, Rutebeuf, and Adam le Bossu were assisted in the production of their plays by their professional colleagues, and in 1392 and 1393 we hear of payments to *joueurs de personnages*, probably specialists, in the accounts of the duc d'Orléans.[2]

For the most part, the players in the great biblical spectacles of the fifteenth and sixteenth centuries embraced persons of all classes. The clergy might direct and censor but they are also to be found in the more dignified stellar roles. Similarly the nobility gravitated to the parts of kings and members of the aristocracy. However, such spectacles were usually organized by towns, and townspeople assumed most of the roles. Until the middle of the sixteenth century young lads regularly took the parts of women and choirboys appeared as angels and children. They also represented various protagonists in their youth. Thus in the *Mystère du Viel Testament* we read 'fin du petit Joseph' and 'le grand Joseph commence'. There are also a *petit* and a *grand Samuel*.

Doubling in roles became a necessity in the very long mysteries. In the *Actes des Apôtres* there are some 494 roles but less than 300 actors, in the *Mystère de S. Martin* some 152 roles and only about 120 actors. There were selective trials for the different parts and a proclamation of 1540 in Paris asks those of

[1] Similarly in ancient Ostia the carpenters' guild carried a tree in the Magna Mater procession and in medieval England shipwrights were responsible for plays about Noah's ark.

[2] *Histoire litt.* xxiv. 200. On actors in general in the medieval theatre see Petit de Julleville, *Mystères*, i. 340 ff.; Cohen, *Mise en scène*, pp. 196 ff., and *Livre de conduite*, pp. lxx ff. and xcix ff.; Chambers, ii. 114, 139, appendix W, *passim*; Sadron, *Mélanges Cohen*, pp. 205–18.

bonne volonté to come to *la salle de la Passion* to be tested. We hear
of a similar procedure at York, where the guilds in like fashion
attempted to find good actors for their plays.

Actors had to bind themselves before a notary to play on the
prescribed days unless ill, to be on time, accept the roles assigned
them by the superintendents, attend rehearsals or pay fines, and
not to find fault or get drunk. In some localities the actors paid
a sum in advance in order to take part in any benefits accruing
from the performances, to help defray expenses in case of need,
and also to serve as a deposit against potential fines. Occasionally
payments to actors are mentioned; these were usually small and
sometimes consisted merely of food and wine. On the other hand,
actors usually were obliged to provide their own costumes.

Such costumes might, of course, be simple or elaborate. God
the Father was usually dressed as a pope or emperor and other
divine persons wore ecclesiastical garb. Anachronisms bothered
no one; Jews, Roman soldiers, and ancient heroes were clothed
in the distinguishing garments of the Middle Ages. Mary Magdalen's dress and jewellery were apt to be those of a medieval
prostitute. Payments for wigs and false beards are recorded.
For the sixteenth-century *Actes des Apôtres* we hear of some
very costly costumes made of silks, taffetas, velvets, and
damasks, as well as of robes with gems sewn upon them for
the Orientals.[1] The brilliant colours of these costumes must
have produced a splendid effect: for example, Satan appeared
in crimson velvet and one queen had a gown of violet velvet
with sleeves lined in cloth of gold over which she wore a purple
satin cloak lined with silver. The blind man in another play was
clothed in gray satin and the paralytic in changeable taffeta. It
is comforting to learn that in some instances rich non-players
were assessed to help less affluent actors pay for their costumes.
Usually, however, this would have been unnecessary, since for
the most part simplicity and restraint obtained.

The organization of the great Passion plays usually involved
the energies and talents of a whole community. Towns were
interested because the influx of people likely to make purchases

---

[1] Cf. the Latin *Presentation of the Virgin*, discussed on pp. 70–71, above. On
costumes in general see Cohen, *Mise en scène*, pp. 220 ff., and on those of the *Actes
des Apôtres*, Petit de Julleville, *Mystères*, i. 377–8.

of various sorts brought in a considerable amount of money. The mayor and town council often appeared in the preliminary *monstre*[1] or procession which, like the proclamations and banns in England, advertised the plays in advance, and these men sometimes helped defray costs themselves, levied special taxes, or took what was needed from the public treasury. Occasionally a few citizens, instead of representatives of the whole community, assumed all risks and shared both expenses and profits. More often, however, the responsibility for costs and production fell upon a larger group which included, among others, all the actors involved.

In such cases, first of all, supervisors or superintendents were chosen. They in turn decided on a director or directors (*maîtres des jeux*). Such organizers of mysteries often became so famous that their services were in great demand. Communities from Bordeaux to Bourges tried to obtain Jean Bouchet to direct their plays and some even bribed or threatened in order to acquire his services. A *maître du jeu* had tremendous responsibilities : often he was at once director, prompter, machinist, actor, trainer, and reviser. He often spoke the prologues or sermons, and advertised the following day's programme by way of epilogue. This role might be quite arduous, for the great spectacles of the fifteenth and sixteenth centuries lasted many days, three or four on the average, though frequently more, even as many as the forty days required by the performance of the *Actes des Apôtres* at Bourges in 1536.[2]

Work was usually suspended during the performances, which might begin at eight in the morning and continue till dark, with a noonday pause of an hour or two for lunch, a pause sometimes announced in our texts. The spectators included men, women, and children and embraced all classes—ladies and

---

[1] The *monstre* usually occurred a few days before the plays, all actors marching in costume or appearing on floats that showed some of the *mansions*. We have a description of such floats from Bourges in 1536. There was a magnificent paradise with richly dressed virtues at the four corners, a garden of beautiful flowers and fruits, angels playing on flutes, harps, and other instruments, and there was also a terrifying hell that discharged flames and showed Lucifer inside with fire-spouting serpents in his hands while the damned suffered various horrible forms of punishment. See Cohen, *Mise en scène*, pp. 91–2, 95.

[2] See Petit de Julleville, *Mystères*, ii. 130–4. On the Bourges performance of the *Actes des Apôtres* see also Chap. XVII below.

knights, bourgeois, and peasants were frequently saluted from the stage. It is recorded that some of the common folk arrived as early as four o'clock in the morning in order to secure good places. Many of these sat on the ground (*par terre*) or brought their own stools, but for the more fortunate, *loges* and tiers of seats were occasionally erected. Audiences and actors were apt to be on friendly terms and to mingle freely during and after performances. Indeed festivities on the occasion of the giving of the plays might continue well into the night, the holiday mood producing a number of incidents that have been recorded for posterity in legal documents.

Many details about the organization of the huge spectacles are also contained in the *Abregiés* found at Mons and dated 1501. These are two directors' copies, one for each director of the play, and it is clear from them that Greban's *Passion*, with changes and additions, many from Jean Michel's later *Passion*, served as the basic text used in the performance. The *Abregiés* give the names of the characters in the play followed by the actors' real names, adding their addresses when the actors were children or servants. The first and last lines of all the speeches appear with a Roman numeral beside them in the margin indicating the number of lines between. Careful directions are provided for the manner of entrances and exits, for orchestral interludes, and especially for the functioning of the mechanical contrivances (*secrets* or *feintes*) to be used. Also from Mons comes an account-book dated 1501 which reveals further details about the performance there, for instance that the manuscripts of the play were obtained from Amiens, the machinists from Chauny in Picardy, and that the market-place was used for the production of the spectacle. A contract of 1547 from Valenciennes supplements our information from Mons by indicating how superintendents for plays of this sort were elected, powers and profits divided, roles assigned, and how actors were held to their duties upon pain of the payment of fines.[1]

[1] The *Abregiés* and account-book of Mons are printed by Cohen, *Livre de conduite*. The Valenciennes contract is printed by Petit de Julleville, *Mystères*, ii. 145. Cf. also Chambers, ii, appendix W, and Sadron, op. cit. The vignettes in the manuscript of the Valenciennes *Passion* of 1547 were painted by Hubert Cailleau, himself an actor in the play. They include the frequently reproduced design for its staging. See Cohen, *Mise en scène*, Planche 1, and Bédier–Hazard, i. 135.

The mechanical devices used to arouse the wonder of the audience by the *facteurs ou conducteurs de secrets* included elevations (*voleries*) with counterbalances, wheels, ropes, and pulleys for bringing saints or divine persons to paradise and dropping Lucifer and the fallen angels down to hell.[1] The executions and tortures were accomplished with the aid of dummies and skilful substitutions—trap-doors and hollow altars for concealing substitutes are mentioned—whereas the instruments employed in floggings were actually fashioned of light materials made to imitate heavy whips. For burnings there were real flames—tow dipped in brandy frequently produced them—but careful provisions were made for actors to slip through hollow furnaces or trap-doors in order to avoid accidents. Brandy was also supplied in connexion with nimbuses and the descent of the Holy Spirit, whereas sulphur evoked both the smoke and odours of hell. In one play Jerusalem, represented by painted drops, was spectacularly destroyed in a great holocaust. Clouds made of cloth concealed *trucs* and performers at need. Water in concrete basins was employed in scenes depicting the Creation, Deluge, Moses striking the Rock, the Sea of Galilee, &c. Automata and humans in skins represented animals. Canons, drums, and the rattling of boxes of stones created sound-effects. Passages under platforms were ingeniously devised and trap-doors above them cleverly screened, sometimes with real sod.

Music played a prominent part in all dramatic performances of the Middle Ages.[2] Plain-chant and well-known church melodies are often specified (in one play, for instance, the shepherds sing the *Stabat Mater*) but also original songs for solo- and part-singing such as *rondeaux*, *ballades*, *motets*, *chants royaux*, &c. Greban, who trained the choirboys of Notre Dame and played its organ, has won high praise for the melodies he composed for his own poetic Passion play, and in the Rouen *Incarnation et Nativité* the angels sing a series of perennially charming

---

[1] In the manuscript of a Resurrection play wrongly attributed to Michel, Jesus, three angels, and fifty-one souls had to be raised. We learn that an *engin* was used for Jesus and the angels and that, while the others secretly ascended to paradise by ladders, their painted figures made of paper or parchment were attached to the robe of Jesus and pulled aloft by the same mechanism. Clouds painted on cloth were to hide the contrivance and helped create the desired illusion. See Cohen, *Mise en scène*, pp. 153-5.

[2] See the works of Gérold, Reese, and Chailley.

couplets. Orchestral music not only provided overtures and accompaniments to dances but also served to summon audiences
to the performances, filled in pauses, and helped mark the passage of time. The word *silete* in our manuscripts usually means
that instruments are to silence the spectators, awaken their
attention, and introduce important persons of the play. The
instruments employed included organs, trumpets, oboes, harps,
flutes, viols and lutes, with fifes and tambourines especially
important for calling spectators to their places. The musicians
were often stationed in paradise, though sometimes behind the
scenes; occasionally angels are directed to pretend to perform
while concealed musicians actually produce the music.

On the authors and directors of the great spectacles we have
considerable information. They are apt to be ecclesiastics like
Mercadé and the Greban brothers, Arnoul and Simon, but
various professions are represented and we hear, among others,
of jurists, notaries, bailiffs, and a physician. Relatively few
purely professional dramatists appear. However, most of the
later authors, unlike their anonymous early predecessors, signed
their works, indicating that such literary texts were held in high
esteem. Indeed we learn from many sources that the plays of
the Grebans and of Jean Michel commanded respect all over
France.

Some of our later authors should perhaps be called redactors or editors.[1] They used older texts which they cut or
padded at need. Their additions usually comprised lighter episodes, and their own characteristics can best be studied in scenes
involving shepherds, torturers, gaolers, devils, patrons of
taverns, and the like. Some authors became widely acclaimed
and wrote to order. Claude Chevalet was asked not only to
compose a play but to criticize the work of another man. It is
recorded that a certain canon Pra had great difficulty with his
supervisors and that Chevalet was brought to town to help.
He tore the poor canon's work to pieces, rewrote much of it,
and when incriminations ensued he left town, saying he could
not work with so wretched an author.[2] We know that in the

---

[1] The author of the Digby *Conversion of St. Paul* frankly speaks of himself as
a 'compyler'. See *The Digby Plays*, ed. F. J. Furnivall, *EETS*, extra series, lxx
(1896), line 357.   [2] Cohen, *Mise en scène*, p. 189.

sixteenth century Jean Bouchet organized festivities at Poitiers,
Saumur, Issoudun, Bourges, and Nantes. He himself describes
his procedure in his *Épître familière* xcii, addressed *Aux habitans
d'Issoudun* :[1]

> Du moule ay prins ce que j'ay bon trouvé,
> Et ce qui est par l'Église approuvé,
> Car il y a ou moule aulcuns passages
> Qui n'ont passé par l'escolle des sages :
> Dont par conseil j'ay fait rescision,
> Et en ces lieux mis quelque addition.

A word should perhaps be said about the preservation of the
later medieval mystery plays. Most of our manuscripts seem not
to have suffered the hard usage of the stage but to have been designed for reading or for preservation in libraries and archives.
The guild plays of York, for example, were entered into a town
register apparently from the *origenalls* kept by the individual
crafts. However, a few practical directors' or prompters' copies
with stage-directions and cues have survived, such as the
Abregiés of Mons and the *Frankfurter Dirigierrolle*. Individual
actors' copies are rarer, but the Shrewsbury fragments illustrate
what they must have been like, for they give us the part of a
single actor who played the Third Shepherd in the *Pastores*, the
Third Mary in the *Quem quaeritis?*, and one of the Pilgrims in
the *Peregrini*.[2] Some of our manuscripts are luxurious, obviously
intended for libraries of the wealthy, whereas others are simpler
and must have been designed for less pretentious owners. The
manuscripts of Greban's *Passion*, for example, range from a
paper copy with two miniatures made for the connétable de
Saint-Pol to a fine parchment copy with numerous miniatures
which belonged at various times to Louise de Bourbon and
Gaston, duc d'Orléans. Other manuscripts were executed for
use at designated performances and providentially a few of
these have survived. Thus the combined text of the beginning

---

[1] See Henri Clouzot, *Ancien Théâtre en Poitou*, p. 35, and Petit de Julleville,
Mystères, ii. 128–30.

[2] On the Shrewsbury fragments see Manly, *Pre-Shaksperean Drama*, vol. i,
pp. xxviii–xxxvii, and Chambers, ii. 90. Other bibliography on the preservation
of the English plays is given in Chambers, ii, appendix x. For the *Abregiés* of
Mons see Cohen's *Livre de conduite* and on the *Frankfurter Dirigierrolle*, R. Froning,
Das Drama des Mittelalters, ii.

of the *Vieux Testament* and parts of Greban's *Passion*, played at
Troyes in 1490, was bound that same year in three volumes at
the expense of the town and these volumes still exist, although
a lacuna indicates that another volume must have been lost
previous to the binding, presumably during the performance.[1]
With the invention of printing came a profound change. Plays
could now be made available to the general reading public and
the various communities performing them. Printers quarrelled
for the privilege of turning out editions which undoubtedly
sold well. At least fifteen editions of Jean Michel's *Passion* appeared between 1490 and 1542, and most of our later comic
pieces survive only in printed form (cf. Chap. XXIV below).

The influence of the medieval drama on art has been studied,
especially by Émile Mâle.[2] Visualization of biblical scenes upon
the stage and observation of methods of portraying them could
not but have affected any artists in the audience. Mâle indicates
changes in iconography that occurred, for instance, when the
religious drama was popularizing hitherto neglected incidents
in Jesus' life such as the smith and Veronica scenes, or evolving
a new method of seating the apostles around a square table at
the Last Supper. Also attributed to the plays are the representations in art of the shepherds and shepherdesses offering their
humble, characteristic gifts to the infant Jesus and of the four
virtues, Mercy, Truth, Justice, and Peace—the so-called four
daughters of God—who by their contrasting arguments ini-
tiated the Incarnation in the plays of Mercadé and Greban.
These and many other details observable in the paintings,
sculpture, miniatures, tapestries, ivories, and stained glass of the
later Middle Ages may all be found in the Church Fathers and
in earlier narrative literature—whence the drama took them—
but the timing of various transformations in the visual representation of Church history and Church legend indicates a true
indebtedness to the theatre. Even the simultaneous staging of
that theatre left its mark upon the art of the period.

[1] See the Paris–Raynaud ed. of Greban's *Passion*, p. xxv.
[2] Mâle, *Fin*, chap. ii. See also Cohen, *Mise en scène*, chap. iii. For the reciprocal
influence of art on the theatre and bibliography on the subject see Kernodle,
From Art to Theatre. Illustrative material pertinent to the medieval French theatre
can be found in Cohen, *Théâtre*, and in the *Histoire générale illustrée du théâtre*, by
L. Dubech and others (especially in vol. ii [1931], pp. 9–163).

XVII

Late Passion Plays and Spectacles

LA PASSION DE SEMUR

THE earliest and simplest survivor of the great Passion plays that served as texts for the fifteenth-century spectacles of France is known as the *Passion de Semur* and its unique manuscript is dated 1488.[1] Like the *Passion du Palatinus* and the *Passion d'Autun*, which it sometimes resembles, it seems to emanate from Burgundy. Its length, however—9,582 lines—greatly exceeds theirs and it required two days, with frequent pauses, for its performance. At the end of the first day (line 4,295) the audience is told to go home and return on the morrow to view *le prix de no redempcion*.

Although shorter than the later plays of Mercadé and Greban, it includes more Old Testament material than theirs. Indeed the compass of the Semur text is enormous, extending from the Creation (with God the Father enthroned among His angels in paradise saying 'Let there be light!' and with Lucifer and his devils being routed by Michael, Gabriel, and other heavenly cohorts) to the Appearances and the Ascension. Within this gigantic framework are ranged scores of biblical, legendary, and purely fanciful scenes, as well as many original characters allegorically or imaginatively named. The effect is at once grandiose and yet compact.

Among the Old Testament scenes are the Creation of Adam and Eve, the stories of Cain and Abel, the Flood (with dialogue depicting Noah's family life), the Sacrifice of Isaac, and the advent of Moses. Prophets with their predictions and an unusual scene between God, Hope, and Charity usher in a charming dramatization of the legend of Joseph's flowering rod and his espousal of the Virgin Mary. There follow the Visit to Elizabeth, the Doubting of Joseph, &c., and the first day ends with

[1] This is the date of the copy; the play itself was probably earlier. Ed. É. Roy, *Mystère*, pp. 73* ff. See also E. Streblow; Jeanroy, *JS*, N.S., iv (1906), 476–92, *RLR*, xlix (1906), 220–9, and *Rom.* xxxv (1906), 365–78; E. Stengel, *ZFSL*, xxix² (1906), 165–90; and Frank, *PMLA*, xxxv (1920), 479.

a dance of Herod's daughter, the death of John the Baptist, a scene in limbo showing the souls who await Christ's coming, and finally the Temptation of Jesus.

The second day proceeds along more familiar paths with the Public Life, the Last Days, the Resurrection, Appearances, and Ascension. At the end it is the Risen Christ who, after silencing the doubts of Thomas, invites the singing of the *Te Deum laudamus*. But even in this part of the play details not encountered before are to be found, for example in the scenes dramatizing the summoning of the Apostles, the curing of the sick, the council of the Jews, in the development of Judas's role, and in the incidental characters and the various *diableries*.

Allegorical and original names appear throughout. In Lucifer's train, for example, are Orgueul, Despit, and Dame Oyseuse. Esperance and Charité are daughters of God (though the four daughters of Psalm lxxxv. 10, so necessary to later plays—Mercy, Truth, Righteousness, and Peace—are absent). Sinagogua disputes with Ecclesia who is accompanied by Innocencia and Temperantia. We find priests named Damp Godiber and Damp Brun; two maidens of Jerusalem (present on both days) are called Sarrom and Plaisance; the shepherds and their wives bear names like Josseret, Menecier, Guarin, Hersen, and Flamberge; Herod's daughter is Esglantine; the wife of the smith who forges the nails is Grumaton, and various minor characters have whimsical patronymics like Cirinet, Goguery, Doucet, Beric, Mirofflet, Gonbault, &c.

Realism and comedy, sometimes descending to farce,[1] conspicuously brighten this play and make it much livelier than some of its successors. The individual scenes are relatively short and the humorous elements have been artfully introduced to effect transitions and leaven the more serious portions without disrupting the flow of the action. The text, indeed, is remarkably well knit. In part this has been accomplished by the appearance and reappearance of some of the same minor characters. Named as they are, these messengers, Jews, daughters of

---

[1] Such are the scenes involving Canaan (confused with Ham) who turns into Rusticus and the coarse scenes between Rusticus and his family which punctuate the text at intervals. Cf. 1157 ff., 2224 ff., 5513 ff. The *diableries* are also numerous and entertaining.

Jerusalem, shepherds, torturers, Roman soldiers, and the rest also create an impression of individual personalities.

Combined with its free use of realism and comedy the Semur text introduces a new note of pathos. The sufferings of the Virgin Mary accompany those of her Son, and add to the tragic implications of her role. Her maternity becomes human as well as divine. This more emotional portrayal of the Mother of God marks a new spirit rather than the consummation of an old one and seems to derive, directly or indirectly, from the *Dialogus Beatae Mariae et Anselmi* which exerted a tremendous influence not only on other theological works such as the *Meditations* of Pseudo-Bonaventura, but on practically all the later narratives of the Passion. Apparently from the *Dialogus* also comes a new and more harrowing conception of the manner of the Crucifixion. Older writers assumed that Christ met His death on a cross previously raised (*sublime*), but later commentators prefer to believe that He was nailed to the cross while it lay on the ground (*humi*) and that the recumbent cross was then raised into position. With this conception the scene of the Crucifixion could be even more gruesomely portrayed, the executioners pulling, stretching, and cursing while the Virgin suffered with her Son, the other Marys uttered their lamentations, and the audience winced at each hurt.[1]

The lighter scenes, certain realistic interpretations, and the conscious integration of the whole text seem to be the work of a skilful author (or redactor) who did not hesitate to adopt material from his predecessors. Thus lines reminiscent of the old narrative *Passion des Jongleurs* and the earlier Palatine and Autun texts can be recognized and one or two short scenes recall lines in the Ste Geneviève *Passion*.[2] In general, however,

[1] For the *Dialogus* see Migne, *PL*, clix, col. 271, and on the two traditions Duriez, *Théologie*, p. 417, and Mâle, *Fin*, pp. 19 ff. Among theologians St. Bernard and St. Bridget believe that the manner of the Crucifixion was *sublime* and Pseudo-Bonaventura, though contemplating both possibilities, also prefers to conceive of the cross as previously raised. Among the vernacular texts following this conception are the narrative *Passion des Jongleurs*, the *Passion du Palatinus*, and the *Passion d'Amboise*. On the other hand the *Dialogus*, the narrative *Livre de la Passion*, one of the manuscripts of the *Passion d'Autun* (by Biard), the *Passion de Semur*, and all the later French Passion plays portray the execution on a recumbent cross.

[2] See Roy, *Mystère*, p. 90*; Jeanroy, *JS*, N.S., iv (1906), 488 ff.; Creizenach, i. 258; Frank, *PMLA*, xxxv (1920), 479.

the dramatist exhibits both daring and originality not only in the conception of his whole vast project but in the development of its individual parts.

Moreover, the variety of his versification reveals an accomplished technician. His verse structure is far more complex and subtly adapted to its purpose than was at first supposed.[1] Lines of four, six, eight, ten, and twelve syllables hurry or retard the action, give it vivacity or high seriousness. Lyrics and stanzaic forms as well as the four-syllabled cue-line frequently occur. Only by the absence of single lines divided between two speakers does the poet seem to betray a certain timidity.

LA PASSION D'ARRAS

Contrasting with the relatively short and lively *Passion de Semur* is the much longer and more serious *Passion d'Arras* attributed to Eustache Mercadé (or Marcadé).[2] Mercadé was famous as one of the great rhetoricians of his day, a man highly esteemed both as theologian and poet. A bachelor in theology and doctor of laws, sometime official of the Abbey of Corbie and dean of the faculty of ecclesiastical law in Paris, he died in 1440. Our play is plausibly assigned him chiefly because it is followed in the same manuscript by the *Vengeance Jésus-Christ*, a play, similar in tone to the *Passion*, which is signed by Mercadé, and because various minor characters in both plays bear the same names.

Though the *Passion d'Arras* with its 25,000 lines is more than two and a half times as long as the *Passion de Semur* and took four days for its performance instead of two, the action covers only the history of Jesus. The first day is devoted to His Birth and Childhood, the second to the Public Life, the third to the Passion, and the fourth to the Resurrection and Ascension. Mercadé apologizes for the length of his play which suggests that this may have been unusual in his time. Actually his

[1] Cf. Jeanroy, *RLR*, xlix (1906), 220 ff. Mistakes of the copyist and of the modern editor as well as the changing rules of versification in the fifteenth century and a text designed only for popular oral presentation must be held responsible for many irregularities in the surviving version. Chatelain, *Recherches sur le vers français*, takes many of his examples of peculiar rhymes from the *Passion de Semur*.

[2] Ed. J.-M. Richard. Cf. plates ix–xxxviii in Cohen, *Théâtre en France*, vol. i. On the attribution to Mercadé see Thomas, *Rom.* xxxv (1906), 583 ff.; Roy, *Mystère*, p. 275; P. Champion, *Histoire poétique du xvᵉ siècle*, ii. 153–6.

prolixity detracts somewhat from his accomplishment, which merits praise for originality, if not for artistry.

Rhetorician, logician, and theologian that he was, Mercadé realized the advantage of an architectural structure capable of giving the drama of the Incarnation and Redemption coherence and unity. He frames his play within the so-called *Procès de Paradis*. At the beginning the Trinity is in paradise and God is shown enthroned, surrounded by a great multitude of angels and archangels, some playing music, others kneeling before Him. Justice, sword in hand, stands up straight beside the throne while Truth, Wisdom, Charity, and Mercy kneel among the angelic hosts. Mercy pleads for the release of the human race from the consequences of Adam's sin, Justice insists that on the contrary man should be eternally damned, while Truth asks whether punishment, however great the crime, must endure for ever. They call upon Lady Wisdom to arbitrate the question before God, and Charity adds her pleas to those of Mercy, Truth, and the archangel Gabriel. God consents to let His Son save the human race and Gabriel is dispatched to Nazareth to tell the Virgin Mary that she will bear the King of Glory destined to redeem man from his captivity. Thus motivated the great drama proceeds to its conclusion, when Jesus, His pilgrimage and martyrdom accomplished, returns to His Father in paradise and the three virtues, Mercy, Justice, and Truth, kiss and embrace while the celestial hierarchy, exhorted by Gabriel, sing and make joyous music to celebrate the reconciliation and to give thanks and praise to the Trinity.[1]

Mercadé, like many of his predecessors, uses a *Prescheur* to speak prologues and epilogues. The prologues are little sermons, complete with Latin texts, but usually summarize the events

[1] The so-called *Procès de Paradis*, or theme of the Four Daughters of God, derives ultimately from Psalm lxxxv. 10: 'Mercy and Truth are met together; Righteousness and Peace have kissed each other.' Various commentators, notably Hugh of St. Victor, Bernard of Clairvaux, and Bonaventura, followed by writers like Grosseteste and Deguilleville, modified and developed this theme. Deguilleville is credited with first using it as a framework in his *Pèlerinage de Jésu-Crist* and with introducing Sapience as arbitrator. So far as we know Mercadé first introduced the theme into drama, though he owes to Deguilleville his most striking additions to the old allegory, i.e. the use of the *Procès* as a framework and the addition of the roles of Sapience and Charité. See Hope Traver, *The Four Daughters of God*, and A. Lângfors in *Notices et extraits*, xlii. 1932.

about to be witnessed in each day's performance and suggest their theological interpretations.[1] The shorter epilogues invite the spectators to return next day with hints of what they will see, apologies for any inadequacies they may have discovered, and prayers for their happiness and welfare. These prologues and epilogues, like the *Procès de Paradis*, give the text a kind of unity, but the initial sermons resemble the arguments of the Virtues in sometimes proceeding to a wearisome length. Many other prolix speeches, too, would probably tax the patience of a modern audience.

Nevertheless the *Passion d'Arras* contains details that are still good theatre. Some of the popular scenes present delightfully realistic touches. The lamentations of the Jewish mothers are truly affecting, the shepherd scenes have a fresh charm, and the farewell to *la terre de Judée*, as Notre Dame turns to leave her old home, moves one by its pathos. Magdalen's characterization contrasts favourably with that in the earlier plays: no woodenly repentant sinner like her predecessors, Mercadé's Magdalen is a *fille de joie* who loves pleasure for its own sake, wants to enjoy her youth in gaiety, pretty clothes, and song; she spurns money and offers her fair body—*les mamellottelles poinnans* and all the rest—from sheer wantonness. Indeed her penitence seems to stem more from failure to attract prospective lovers than from memory of her brother's resurrection at the hand of Jesus.[2]

Mercadé's versification is careful, if not inspired. The octosyllabic couplets are unrelieved by other measures, although lines are occasionally lightened by being broken up and attributed to more than one speaker. On the whole this long play, despite the merits of a grandiose conception and of many excellent individual scenes, gives an impression of stiffness and verbosity which the technique of its poetry does nothing to relieve.

LE MYSTÈRE DE LA PASSION
BY ARNOUL GREBAN

Greban's play is the most famous of all the great French *Passions*, the most popular in its own day and in ours. Many

---

[1] On the second day it is John the Baptist who preaches the sermon-prologue and by exception there is no epilogue.

[2] See lines 9938 ff. On the early identification of Mary Magdalen with Mary the sister of Lazarus see Duriez, *Théologie*, p. 81, n. 157.

manuscripts of it survive and, as we have seen, from Mons come two revealing *Abregiés*, or directors' copies, of a text that in large measure follows Greban's. A handsome manuscript of the first day's contents has always remained in Le Mans and may be contemporaneous with the play itself, possibly even an author's copy, because of the elaborate directions it provides, especially for the music used in the play. Other manuscripts transcribe the long drama in whole or in part or incorporate portions of it in the works of later dramatists.[1] Together these manuscripts testify to the remarkable success of a play, written at the instigation of Parisians, yet performed complete, abridged, or in combination with other texts, not only in Paris but also far from the capital. Thus Abbeville asked for a copy of the piece as early as 1452; it was apparently played in some form at Le Mans, Amiens, and Mons; we know that parts of it, annexed to the beginning of the *Vieux Testament*, were performed at Troyes in 1490; and Jean Michel in his later *Passion*, which succeeded Greban's after the invention of printing and was often played in the sixteenth century, borrowed heavily from his predecessor.

'Maistre Arnoul Greban, notable bachelier en theologie', as he is called in one of the manuscripts of his *Passion*, probably was born and died at Le Mans, but he passed many important years of his life in Paris.[2] While studying theology he lived in the cloister of Notre Dame de Paris, playing the organ and training the choirboys of the cathedral, and it was there that he wrote both the words and music of his *Passion*. Champion paints a vivid picture of the man at this time. The role of choirmaster irked him, for the boys had to be kept virtual prisoners and the master

---

[1] Ed. by Gaston Paris and Gaston Raynaud with a valuable introduction. See also Champion, *Histoire poétique*, ii. 133–88; Cohen, *Livre de conduite*; Y. Rokseth, *La Musique d'orgue au xve siècle*, pp. 55–56; R. Lebègue, *Mystère*, and in *Rom.* lx (1934), 218. On the *Abregiés* see Chap. XVI above. The enigmatic figure of *Humain Lignaige* appearing in them (Cohen, op. cit., p. xxxii) is also found in the *Ystoire de l'humain lignage et Resurrection* played at Nevers in 1425 (Petit de Julleville, *Mystères*, ii. 644). Champion, op. cit., pp. 175 ff., Lebègue, and Rokseth discuss the Le Mans manuscript which was unknown to the original editors.

[2] Lebègue in *Rom.* lx (1934), 218 ff., shows that this MS. *A*, which the editors thought earliest and nearest the original, is actually a curtailed version of *BC* and that the reviser of *A* suppressed or abridged *rondeaux*, *diableries*, and various comic episodes.

had constantly to be an example and a disciplinarian, attending the while not only to their education but to their housing and provisioning. In 1452 Greban asked to have a key to the library and his request was granted on condition that he have one made at his own expense. It was doubtless in the library of Notre Dame that he consulted the theological works he used in fashioning his play.

Gradually he became more and more tired of his restricted life and in 1453 he petitioned for the privilege of having certain hours allotted him for his own devices. The chapter consented, but presently accused him of diverting funds assigned for the sustenance of the choirboys to the entertainment of his friends. Two years later, after having had a month's leave to visit Charles d'Anjou, he departed from Notre Dame. He became *bachelier en théologie* in 1456 and probably left Paris soon afterwards to go back to Le Mans, where he may have become canon of the cathedral and where he seems to have died before 1471, though these last two hypotheses have not been firmly established.[1]

Greban's play grew in the shadows and petty irritations of a cloistered existence, but it also took shape in an institution devoted to the worship of the Mother of God. It benefited from an excellent library and from the musical training of its author; it likewise shows signs, despite his competence, of considerable indebtedness to its predecessors; above all it reflects an overwhelming sympathy for the Virgin Mary. Written for performance in Paris, it was played there at least three times before 1473, perhaps by the Confrérie de la Passion, perhaps for some celebration of the cathedral of Notre Dame by members of that community. At various times in our own century, notably at the bi-millennial celebration of 1951, modern adaptations of Greban's work have been successfully performed 'sur le parvis de Notre Dame'.

This *Passion* has always been admired for its originality, its artistic qualities, the charm of its interspersed lyrics, the swiftness of its movement, the lightness and grace of its versification.

---

[1] His brother Simon is known to have been in the service of Charles du Maine in 1468, to have lived in a canon's house in 1471–2, and to have died about 1473. See Lebègue, *Mystère*, pp. 4–5.

The different manuscripts vary in length, but in its original form it seems to have had well over 30,000 lines. Except for the introductory scenes of a Prologue of some 1,740 lines—perhaps designed for readers (which is called a *creacion abregée* and which includes, besides the Creation, the quarrel between Cain and Abel and Seth's dispatch for the Oil of Mercy, but omits for the sake of brevity, as it says in line 1,720, the stories of Abraham, Isaac, and Jacob),[1] Greban's play covers in its four days approximately the same events as Mercadé's, and its prologues and epilogues, though shorter than his, follow similar lines. Like Mercadé's text it also invents numerous secondary characters and endows them with differentiating qualities. Moreover, it interprets the events that it represents, thus attempting to give meaning to biblical history, and, while using the same framework as Mercadé's play, it motivates the drama of the redemption even more skilfully. The architectural structure is reinforced by the presence of Satan at critical moments, the jubilation and depression of the spirit of evil accompanying in reverse the tragedy that ends in the triumph of the powers of righteousness.[2]

Greban prided himself on accepting no apocryphal material, but he defined 'apocryphal' in the manner of his time. His classical references, as well as the theological and didactic elements of the piece, reveal a man of wide learning. He knew, besides the evangelists and various earlier Passion plays, the *Gesta Pilati*, the *Dialogus* of the Pseudo-Anselm, the *Meditations* attributed to Bonaventura, the *Historia Scolastica* of Peter Comestor, the *Summa* of St. Thomas Aquinas, the *Postillae* of Nicolas de Lyre, the *Golden Legend*, a prose French *Passion* written in 1398 for Isabel of Bavaria, and perhaps a French version of the *Gospel of Gamaliel*.[3]

---

[1] It is possible that Greban wrote or collaborated in some of these scenes in the *Vieux Testament*. See Roy, *Mystères*, p. 303.

[2] One manuscript accounts for the *creacion abregée* by sayingt hat it is solely to show the difference between the sins of the devil and of man and why man's sin was redeemed, while that of the devil was not.

[3] On these see Roy, *Mystère*, pp. 97* ff., 207 ff., and 243 ff.; P. Champion, *Hist. poétique*, ii. 184; J. Wright, *Study*, especially the conclusions to each chapter which often correct statements by Roy and Champion. Cf. also on the sources used over and over in all medieval *Passions*, G. Duriez, *Théologie*, pp. 22 ff., and *Apocryphes*, *passim*.

Mercadé's outline and many of his original scenes directly inspired Greban who, however, knew how to break up, abridge, and simplify the verbosities of his predecessor. At times, indeed, Greban deliberately reverts to the traditions of the earlier plays when Mercadé introduces diffuse complexities. But Greban's indebtedness to Mercadé for the grandeur of his framework— the *Procès*—and for many another addition to the drama has long been established.[1]

Much of the charm of Greban's work resides in its tenderness and the delicacy of its feeling. The author also combines a sense of the dramatic with a unique poetic lyricism, and technically his accomplishment far surpasses that of any of his predecessors. The role of Notre Dame in this play is exceptionally beautiful. Theological works of Greban's day reflect a sense of the humanity of Christ's mother, but our author portrays her throughout with understanding and compassionate affection. Consider, for example, the scene at the end of the first day (lines 9,863–76) when Notre Dame finds her missing boy among the doctors. She has been pathetically distraught at losing him and is overjoyed when he is discovered. She praises his *doulx viaire*, his *bouchete*, his *rians yeulx*, and then she exclaims : 'Even if they are doctors and senators, no one shall keep me from kissing and embracing my child before them all !'

Greban's sense of the tragic conflict between the Virgin Mary's humanity and divinity, between her passionate maternity and her humility before God's will, is obvious everywhere. The author's lighter touch is reflected in the innocent grace of his pastoral scenes, especially in a scene where the shepherds in turn refuse to offer the *petit rois* their crook, dog, and dark bread, but give him gladly a new whistle, a little bell, a teetotum, a rattle 'qui dira clic clic a l'oreille', a 'beau kalendrier de bois / pour savoir les jours et les mois'. One has only to compare the famous scene in which Notre Dame makes her four last requests of her Son—a scene admired in their several ways by Sainte-Beuve and Petit de Julleville—with its probable source, the prose French *Passion* written for Isabel of Bavaria

---

[1] See Roy and Wright, op. cit., and Hope Traver, *Four Daughters*, p. 93. Greban introduces an extra, third *Procès* at the time of Christ's agony in Gethsemane and adds various arguments not used by Mercadé.

in 1398, to realize the sympathy and the balanced economy of diction with which Greban has tightened and strengthened the original:[1]

La premiere chose est que ce rachat qu'i[l] te plaist a faire de *l'umain lignage* tu le faces *sans mort souffrir* et endurer, consideré que tu le peulx faire. La seconde chose que je te requier si est, se autrement ne peult estre qu'il ne te conviengne mort et passion souffrir, au moins que celle mort soit *sans doulleur et affliction.* La tierce chose si est, se tu ne veulx ce fere, que ne seuffres mort douloureuse, fay moy ceste grace que *je meure* avant que je voye ta mort. La quarte si est, se tout [ce] ne me veulx octroyer, ne aucune des choses dessus dictes, a tout le moins fay pour celui temps que *je soye insensible comme une pierre,* et que je n'aye connaissance ne aucun sentiment de ta mort et passion. He! mon tresdoulx enffant, *je n'ay pas desservi,* s'il te plest, que au moings je n'aye par ta bonne grace et pitié *l'une de ces quatre choses* ou demandes qui *toutes te sont possibles.*

Roy, *Mystère,* p. 259

Pour oster ceste mort dolante
qui deux cueurs pour ung occiroit,
il m'est advis que bon seroit
que *sans vostre mort* et *souffrance*
se fist *l'humaine delivrance;*
ou que *s'il vous convient mourir,*
que ce soit *sans peine souffrir;*
ou se la peine vous doit nuyre,
consentez que *premier je muyre;*
ou s'il fault qe mourir vous voye,
comme pierre insensible soie.
Filz, humblement vous ay servy:
si *n'ay pas vers vous deservy*
chose par quoy doyez debattre
a m'ottroier *l'un de ces quatre,*
car *tous sont en vostre puissance.*

Greban, edition, p. 214,
lines 16,523 ff.

The poet's technical facility, his dexterity with rhymes and musical cadences, appears from the very opening lines of his prologue where octosyllabic stanzas rhyming *aabaabbbabba* flow from his pen. Throughout, *rondeaux, ballades,* and other lyrical forms embellish the dialogue and, instead of being separated from it, as in the *Miracles de Notre Dame,* they are woven tightly into the texture of the drama. The delightful scene among the shepherds (4,638 ff.) with its gay, complicated rhythms and

---

[1] See *Nouveaux lundis,* iii. 411–15 (Sainte-Beuve used the version of Greban found in Jean Michel's *Passion*) and Petit de Julleville, *Mystères,* i. 213. On the character of Notre Dame, cf. G. Paris, ed. p. xvii. None of these critics knew Greban's source for this scene, on which see É. Roy, *Mystère,* pp. 97*, 243, 259. For the reader's convenience the similar expressions in the source and play have been italicized.

harmoniously spaced refrains sounds as if it might have been danced as well as sung,[1] and some of the *diableries*, with their refrains broken in mid-line and assigned to two different speakers, suggest similar eurhythmic gambollings and cavortings (cf. 10,527 ff.). In fact throughout the play Greban shows complete mastery of the divided line as well as of an endlessly varied vocabulary and strophic structure. The important role of both songs and instrumental music in the various performances of the play is obvious from the manuscripts and, given the musicianship of the author, it is certain that the frequent singing and the playing of the organ before divine and angelic utterances must have stressed the solemnity of the occasion and contributed much to its value as entertainment.

MICHEL'S *PASSION* AND THE MERCADÉ-GREBAN-MICHEL TRADITION

Jean Michel, called 'tres eloquent et scientifique docteur maistre Jehan Michel' in our first printed text, appropriated much of Greban's play, even as Greban had used Mercadé's and as later compilers used them both. Actually in the early editions Michel is credited only with *addicions et corrections*, but after the invention of printing it was his *Passion* that frequently replaced the works of his predecessors. There exist many such editions (at least fifteen between *c.* 1490 and 1542), as well as many manuscripts based on them, although the play has not been re-edited in modern times. The earliest surviving edition says that the play was played at Angiers *moult triumphanment et sumptueusement* in 1486.[2]

Michel stretches the events of Greban's second and third days —with a short borrowing from the first—to four, and devotes some 30,000 lines to them, thus expanding individual speeches to wearisome length. Though he lacks the delicate restraint and artistic facility of Greban, he prepares his scenes with a feeling for their theatrical possibilities and betrays a highly developed sense of the dramatic. He displays no conscience about incorporating apocryphal material, no regard for historical facts, and

---

[1] In the production of Mons after a somewhat similar scene the shepherds sing and dance. Cf. Cohen, *Livre de conduite*, p. 74.

[2] See Petit de Julleville, *Mystères*, i. 218 ff., and ii. 437; Roy, *Mystère*, pp. 280 ff.; Creizenach, i. 265 ff.

seizes upon promising new themes wherever he can find them.
His Lazarus is a man of the world, shown with falcons and
hunting-dogs; his Mary Magdalen, among her flattering maids,
her paint-pots and perfumes, behaves like an elegant demi-
mondaine; his Pilate is a craven politician belatedly blaming
those to whom he has capitulated.[1] Mary Magdalen's dialogue
with her sister Martha as well as the short dialogue which
Michel adds to Greban's scene depicting Notre Dame's four
requests to her Son seem to reveal a writer influenced by the
strophes and antistrophes of classical literature. There is also a
Renaissance flavour about the names of many secondary characters invented by Michel. His play relies for its effectiveness
largely upon his sense of theatre, its legendary additions, com-
plications of plot and action, new roles, and new interpretations
of old themes.

Michel's *Passion* was immensely popular, and it, together
with Mercadé's and Greban's, formed the basis of numerous
spectacles. They were revised, cut, expanded, and combined with
other works in many ways. Michel's text seems to have become
more popular in Paris at a time when the others remained
influential outside the capital, but the process mentioned by
Jean Bouchet (see above, Chap. XVI, p. 174) continued everywhere: arrangers took from their *moule* what seemed best,
omitted what they did not like, and when they pleased added
something original of their own. Thus the Creation, the Nativity, or the Resurrection might be played independently, and
the contents of a single day or several days in the original might
form the basis of a whole long play.

A text embracing many scenes taken verbatim from Greban's
Passion as well as some scenes from the *Vieux Testament* was
played at Troyes in 1490.[2] A fusion of the works of Greban and
Michel was performed in Paris in 1507, according to its printed
version, and the playing of its 65,000 lines occupied six days.[3]

---

[1] On Pilate in the medieval drama see Arnold Williams, *The Characterization
of Pilate in the Towneley Plays*.

[2] This text is notable for marginal directions in a late hand introducing a comic
Fool's part. Petit de Julleville, *Mystères*, ii. 58 and 411 ff.

[3] Ibid. ii. 439. In studying the late plays, however, it is well to remember that
the word *journée* may not always correspond to the playing-time as it did in the
earlier mysteries.

Many other redactions and arrangements of these texts survive, notably two very long, late ones associated with Valenciennes, the performance of which took, respectively, twenty and twenty-five days. The attribution of one of these to the rhetorician Jean Molinet has been both proposed and rejected, and Roy suggests that, though the longer play may have been performed at Valenciennes, the destination of the shorter was Douai.[1] In any case a contract of 1547 from Valenciennes contains valuable information concerning the organization of great spectacles like these (cf. above, Chap. XVI, p. 171), and the plays themselves are in the main merely differing compilations of the works of Mercadé and Michel with additions from the *Vieux Testament* and from an anonymous *Conception* based largely on the first day of Greban's *Passion*.

OTHER LATE PLAYS

Certain texts also exist that bear no relation to the Mercadé-Greban-Michel tradition. Thus a *Resurrection* which Vérard, battening on Michel's reputation, repeatedly printed as his but which is surely not by Michel and may be by Jean du Prier, was played before René d'Anjou in 1456 as a sequel to a performance in 1446 of a lost *Passion* possibly written by the same author.[2] The fragmentary *Passion d'Amboise* had a great success in its vicinity and seems in certain scenes, notably that of the Crucifixion and that in which Judas counts his thirty pieces of silver one by one, to return to the earlier traditions of the *Passion des Jongleurs* and the Palatine *Passion*.[3]

L'Incarnation et la Nativité played in the market-place of Rouen at Christmastime, 1474, also represents an independent effort, and the single ancient edition carefully indicates its sources and describes its staging. The sources, cited in Latin in the margins, show that the anonymous author most frequently used, in addi-

---

[1] See Dupire, *Rom.* xlviii (1922), 571; Lebègue, *Rom.* lix (1933), 438; Lebègue, *La Tragédie religieuse en France*, pp. 29–30; Roy, *Mystère*, pp. 310 ff., and Greifswald dissertations by A. Kneisel, H. Schreiner, K. Mokross, O. Schaab, and B. Koeppen. On the vignettes of the Valenciennes MS. see above, Chap. XVI, p. 171, n. 1.

[2] See Creizenach, i. 260, n. 1; Roy, *Mystère*, p. 313.

[3] Ed. Picot in *Rom.* xix (1890), 264; Roy, *Mystère*, pp. 313 ff. Cf. above, pp. 127, 178. On the Provençal *Passion* of the Didot MS. see the edition by William P. Shepard, *SATF*, 1928, and on other southern texts Roy, *Mystère*, pp. 319 ff.

tion to the scriptures, the works of Peter Comestor and Nicolas
de Lyre and the *Golden Legend*. But he follows liturgical precedent for his *Prophetae* and explicitly states concerning the speech
of the Sybil: these verses are in the sermon that Augustine
made 'contra Judeos et incipitur sic, Vos, inquam, convenio,
o Judei' (edition, i, p. 24). Unusually detailed rubrics set forth
such matters as 'l'ordre comment estoient faictes les establies:
Premierement, vers Orient, Paradis ordonné comme il est
dessus dit au feuillot vingt neufieme . . .'.[1] The action is divided
between paradise, Nazareth, Jerusalem, Bethlehem, Syria,
Rome, hell, and limbo, and we are told where the seventy-
eight characters involved are to be stationed. Some of these
places contain more than one *establi*, for instance at Nazareth
there were 'la maison des parens Nostre Dame, son oratoire, la
maison de Elizabeth en montaigne'. In fact there were twenty-
five *establis* in all, besides six separate scaffolds for the prophets.
Paradise adjoined the Holy Land; hell, with an entrance represented by the jaws of a dragon that could open and close, was
placed next to Rome; and limbo, fashioned to look like a prison,
formed part of hell. In one stage-direction (ii. 247) we learn that
the devils are to cry out and make a terrible noise, aided by
drums and *autres tonnerres fais par engins*; that they are to hurl
serpents and flaming brands, that fire is to issue from the jaws,
eyes, and ears of hell, that after this scene hell is to close up
with the devils inside and that angels are then to appear at the
crib, adoring Jesus.

The events of the play were covered in two days and in about
12,800 lines. It begins with the prophecies of Balaam, the prophets, and the Sybil, uses the dispute between the Four Daughters of God, and emphasizes the idolatry of the pagans and
the many wonders accompanying Christ's birth. The first day
ends with the Annunciation, the Doubting of Joseph, the
angel's explanation to him, his return to Mary and her forgiveness of him. The second day opens with a scene in Rome showing Octavian's decision which in turn motivates Joseph's
departure for Bethlehem; it terminates with Octavian sacri-
ficing to Notre Dame at the order of the Sybil. Many shepherd
scenes enliven the second day and these *pasteurs* are individually

---

[1] Ed. Pierre Le Verdier, 3 vols., 1884–6. See ii. 473 ff., and also i. 64, 86, 106, &c.

named and also designated as *maistre*, *prudent*, *fol*, and *niais*. They furnish some comedy and frequently sing—at one point the manuscript reads (edition, ii. 130): 'Adonc chantent tous ensemble Requiescant in pace, ainsy qu'il est noté en icelle pagee'—and the scene of their adoration of the Child is very fully developed. The conversation between Joseph and Mary just before the Birth has an appealing quality: in a series of stanzas Joseph complains that the manger is an unsuitable birth-place for a king and after each Notre Dame simply replies, 'Il plait a Dieu que ainsy se face.'[1] Topical allusions to Paris and Rouen animate a *diablerie* that follows the fall of the idols at the Birth when Lucifer asks for news of these idols. 'Mars', says one of the devils, 'still reigns in Paris in the famous Mommartre which has received its name from him' (ii. 230). In general, the versification and other literary qualities of the play are feeble— there is an especially unfortunate tendency to indulge in tire-some tirades on a single rhyme—but the author manages at times to introduce vivid dramatic contrasts and to approach his subject with imagination and humour.

Two plays concerned with the *Vengeance de Nostre Seigneur Jhesucrist sur les Juifs par Vespasien et Titus*, one of them (of *c.* 14,000 lines divided into three days) by Mercadé and the second anonymous (printed often by Vérard, Trepperel, and others from 1491 on), present signs of some relationship. Oldörp concludes that the anonymous version copies Mercadé's directly at times, but also reworks and expands it independently.[2] This second play, which occupied four days and some 22,000 lines in the telling, reveals the punishments visited on the Jews because of the Crucifixion. It ministers to the sadistic impulses of an audience in a series of massacres and unspeakable physical horrors: Nero has his mother killed and her body opened in his presence; a starving woman devours her own child; Jewish soldiers swallow their gold to keep it from falling into the hands of the Romans who, however, disembowel their victims to recover the loot. A 'meneur du jeu ou un predicateur, lequel

---

[1] See edition, ii. 138 ff.; this scene is also in Petit de Julleville, *Mystères*, ii. 434.

[2] On these two texts, unedited in modern times, see B. Oldörp, *Untersuchungen*; J.-M. Richard, *Mystère de la Passion . . . d'Arras*; P. Champion, *Histoire poétique*, ii. 153; A. Thomas, *Rom.* xxxv (1906), 583; Petit de Julleville, *Mystères*, ii. 185, 415, and 451.

on veult, prononce l'epilogue et résume le mystère et la moralité qu'il faut en tirer'. For a modern audience the *moralité* of this orgy of hatred and cruelty would be difficult to stomach. We know, however, of at least twelve performances of a *Vengeance Jésus-Christ* between 1396 and 1540.[1]

A phenomenally long play of 61,908 lines, said to have taken forty days to perform in the version of 1536 played at Bourges, is the *Actes des Apôtres* attributed either to Simon Greban, perhaps aided by his brother Arnoul, or to Jean du Prier, and dated between 1452 and 1478.[2] The earlier Ste Geneviève collection contains legends of the martyrdoms of some of the disciples, but the nine books of the *Actes* include stories about all the apostles except Judas and John and add to them legends concerning Matthias (who, of course, succeeded Judas), Stephen, Paul, and Barnabas. In the Middle Ages apocryphal accounts of the lives and martyrdoms of the disciples circulated widely through the *Golden Legend* and Abdias's popular *Historia*.[3] Our play not only weaves them together deftly but also sets them off against a tapestry of putative historical events. Intermingled with the saints' lives are many *diableries* and scenes depicting the Ascension, the Descent of the Holy Spirit, the deaths of Tiberius, Caligula, Herod, and Nero, the death, burial, and assumption of the Virgin Mary. The disciples go to their far-flung posts, convert Ethiopians, Indians, Armenians, Greeks, Babylonians, Scythians, &c., perform prodigious miracles of healing and resuscitation, and eventually suffer various hideous forms of martyrdom. Humorous touches abound especially in the *diableries*: in the seventh book, for example, various devils decide that Christianity has made such conquests that nothing is left them but to live as mortals; Satan will be a usurer and the

---

[1] For additions to the eight performances listed in Petit de Julleville, *Mystères*, ii. 185 and 644, see J.-M. Richard, *Mystère . . . d'Arras*, pp. xxi–xxii. Obviously the 1396 performance at Nevers must have been of a text antedating the existing versions.

[2] See A. de Girardot, *Mystère des Actes des Apôtres*, and R. Lebègue, *Mystère*. See also Petit de Julleville, *Mystères*, i. 377; ii. 130 and 461, and above, Chap. XVI. Lebègue compares the five known editions, all of the sixteenth century, and shows the changes introduced during the Renaissance. The division of this play into nine books or parts was a matter of convenience in its transcription (cf. p. 188, n. 3 above).

[3] *De Historia certaminis apostolici libri decem, Julio Africano . . . interprete.*

others elect to be, respectively, a lawyer, jockey, sorcerer, messenger of love, and simoniac. There are nearly 500 roles in the play which moves swiftly from place to place and dramatizes an astounding amount of action. Plot succeeds plot with suspense and excitement at every turn, and there is tremendous variety in the hair-raising incidents.

Several contemporary accounts survive of the 1536 performance of this play at Bourges that impress the reader with the prodigality of effort and expense involved. The performance was in the ancient Roman amphitheatre which, to shield the spectators from sun and inclement weather, was covered with a canopy painted gold, silver, blue, *et autres riches couleurs*. The most distinguished persons of Bourges, laity and ecclesiastics, co-operated in the undertaking and the cathedral even granted participating members of its chapter dispensation from taking part in the regular offices of the church. An enormous procession before the play included officers of the town and all other participants dressed in their brilliantly coloured silk, satin, velvet, and jewel-strewn costumes; they went on foot or in carts from the Abbey of St. Sulpice to the amphitheatre accompanied by a fanfare of drums, fifes, and trumpets. The sumptuous properties and decorations, the elaborate mechanical devices employed to produce thunder, to simulate camels, serpents, ravening lions, flying owls, dragons spouting flames, and other performing animals, the *trucs* used to lower or raise persons and beasts or to conceal them in clouds, to burn and decapitate saints, permit magicians to fly, fountains to spout milk, ships to sail across the stage, all these and many more marvels were faithfully described by bedazzled contemporaries. Even the actors come in for praise, those *hommes graves* 'qui sçavaient si bien feindre par signes et gestes les personnages qu'ils representaient, que la plupart des assistants jugeaient la chose estre vraie et non feinte'.[1]

---

[1] Cited by Petit de Julleville, *Mystères*, ii. 133. On this performance and that by the Confrérie de la Passion of Paris in 1541 see Lebègue, *Mystère*, chaps. iii and viii. Cf. also Chap. XVI above. The Paris performances lasted thirty-five days and took place in the Hôtel de Flandres. In 1548 Parliament forbade *mystères sacrés* in the capital, but they continued to be played in the provinces, where they were attended by the common people, the bourgeoisie, and the lower clergy (see Lebègue, op. cit., p. 231).

References in the fifteenth and sixteenth centuries to performances of the *Vieux Testament* probably allude to performances of individual plays rather than of the whole vast disparate
compilation which survives.[1] No manuscripts of the entire text
are known but at least three editions of it were made between
c. 1500 and 1542, and separate parts of the whole, such as *Le
Sacrifice d'Abraham*, *La Vendition de Joseph*, and *L'Hystoire de Ste
Susanne*, appear in individual early printings. The compilation
is not divided into *journées*, though there are at times definite
indications of pauses or breaks; the length of the individual episodes varies greatly; and connexions between some of them are
uncertain or non-existent. It would seem, therefore, that the
surviving text is a collection of plays by different authors, for-
tuitously assembled by early printers, and that though some of
these pieces might have been performed together, the whole
does not present any intrinsic unity.

The earliest edition tabulates or indexes the work as having
forty episodes, but these do not correspond to divisions of
playable length. The vast expanse of 49,386 lines contains a long
compilation (36,535 lines) of scenes extending from the Creation
to the Visit of the Queen of Sheba, which is followed by six
short plays, clearly defined as such, about Job, Tobias, Susannah
and Daniel, Holofernes and Judith, Esther, Octavian and the
Sybils (these six together contain only 12,851 lines). Obviously
a group of players or a *meneur de jeu* might extract from this
material whatever stories suited their purposes. Some of the
scenes of the long compilation originally developed within the
liturgical drama, some form part of the more comprehensive
Passion plays, but others represent accretions to a well-established tradition. In any case the whole work does not seek to
dramatize Old Testament history in orderly fashion and the
unequal proportions allotted various episodes—for example,
the detailed treatment of the stories of Abraham and Joseph

---

[1] Ed. by J. de Rothschild, *SATF* (1878–91) in 6 vols. from the earliest print
of *c.* 1500. We know of performances referred to as of the *Vieux Testament* in
Abbeville (1458), Paris (1500, 1542), Lyons (1538 and probably later), Meaux
(1547), Draguignan (1557), and mention is frequently made of individual plays
that may be parts of the whole, a Murder of Abel, a Sacrifice of Abraham, a Daniel,
Esther, Job, Jonas, Joseph, Susannah, and Tobias (Petit de Julleville, *Mystères*,
ii. 180 ff.).

versus the barely mentioned story of Samson—must be attributed not only to the evolution of this particular text, but also to the fact that Church usage stressed certain subjects at the expense of others. Throughout the Middle Ages, as we observed in Chapter VIII above, the drama, like vernacular literature, painting, and sculpture, tended to represent scenes that were emphasized by the liturgy.

Different parts of the *Vieux Testament* vary so much in prosody, language, and literary value that it is generally agreed that different authors must be responsible for them.[1] The characterization of the same person as well as the form of his name may change from one portion to another. Some parts seem tiresome and flat: the Adam and Eve episodes, for instance, are much less animated than those in the old *Mystère d'Adam*, and the Judith play, despite the potentialities of the story, is crude and prolix. On the other hand, the Cain and Abel scenes contain many original and spirited passages. Cain's soliloquy (i. 2867 ff.), the expression of a contrite sinner certain of damnation, has a moving eloquence. In the long compilation certain economic questions are entertainingly discussed; they include such matters as the division of labour, the founding of cities, and the inequalities of social status among men. That the pathetic *Sacrifice of Isaac* and the exciting story of Joseph were admired in their own day, as well as by modern critics, is apparent from their appearance in separate editions. Throughout, much legendary and unhistorical material is introduced. Thus the wisdom of Solomon (vol. iv) is considerably enriched in the present work by many medieval proverbs, and the King judges not only between the two women who claimed the same child but also between three brothers unknown to the scriptures. The feast offered the Queen of Sheba by King Solomon has a medieval atmosphere much enlivened by trumpets, minstrels, singing, and jousting *contre la quintaine*. The famous debates between the Four Daughters of God, seemingly derived from Greban, furnish recurrent scenes in heaven that accompany and point up the scenes on earth and sometimes stress Old Testament occurrences as prefigurations of those in the New Testament. Not unexpectedly, there is great variety in the

---

[1] Cf. edition, vol. i, p. vi, and vol. iv, pp. xix and cxii.

versification. Passages of derivative, pedestrian facility may follow others of great beauty and originality. Lyrics of fixed form are introduced at intervals and much use is made of long, eloquently serious lines as well as of short, lively ones. Elaborate productions were evidently taken for granted: at the Creation trees and flowers had to spring from the earth, water had to be provided for the Deluge, fire for the destruction of Sodom and Gomorrah, and so on.

These plays from the Old Testament must have been very popular. A special performance by the Confrérie de la Passion was given in Paris in 1542 for the Duke of Vendôme who apparently had heard so much about the *Vieux Testament* that, unable to attend a regular performance, he requested that the *maistres entrepreneurs* be allowed to play for him after dinner.[1] To those acquainted with the more familiar scenes of the Passion plays, Old Testament history offered variety, colour, and an element of suspense, and certainly some of the episodes in the long compilation merit the success they achieved.

[1] Obviously only a short extract from the whole could have been performed then. Other evidence indicates that the usual performances of the play at this time began at one o'clock, ended at five, were permitted only on *festes non solennelles*, and that the playing of the entire compilation, if it were ever performed as a whole, would have occupied about twenty-five days. We know that at one time Parliament wanted to forbid the spectacle altogether but that the King permitted it on certain conditions. See edition, vol. i, pp. xiv–xv.

XVIII

Late Saint Plays

OF the numerous plays performed during the fifteenth and sixteenth centuries by guilds, towns, and societies in honour of their patron saints many manuscripts and early editions survive, as well as many records of others that have disappeared.[1] In general these saint plays follow hagiographical sources and tell of the early life and conversion of some saint, his preaching and the miracles performed by him, the sufferings he endured at his martyrdom, and the wonders associated after his death with his tomb and relics. The plays owe much not only to Latin and vernacular saints' lives and earlier saint plays, but also to the dramatized miracles of the Virgin Mary and to the universally popular Passion plays. The corporeal intervention of God, His Mother and their angels, the alternate rejoicing and despair of Satan and his demons, the humorous *diableries*, the terrible sufferings and prolonged torturings of the martyrs, the arguments and sermons that accompany conversions, the miraculous resuscitations of the dead and the prodigious cures of lame, halt, and blind, all these we have met before.

Some of the late saint plays are relatively short, others lasted many days and involved great numbers of roles. Some served small communities or unpretentious groups, others were played by the great Confrérie de la Passion in Paris. Some were written by unknown hacks, others by skilful professionals like Jean Molinet or Jean du Prier. Yet they all have in common their emphasis on plot and the special appeal of their protagonists for a selected audience. However stereotyped their characters and technique, these plays could make effective use of movement and suspense, of local piety and patriotism. To see in the flesh the guardian of one's guild throughout his life's vicissi-

---

[1] The most comprehensive survey of the late saint plays is in Petit de Julleville, *Mystères*. The Parfaict brothers analysed some and some have been the object of more recent studies. When the latter are not specifically mentioned below, see Petit de Julleville, op. cit., especially vol. ii, chap. xx.

tudes, to participate in the agony of a saint whose relics one
daily worshipped, to witness miracles being performed before
one's very eyes by the founder of one's monastery or by the
holy man from whom one's town took its name, these were
experiences calculated to hold the rapt attention of medieval
spectators. Moreover the lives of most saints presented dramatic
contrasts of emotion and an exotic diversity of social and geo-
graphical backgrounds that heightened the other elements of
their impressiveness. Nor were the authors of these plays averse
to spicing holiness with humour or legendary incidents with
contemporary realism. In short, many of the saint plays, despite
their shortcomings, were good theatre.

Jean Molinet's *Mystère de S. Quentin*, for example, presents
the youthful martyr who introduced Christianity into the
ancient town named after him, shows him first at Rome, questioning the pagan beliefs of his teacher Cato, next receiving
baptism at the hands of the Pope himself, and eventually leaving
Rome with eleven newly converted comrades to spread the
gospel abroad, where they all suffer martyrdom after submitting
to horrible atrocities. The play dates before 1465, since citations
from it appear in Molinet's *Art de rhétorique*. As might be expected, the rhetorician exhibits in it complete mastery of many
elaborate rhymes and complicated rhythms.[1]

A saint play notable for its humour is that devoted to the
conversion, flight, preaching, and miracles of St. Martin. After
his death the saint's relics possess such power that two beggars,
a blind man and a paralytic, fearing to lose their livelihood by
forcibly recovering their sight and use of limbs, try to escape,
but the relics of the saint overtake them and they are cured
despite themselves, belatedly giving thanks none the less. This
scene became a separate 'moralité joyeuse', *L'Aveugle et le
Boiteux*, when Andrieu de la Vigne expanded and reworked the
story of St. Martin in 1496.[2]

An involved play using 116 characters and three days in its
performance is Jean du Prier's *Mystère du Roy Avenir*, which

[1] Ed. by H. Chatelain. Cf. N. Dupire, *Jean Molinet*. Ascription of the play to
Molinet had been questioned, but Langlois plausibly restored it to him (*Rom.*
xxii [1893], 552–3).
[2] Cf. Petit de Julleville, *Mystères*, ii. 535 ff.

dramatizes the well-known story of the saints Barlaam and Josaphat. In one of the most admired scenes of the play Josaphat, who has been kept by his pagan father, King Avenir, completely ignorant of human misery so that he may not seek in Christianity the only true remedy against all the ills of the world, accidentally meets a leper, a beggar, and a wretchedly infirm old man. Josaphat's reaction to the sight of sickness, poverty, and approaching death is moving as he asks:

> Qu'esse a dire? fault-il mourir?
> Qu'esse a dire de ceste mort?
> Qu'esse a dire? fault-il pourrir?
> N'y a il quelque reconfort?

This scene is embedded in a multiplicity of colourful actions, battles involving the rulers of many oriental countries, the massacre of monks and hermits, the predictions of astrologers, the ruses by which Barlaam succeeds in entering Josaphat's tower, converting and baptizing him, the furious acts of revenge upon the Christians undertaken in return by King Avenir, the attempts of the King to lure his son back to paganism through the wiles of a magician and a beautiful young princess, &c. The famous narrative attributed to John of Damascus has been fully exploited by Jean du Prier and it may be assumed that his patron, René of Anjou, was well pleased with it, since in 1455 the King rewarded him with a pair of *esperons dorez* because of the *mystère* which, according to the prologue, was composed at René's request.[1]

The *Mystère de S. Genis* by Jean Oudin dramatizes a tale used later by Lope de Vega and by Rotrou, the tale of the mime, Genesius, who, performing before the emperor Diocletian, is about to mock the rite of baptism when he suddenly becomes converted to Christianity. Later he suffers a series of cruel tortures without swerving from his faith and is finally beheaded. From Oudin's medieval roots springs the prolonged *diablerie* in this play; the devils rejoice in the record of the mime's sins but break forth in abuse of the Mother of Jesus when they see the

---

[1] Cf. Lebègue, *Mystère*, pp. 6–7; Petit de Julleville, *Mystères*, i. 299–309, ii. 474; Max Hippe, *Le Mystère du Roy Avennir*. On sources and narrative versions see C. Appel's edition of Gui de Cambrai, *Balaham und Josaphas*, Halle, 1907, and E. C. Armstrong in *Elliott Monographs*, x, 1922.

record erased after the saint's conversion and martyrdom. The fifteenth-century manuscript is of considerable interest because it seems to have served for a performance of the play: it shows hard usage and various marginal notes reveal how the text could be cut, if desired.[1]

At least two plays about St. Barbara survive, as well as records of a dozen performances of plays about her.[2] The two surviving texts—one with only thirty-eight roles, the other with 100 roles that required five days for its performance—suggest some of the sources of her popularity. The longer play indicates, sometimes in Latin, sometimes in French, how the elaborate production was to be staged and how the scenery was to be transformed from one day to the next. Like other saints, Barbara protests against the teaching of her pagan masters (who, strangely enough, require her to read Boccaccio among many other authors). But it must have been the peculiarly sadistic treatment of the young virgin that aroused the emotions of the audience: bound to a stake, naked, she is beaten, burned, and her breasts are torn off; at the instigation of her own father she is rolled in a barrel studded with nails and dragged by the hair over a mountain before being finally decapitated. A *stultus* improvised quips and drolleries during the performance which was otherwise relieved by various amusing touches (in it, for instance, wives and young girls were reproached for faults as prevalent today as in the fifteenth century), but on the whole the play makes dreary reading with its succession of brutal episodes, its long theological disquisitions, and its unimaginative style.

Some of the saint plays bear obvious indications of the purpose for which they were written. A play about St. Didier, Bishop of Langres, was composed by a canon of Langres for the Confrérie de S. Didier of Langres.[3] St. Clement, Bishop of Metz, and St. Remy of Rheims seem to have generated local performances for the furtherance of their cults, and similarly

---

[1] Ed. by Mostert and Stengel in *AA*, xciii (1895). An acrostic at the end gives the name of the author and this must, of course, have been intended for the reader.

[2] Cf. P. Seefeldt, *Studien*; Petit de Julleville, *Mystères*, ii. 478, 486; and A. J. Denomy in *Mediaeval Studies*, i (1939), 148.

[3] Analysed at length in Petit de Julleville, *Mystères*, i. 231 ff.

the relics of Ste Marguerite and St. Christopher are probably responsible for the plays in their honour. Two differing manuscripts survive of a *Mystère de S. Crespin et S. Crespinien*, patrons of the shoemakers, and one of them states that it is from the 'confrarie monseigneur S. Crespinien fondée en l'eglise Nostre Dame de Paris aux maistres et aux compaignons cordouenniers'.[1] An inmate of the monastery of S. Bernard de Menthon wrote of his patron, showing how St. Bernard fled marriage to become a churchman, preached and converted sinners, how he conquered the demons who had attacked pilgrims on the site of the monastery he founded, and how he performed many miracles during his life and after his death.[2] A late St. Nicholas play was written for a society of lawyers,[3] and Gringore wrote his *S. Louis* for a guild of masons and carpenters. Two manuscripts survive of plays about St. Sebastian and one of them mentions a performance at Lanslevillard in Maurienne in 1567, whereas a play concerned with St. Vincent seems to have been written especially for performance before René d'Anjou, probably at Angers in 1471.

Some of the saints known to us from the Ste Geneviève collection reappear in later plays, notably SS. Stephen, Fiacre, Peter, and Paul. And many of the characteristics of the earlier saint plays survive in exaggerated form as time goes on. The realistic and comic incidents tentatively introduced in the Ste Geneviève collection become almost universal in the later saint plays, consciously added for their intrinsic value as entertainment, sometimes decidedly at variance with the simple faith underlying the original inspiration of the tales they dramatize. The plays about SS. Barbara, Didier, and Sebastian contain a fool's part; in the case of the St. Barbara play this was to be improvised, but in one of the St. Sebastian plays the role is inserted and is so irreverently conceived as to be censored in one of the surviving manuscripts.[4] Deaf men by their misunder-

[1] Ed. by Dessalles and Chabaille. Cf. Ostrowski, Greifswald diss., 1909. In this play the old four-syllabled cue-line is used and the influence of the *Miracles de Notre Dame* is apparent not only in technique but in plot: the Virgin Mary and her angels, Gabriel and Michael, take a prominent part in the action, appearing often to visit and comfort the martyrs and eventually to overcome the discomfited Satan and his demons.

[2] Ed. by A. Lecoy de la Marche.   [3] See Roy, *Études*, p. clii.

[4] In another St. Sebastian play *Rusticus ou le Villain* replaces the fool of this

standings provide amusement in the plays about SS. Vincent and Marguerite, and in other plays labourers, peasants, messengers, and devils with picturesquely revealing names help to alleviate the monotony of the endless sufferings attending martyrdom.

Quite different, however, from the plots concerned with early martyrs of the Church, is the story of the *Vie* (or *Mystère*) *de S. Louis.*[1] This play was written before 1472 and played in Paris by the Confrérie de la Passion. Over 280 characters are involved —two different actors played the part of the King in youth and manhood—and the action extends from the coronation and marriage of the young monarch through his war against England, the birth of his son Philip, the expedition to the Holy Land, the battles against the pagans, the King's capture and release, his pilgrimage to Syria, return to France, resolve to undertake a new crusade, arrival in Tunis, illness and death there, followed by the return of his body to France and the marvels wrought by his holy relics. Potentially a historical and realistic play, it nevertheless betrays its hagiographical sources by the emphasis placed on the role of the devils and the wonders worked by the saint after his death. These devils include one Penthagruel,[2] also known to the *Actes des Apôtres* before Rabelais immortalized him, and the topical remarks of the demons, together with the deformed French spoken by the English king and his court, reveal an amusing satirical intention on the part of the author. With a shift of stress this play might have become the kind of chronicle play so well known to us from the Elizabethan period, but even Gringore, writing his *Vie de S. Louis* in the sixteenth century, did not quite achieve this transformation, since, though he excluded all supernatural characters, he nevertheless ended his play with scenes depicting the miracles of the saint.[3]

and other plays and amuses the spectators by his crude and obscene sallies. See Petit de Julleville, *Mystères*, ii. 557–61.

[1] Ed. by Francisque Michel, 1871, for the Roxburghe Club. The title in the manuscript is *Vie*, in Michel's edition, *Mystère*.

[2] On the name Pantagruel see Lebègue, *Mystère*, pp. 242–3.

[3] Clovis, of course, is the hero of the thirty-ninth of the *Miracles de Notre Dame* and he reappears in the *Mystère de S. Remy*, but in both these plays the religious note everywhere predominates. Gringore's play is in vol. ii of the *Œuvres complètes*, ed. by Montaiglon et Rothschild.

XIX

Serious Non-Religious Plays of the Fifteenth Century

Two non-religious plays of the fifteenth century, rich in unrealized possibilities, remain to be considered, the anonymous *Mystère du Siège d'Orléans* and the *Istoire de la Destruction de Troye la grant* by Jacques Milet. The anonymous play connects in form and to a certain extent in spirit with the biblical and saint plays, but not in theme, for it is unique in being the only extant medieval dramatization in French of an almost contemporary event, an event probably experienced by the author. Milet, too, may lay claim to originality both in his choice of subject and in his development of that subject, and his play, though of medieval heritage, contains seeds due to ripen in the Renaissance.

LE MYSTÈRE DU SIÈGE D'ORLÉANS

In the *Siège d'Orléans*, Joan of Arc makes her initial appearance upon the stage. The play[1] is preserved in a single paper manuscript, now in the Regina collection of the Vatican but formerly in the library of Fleury, which was copied in the second half of the fifteenth century. The long text of 20,529 lines contains 140 roles, not counting characters appearing in groups, and it may have been performed in two days, though this is not definitely indicated by the manuscript. The unknown author was undoubtedly a citizen of Orléans and the tone throughout

---

[1] Published by Guessard and de Certain. Modernized extracts are to be found in Joseph Fabre's *La Délivrance d'Orléans*, pp. 141 ff., and in Lenient, *La Poésie patriotique en France*, pp. 389 ff., and selections with an English translation in Evans and Studer, *Saint Joan of Orleans*. The historical reliability is tested by Alfred Meyer, *Das Kulturhistorische in Le Mystère du Siège d'Orléans*. H. Tivier's *Étude* tried to establish Jacques Milet as its author, but Häpke, *Kritische Beiträge*, and other students of Milet's work, reject this attribution. Tivier's argument was largely inspired by the fact that Milet was a student at Orléans. Carl Becker showed differences of language between this play and Milet's *Istoire* and Häpke remarks that contemporary references to Milet are so frequent that they would surely mention the *Siège* if he had written it. See also Petit de Julleville, *Mystères*, ii. 576–82, and Hanebuth, *Ueber die hauptsächlichsten Jeanne d'Arc-Dichtungen*.

is one of local patriotism. The town, rather than Joan, is the protagonist and the playwright seems unconcerned about his heroine's fate. He ends his play with the raising of the siege (8 May 1429) and an invitation to institute a procession in honour of this victory every year on the anniversary of the town's deliverance. Joan's death in 1431 is therefore not in question.

Records survive of some sort of performances on the anniversaries of 1435 and 1439, but these seem to have been of *mystères mimés*. Could our play have developed from these dumb shows by the gradual addition of more and more speeches from year to year? This has been conjectured, but it seems more likely that the play replaced the earlier pageants, itself suffering various revisions in the course of time. The date of the surviving text is uncertain. Some authorities would put it before 1440, others after 1453, 1456, 1461, or even 1467. Since Gille de Rais, the prototype of Bluebeard, appears in a favourable light in the play, although he was put to death in 1440 because of abominable crimes involving children, it has been argued that the piece must have been written before his condemnation. On the other hand, Talbot's death is referred to, and he did not die until 1453. It has also been proposed that the play must have been written after 1456 when an *Enquête* rehabilitated Joan's family, or after the death of Charles VII in 1461, since a monarch would have objected to having his prayers and other intimate details of his life portrayed on the stage during his lifetime, or even after *c.* 1467 when the *Journal du Siège*, which parts of our play closely resemble, was compiled. It seems that the preponderance of evidence favours the later rather than earlier dates and that various discrepancies in the text merely reflect different stages in its composition. Evans and Studer plausibly conclude that the first part (lines 1–5,330) was written after 1439, possibly as late as 1470, and that the second part represents an interpolated reworking of an earlier version.

In any event the play is remarkably accurate, and the author never seems to sacrifice historicity to dramatic exegencies. He incorporates verbatim in prose Joan's famous letter to the English which has been preserved in many documents, and it has been proved that he knew at least three contemporary chronicles besides the *Journal du Siège*, with which he agrees so closely in parts of the play that at one time he was thought merely to have dramatized and versified it. Alfred Meyer indeed found the piece so reliable that he used it as a source in discussing the military usages, religious customs, and social life of the period.[1]

The fidelity of some of its characterizations is remarkable and all critics agree that this picture of Joan resembles her more closely than most subsequent portraits. Despite her visions, she appears as a practical, straightforward girl, simple, humble, and sensible. Her speeches ring true. The poet, Charles d'Orléans, is also lifelike, the man we know from his verses, gentle, never haughty. When the English break their promise to respect his land, he instantly wins one's sympathy by his behaviour under trying circumstances.

Throughout, the role of the supernatural, though medieval in spirit, is restrained and is made to serve the cause of history. The playwright makes good use of the dreams and prophecies so dear to poets of all times, but since he was writing after the events, there was no danger of these predictions being untrue. Sallebry (i.e. Salisbury), for example, meets a soothsayer who sees no future harm to his body, but advises him to look after his head. We know that his head was blown away. Similarly, it is prophesied that Glasidas (i.e. Glasdale) will not die from cannon or wound and will die without bleeding. He was drowned. St. Michael often descends from paradise to direct Joan's acts and it is he who bids her assume male attire, one of the counts against her at her trial. Other scenes in paradise effectively motivate the Maid's visions and the reasons for the raising of the siege of Orléans. In one of these scenes, after duly reproaching France for her many sins, God in His mercy grants the prayers of the Dauphin, and in another it is Notre Dame with two canonized bishops of Orléans beside her who successfully pleads with her Son to save the city.

Technically the playwright's skill was unequal to his ambition. Like his contemporary, Arnoul Greban, he adopts lines of

---

[1] A. Meyer, op. cit., concluded that details concerning the French are surely accurate and those concerning the English probably so, since the two countries varied little in such matters at the time.

different lengths, divides them between speakers at times, and he too likes crossed rhymes, triolets, and other fixed strophic forms. But he does not attempt the more elaborate kinds of stanzaic structure and shows little facility in handling even the simpler rhythms. Moreover, although his language, like his sentiments, can occasionally rise to a certain distinction, it is usually quite commonplace. On the other hand, our manuscript betrays much interest in the complicated staging and music required by the play. Detailed rubrics give directions for the manner in which the English are to set sail and disembark before the spectators' eyes, how great battles are to be fought and various parts of the town are to go up in flames. They also indicate exactly which instruments are to be played during the intermissions.

In sum, the originality of its theme, its patriotic tone, the undistorted portrait of Joan, the vivid battle scenes, its regard for veracity and concern for the music and staging of the performance, all make this play unusually interesting and largely compensate for its flat, dry style and for the imperfections of its verses.[1]

L'ISTOIRE DE LA DESTRUCTION DE TROYE LA GRANT, BY JACQUES MILET

From the number of manuscripts and early editions of *L'Istoire de la Destruction de Troye la grant*, by Jacques Milet, it would seem that the play was exceedingly popular, even though no certain records of its performance have survived. More than twelve manuscripts of the fifteenth and sixteenth centuries exist, about as many different editions dating between 1484 and 1544, and the 1544 edition states that the play had then been newly revised and 'reduite en la vraye langue françoys'. It contains over 27,000 lines and took four days to perform in its entirety,

---

[1] It must be remembered that the so-called imperfections of fifteenth-century versification often reflect the changing language of the day, a time when final consonants were becoming silent, the reduction of hiatus was taking place, &c., and that 'imperfect' verses destined for the popular usage of the stage might satisfy—or be readily made to satisfy—contemporary pronunciation. Cf. above, Chap. XVII, p. 179, n. 1. Of philological interest also are the transcriptions of the English proper names which show French linguistic predispositions of the period.

though parts, marked by the frequent playing of minstrels during pauses, could perhaps have been played separately.[1]

The play illustrates once again the perennial interest in the Trojan tale—and in Helen of Troy. Indeed the prologue reflects Milet's consciousness of this interest, for he says the tale has been told before 'en latin et en prose laye'. This prologue transfers to the stage a conventional opening of the romances : the author, wandering in a flowery meadow, espies a beautiful tree beside a spring. A shepherdess tells him that this is the tree of the lineage of France, a kind of genealogical tree; he digs towards its roots and finds the weapons of the Trojans from whom the French are descended. Then he bethinks him to write the history of Troy, but since, he says, others have told it in Latin and in *prose laye*, i.e. the vernacular, he has decided to tell it *par parsonnages seullement*.[2]

It is, of course, well known that a French versified form of the story was written in the twelfth century by Benoît de Sainte-More, a writer who lived at the Norman-French court of Henry II of England. His *Roman de Troie* (usually dated *c.* 1155–65 but possibly later) is a work of some merit, much of it apparently original, although he alleges his dependence on Dares and to a lesser extent on Dictys.[3] In the thirteenth century

---

[1] A reproduction of the first edition of 1484 was published by Stengel in 1883. See also T. E. Oliver, *Jacques Milet's Drama*, Gustav Häpke, *Kritische Beiträge*, E. Meybrinck, *AA*, liv (1886). On Guido delle Colonne see edition by N. E. Griffin, 1936, and E. B. Atwood and V. K. Whitaker, edition of *Excidium Troiae*. Creizenach and Petit de Julleville—and their opinion is echoed by Hofer's edition of Gröber's *Geschichte*, i (1933), 236-7—found no record of any performance, though the play was obviously destined to be performed. They concluded that it may have been too elaborate, especially since it was not religious in theme, to justify the effort and expense. Champion, *Histoire poétique*, i. 329, assumes that it was performed, and there is in F. J. Faber, *Histoire du théâtre français en Belgique*, i (1878), 13, a reference to an intended performance of '*l'histoire du Siège de Troie*' at Tournai in 1472 which may or may not have been our *Destruction*.

[2] See the Prologue, lines 277 ff.:

> Et pource que bien je savoye
> Que aultreffois a esté escripte
> En latin et en prose laye
> Si ay voulu eviter reddicte
> Si ay proposé de la faire
> Par parsonnages seullement.

[3] It was ultimately from two mediocre writers of the early Middle Ages, Dares and Dictys, and naturally not from Homer, that the story became known to medieval authors. Dares and Dictys both wrote a lifeless Latin prose, but they

(partly in 1272, partly in 1287) Benoît's poem was translated into poor Latin by Guido delle Colonne (Guido de Columnis), who never mentions the work that he slavishly followed but, like his source, depends upon Dictys and Dares as his authorities. Now it has been conclusively proved that Milet followed Guido's version, rather than Benoît's.[1] Some of the manuscripts of the play state that it was translated from Latin, and Milet himself refers to the tale as having been told in Latin as well as in *prose laye*. However, his knowledge of vernacular versions and his use of the words *par parsonnages* suggest that he, like the author of the *Estoire de Griseldis*, may merely be dramatizing some French translation of his ultimate source. Various different French translations of Guido are known and it seems at least possible that Milet may have used one of these.[2]

The facts about Jacques Milet are furnished by the colophons of the manuscripts and early editions of his play and by other authors' references to him. Born about 1425, he died in Paris in 1466, and his death at so early an age became the subject of several *Complaintes* composed in his honour. He began writing his *Istoire* in 1450 when he was 'estudiant es loys en l'université d'Orléans' and finished it as *maistre* by 1452, the date of its epilogue. Simon Greban calls Milet a *notable homme et scientifique* and other poets group these two together as men of great distinction. Octovien de Saint-Gelays, too, was among his admirers.[3]

claimed to have been eyewitnesses of the events they described, which gave them considerable standing. Benoît's dependence cannot always be verified from the texts that survive, so that it is sometimes assumed he used expanded versions now lost. But in any case he himself greatly expanded his sources.

[1] See Oliver, op. cit.

[2] Doutrepont, *La Littérature française à la cour des ducs de Bourgogne*, pp. 171–6, mentions some of these versions and so does Pierre Champion in his *Histoire poétique*, i. 329. But neither suggests the possibility that Milet may have given one of them dramatic form. Doutrepont says that in 1467 the library of Philippe le Bon possessed seventeen manuscripts of the Troy story, including two manuscripts of Milet's play and various French translations of Guido's work. The manuscripts of the dukes of Burgundy are now in Brussels and the British Museum, and the Brussels catalogue of the Bibliothèque royale de Belgique, *Section des manuscrits (Bibliothèque de Bourgogne)*, [1832]–42, ii. 201–2, as well as H. L. D. Ward's *Catalogue of Romances in the British Museum*, 1883, i. 54 ff., lists a number of French translations of Guido—one dated as early as 1380—which Milet could have known.

[3] See Piaget, 'Simon Greban et Jacques Milet', *Rom.* xxii (1893), 230–43, and

Milet is praised by modern critics for seeking material in classical fields at a period when, almost without exception, the serious drama concerned itself only with religious themes. He displays originality also in his departures from his source. His characterizations are especially happy. Like Guido he treats the Greeks harshly and his patriotic sympathies are entirely with the Trojans, reputed ancestors of the French, but he goes further than Guido in making Achilles a weakling, coward, and traitor who is ignominiously beaten with a stick. Helen's lament at the death of Paris and Priam's long speech mourning over his son Hector reveal authentic emotions. Though Milet's Greeks and Trojans for the most part mirror fifteenth-century Frenchmen, he makes some effort—not altogether successful—to picture their times and especially their religious customs as he imagines them.

Yet for all its faint hints of the coming Renaissance, the play is essentially medieval. The Troy story itself had appealed in similar fashion to the earlier Middle Ages, and the religious drama contributed much to Milet's technique of telling it *par personnages*. In the use of many mansions for its staging it recalls the usual medieval *mise en scène*, and the minstrels who perform during its pauses fill very much the same role as the angelic musicians of the biblical and saint plays. The versification is elaborate and, like Greban's, includes a great variety of rhythms. Like Greban, too, Milet experiments with many types of stanzas, makes effective use of *rondeaux* and other fixed forms, and indeed seems to have tried almost every rhythmic combination prevalent in his day.

Obviously the material for a serious, non-religious drama was available. Lay and historical themes had been used not only in the two plays just considered but in the earlier *Miracles de Notre Dame*, in the *Estoire de Griseldis*, in some of the morality plays, and in the plays about the royal St. Louis. Records of other performances that suggest a non-religious theatre have come down to us, though the plays referred to have been lost. Some of these may have been modified *mystères mimés*. We hear,

Häpke, op. cit., pp. 1-4. In 1459 Milet wrote an allegorical poem called *La Forêt de Tristesse* which Piaget recovered for us.

for instance, of *La Fieste des enfants Aymery de Narbonne* performed at Lille in 1351, *Le Pas Saladin* in Paris *c.* 1389, a *Mystère
de Jules César* at Amboise in 1500. However, a Narcissus play
and various moralities with secular characters survive.[1] It must
also be remembered that comedy early played a large role in
such a play as Bodel's *Jeu de S. Nicolas* and that from the thirteenth century on, comic and farcical episodes appear not only
in the religious plays but as independent dramatic offerings. In
their isolated form we may somewhat arbitrarily call them
comedies and for convenience treat them separately, but since
chronologically they existed side by side with the serious religious plays they too furnished sources from which a serious
non-religious drama might have sprung.[2]

[1] The Narcissus play is edited by Hilka, *ZRP*, lvi (1936), 275–321, who classi-
fies the text as a morality. On the lost plays see Creizenach, i. 376–7. On *Amery de
Narbonne* see Petit de Julleville, *Mystères* ii. 4 and on the *Pas Saladin* cf. L. H.
Loomis, *Speculum* xxxiii (1958), 251.

[2] Cf. Chap. X above, and Chaps. XX, XXIV below.

XX

The Beginnings of Comedy in France

As suggested elsewhere in this book, the advent of formal comedy in France cannot be regarded as an isolated phenomenon. Scholars have been inclined to seek origins in the potentially comic elements of the liturgical drama, or in the fun furnished by jongleurs at entertainments and later introduced by them into the religious plays, or in Latin school-pieces like the *Babio* and *Pamphilus*, or even in such folk festivities as May-games, dances, and mummings of various sorts. But all these proposals are open to objections and it seems best to consider our earliest comedies themselves before generalizing.[1]

In approximately chronological order these are Bodel's *Jeu de S. Nicolas*, *c.* 1200, the anonymous *Courtois d'Arras*, before 1228, the anonymous and undatable *Garçon et l'Aveugle* (possibly 1266 or 1282), Adam le Bossu's two plays, *Le Jeu de la Feuillée* (1276 or 1277) and *Robin et Marion* (between *c.* 1282 and 1288). Now, what are these plays? Bodel's *Jeu de S. Nicolas* is a miracle play that derives its humour largely from its scenes of low life, the drinking, dicing, and quarrelling of thieves and tipplers. *Courtois d'Arras* is a dramatization of the parable of the Prodigal Son, which becomes a comedy only because its author stresses the life of the prodigal while he is wasting his substance with riotous living among gamblers and harlots. Both plays end with the *Te Deum laudamus* and are so alike in their mingling of humorous and serious scenes that they might have been written by the same author and played by the same *puy*. In any case they indicate one way in which the profane drama may have developed from the religious. It is evident that from a very early period the desire to enliven the teachings of the Church was present and that humorous elements made their way not only

---

[1] Parts of this chapter appeared in *MLR*, xxxi (1936), 377–84. For the various points of view mentioned see that article and also Wilmotte, *Études critiques*, pp. 93 ff.; Faral, *Jongleurs*, pp. 226 ff.; J.-P. Jacobsen, *Essai*, p. 32; and G. Cohen, '*Comédie' latine*, Introduction. Cf. also J. Bédier, *Commencements*, pp. 869 ff., and P. Toldo, *Études*, pp. 181 ff. For additional bibliography see Petit de Julleville, *Répertoire*, *Comédiens*, *Comédie*, and Rolland, *Théâtre Comique*.

into the two plays referred to, but also into others like the *Mystère d'Adam* where the tone is nevertheless preponderantly serious. In fact the classification of Bodel's play and *Courtois d'Arras* as 'comedies' or 'religious plays' is equally possible and, involving as it does matters of emphasis and relative proportions, is necessarily arbitrary.

Our next examples, however, show no connexion at all with the religious plays. *Le Garçon et l'Aveugle* has but two characters, a scamp of a blind beggar and his rascally boy. It turns upon the ageless theme of the hoodwinker who is hoodwinked. This is the kind of dialogue that might have been recited at any time and contains the universal characteristics of farce. The *Jeu de la Feuillée* is an admixture of personal satire and fairy-tale fantasy. It was written by Adam le Bossu when he was about to leave Arras and was obviously intended to amuse his friends, some of whom appear as characters in the play. *Robin et Marion* by the same author is often described as an operetta or musical comedy. It is in fact a realistic dramatization of the lyric *pastourelle* in which music plays an important part: Robin, Marion, and the other shepherds and shepherdesses sing snatches of songs known to us from various collections of lyric *pastourelles* and *bergeries*.

There is good reason to believe that these five texts are typical of the earliest lay theatre in France. It is, of course, certain that much of the patter of the jongleurs—if it was ever written down —has been censored out of existence, that early farces have vanished, that some scenarios of folk and courtly dances have disappeared and that, besides the *Jeu de S. Nicolas*, other dramatizations of saints' lives containing humorous scenes may have been written but have not survived. However, three of these five plays exist in more than one manuscript and none of them presupposes an elaborate evolution from a long line of lost originals. Their immediate antecedents can be readily indicated. The earliest of them, the *Jeu de S. Nicolas*, can be connected in its main theme with two Latin miracle plays and a narrative life of the saint that survives in various Latin and French recensions, and, whether Bodel knew any of these or not, he depended upon some such material for the more serious elements of his text. He seems also to have been influenced by certain characters in the Easter and Christmas plays (see above, Chap. X). Similarly, the author of *Courtois d'Arras* drew his primary inspiration from the parable of the Prodigal Son, even as the author of the liturgical *Sponsus* used the parable of the Wise and Foolish Virgins. *Le Garçon et l'Aveugle* is the type of farcical dialogue so readily written and recited at any time that analogues to it have been discovered in a Latin school-piece and in a late Resurrection play. It belongs, not to the category of formal comedy, but to the slap-stick variety of entertainment represented as well by the Atellan farces of the ancients as by our own vaudeville turns. Adam le Bossu for his *Jeu de la Feuillée* needed only his friends, their foibles, anecdotes about the citizens of Arras, and the fairy-tales he had heard in his youth; for his *Robin et Marion* he had at hand the lyrico-narrative *pastourelles* that he and his companions were wont to write.

Nor is the source of the humorous elements in these five plays far to seek. The scenes of drinking, gaming, and quarrelling, the characters of beggars and thieves, of priests and clerks, of prostitutes and peasants, all took their rise in the taverns of Arras, in the countryside of Picardy, in the streets and fields familiar to men like Jean Bodel and Adam le Bossu. The writers of our earliest surviving comedies turned for their main themes to a saint's life, a biblical parable, a well-known anecdote, certain contemporary experiences, and the lyric *pastourelle*. Their innovation, or the innovation of their predecessors, was to present not only serious but humorous elements *par personnages*, that is, by means of actors playing roles.

We have met the term *par personnages* in the *Estoire de Griseldis*, the *Istoire de la Destruction de Troye*, the *Vieux Testament*, in other plays, and in various documents. It is evident that for the Middle Ages there was less distinction between narrative and dramatic genres than for us. Narrative works depended for their circulation upon a single jongleur, the usual means of distribution at a time when manuscripts were relatively scarce and printing had not yet made books easily accessible to a wider reading public. The recitations of jongleurs constituted one type of entertainment. But when such narratives were reworked so that their dialogued portions might be spoken by a group of persons, whether jongleurs or members of some *puy*, guild or other society, each impersonating a character, and when their descriptive portions might be replaced by mimetic action or suitable *mise en scène*, then they were presented *par personnages* and another type of entertainment resulted which we call drama. When this second kind of entertainment seems to us today to rely for its interest largely upon its humorous elements we classify it as comedy.[1]

The original impetus toward this method of presenting humorous material may well have come from the religious plays, or the fecundating germ may have lain inherent in the jongleur's method of transmitting all types of vernacular literature in the Middle Ages. Probably both factors contributed to the final result. In the case of the plays on saints' lives, which were apparently presented by societies animated by a religious purpose, the liturgical drama lay near at hand for imitation. Since scenes from the Bible were regularly presented *par personnages* at Easter and Christmas time, why should not scenes from the lives of saints be presented—*par personnages*—on saints' days? The presence of the hymn *Te Deum laudamus* at the close of the *Jeu de S. Nicolas* and *Courtois d'Arras* is clearly a heritage from the liturgical drama. That comedy should creep into such plays in the gay, prosperous towns of Picardy and in other communities like these was inevitable and in no wise especially significant to author or actors. The guilds, *puys*, and societies of various sorts were entertaining their fellow members and guests in their own fashion. They were unaware of creating a new genre by incorporating realistic scenes in a saint's life presented *par personnages*.

In the case of *Le Garçon et l'Aveugle*, of the plays by Adam le Bossu, and of the later farces—*Maître Pierre Pathelin* and all the rest—no connexion with the religious drama is evident. Of course, even here, the fact that the Church regularly presented certain biblical scenes *par personnages* may not have been with-

[1] For Bodel's play and *Courtois d'Arras* the classification is obviously arbitrary and its only justification is that in both these texts, despite their religious background, comic scenes occupy about half of the play. Because the *Jeu de S. Nicolas* could be profitably studied in connexion with other miracle plays, it was treated in the earlier part of this book. *Courtois d'Arras*, on the other hand, as the dramatization of a parable rather than a saint's life, holds a position somewhat apart and has therefore been considered in this and the following chapters. It is clear, however, that from various points of view both plays might have been grouped and discussed together in either place.

out influence in the beginning. Adam le Bossu was a clerk and would naturally be acquainted with liturgical practices. However, he was also a professional poet and musician, a trouvère as well as a clerk, and for a man who wrote *chansons*, *motets*, *rondeaux*, and especially *jeux-partis*, the idea of presenting poems *par personnages* would grow quite regularly out of his métier. His *Robin et Marion* is a characteristic product of the trouvère's art, a *pastourelle*; his own innovation—if it was his—consisted in presenting this *pastourelle par personnages*.

It is not necessary to suppose that Jean Bodel and Adam le Bossu—or their predecessors—turned directly to church performances and the jongleur's art for their inspiration in writing comedies. The first writer of profane plays, whoever he may have been, had but to present narrative poems *par personnages*, inject humour into the situation portrayed, and a comedy would be born. The principle of dramatic representation was constantly made visible to every medieval writer in the liturgical drama; it also inhered in the method by which all medieval vernacular literature was transmitted. One has only to assume a single author with a story to tell who decided to tell his story as directly as possible to his audience. He may have been a clerk well acquainted with the drama of the Church, who wished to set forth in the vernacular some saint's legend or biblical tale and used the Church's own means of dramatic representation. He may have been a trouvère, well acquainted with the technique of oral delivery, who decided to turn his narrative into dialogue and add thereto impersonation, mimetic action, a more pretentious script, and some *mise en scène*. The incorporation of humorous or realistic detail would in either case make the modern critic call his production a comedy. If the tale he desired to tell were of the *fabliau* type and more coarsely conceived, the modern critic would call his production a farce.

The earliest author of comedies in France was probably a professional writer. On some occasion when a saint's day was to be celebrated by a guild, when a group of fellow citizens was to be amused or when a nobleman's court was to be entertained, he conceived the notion of presenting a remembered tale or some original fancy of his own *par personnages*. The jongleurs and the literary and religious societies of his native town—perhaps it was Arras—would furnish him with actors used to reciting verses, men capable of being both serious and gay, versatile bourgeois like those Parisians who in 1398 were forbidden by the provost to play 'aucuns jeux de personages par maniere de farces, de vies de sains, ne autrement'.[1] He was probably not conscious of creating a new literary form or of re-creating an old one. It seems unnecessary therefore to posit for the origins of French comedy any survival of the cults of pagan deities or of a classical *mimus*, unnecessary to decide whether comedy first made its way into or out of the religious play, unnecessary to suggest the influence of learned Latin school-pieces like the *Babio* and *Pamphilus*. For the beginnings of comedy in France, for the plays of Jean Bodel and Adam le Bossu—or their predecessors—we need assume only a knowledge of the principle of dramatic presentation, a desire to entertain, a story to tell, and a sense of humour.

[1] Petit de Julleville, *Mystères*, i. 415.

XXI

Courtois d'Arras. Le Garçon et l'Aveugle

COURTOIS D'ARRAS, a sprightly dramatization of the parable of the Prodigal Son in Luke xv. 11–32, recalls in its tavern scenes the humorous elements of Bodel's *Jeu de S. Nicolas* and is so like that play stylistically, as well as in its mingling of comedy with a religious subject, that Guesnon would attribute it to the same author.[1]

The biblical parable, of course, illustrates the importance of repentance and devotes considerably more space to the younger son's contrition than to how he wasted his substance. The play, on the contrary, after a realistic dialogue of ninety lines between a father, his elder son and his younger, here named Courtois, proceeds directly to an Artois tavern where the innkeeper's boy is advertising delightful hospitality on easy terms and where Courtois, rich with the portion of his father's wealth that he has just obtained, is soon wantoning with two girls, Pourette and Manchevaire. Between them he is lured into drinking too much, promising to pay all their debts as well as his own, and even into giving one of them his purse for safe keeping. The girls soon disappear, the innkeeper demands payment, and Courtois, obliged to leave all his clothes as pledges for the scot, goes off in an old garment lent him by his host. These scenes occupy some 340 lines. The next 169 verses show the disillusioned Courtois accepting the offer of a *bourgeois* to become a swineherd and presently growing so hungry that he is eager to return to his father's house. The biblical famine is implied and Courtois's remorse is evident, but the author gives realistic emphasis to the Prodigal's hunger, the poverty of his fare, and his humiliation at the thought of how much his elder brother

---

[1] See A. Guesnon, *Moyen-Âge*, 2ᵉ série, xii (1908), 67. E. Faral's edition, *CFMA*, 1922, finds this hypothesis not unlikely, though lacking proof. P. Groult in *Mélanges Cohen*, pp. 47 ff., refuses to classify the piece as a comedy, though he recognizes (p. 53) that in some ways it *a faussé compagnie à l'évangile*. Cf. Chap. XX, above.

would gloat over his plight, if he knew of it. The final two scenes (of only sixty-five lines) chronicle the meeting of Courtois and his father, the latter's forgiveness and eagerness to kill the fatted calf in honour of his son's repentance, the elder brother's indignation at such proceedings ('for me who have served you night and day like a servant, you wouldn't kill a chicken'), and the father's final pointing of the moral that there is more joy in heaven over one sinner that repenteth than over ninety and nine righteous persons who need no repentance.

Not only does the play vary the proportions of the parable, devoting comparatively much more space than its source to the Prodigal's life in sin by dwelling on how he devoured his living with harlots, but it carefully motivates the Prodigal's reasons for asking for his portion by characterizing him as an arrogant wastrel, spoiled by his father and hated by his virtuous elder brother. His losses at the inn and his lowly state as a hungry swineherd because he has 'spent all', rather than the implied famine, slowly lead up to his repentance which occurs convincingly after considerable hesitation and fear of his elder brother's taunts. And the end of the play, proportionately shorter than the biblical version, differs in various details from it : the father does not recognize his son from afar, but fails at first to know him at all—or perhaps pretends not to know him —then, as soon as he admits recognition, he overwhelms the boy with kindness, stressing the virtue of penitence though not, as in Luke, ordering for him ring and shoes. Certain other drama-tic possibilities in the last verses of the parable are not devel-oped, i.e. no servant appears and, to judge by the manuscript, no music and dancing occur. However, neighbours are to be invited and the elder son, arriving home for dinner, finds the household in a turmoil, so that unchronicled festivities may have been introduced. In the final short scene between the father and his elder son, the latter does not refuse to enter nor does his loving father say 'Son thou art ever with me, and all that I have is thine'. Instead, the elder son's anger takes a whim-sical and original turn when he substitutes a *poulet* for the biblical kid and asks if his brother has returned to get yet another share of the family fortune. After the father's words echoing Luke xv. 7 and rejoicing in the killing of his *buef* because of the Prodigal's home-coming, the play concludes with the singing of the *Te Deum laudamus*.

The text is dated before 1228[1] because Gerart Lenoir, a rich man of Arras whose *tresor* is mentioned in line 81, is represented as alive, whereas he died in that year. Various other references, as well as the language of the piece, clearly place the text in Picardy, and its popularity is attested by its preservation in four manuscripts.

None of these manuscripts indicates the division into dialogue or the names of the speakers. The absence of such indications is usual enough in medieval plays, but in this case the question of whether we are dealing with a true play or a mime (i.e. performance by a single person) has sometimes been raised. There can be little doubt, however, that this is a play. To be sure, the characters are few, Courtois's lament (486–599) is of exaggerated length, a few narrative lines occur, the stanzaic structure at the beginning does not correspond to the speeches, and the incipit and explicit of manuscript *A* refer to the piece as a *lais*. But all these factors can be found in true plays, and the evidence for performance by more than one actor is impressive. The use of mnemonic rhymes, the occasional division of single lines between two speakers, and the *Te Deum* at the end indicate it; so does the fact that the action would be clearer and far more amusing if the roles were assumed by different actors.

Amusing the play certainly is. Its gifted author has freshly visualized the old parable, located it in Arras, and made the action both plausible and witty. His persons are real, not abstractions, and his hero bears a local name, probably not without special significance. The elder and younger brothers are carefully differentiated with definite traits of character emerging from their words. Above all, the scenes at the inn are cleverly motivated and the behaviour of the naïve but bragging Courtois, of the expert *filles de joie* out to fleece him, of the innkeeper and his boy, all reveal a writer of unusual deftness and imagination. Courtois, leaving his father's house with his new wealth, is ready for just such fare as the innkeeper's boy advertises when he promises good wine of Soissons in silver cups

---

[1] How much before we do not know, but if Bodel should be the author, then probably before 1202. Cf. above, Chap. X.

amid pleasant surroundings and on easy credit, 'as the girls,
Manchevaire and Pourette, can testify who eat and drink at the
inn without paying a penny'. Then the host appears and praises
not only his wine but his rooms, beds, linen, and cleansing
facilities. Pourette, who takes the lead in all that follows, ably
abetted by Manchevaire—the audience has been well advised
in advance of their nature—proceeds with plans to separate the
fool from his money by offering him copious doses of wine and
seduction. And how adroit Pourette is! She flatters and pretends to make love while she keeps praising the wine and
ordering more of it, until finally she has her victim thoroughly
cozened and befuddled by her wiles. Then after getting rid of
Courtois temporarily by suggesting that he should not be bash-
ful about relieving himself in the garden, she informs the host
of the Prodigal's heavy purse and agrees to leave her dupe
behind to pay for her debts, old and new, as well as his own.
She even begs the host not to be timid about taking Courtois's
money and clothes away from him and then throwing him out.
All the while, however, she intends to acquire Courtois's wealth
for herself. She tells the simpleton that she must go home for
a bit and warns him not to gamble and lose his money during
her absence. To reassure her, the trusting Courtois hands over
his purse, saying he prefers to have it hidden in her fair bosom
rather than put to evil use at dice. As soon as the girls have left,
however, the host and Lequet, his helper, tell Courtois he has
been hoodwinked. At first the poor fool refuses to believe them
and offers his cloak as pledge. But the host replies that if he
really wants news of the girls he'll have to go to Béthune and
that, moreover, he must forthwith give up not only his cloak,
but all his clothes and money as well. Since Pourette has made
off with Courtois's wallet the host, too, has been deceived and
he protests vehemently that his guest's clothes will hardly cover
half the girls' debts. In the end he takes everything, but out of
pity gives the wretched Courtois a single tattered garment to
cover his nakedness. It is during the end of this scene that the
Prodigal begins to regret not heeding his father's advice. This
and the further development of his sense of sin and repentance
after he has become a humiliated, hungry swineherd capitally
motivate the return to his father. The culprit's remorse here

has none of the abruptness that so shocks the modern reader in most medieval miracle plays.

The way in which each twist of the plot is convincingly prepared for in advance combines with the verisimilitude of the persons, their imaginatively conceived surroundings, and their realistically argotic speech to make this slight text unusually effective. The technical facility of its varying metres indicates a professional poet: octosyllabic stanzas rhyming *aabccb*, such as we shall find again in Adam le Bossu's *Jeu de la Feuillée*, compose the first scene between the father and his two sons; the tavern scenes and the end of the play are developed in swift, diversified octosyllabic couplets in which some single-lined speeches and a few lines divided between two speakers speed the action; on the other hand, the beginning of Courtois's penitence (431–50) takes on seriousness and significance because of its twelve-syllabled monorhymed quatrains. In short, within its small compass of 664 lines, *Courtois d'Arras* provides us with expert entertainment.

LE GARÇON ET L'AVEUGLE

Le Garçon et l'Aveugle has only two characters and tells its anecdotal story in a mere 265 lines.[1] A blind man, singing and unsuccessfully begging for alms, longs for a boy to lead him. 'Even if he can't sing, he'll be able to ask for bread and direct me to the large inns.' Jehannet appears who shows his true character at once by offering his services, but at a stiff price: he must have an *escuçon* (little crown) a day. He is accepted, the two of them sing, and the boy pretends to beg to the amusement of an audience well aware that no bystanders are present. The boy's deception is matched by his master's, however, for the latter soon confesses that begging is actually not a necessity to him: he has a nice hoard put away. Jehannet at once cajoles him into sharing this wealth and, among other things, offers to procure for him a pretty girl, whereupon they exchange obscene pleasantries about the joys of copulation. Pretending to leave the blind man, the boy disguises his voice, assumes the role of bystander, beats him for his filthy language, and compounds the

---

[1] Ed. Mario Roques, *CFMA*, 1921.

deception by saying, in his own voice, that if only he had been present the beating would not have occurred. He kindly offers to take his master home and heal his wounds—with the dung of a fat chicken. Once in the house, the blind man directs Jehannet to his big purse and asks him to fetch food, wine, and his own *amiete*. The boy promises to do so and also to have his master's cloak, belt, and buckle mended. Then, as he makes off with purse and clothes, Jehannet turns first to the audience and then to his master, bragging of the deception he has practised on the blind man who claimed to have neither cloak nor money and who, were it not for his fellow beggars, would be worth a thousand millions. In his last words Jehannet taunts his ex-master: 'Get yourself another boy . . . I'm off now. . . . If all this doesn't suit you, just follow me.'

The humour in this trifle, such as it is, consists in the specta-tors' awareness of the various deceptions being practised and of the fact that one trickster has been outwitted by another. The emphasis in the play is not on the blind man's infirmity but on the fraud and guile made possible by it, and much of the fun derives from the audience's participation in knavery invisible to the deluded impostor. The feigned begging from non-existent bystanders, the disguised voice and subsequent beating, the absolute trust placed by the old rascal in the young one as he so cheerfully and unguardedly puts his hoarded wealth in itching palms, the contrast between the state he claims to be his and the luxury he can command—these are funny and, like the few obscenities and other realistic touches, would amuse a simple, unexacting public. The piece is further enlivened by three short songs, two of them of a topical nature.

These two songs refer to the King of Sicily, who has called for troops from everywhere and who is daily put to the test against his enemy, and they also refer to those who serve the King's son. Charles d'Anjou, brother of Louis IX, received the title of King of Sicily in 1266; he needed troops that year to conquer his realm and again after the Sicilian Vespers in 1282 when his son, the Prince of Salerno, tried to help him raise them. It is assumed that the references in these songs are to Charles and his son and either to one of the special levies or to the constant call for troops during their time. Our play may be

definitely associated with Tournai, and it is known that men of
Flanders and the region around Tournai joined both Charles
and, later, his son. The two songs, of course, might be interpolations but they are alike in rhyming $a^8b^6a^8b^6b^6c^8c^8b^6$, which
is the pattern of the opening song in which the blind man begs
for alms, and they are tightly tied to the rest of the text by
mnemonic rhymes. Some date after 1266 is therefore indicated,
and the piece, like its single manuscript, may be confidently
ascribed to a Picard writer of the second half of the thirteenth
century.

Mnemonic rhymes, lines divided between the speakers, and
plurals like *cantent endoi ensemble* show that two performers recited the piece, and the clear differentiation between the two
scamps, the wit in their interchanges, and the verve of the octosyllabic couplets in which most of the skit is written suggest
that it is the work of a facile and practised author.

Analogues to its subject have been discovered in the late
French religious plays, in farces and moralities, as well as in
Spanish literature of the sixteenth century.[1] Usually these involve a humorous dialogue between a blind man and his boy,
but there is little resemblance in detail except for a few instances
in which a disguised voice is used. Some critics believe that
unpretentious skits like ours were recited by jongleurs throughout the Middle Ages and made their way into the religious
drama. Others hold that the comic scene between the blind man
and his companion came from the religious drama (from scenes
involving Longinus or the man born blind who was healed by
Jesus) and later developed farcical elements.[2] In view of the
fact that the idea of a blind man deceived by his boy is so simple
and so widely prevalent, its reinvention any number of times
seems likely enough. The early religious plays were too reverent
in tone to admit of Longinus as a comic figure, but the later
ones may well have been influenced in this and other themes,
like the spice-merchant's harangue, by current farcical interludes.

[1] Cf. G. Cohen, *Rom.* xli (1912), 346–72, Wilmotte, in *Études*, pp. 93–126,
J. P. Wickersham Crawford, *Spanish Drama before Lope de Vega*, 2nd ed. (1937),
p. 52, Jean Wright, *Study*, chap. i, especially pp. 13–14 .

[2] For the first opinion see Creizenach. i. 205 ff., 409 Faral, *Jonleurs*; and
J. Wright, loc. cit. For the second, G. Cohen and Wilmotte, loc. cit. Cf. also
Chap. XX, above.

It would seem, accordingly, that there is no good reason to posit any connexion between our unpretentious little dialogue from Tournai and other treatments of the same subject, and that both the ancestry and progeny of this, the earliest surviving French farce, may best be regarded as Legion.

XXII

The Plays of Adam le Bossu

ADAM LE BOSSU, or de la Halle, or d'Arras, as he was variously designated at home and abroad,[1] came from the same general milieu as Jean Bodel, that is, from a well-educated circle in the gay and relatively prosperous town of Arras.[2] Adam, like his father, achieved the title of *maître*, but soon afterwards interrupted his studies, begun in Paris, to marry. He speaks freely in several of his poems of giving up school, friends, and possessions for the sake of his young wife. However, in the *Jeu de la Feuillée* and in a lyrical *Congé* of about the same date (1276–7), we find him in Arras, taking leave of his family and friends, resolved to return to Paris to continue his studies. He must have been about twenty-five or thirty at this time. He planned to leave his beautiful young wife, Marie, in the care of his father, and he was so deeply and obviously devoted to her that he could publicly make fun of his uxoriousness. In both the play and the *Congé* he gracefully expresses his affection for Marie, and even when he is pretending to disparage her charms, it is in the teasing tone of one who loves. Concerning his life in Paris, which may have lasted three or four years, we know nothing, but in two of his lyrical pieces he speaks of a long absence, his delight in coming back to his own land, and these poems may have been written upon his second return to Arras.

His unfinished poem, *Le Roi de Sezile*, was written after the death of Charles d'Anjou in 1285, and we know that the poet himself died far from home in the south of Italy between 1285 and 1289, perhaps in 1288. Employed by Robert, Comte

---

[1] In the *Jeu du Pèlerin* we read (line 25): 'Maistre(s) Adans li Bochus estoit chi [i.e. in Arras] apelés / Et la [in Apulia] Adans d'Arras.' His father, who was in the service of the aldermen of Arras, is referred to either as Maître Henri le Bossu or Henri de la Halle.

[2] On Adam see the latest editions of the *Jeu de la Feuillée* and *Robin et Marion* by E. Langlois in *CFMA*; Henry Guy, *Essai sur la vie et les œuvres*; Guesnon in *Moyen-Âge*, 2e série, xix (1915–16), 173–233; E. de Coussemaker, *Œuvres complètes*; Thomas Walton, in *MLR*, xxxvi (1941), 344–50.

d'Artois, as court poet and musician, he had probably accompanied that nobleman to Italy where in 1282, after the Sicilian Vespers, the count had been sent by the King of France to help Robert's kinsman, Charles d'Anjou, King of Naples and Sicily, brother of Louis IX of France.

The poet's nephew, Jean Madot, writing in 1289 after Adam's death, said that the poet had left Arras *por revel et compaignie*, and that this was foolish for he was both feared and loved at home. In reading Adam's pointed gibes at some of the town's well-known citizens—their miserliness, gluttony, and various other sins and follies—one may well believe that he might have inspired apprehension. Moreover, class warfare was disturbing the town in his day, the local government was levying heavy imposts, and so-called 'bigamous' clerks—that is, clerks married more than once or married to widows—had recently been forced to give up their exemption privileges, pay taxes, and be classified with the laity. Some of the satire in Adam's *Jeu de la Feuillée* concerns these *bigames*.

However, it is certain that he was also admired. In Arras and even outside Picardy he achieved great fame as a poet and musician. Many references to his skill and renown survive in the works of others, and his own versatile compositions—two plays, the *Congé*, many *chansons, motets, rondeaux, jeux-partis*, a poem concerned with death, a *Dit d'Amour*, and the first nineteen stanzas of his incomplete epic about the King of Sicily—testify to his originality and technical proficiency.

The *Jeu de la Feuillée* which can be definitely dated in 1276 or 1277[1] was written to amuse a group of the author's friends when he was leaving them to return to his studies in Paris. It is a strange mixture of topical joking and fantasy used for realistic purposes; people of the town encounter fairies and both groups serve to lampoon the author's contemporaries. The play abounds in humorous allusions to identifiable persons, those called sick of avarice, fools needing a cure, heavy eaters and drinkers, scolding wives and henpecked husbands, a woman of ill repute and her supposed lovers, certain 'bigamous' clerks unwilling to pay the new taxes imposed on them. Adam's own

---

[1] By references in the play to Pope Gregory X, who died 10 Jan. 1276, as being deceased and to Ermenfrois Crespin, who died in 1277, as being alive.

family does not escape. He pretends that his wife's charms have
begun to pall on him, thus giving him an excellent chance to
describe them in detail. He also pretends that he greatly fears
her. At the same time he reveals his devotion and pokes fun at
himself for his uxoriousness. He charges his father, Maître
Henri, with being stingy, fat, a *bigame*, liking the bottle too
much, and trying to curry favour with the aldermen. Adam's
friends, Gillot and Rikier, are clearly characterized, the first as
a mischievous trouble-maker and a kind of clown, the second
as a rich clerk, bald, afraid of his wife, yet a ladies' man, ready
to take on Adam's wife if he doesn't want her, and involved
with the loose woman, Dame Douche.

These together with a young merchant, a tavern-keeper, a
physician and his helper, a fool named Walet, a gullible monk,
an idiot boy and his father, three fairies, and the messenger of
King Hellekin comprise the motley characters of the play.
There is little that can be called a plot. The action supposedly
takes place at Pentecost, a time when the women of Arras were
wont to go to the Crois ou Pré in the hope of seeing fairies and
when the shrine of Notre Dame was exposed in the Petit-
Marché under a canopy of green foliage, a *feuillée*. Adam and
his young friends discuss his imminent departure and his supposed change of heart toward his wife. His father deplores the
fact that his son has lost so much time in his wife's company
and urges him to go back to his studies in Paris. Adam's friends
twit the old man with not giving his son enough money for the
trip, but Maître Henri complains that he is poor, old, and infirm. However, a physician appears who diagnoses his ailments
as avarice and gluttony and names a good many other Artesians
who are suffering from the same ills. Then Dame Douche
arrives; she too suffers, for her stomach is bothering her, but
her malady is soon shown to be an unborn child. She admits
this is true and accuses Adam's friend, Rikier, of being the
child's father. Despite the supposed father's prompt and terrified denial, Gillot threatens to tell Rikier's wife the news and
this leads to a discussion of various wives who are feared and
spoiled by their husbands, Adam's wife among them. 'I don't
care,' says Adam, 'but just don't let her hear of it.'

At this point a monk presents himself, praising his relics of

S. Acaire, patron of fools and madmen, and promising miraculous cures in return for small offerings. The monk is invited to try his miracles on Walet, the biggest fool there is, and on various other foolish Artesians, proposed by the company as needing his help. Then an idiot's father brings his son forward to be healed and the idiot's chatter introduces a discussion of the troubles of the 'bigamous' clerks. It seems that Maître Henri, Adam's father, is in this category since he has had more than one wife, but he remarks dryly that holy matrimony is better than the sins of the unmarried prelates. However, various legal steps are being taken to plead the cause of these *bigames* and Gillot tells Maître Henri that this will cost him money. Henri once again insists on his poverty and claims besides that he serves the aldermen and dare not lose their favour. At this Gillot accuses him of always fawning upon the powers that be.

Presently we learn that fairies are expected and Rikier and Adam prepare for their coming by setting a table for them. The fairies are preceded by Crokesot, messenger of Hellekin, king of the wicked elves. Crokesot has been sent to pay court to Morgue la fée on behalf of his master, and soon Morgue arrives with her companions, Arsile and Maglore. The first two fairies are content with the arrangements and suitably reward Rikier and Adam: Rikier is to have plenty of money and Adam is to be handsome, a good composer of songs, and the most amorous man in the country. Maglore, however, finds no knife at her place and she proceeds to wreak vengeance on the careless clerks: Rikier shall be bald and Adam shall be so debauched by his companions and shall so forget himself in the soft arms of his wife that he will hate learning and delay his journey. Crokesot pleads the suit of Hellekin, but Morgue says her heart belongs to Robert Sommeillons, a rich citizen of Arras and the new prince of the *puy*. There is jesting about Robert's character and his recent mishaps at jousting. At first Morgue defends him, but suddenly she changes her mind and promises Hellekin her friendship. At this point Fortune and her wheel are discovered and this leads to a rehearsal of the shifting destinies of various men of Arras, especially of those who have fallen to low estate from former heights. The bad fairy, Maglore, true to character, takes the lead in being malicious about them. Before the fairies leave for the Crois ou Pré, they encounter Dame Douche who says she has been awaiting them there all night. She complains of being maligned by someone and wants to punish this man *en sen lit* even as she recently did two other men whom she names. The fairies invite her, her daughter, and another pitiless woman known to the audience to accompany them, and they go off singing.

Now the monk, who has been asleep, wakes up and joins Adam and his circle at the tavern. There is drinking, eating, horse-play, and more joking. The tavern-keeper proposes to charge the debts of all of them to the gullible monk, who is persuaded to believe that while he slept one of the company shook dice for him and lost. He leaves his relics in pawn for the scot and, as the bells of the church of St. Nicholas begin to peal, the play ends with Adam and his friends departing to kiss the shrine of Notre Dame and offer her a candle.

It has been plausibly assumed by Walton that the actors in this piece were for the most part the persons portrayed, that they sat among the audience when not performing, and that they went to and from the playing-space only when needed. At any rate, relations between actors and audience must have been unusually close. The playing-space seems to have represented the approach to a tavern situated in or near the Petit-Marché, a convenient meeting-place for the assorted characters. Walton thinks that the performance may have taken place at night at the very time when the fairies were to be expected and that some of the fun consisted in having them come to the tavern while Dame Douche and her friends were awaiting them elsewhere.

The name of the play appears in the only one of three surviving manuscripts that is complete. This copy reads at the end 'Explicit li jeus de le Fuellie'. We know that the shrine of Notre Dame mentioned in line 1078 was displayed annually at Pentecost in the Petit-Marché of Arras and that a *feuillée*, or canopy of green leaves, was placed over it. This seems the likeliest explanation of the Explicit, as Guesnon, Langlois, and Walton agree, though the possibility of an arbour (*feuillée*) outside the tavern where the action takes place cannot be ruled out. The introductory title of this same manuscript is simply *Li jus Adan*.

The other two manuscripts, which give us only the initial 174 and 170 lines respectively, entitle it 'C'est le Jeu Adan le Boçu d'Arraz', and 'C'est li coumencemens du Jeu Adan le Boçu'.

The two manuscripts that preserve only the beginning of the play show that one of its most famous passages could be recited and enjoyed separately. This passage contains Adam's description of his wife as she seemed when he first knew her in the springtime of youthful love and as she now appears to him in the disillusionment of marriage. Something of the contrast of Villon's *Vieille en regrettant le temps de sa jeunesse* is in these lines, but nothing of its bitterness and pain: Adam so delights in picturing the beauties of his wife that although his purpose is supposedly to compare the ideal that lovers see with the reality that actually exists, he ends by describing all her loveliness in great detail and tells us how she made his desire and passion—mingled, to be sure, with jealousy, despair, and madness—grow and grow until no human body could have been as beautiful as love made hers seem to him. Now, he says, he must come to his senses and leave her, and one realizes that he is trying to conceal the sorrow of parting under a light veil of mockery which actually succeeds in revealing his devotion.[1]

Elsewhere in the play the humour is broader. Many of the people ridiculed must have been in the audience and some of the barbs may well have struck home. Adam shrewdly places the sharpest of them in the speeches of the idiot, the fool, the wicked fairy, and various of his anonymous characters. But Maître Henri's defence of the *bigames* and Gillot's words about the Pope whose edict deprived some of the clerks of their exemption from taxation have a biting edge that is not to be hidden. The meaning of some of the attacks escapes us and even those we understand would naturally have had more relevance for Adam's contemporaries. Occasionally the horseplay seems pointless and a few phrases are crude. But on the whole Adam's wit matches the grace and delicacy of his tributes to his wife.

The construction of the play is far less loose than it at first appears. Adam had the problem of introducing a series of ideas amusing to his audience by way of real and imaginary characters,

[1] A similar description of Marie occurs in one of Adam's *motets*. See Langlois's note to line 152.

and in their conversations one subject grows plausibly out
of another. Even the coming of the fairies is well prepared for.
Only at the end does the comedy limp. Once the lampooning
is over, Adam seems to lose interest.

Technically the versification is facile. The opening dodeca-
syllabic quatrains, perhaps a kind of satire on the solemn
beginnings of more serious plays, boldly merge with the usual
octosyllabic couplets via a line divided between two speakers,
and thereafter lines divided between speakers become frequent.
Mnemonic verses are, of course, the rule. In a few places Adam
introduces stanzaic structure (*aabccb*) for no discernible reason
except his own pleasure, and he further enlivens his comedy
with a song or two.

This piece, probably destined as ephemeral entertainment for
a selected group of friends and written for a special occasion,
may never have been performed in its entirety more than once.
Yet its wit still sparkles and the unexpected charm of Adam's
mocking adoration of his wife continues to captivate the dis-
criminating.

The plot of *Le Jeu de Robin et Marion*, which in its simplest
terms merely reveals how Marion, a shepherdess, repulses the
advances of an amorous knight in favour of her rustic lover,
Robin, is the theme of hundreds of lyrico-narrative *pastourelles*
and the piece may rightly be called a *pastourelle par personnages*.
Because it is embellished with songs and dances it is sometimes
referred to as the first French comic opera, and a resemblance
has also been seen to the *divertissements*, the *ballets*, and the *inter-
mèdes rustiques* of Molière. But perhaps Gérold's unpretentious
description best fits it: *une pastourelle dramatique*.[1]

What Adam has done is to give dramatic form to a conventional and stylized form of lyric widely appreciated in his time.
The *pastourelles* almost invariably begin with some slight variation of the words, 'The other day I was riding along and spied
a pretty shepherdess'. The narrator is regularly a knight, the
maid's name is Marion, her rustic lover is Robin. Sometimes a

[1] On this play see Langlois's latest edition in *CFMA*; Th. Gérold, *La Musique
au moyen âge*, pp. 302 ff.; Chambers, i. 171 ff.; Bédier, *Commencements*, p. 895;
H. Guy, *Essai*; Cohen's transposition; Bahlsen, *AA*, xxvii (1885); J. Chailley,
in *Mélanges Cohen*, pp. 111–17, and his *Histoire*, pp. 212 ff. See also W. P. Jones,
The Pastourelle.

wolf makes off with a sheep, Robin chases the animal, and the knight tries to profit by the peasant's absence. The knight may or may not be repulsed by the girl; the shepherdess may be chaste or more than receptive. Robin's friends occasionally appear to help him and the knight receives blows, but more often it is Robin who is discomfited by the *chevalier*. Some of these lyrics omit the amorous adventure and chronicle only the games and pastimes of shepherds and shepherdesses seen by the knight as he rides by, and such poems have been distinguished from the true *pastourelles* and termed *bergeries*.[1] But all have similar introductions and depend for their interest and charm upon slight variations in background, development, and denouement, and especially upon differences in their melodies both verbal and musical: the versification is artfully devised, refrains or bits of popular songs are incorporated—many of these known from other poems—and the whole has the swing of the dance. Whether prototypes of these lyrics were popular or courtly, whether the *pastourelle* 'forms a link between folk-song and drama', need not concern us. Adam's originality consists in adapting a kind of well-known courtly lyric for the stage. In so doing he has kept the framework—names, incidents, popular songs, and refrains with their inherited music—but he has realized the background and wittily amplified or twisted certain elements of the scenario.

The play opens with an exchange of songs between Marion and the Chevalier. These are in traditional vein and even their music is not by Adam, although he was an accomplished composer. But Adam's graceful wit appears in the following dialogue between the knight and Marion, when the girl misinterprets the Chevalier's remarks in a series of puns and guilelessly expresses her preference for Robin with his gifts of bread and cheese and his plodding plough-horse to the Chevalier's foolish falcon and his spirited steed that kicks. After more songs have been sung Robin appears, and when Marion tells him of the knight's proposals he boasts that, had he and his two cousins been present, the fellow would never have left without a fight. Marion and Robin eat their rustic fare and

---

[1] *Sic* Chailley, *Mélanges Cohen*, pp. 111–12. Cf., for example, Bartsch, *Romanzen und Pastourellen*, pp. 135, 147, 154, 160, 163, 179, &c.

proceed to dance and sing together in a charming antiphonal *balerie*. Then while Robin is off inviting his cousins to help him with rake and club, in case the Chevalier should reappear, and is promising them a feast of fine bread, cheese, and clear spring water, the knight again accosts Marion. Repulsed once more, he leaves her only to come upon Robin who is holding a falcon that he has just killed lest it 'escape'. The knight is naturally furious at the death of his bird and slaps the peasant who cries out as though he were badly hurt. Marion hears him and comes running to his defence. The knight then offers to forgive the crime, but only if the girl will accompany him, and he proceeds forthwith to lift her on his horse. She begs Robin to rescue her, but the former braggart can only call for his cousins and bleat weakly, 'I'm losing Marion and being beaten and my clothes are getting torn!' The others hurry to him and, though he paints a terrible picture of the mad knight with his great sword and terrible blows, his courage somewhat returns—he is now ready to succour Marion, if his cousins will help him. All three prudently hide in the bushes to await developments. Meanwhile Marion extricates herself quite alone: she tells her aristocratic wooer that she still prefers her own bread and cheese to the fine-feathered bird he offers her, and he departs cursing himself for a fool in having had dealings with such a goose. When the coast is clear Robin comes out of hiding, saying he is all right now that he sees Marion, and the play is about at its half-way point.

The rest is more *bergerie* than *pastourelle*. Marion and Robin, joined by the two cousins, another peasant, and a young shepherdess, begin to tease each other. Robin is twitted about his timidity, his public love-making and jealousy, and Gautier, one of the cousins, about his indecency. All of them play games, feast, sing, and dance to the accompaniment of musical instruments. Their rustic pleasures are only momentarily interrupted when a wolf carries off one of Marion's lambs and Robin, again the bravest man alive, recaptures it. The play ends with Robin and Marion leading the others off stage as all sing and dance.

We know something of the circumstances in which this play was first performed. It was after Adam had accompanied Robert, Comte d'Artois, to southern Italy in 1282 that he wrote it, and the piece was apparently designed to entertain Robert's kinsman, the old King Charles d'Anjou, and his veteran warriors as they rested between battles. Tired men, they would approve its lightness and gaiety, its graceful songs and dances, its artfully simple rusticity. They would enjoy the verses that trip along so smoothly, varied in metre, yet realistically divided between speakers.

They would know Adam's characters from the courtly *pastourelle*, but they must have been delighted by the naturalistic details added to the traditional figures. The knight, though rebuffed, is not discomfited, he takes his defeat lightly and merely cuffs Robin for killing his falcon. Robin is a peasant *miles gloriosus*, braggart and coward by turns, an awkward lout of a lover, crudely affectionate. Marion may be ignorant, but she resourcefully manages to outwit the knight and is staunchly faithful to Robin. Their games are real games : that of S. Cosme is still played in Normandy, and in another game the method of choosing a king by counting hands still obtains the world over. The speech of these peasants is coarse at times and Boileau reproached Adam with making his shepherds speak 'comme on parle au village'. To this Victor Hugo replied, 'Et comment voudriez-vous qu'ils parlassent?' Bédier gives a somewhat surprising answer when he says that the shepherds should speak as they do in the conventional *pastourelles*. But surely some of the charm of Adam's flavorous and original composition would have evaporated if his audience had not been titillated by the unexpectedly real behaviour and conversation of his rustic characters.[1]

In addition to sprightly dialogue and reasonably natural peasants who make love, feast, and play games in diverting fashion, Adam regaled his audience with well-known songs, graceful dances, and instrumental music. Only two of the three manuscripts conserve the melodies, and these are of only some of the songs, but their words and music have been found in various other texts, and it is plausibly conjectured that they are older than the play and that Adam deliberately inserted them,

[1] See Bédier, op. cit., pp. 893–4. In the religious and serious plays, of course, realistic shepherds abound. Cf. the plays of the Ste Geneviève collection and the Griseldis play. See above, Chap. XIV, p. 154, n. 2.

knowing that they would be recognized and enjoyed as old friends. Many of the dances were accompanied by singing alone, but others had an instrumental accompaniment probably provided by the *chevrette* and *musette* (forms of the bagpipe), the horns or cornets, possibly by the flutes too, that are mentioned in the dialogue and that are generally associated with rustic diversions in the *pastourelle*.[1]

The play seems to have been revived in Arras shortly after the author's death, since a curious prologue, designed to introduce it on that occasion, has come down to us in a piece known as the *Jeu du Pèlerin*. This is no true *jeu* but merely an awkward, commonplace introduction to Adam's work in which a pilgrim who has been in southern Italy and elsewhere, as well as various other characters, extol the poet; everywhere the pilgrim has heard of the dead clerk's virtues and talents, his songs and music, his *partures* and *motets*, and of how he was loved and honoured by the Comte d'Artois. The last line spoken by one of the characters rhymes with the opening line of the *Jeu de Robin et Marion*, and the only manuscript (*P*) containing this prologue also interpolates in the play itself eighty-eight lines attributed to some of the persons addressed by the pilgrim. Apparently the author of the pilgrim-prologue wanted not only to praise Adam but to localize the scene of the play near Arras (in its original form it was unlocalized) and to identify the poet with that town in view of a contemplated revival of the play there, perhaps an anniversary performance.[2]

We know of a play about Robin and Marion performed at the Pentecost fairs of Angers each year 'tant par les ecoliers et filz de bourgois comme aultres', but the reference is in a document of 1392 and we cannot be sure that this was Adam's play. It seems to Guy and others more like some sort of popular dance than a true play.[3] However, the number of roles—seven or eight—corresponds, and at least one of the manuscripts of Adam's play is dated in the fourteenth century while the other

---

[1] Gérold, op. cit., p. 304, points out that MS. *A* shows a later version of the music than *P*. Cf. also Chailley, op. cit. For a picture of dancing shepherds and shepherdesses from a fifteenth-century manuscript see Bédier-Hazard *Histoire, de la littérature française*, i. 68.

[2] On the *Jeu du Pèlerin* see Langlois, *Rom.* xxiv (1895), 437–46.

[3] See Guy, op. cit., pp. 197–9.

two are of the end of the thirteenth or beginning of the fourteenth, so that memory of the piece must have survived long
after the author's death. In any case this light, gay *balerie* has
a timeless quality which with its songs and dances and its *air
champêtre* would make it a delicate entertainment for almost
any audience. It needed little scenery, could be played indoors
or out, and, like the stories about the English Robin Hood,
would appeal to the young of all ages.[1]

---

[1] Chambers, i. 171 ff., has suggested that the French Robin of the *pastourelles*
connects with the English Robin of the May-games who is also the May King
and Robin Hood. He thinks that the Robin and Marion of the French *fêtes du mai*
merged in England with Robin Hood, and that it is because of this merging that
Robin Hood and Maid Marion became in England the May King and Queen.
On the staging of the play see Cohen's introduction to his modern transcription
and Bahlsen in *AA*, xxvii (1885).

XXIII

Aucassin et Nicolette

SOMETHING may perhaps be said here about *Aucassin et Nicolette* because, although it is not a play, it illustrates the thesis often presented in this book that during the Middle Ages the dividing line between the recitation of narrative material and the dramatization of such material was frequently a narrow one. The anonymous thirteenth-century text of *Aucassin et Nicolette*, which survives in a unique copy of the same century, calls itself a *chante-fable*, or song-story, and the tale progresses by means of alternate passages of prose that was recited and of verse that was sung. Incidentally, neumes give us the music of the songs and their haunting melody retains its charm to this day. Two persons, a narrator and a singer, seem to have been entrusted with the performance, and both their parts contain direct discourse which they may well have pronounced with the aid of impersonation, voice-changes, and mimetic action. Long ago Gaston Paris wrote: 'Cette prose a été faite pour être récitée, presque jouée, et non pour être froidement lue.' Meyer-Lübke indeed tried to argue that *Aucassin et Nicolette* is a play by emphasizing the importance in it of monologues and dialogues and by reducing the connecting tissue to the status of stage directions. But this hypothesis does an injustice to the narrative portions, which mesh with the direct discourse and cannot be removed without mutilating the style and rhythm of both prose and verse. If such parts were suppressed or spoken by a third performer, much of the charm of the *chante-fable* would be lost.[1] As has often been remarked, no more than two persons are ever involved in any conversation; if others are

---

[1] The best editions are by M. Roques in *CFMA* and H. and W. Suchier. See also G. Paris, *Poèmes et légendes*, pp. 97–112. Meyer-Lübke argued that the piece was a play in *ZRP*, xxxiv (1910), 513–22. He was answered by Aschner, *ZRP*, xxxv (1911), 741–3, and Roques, loc. cit., among others. For the hypothesis that the words *Or se cante* and *Or dient et content et fabloient* are cues to the two performers see Frank, *MLN*, xlvii (1932), 14. Cf. also Pauphilet, *Le Legs du moyen âge*, pp. 239–48, and my interpretation of line 2 in *RR*, xl (1949), 161.

present they remain mute. A competent performer could readily mimic two people. The *chante-fable* was undoubtedly designed for performance, but it is not a play in the accepted sense of the word. It owes its consideration in this book to the fact that it stands on the threshold of dramatic comedy.

The initial song tells us that we are about to hear the story of two fair lovers, Nicolette and Aucassin, of the pains he suffered, and the valiant deeds that he performed for his mistress, and it promises us that the words will be gracious and fitly fashioned, the music sweet. Then in alternate prose and verse we learn of the love of a noble lad for a slave-girl, of how they were kept apart, and how they finally came together after many adventures. This is a theme sanctioned since the beginning of time and still universally potent, but our tale highlights the old, old story with wit and a rare combination of fantasy and realism, giving us a picture of the never-never land of far away and long ago with the patina of ageless truth and humour illuminating the whole canvas. It has grace and delicacy, freshness and idyllic charm, all seasoned with gentle irony at the expense of delectable youngsters in the springtime madness of love. Gaston Paris observed that the author sometimes seems to be making fun of his hero and heroine, but as one who has himself experienced their emotions.[1]

Pauphilet and others have detected an element of parody in the *chante-fable*, suggesting that the author, like Chaucer and Cervantes, was lightly mocking the serious romances of his own day and deliberately turning the motives of the chivalric stories upside down. Where chivalry dictated that heroes must fight for their ladies and undertake difficult adventures to show their prowess, Aucassin scorns knighthood and mopes because he cannot have his Nicolette. He even falls off his horse from too much thinking of his sweetheart. And where the heroines of the romances usually remain placidly on their pedestals to be worshipped, the enterprising Nicolette initiates such slight action as the story possesses. Obviously, neither of these young people quite fits the traditional pattern of chivalry or the courtly romances. Yet one must not exaggerate. If parody alone were the author's motive, then his sense of reality and his delight in

[1] *Poèmes et légendes*, p. 108.

his own playfulness got the better of him. And mere parody of
forgotten chivalric romances would hardly charm us today, as
this unpretentious trifle continues to do.

United to the mockery is the author's affection for his young
lovers, his sympathy and tenderness. Both hero and heroine are
fair, and the beauty of Nicolette is effectively suggested both
directly and indirectly. Aucassin sometimes seems too plaintive
to us, too lacking in decisiveness, but he is always generous
and devoted, and he can act aggressively on occasion. Nicolette is obviously the more resourceful of the two, though in
a thoroughly feminine fashion. Indeed the forthright way in
which she expresses her love and obtains her man has a modern,
not to say a universal, flavour.

The author gives plentiful evidence of his puckish sense of
humour, whatever its intention. In the famous passage in which
Aucassin says he prefers hell with Nicolette to paradise without
her, he proceeds to paint an impudent picture of those who go
to each, a picture as unflattering to the saved as it is gracious to
the damned, and the damned, it will be remembered, include
not only brave warriors, luxury-loving knights, and beautiful
ladies who have two or three lovers, but also those obviously
even nearer the author's own heart, the fair clerks, harpers, and
jongleurs. Another instance of his playfulness occurs when
Aucassin rides into battle thinking only of his true love and is
captured by the enemy. Our hero would have been speedily
destroyed, had he not remembered just in time that, once his
head had been cut off, he could never speak to Nicolette again.
Impish, too, is Aucassin's behaviour when he goes into the fray
only upon his father's promise that, if he survives, he may see
his true love, and when, after his father refuses to honour this
covenant, telling him Nicolette is unworthy of him, the lad
turns fiercely upon the old man with 'Preach me no sermons'
and releases his father's enemy whom he has captured in the
battle, extracting an oath from the startled enemy that the war
against his father will continue to be harshly waged. There are
both wit and realism in the author's portrayal of a forthright
shepherd and a surly cowherd, as well as in his whimsical picture of the topsy-turvy kingdom of Torelore where the king
lies in childbed while the queen fights with an army that uses

apples, eggs, cheeses, and mushrooms as weapons.[1] A subtler kind of humour pervades the piece when Aucassin is in prison and Nicolette, fleeing for her life, pauses to speak to him. The lovers are in grave danger and may never meet again, yet they spend these few precious minutes in arguing about who loves whom most.

The 'plot', of course, is of the simplest and motivation in the modern sense is often lacking. Much happens with the sketchiest of preparation, or none at all. Nicolette leaves Aucassin without telling him where she is going, and yet, once in the forest, she expects him to come and find her. And he does so—on the advice of a knight of whom we have never heard before and of whom we never hear again. At the end of the tale pirates separate the lovers, carrying Nicolette off to Carthage, but, like the pirates of Penzance, they serve a kindly purpose. The King of Carthage recognizes Nicolette at once as his long-lost daughter. And soon she makes her way over the sea without too much difficulty, disguises herself as a minstrel, and is reunited to Aucassin.

But plot was not our author's concern. It is the unexpected twists in dialogue and the surprising contrasts of situation that obviously pleased him: the effrontery of Aucassin in the presence of his father; the saucy shepherd and the churlish cowherd in conversation with our infatuated young lovers; the sudden boldness of Aucassin in the Utopian kingdom of Torelore. And the author delighted in artistically posing and lighting his scenes. Nicolette leaves her prison in the soft air of a May night, crosses the garden, and tucks up her dress against the dew, her white feet making the little daisies seem black beside their whiteness. Or again, Nicolette with the moonlight brightening the street crouches in the shadows of Aucassin's tower and seeks a crevice through which to commune with her lover. Or again, the lovers meet in the forest in a bower that Nicolette had fashioned of leaves and flowers and used, like a child, to test the love and discernment of Aucassin. Or again, Aucassin with Nicolette in his arms rides over dale and down, he knows not where. And throughout these scenes

---

[1] On the so-called *couvade*, still observed by the Basques and widely prevalent elsewhere, see W. Suchier's note to 28, 18.

the background may be romantic, but the foreground is real, and the lovers are always real in their devotion to one another.

Moreover our author was a poet: he could be lyrical, precise, intense, and musical, with an ear for tonal colour and fitting sound. His use of diminutives, of liquid consonants, and feminine endings is especially evocative. The versified parts are in a somewhat unusual rhythm. Each division contains a varying number of seven-syllabled lines, linked together not by rhyme but by assonance, with a short four-syllabled refrain at the end. This rhythm was archaic for the author's time and helped, I think, to throw the tale into the distant past. It should also be remarked that the versified sections, although they were sung, nevertheless form an integral part of the whole: they are not mere embellishments and can seldom be omitted, because they usually carry the narrative forward.

As for the prose portions, they are often as poetic, sometimes even more poetic, than the verse. They contain many stylized repetitions. Such repetitions occur in almost all medieval poetry. They served a special and useful purpose in the Middle Ages, as in the days of Homer and in all ages when poetry has used the ears of auditors rather than the eyes of readers. These repetitions give us today the lilt and flavour of ballads and folk-tales. But they belong to the conscious artistry of medieval writers, and in their own time, as now, they heightened the hearer's sense of recognition and identification, even as they soothed him with their remembered cadences.

So many things about *Aucassin et Nicolette* are unique—beginning with its form—that efforts to find sources, influences, and parallels have merely served to emphasize its originality. Analogues have been sought in Greek, Byzantine, Latin, Arabic, Celtic, and Old Norse tales, in the lyric *tensons*, *partimens*, *albas*, *pastourelles*, and *razos* of Provence, as well as in the Old French romances of Chrétien de Troyes and other authors.[1] In seeking to establish its dramatic heritage, Meyer-Lübke tried to equate it with the *Sponsus* and the Anglo-Norman *Resureccion*, with

[1] See among many others Meyer-Lübke, Aschner, W. Suchier, and Roques, op. cit.; J. R. Reinhard, *Speculum*, i (1926), 157–69; Faral, *Recherches sur les sources latines*, pp. 26–33; Leo Jordan in *ZRP*, xliv (1924), 291–307; Scheludko, *ZFSL*, li (1928), 255–93.

Bodel's *S. Nicolas*, with *Courtois d'Arras*, and the plays of Adam le Bossu.[1] None of these explains the magic of our *chante-fable*. One may relate the prose-verse form to some, the series of romanesque adventures to others, the watchman's song to the *alba*, the forthright peasants to those in *Robin et Marion* and in some of the *pastourelles*, the mockery of the powerful to a similar attitude in the *Jeu de la Feuillée* or in the widespread oral parodies of church doctrine.[2] But the fact remains that nowhere else in Old French literature does one find all the essential elements of our text united, nor does one find anywhere in the posited analogues its delicate whimsicality, its gentle air of raillery, or its application of the test of reality to romantic themes. In form and content *Aucassin et Nicolette* owes little to its predecessors, almost everything to the imagination of a gifted poet.[3]

[1] See Meyer-Lübke, op. cit.
[2] See especially W. Suchier's note to 6. 26.
[3] For a lengthy examination of the *chante-fable* see K. Rogger in *ZRP* lxvii (1951), 409–57 and lxx (1954), 1–58.

XXIV

Comedy in the Fifteenth and Sixteenth Centuries

THE prolific production of dramatic works of a serious and religious nature in the fifteenth and sixteenth centuries was matched in comedy by a spate of farces, *sotties*, moralities, and humorous monologues of various sorts. The invention of printing has conserved a relatively large number of these offerings, many of them on long, narrow pages, the so-called *agenda* form. The desire of those who witnessed performances to own copies of the plays, the needs of actors reading their roles, and the collecting instincts of men with private libraries were all served by such editions which were made by popular printers of the day—Trepperel, Levet, Pierre Le Caron, and others of Paris, Lyons, Rouen, and elsewhere—who seem to have exploited this trade.[1]

The dividing line between farces, *sotties*, and moralities was not clearly established in the Middle Ages; such titles as *sottie et farce*, *farce ou sottie*, *farce moralisée* are frequent, and the subject-matter often makes exact definition difficult. Nevertheless, even while realizing this difficulty, modern editors find it convenient to distinguish between the various types, and there is testimony to the fact that certain differences have always been recognized. Gringore's *Prince des Sots et Mère Sotte*, for example, has an explicit 'Fin du Cry, Sottie, Moralité et Farce composez par Pierre Gringoire, dit Mère Sotte, et imprimé pour iceluy', and it has been conjectured that this represents the order of theatrical performances sometimes observed in his time, namely a *sottie*, preceded by a humorous proclamation or *cry* to amuse the noisy crowd, then a morality (or mystery), and finally a farce.[2] And yet the question of whether a given piece should be

---

[1] On the late comedy see E. Droz, *Recueil Trepperel*; E. Picot, *Recueil général des sotties*; H. G. Harvey, *Theatre of the Basoche*; I. Maxwell, *French Farce and John Heywood*; Cohen, *Recueil*, and in *Convivium* xxiii, N.S. (1955), 16–28. For earlier collections and comments see Petit de Julleville, *Répertoire*, *Comédiens*, and *Comédie*. An analysis of comic devices in the early French theatre appears in Robert Garapon, *La Fantaisie verbale et le comique dans le théâtre français*, Paris, 1957.

[2] See Gringore, *Œuvres complètes*, Paris, 1858, i. 286, and cf. Harvey, op. cit., p. 174. Droz, op. cit., p. xliv, believes it was customary to print plays in such series and sell them during performances.

classified as *sottie* or farce frequently arises and cannot always be settled. In their several collections Picot and Droz attempt to differentiate between the two types, but Cohen does not, and contemporary audiences probably saw little difference between them. As Droz well says, 'on glisse imperceptiblement d'un genre à l'autre'.[1]

The *sottie* was essentially a comedy played by 'fools' in their characteristic costume of cap with asses' ears, staff with bells, and parti-coloured dress. The licence always permitted *sots* appeared early in the ecclesiastical Feast of Fools, not to mention earlier evidence from Greece, Rome, and the Orient. It is obvious in Adam le Bossu's *Jeu de la Feuillée*, in various religious plays and moralities, and persisted long afterwards in the Renaissance theatre and in the practice of royal and court fools. Such licence, translated into rapid patter and acrobatic clowning, characterizes the true *sottie*, even though some of the texts later become almost indistinguishable from the farces. The actors, masquerading as fools, bear various fanciful names like Molostru, Fine Myne, Teste Verte, as well as Premier Sot, le Second, &c., and their leader is apt to be called prince, mother, captain, or general. Since satirical allegory played a large part in the *sottie*, the leader sometimes represented the King of France or some other important figure as well as the director of the society responsible for the piece. In their skits the *sots* deride all kinds of persons and ridicule social, political, or ecclesiastical abuses but, as Thomas Sebillet said in the sixteenth century, their chief aim is dissolute laughter. For the most part, indeed, theirs is slapstick comedy, quick banter uttered amid cries and blows. The *vray sot* had to be agile, young, and intelligent. Some of the later writers of *sotties* endowed the fast chatter of their fools with the subtleties of farce, with clever dialogues and carefully constructed plots,[2] but most of the earlier ones contented themselves with little or no action, depending for laughter on lively interchanges of buffets and on harangues involving puns, obscenities, double meanings, and misunderstandings. It is possible that, as Droz has suggested, the joyous

[1] Op. cit., p. lxix.
[2] Cf. the political *sottie* forming part of Gringore's *Jeu du Prince des Sots* (*Œuvres*, i. 203) and the realistic *Trois galans et Phlipot* (Picot, op. cit. iii, no. 26).

company of fools might transform the more pretentious farces —even a *Maître Pierre Pathelin*—into *sotties* by playing them in fool's costume, changing the *mise en scène* and speeding the dialogue,[1] but the typical *sottie* seems, at least at first, to have involved few roles and to have united the perennial antics of the clown with *menus propos*, a kind of vaudeville patter.

The word 'farce', used in its dramatic sense, first appears in France, so far as we know, in a document of 1398 forbidding the inhabitants of Paris, Saint-Maur, and other nearby places to give 'jeux de personnages par maniere de farces, de vie de sains, ne autrement' without express permission.[2] After the death of Eustache Deschamps, in the table of contents of a manuscript devoted to his works, that author's *Maître Trubert et Antroignart* is entitled a farce, and, though unconventional in form—it has a few narrative lines at the beginning and end— and possibly designed for performance by a single clever impersonator rather than by several actors, the poem does present many of the essentials of farce: swift repartee and a humorous twisting of the widely prevalent farcical theme of the trickster tricked—in this case, as in *Pathelin*, a crafty lawyer fooled by a craftier litigant. Deschamps, who lived at the end of the fourteenth century, also wrote 'un beau dit des quatre offices de l'ostel du roy . . . à jouer par personnaiges', which, while essentially a dramatic debate of the morality type between the purveyors of bread, wine, food, and sauces, each defending his own office, also contains certain farcical elements. Both these pieces carry on the age-old tradition of the dramatic monologue but both also were obviously designed in the tradition of true comedy.[3] The earliest surviving example of a conventional French farce that is so called by the copyist is in the Ste Geneviève collection where we read in the midst of a saint's play, the *Vie Monseigneur S. Fiacre*, 'Cy est interposé une farsse.'[4] But in

---

[1] Droz, op. cit., p. lxviii. Note also the interesting suggestion on p. lxix that the *sottie* may have exercised some influence upon the Italian *commedia dell' arte*, and cf. Attinger, *L'Esprit de la commedia dell' arte dans le théâtre français*.

[2] See Petit de Julleville, *Mystères*, i. 414–15, and above, Chap. XIV, pp. 145–7.

[3] Cf. Faral, *Jongleurs*, p. 237, and Harvey, op. cit., p. 71. For Deschamps's pieces see his *Œuvres complètes*, vii. 155 and 175.

[4] The word 'farce' from *farcire* here echoes its original sense of 'filling, stuffing', and may have been used in the meaning of *intermède*. The term, of course, very early has its original sense in the non-dramatic *épîtres farcies*. Harvey, op. cit.,

many ways the earlier *Garçon et l'Aveugle* (cf. Chap. XXI, above) conforms to the type and there can be little doubt that something in the nature of farce was known in France long before the fifteenth century.

In that century and the following one, however, farces flourished. Short and simple, most of them exhibit an admirable sense of unity and structural balance. Like the *sottie*, they needed few characters and made fun of contemporary persons and local abuses. Priests, unfaithful wives or husbands, inept doctors and soldiers, all come in for twitting; fashions and would-be learned ladies are ridiculed; and neither peasant, bourgeois, nor nobleman is spared. Especially typical is the triangle, faithless wife, philandering priest, and cuckolded husband. With plots resembling the *fabliaux* and *nouvelles* which they sometimes dramatized,[1] the farces are mostly comic stories of human frailty, rather than satires on the ills of society. The themes include endless variations involving tricks of different sorts with the duper frequently duped, deflated braggarts of the old *miles gloriosus* type, simpletons who misunderstand instructions and act accordingly, and many marital quarrels between wives and husbands caught in adulteries. Some plays dramatize well-known proverbial expressions.[2] Comic effects include beatings, disguises, reversed roles, confessions to the wrong persons (who are usually the wronged persons as well), and verbal ambiguities, especially puns, equivocations, and obscene plays upon words. Like the *sotties*, the farces vary in literary value: some are vivid, deft, full of keen observation; others seem merely dull and insipid. Many are coarse and most are cynical. But all have a special interest as an expression of the colourful, everyday life and language of their time.

Closely related in subject-matter to the farces are the *sermon joyeux* and the dramatic monologue. The first is a recitation with

p. 112, n. 16, would date the Ste Geneviève farce in the time of Charles VII, but it is more plausibly dated *c.* 1420 (see Chap. XIV, above).

[1] Cf. Toldo, *Études*, pp. 181 ff., and Faral, *Jongleurs*, p. 237, who says, 'nous croyons que le monologue fournit logiquement, et peut-être historiquement, un intermédiaire entre le fabliau et la farce . . .'.

[2] Cf. in Cohen's *Recueil*, no. xv, *Farce des femmes qui font accroire à leurs maris de vecies que ce sont lanternes*, and also nos. ix, xix, xx, xxiv, &c. For list see Droz's review in *Bibl. d'Humanisme et Renaissance*, xi (1949), pp. 301–2.

satirical overtones travestying real sermons and the sermons of
the mystery plays, the second a recitation by a single speaker
with appropriate gestures and sometimes with voice-changes
to suggest more than one participant. The *sermons* might be
spoken by *sots*; they often involve facetiously named 'saints'
and make fun of such themes as drinkers and fools, love,
women, and marriage. The monologues represent many different sorts of persons as their speakers—charlatans, valets,
boasting soldiers, villagers, lovers, &c.—and considerable skill
might be demanded of those who recited them. One of the
cleverest of these *farces à un personnage* is the *Franc archier de
Bagnolet*, in which a theme dear to farce—a braggart afraid of
a scarecrow—receives amusing treatment. The usual position
of the *sermons* was at the beginning of dramatic representations,
but they, like the monologues, adapted themselves to many
varied purposes. Both types of recitation participated in the
tremendous vogue enjoyed by the true farces, a vogue that did
not wane even in the seventeenth century.[1]

The morality plays of France, unlike the *sotties* and farces,
could be either serious or gay, but many of the best of them
belong in the realm of comedy. Always didactic in purpose,
they varied widely in subject-matter and treatment, so that some
may properly be considered more edifying than diverting,
whereas others approach farce so closely that the dividing line
is almost invisible. Their dual nature is evident from our texts
and manuscripts as well as from statutes of 1447 concerning
the university of Orléans which forbade students of the
various Nations to give comedies *etiam sub forma moralitatum*.[2]
Allegorical figures usually are present, but since these also
appear in the *sotties* they cannot be considered as a conclusively
distinguishing element. What especially characterizes the true
morality is a didactic intention expressed in symbol and story.

---

[1] On the *sermon joyeux* and the dramatic monologue see É. Picot, *Le Monologue dramatique*.

[2] On slanderous comedies at Orléans see D. Quynn and H. S. Snellgrove in
MLN, lvii (1942), pp. 185–7. The terms *moralité* and *moralisé* in our manuscripts
cover such widely differing texts as André de la Vigne's *Moralité de l'aveugle et du
boiteux*, which differs little from farce, the *Moralité du sacrifice d'Abraham* which
is a fragment of the *Viel Testament*—it is the first piece of the *Recueil Trepperel*
(see p. xv)—and number 34 of the *Recueil Trepperel* (p. xxx), which is called a
farce moralisée although it is a true morality.

It is known that as early as 1390 *gieux* about the seven deadly sins were given at Tours, and the Chantilly collection, as we have seen, contains a morality upon this widely popular theme.[1] Indeed the earliest moralities were for the most part serious in content, concerned with such topics as the salvation of man's soul conceived as a battle between good and evil, a pilgrimage, the siege of a castle or the like. But later the moralities served political, educational, social, and religious ends. There were also historical moralities like *Le Concile de Basle, La Paix de Peronne, La Prinse de Calais*, &c. And quite early, comedy, with plentiful doses of singing and dancing, served to sugar the pill.

Unlike the *sotties* and farces, the moralities could be very long as well as quite short. Some are little more than dramatized arguments—between Knowledge and Ignorance, Flesh and Spirit, &c.—whereas others, embracing many characters and demanding a huge stage, possess intricate plots and may even, like the mysteries, have demanded more than a single day for their performance.

The themes of the more humorous moralities mirror the trends and tastes of the time: the desire for allegorized instruction with personified symbols, the interest in debate, the delight in singing and dancing. Subjects and treatment vary widely. To mention only a few, *Les Enfants de Maintenant* is a satire on the modern children of the day and their parents; the *Condamnacion de Bancquet* attacks the evils of gluttony; the *Blasphémateurs du nom de Dieu* is directed against the sin of blasphemy. Incidentally this last play introduces various realistic games of cards and ends with two of the blasphemers meeting a just punishment after a debate between the Virgin and devils, whereas two others pray for forgiveness and are saved, the morality ending with

---

[1] See Chap. XIV, above, and for other plays on this theme, Chambers, ii. 154. On the moralities in general see Petit de Julleville, *Répertoire*; Harvey, op. cit., pp. 39 ff.; Maxwell, op. cit., pp. 22–23, and earlier authorities cited by them. Cf. too Wm. Roy Mackenzie, *The English Moralities*. I am also indebted to a paper, 'The Morality Play as a Microcosm', by Roberta B. Cornelius, read before the Medieval Section of the Modern Language Association of America, 9 Sept. 1949. As she pointed out there: 'The fourfold interpretation of the scriptures; the endless figurative concepts calling into play the battle, the siege, the castle, the temple, the pilgrimage; the bestiaries and the lapidaries . . . all these repeatedly attest the medieval delight in allegory, symbol, and emblem.'

the *Te Deum laudamus* and in this and other ways recalling the religious plays.

In form the *sotties* and farces show less variety than the moralities and mystery plays. Octosyllabic couplets with mnemonic rhymes are the general rule in both *sotties* and farces. Some repeated li.nes or refrains, stanzaic structure with lines of varying length, many triolets used for specific purposes, and a considerable number of songs help relieve the monotony. A single line often divided into as many as three or four speeches gives great rapidity to the dialogue, and the humorous re-echoing of a phrase in varying circumstances that underscores so many of the plots frequently produces a lilting rhythm.[1]

The moralities, on the contrary, are more ambitious in technique. They introduce much singing, some dancing, and make abundant use of artificial forms like the *rondeau*, *ballade*, and *chant royal*, and in some of them specific metrical patterns serve to characterize particular persons. In fact the diversity of rhythms in the moralities, both comic and serious, serves to emphasize their literary pretensions and to accord with their status as dramatic offerings comparable in importance with the mysteries.

The playing and writing of comic pieces in the fifteenth and sixteenth centuries was largely in the hands of societies devoted, among other things, to that purpose. In Paris these were the Enfants-sans-souci and the Basochiens; in the provinces, various similar organizations. Students also gave plays and so did groups of professional entertainers who wandered from place to place or became attached to noble protectors. The early history of the Enfants-sans-souci is obscure, but we know that their members were the *sots* who played in the *sotties*, and it seems probable that the Enfants were merely a special group of Basochiens, perhaps originally affiliated with the Basoche du Palais in Paris. Each high court of justice in Paris had its separate division of a society of law clerks known as the Basoche, and it has been estimated that before the end of the fifteenth century there were about 10,000 Basochiens in Paris alone, while similar groups were widely prevalent in the provinces.[2]

---

[1] On the art of the farce see Maxwell, op. cit., pp. 37 ff.

[2] See Harvey, op. cit., p. 14, n. 9, and p. 17, n. 12; also Ph. Aug. Becker, *Die*

By the middle of that century the Enfants-sans-souci and Basochiens, who had both been playing *sotties*, farces, and moralities in competition with the Confrérie de la Passion, seem to have arranged some sort of partnership with them, and from that time on these societies played their comedies in conjunction with the religious plays of the Confrérie, first at the Hôpital de la Trinité and later, until the end of the sixteenth century, at the Hôtel de Bourgogne.[1]

Though many of our comic pieces of this time can plausibly be attributed to the law clerks, we know that students, ecclesiastics (many prohibitions show they took part), artisans (we hear of a shoemaker writing a farce for a legate), and professional jongleurs were also concerned in both their authorship and their performance. We hear, too, of *farces d'échafaud, farces de noces, de collège*, and *de bande* (i.e. composed for a regular company).[2] These pieces might be given indoors or outdoors, in private halls or public squares; they might be performed before sponsoring societies, at town or guild festivals, at weddings or in conjunction with the religious plays. Comedies parodying the schools and learning can be confidently ascribed to students,[3] and the *sotties*, as we have seen, largely belonged to the Enfants-sans-souci, but all types apparently were included in the repertory of the Basochiens.

It is difficult to date most of the compositions except for those signed by their authors or those that lampoon definite

Narrenspiele, p. 7. Harvey, op. cit., pp. 174–5, says there were many short-lived groups of *sots* and *badins* both in the provinces and in Paris that had no connexion with the Basoches, but that the *sots* of the Basoches formed permanent organizations and finally became the chief players of *sotties* in Paris.

[1] Harvey, op. cit., p. 24. Harvey has shown *passim* that although satires on nobles, clerics, and specific contemporary abuses were frequent in the comic pieces, the legal profession was largely exempt from attack. He believes that authors and spectators alike belonged in large measure to legal circles.

[2] See the *Sottie des Coppieurs et Lardeurs*, lines 173 ff., in Droz, *Receuil Trepperel*, p. 164. *Pathelin* is considered outmoded in this *sottie* and the discussion there of other plays is also enlightening.

[3] Droz, op. cit., p. xxiv, describes *La Cene des dieux* (unprinted as yet) as 'le type de la revue de collège, d'inspiration savante'. The earliest morality known to have been played by students was 'faite au collège de Navarre le jour de Saint-Antoine, 1426' and has been identified by Morawski in *RLR*, lxv (1927), 71 ff. as in MS. Bib. Nat. fr. 25.547. Harvey, op. cit., p. 14, notes that graduates of law schools would perhaps have played in school plays and in any case would have been accustomed to appearing in public.

events. Many that appear in collections printed in the sixteenth century doubtless were written in the fifteenth; they were, in Droz's words, *vieilles, mais non vieillies* (p. lxxii), or wary printers would not have printed them.[1] Sometimes earlier and later, or shorter and longer, versions of the same play survive (e.g. in Cohen's *Recueil*, XXI and XXXV). The same piece may also appear in several collections made at different times, and the same characters—Thévot, Maître Mimin, Maître Alliborum, &c.—may reappear in more than one play. The popularity of farces and *sotties* is attested by our many surviving texts (no doubt a small part of the whole repertory), but they are infrequently mentioned in our records of performances. References to the playing of moralities, on the other hand, occur often and bear witness not only to their attraction for their audiences but also to their prestige. Nevertheless, with certain exceptions, accurate chronologies have not been established, and accordingly, though it is possible to select characteristic comic pieces, classify them in various ways, and separate the better from the worse, it is as yet impossible to write a history of the development of the various types. Some of the keenest and most original writers of the day used their talents in composing humorous plays, but simultaneously many hacks also engaged in their manufacture. It may be as well to conclude this chapter therefore with an analysis of a few of the worthier or more typical examples of each genre.

LES VIGILES DE TRIBOULET

A characteristic and revealing *sottie* in the *Recueil Trepperel* is *Les Vigiles de Triboulet*,[2] to be played by four actors, Sotouart, Croquepie, Mère Sotie, and Rossignol. The play opens with typical banter and clowning. Sotouart's first words are:

> Ou estes vous, folz afollés,
> Follement follant en folie?

The young fools, Sotouart and Croquepie, exchange jests and exhibit acrobatic skills, probably singing and dancing as they

---

[1] For a list of French farces and an attempt to date them see Maxwell, op. cit., pp. 121 ff. Cohen's *Recueil* appeared after it was made. The lists of Petit de Julleville's *Répertoire* for the moralities and those of Picot and Droz for the *sotties* are useful.

[2] Droz, op. cit., pp. 217 ff. The editor dates it *c.* 1480.

do so, while Mère Sotie on a lower level implies in asides that she has heard bad news. Suddenly she weeps and announces to her companion, Rossignol, that Triboulet, fine player of farces and unexcelled guzzler of wine, is dead. The young fools above become aware of their mother's grief and urge her to leave off mourning and join in their sports. But she and Rossignol beg them to desist from fooling today since they must bury Triboulet, their master, captain, father, head, and leader of all fools hereabouts. There follows a mock service for Triboulet, sung antiphonally by the four actors, in which we learn much about this good actor who composed many *sotties*, no less than 400 moralities, and an equal number of farces. He was a prodigious eater and drinker and his bauble could perform miracles. He died with his muzzle in the pot, sucking up wine so gently that he lost consciousness, but whether he died of thirst is unknown. Before his death he spoke diverse languages, Latin, Picard, Flemish, French. 'Oncques maistre Françoys Villon / Ne composa si bon jargon' (lines 223–4).

In lessons and responses, the fools continue to give us the legend of Triboulet. He was associated with the famous fool named Maître Mouche and he is to be buried in a copy of the farce of *Pathelin*. When he lay dying he began to recite this and other farces, as well as *La Belle Dame sans mercy*. Then he gave a great leap and demanded that a scaffold be erected so that he might play his role But his body was so hot that it melted like a fat cheese, and after his death enough red wine issued from his eyes to water a garden. Mère Sotie, in a final eulogy (lines 311–12), pronounces him 'ung sot autentique / Prest a jouer et a tout faire'. She says that a wake must be held for the dead and that the fools must drink so that they may keep his memory fresh.

The name Triboulet, synonymous with that of the professional fool, was borne by numerous men from at least 1447 on. Our *sottie* associates him with another frequently mentioned professional fool, Maître Mouche. (Both are referred to by Rabelais.) Droz believes that the Triboulet of our *sottie* was a real person, that his decease in this play is fictitious, and that the piece was actually written by him, with the author himself perhaps playing the role of Mère Sotie. Certainly it would add to

the piquancy of the performance to have a famous actor present
at his own obsequies, listening to his own satirical eulogies and
the details of his vinous death. In any case, the references to
Villon and *Pathelin*, to the scaffolds used for performances, and
to an actor who wrote *sotties*, farces, and moralities and recited
not only these but *La Belle Dame sans mercy*, give this work a
special fillip for the modern reader.

On the other hand, typical in this *sottie* are the characters and
the names they bear—Croquepie connotes a tosspot, Sotouart
a dunce, and Rossignol perhaps a picklock. The role of Mère
Sotie, as usual, has a prominent place. Typical too is the absence
of flesh and blood in the characters and of any true feeling in
their words. Nor is the parody of a church office unknown to
other *sotties*. And, of course, the initial repartee and horseplay
prevail in all pieces of this type. Hard and brittle, sometimes
coarse, with a theme of contemporaneous interest, with quick
interchanges in lines divided between speakers, and with rhythmic repetitions that point up humorous phrases (cf. lines 196-7,
212-13, 231-2, 'Or est il mort et trespassé / Mais se c'est de soif,
je ne scay'), this *sottie*—better than average, but not the best of
its kind—will perhaps serve as a fair illustration of its genre.

MAÎTRE PIERRE PATHELIN

Among the farces there can be but one choice, since *Maître
Pierre Pathelin* far outranks all the others.[1] Its witty delineation
of character and the subtle convolutions of its plot have always
been admired, and the changes rung on the widely prevalent
theme of the duper duped carry conviction even as they awaken
amused surprise. The very first scene between Maître Pierre and
his wife Guillemette initiates the action while revealing the
characters through their own words. We soon know that Pierre
has seen better days but is now a penniless lawyer, ignorant and
dishonest, scorned by all. Self-confident none the less, he is off

[1] Ed. by R. T. Holbrook in *CFMA*, 2nd ed., 1937. See bibliography there,
pp. xxii ff., for the controversy about its authorship. The attempts of Holbrook
and Cons to prove the play by G. Alecis and of Norman origin have met with
little success. Cf. especially Roques in *Rom.* liii (1927), 569, and lviii (1932), 88;
Cazalas in *Rom.* lvii (1931), 573-7, and P. Lemercier in *Rom.* lxxiii (1952), 200.
On legal connexions see Lemercier, op. cit., and Harvey, op. cit., pp. 144 f.
On the word 'pathelin' and its meaning see Frank in *MLN*, lvi (1941), 42-47.

to the fair to obtain cloth to replace the rags worn by himself and his wife and he boasts he will get anything his wife likes without spending a sou. Guillemette understands him perfectly : she tells him he has neither learning nor good sense, and that he is no master of law but only of trickery. However, Pathelin proceeds to the booth of Guillaume Joceaulme, a cloth merchant, and so flatters and cajoles him, so mingles praise of the merchant, his father, and his aunt with praise of his wares and intimations of hidden wealth awaiting a good purchase that presently the bemused merchant, forgetting his well-founded suspicions of his customer, is ready to sell. Indeed Guillaume, foolish gull that he is, thinks he has the better of the bargain since Pathelin is buying cloth at twenty-four sous the ell which is not worth twenty. Pathelin promises to pay in gold, piously seals the sale with God's penny, and asks the merchant to trust him until they shall both have had a drink and some fine roast goose at his house. Guillaume, still suspicious—though even more greedy—demurs, but eventually consents to carry the cloth and go home with the lawyer to pick up his money and eat the promised feast. Pathelin insists, however, that he cannot allow the draper to be burdened with the cloth, no indeed, he will carry it himself, though Guillaume must follow speedily to wine and dine at the house. The merchant is won over by renewed flattery and promises, and the lawyer departs. And now in asides to the audience each man boasts of how he has cheated the other.

Pathelin returns to Guillemette with enough cloth for the two of them, big with pride in his chicanery.

'By St. Mary,' he says, 'I so flattered the fellow that he almost gave me the stuff. I told him how intelligent his late father was. "You come of good stock," I said. But may I be damned if he doesn't come from the worst scum in the realm. "Ah, my friend," I said, "You're like your father in every way." God knows how I heaped it on and all the while I interlarded my praise with talk about his wares. "And then," I said, "by St. Mary, how readily your father trusted his customers. Why," said I, "you're his spit and image !" Yet one could have pulled the teeth of that porpoise, his late father, and of his baboon of a son before either of them would have trusted anyone. But I kept talking so fast and so loud that finally he let me have the cloth on credit.'

What next? Well, the merchant will come for his money, Pathelin will pretend to be sick in bed, and Guillemette must sigh, look sad, and say he has been ill there for weeks. If the draper becomes too urgent she must scold him for joking. Guillemette falls in with the scheme but warns her husband that if it fails he'll suffer even worse than when he was in the pillory. Guillaume appears, eager for good food and wine, as well as for his pay. He calls aloud for Maître Pierre, but at every sound, Guillemette asks him to lower his voice, her poor martyr of a husband is so very ill. Why, says the draper, he was just now at my shop. That couldn't be, Guillemette exclaims. But, the merchant insists, he took home my cloth only half of a quarter of an hour ago. Each begins shrieking at the other. Guillaume demands payment, Guillemette contends that Pathelin is at death's door and that the merchant must stop screaming; he returns to the attack, telling her that she is shouting four times as loud as he. Then suddenly Pathelin in a weak voice calls for help and pretends in a faked delirium to mistake the draper for a physician. The latter continues to press for his payment, but between the various dodges of husband and wife he is at last half-persuaded that no roast goose awaits him, that some mistake has occurred, and he goes off muttering to himself in confusion: 'But he *did* take my cloth. No, he couldn't have. I've seen death in his face. But he did, he put my cloth under his arm. No, he didn't. I don't trust people with my stuff, sleeping or waking. I wouldn't have given him credit. But I did—he took my cloth . . .', &c.

However, while Pathelin and his spouse are rejoicing at the success of their ruse, the merchant unexpectedly returns. He has heard Guillemette laughing, and he angrily demands his money at once. As they argue anew and Guillemette urges that he quit tormenting a dying man, Pathelin again begins to rave, this time in many languages, first in Limousin which his uncle used to speak, next in Picard because his mother came from Picardy, and then at intervals in Flemish, Norman, Breton, Lotharingian, and Latin, all for equally cogent reasons.[1] The

---

[1] The 'Latin' is especially funny: 'Quid petit ille mercator? / Dicat sibi quod trufator, / ille qui in lecto jacet / vult ei dare, si placet, / de oca ad comedendum' (lines 962–6).

poor draper is at last convinced that he is in the presence of
death and begs pardon for his error.

But it soon appears that everyone is out to deceive Guillaume.
Even Thibault Aignelet, his shepherd, to whom he has always
been so kind, has taken to slaughtering his sheep, pretending
they died of the scab, and then eating them. However, he will
bring this Thibault Aignelet to justice! The shepherd appears,
trying to soften his master's wrath and escape the penalty of his
misdeeds, but the merchant, sore after his troubles with Pathelin,
begins to babble incoherently of the slaughter of his sheep and
of getting paid for his six ells of cloth, and he indignantly tells
the shepherd he must stand trial. The frightened Thibault
thereupon appeals to a lawyer—none other than Maître Pierre
Pathelin—to defend him and, though he does not mention the
name of his employer, he makes a clean breast of his guilt.
When he slyly promises payment in gold, Pathelin pledges that
his case shall be won, even were it half again as bad as it is.
They then prepare for the trial. Thibault has killed and eaten
more than thirty sheep in three years and there are plenty of
witnesses who will testify against him. 'That's a fact which will
very much hurt your case', says Pathelin. So will anything the
shepherd may say—'confessions are so very prejudicial'. The
best plan will be for Thibault to pretend he does not know
Pathelin and merely answer 'baa' to any question put to him.
Then the lawyer can come forward and say the poor fellow is
a simpleton unaccountable for his actions. However, the shepherd must promise faithfully never to answer anything except
'baa', even to Pathelin himself—and to pay his lawyer well
after he is free.

Off they go to the trial. Guillaume begins his complaint
against Thibault but suddenly catches sight of Pathelin and is
thrown completely off balance. 'Why, it's you, you to whom I
sold six ells of cloth!' 'What's this about cloth?' asks the judge.
'He's wandering', says Pathelin, 'he can't state his case because
he hasn't learned it.' And as the trial proceeds, Pathelin continues to goad his adversary who, incoherent with rage, gabbles
now of cloth and now of sheep until the court commands, in
words become famous, 'Revenons à ces moutons!' When the
shepherd in his turn is examined, he follows orders and answers

only 'baa'. As the merchant continues to sputter, intermingling his case against the shepherd with that against the lawyer, Pathelin pricks him further by saying he believes Guillaume must have been holding back the shepherd's wages and that he, Pathelin, will undertake to defend the poor fellow. Alternately cajoling, scolding, and reasoning, he interrogates his client who obediently replies to every question with his 'baa'. The court is persuaded to adjudge the shepherd a born fool, and send him back to his sheep. Naturally, the merchant who has lost his suit is furious. He accosts Pathelin and begins once more to berate him. But the lawyer in mock-innocence tries to prove to him that this must be an instance of mistaken identity: he, Pathelin, has bought no cloth, nor has he been ill. 'Well,' says the merchant, 'I shall go to your house and see if you're there.' 'Do that,' says Pathelin, 'and then you'll find out.'

But now it is Pathelin's turn to be outwitted. He asks the shepherd if he is satisfied. 'Baa!' says the shepherd. Pathelin demands payment. 'Baa!' says the shepherd. Then Pathelin in turn flatters his client, pleads, threatens, wheedles, rages, begs— he even pretends Thibault must be joking and invites him home to dinner. Finally he menaces him with prison. Each time he is paid *à son mot*, the inevitable 'baa!' And at the end Thibault, safe in the judge's assurance that he need never again answer any summons, takes to his heels, scot-free.

Everything about this farce sets it above others of its kind. Each new incident grows plausibly from its predecessor; the element of surprise evolves from the characters and is not super-imposed upon them. Pathelin's essential qualities emerge in the first scene, but each new revelation of his ability to deceive is unexpected: his flattery and cozening of the merchant, the feigned illness, the raving in 'divers langaiges', his preparation of the shepherd's case, his whole behaviour in court from his playing upon the merchant's anger to his winning of the verdict so cleverly that even the judge is fooled and proposes that they later dine together. Pathelin's lack of real keenness—early sug-gested by Guillemette—is not revealed to the audience until the shepherd takes him at his word, when the lawyer's combined ingenuity and low cunning unexpectedly meet their match.

The shepherd is realistically portrayed: ungrammatical and

confused, he is sly and suspicious, as the ignorant often are. In appealing to his master, he pretends to be humbly innocent, but he soon detects the fact that the merchant's anger is not directed solely against himself. With Pathelin he openly admits all his guilt, craftily consents to his lawyer's wiles, promises to pay him *à son mot*, and then in the climactic scene stands up to him, baaing, while his increasingly bewildered lawyer tries in turn his every skill to obtain his fee. Guillemette, too, contributes her share to the fun. Neither better nor worse than her husband, though more intelligent in some ways, she ably assists him in confusing the merchant and cleverly covers up her mistake when her laughter is overheard by pretending to have been both laughing and weeping at her husband's delirious ravings. But it is the diddled merchant who probably furnishes most merriment. After the cynical manner of farce he is, except for the judge, the relatively least guilty of the lot. Yet he comes off worst in the end. To be sure, he has sold cloth for more than its worth, but in general he is a fool, not a thief. His readiness to yield to flattery, the way in which his anger can be turned against him, his vacillations between disbelief and credulity, and all his distracted sputterings are infinitely funny. As for the judge, he is not venal, as sometimes alleged, but rather hurried and misguided, acting under the twin pressures of time and two exasperating litigants. Indeed the plot leaves no loose ends, proceeds with cumulative effect to the climax, and is neatly worked out with an art that conceals itself and in language that has the naturalness of everyday speech.

The author of this farce is unknown. Obviously a competent craftsman, he has been inconclusively identified with Villon and Guillaume Alecis among others. He may well have been a member of the legal profession, for Pathelin seems to be a lawyer of a lower court, whether ecclesiastical, as Harvey believes, or seigniorial, as Lemercier seeks to prove, in either case a fair butt for the ridicule of his superiors. The author probably lived in Paris and his farce would admirably suit the taste of the Basochiens. Its date is uncertain but surely before 1470 when the words *pateliner et faire du malade*, which occur in a legal document of that year, can only refer to the farce.[1] Hol-

---

[1] Cf. *MLN*, lvi (1941), 42.

brook's exact date of 1464 rests on insufficient proof, but most authorities agree in ascribing the play to around 1465.

The popularity of the piece is attested by numerous editions from *c.* 1489 on, all based upon Levet's edition of about that time.[1] There are also many references to *Pathelin* in contemporaneous and later comedies, both to the farce itself and to phrases like 'revenons à nos moutons', 'divers langaiges', and to the words *pathelin, pateliner, patelinage, patelinois* in meanings derived from the play. As we have seen above, in the *sottie, Les Vigiles de Triboulet*,[2] the famous actor being mourned by other *sots* spouted Pathelin's dialectal ravings before his death and was to be buried in a copy of the farce. Rabelais, of course, knew the play well; he makes use of it frequently in *Pantagruel*, and in fact English owes the phrase 'to return to our muttons (or wethers)' to a translation of Rabelais's works rather than to the original farce from which Rabelais took it.

In our own day numerous successful performances bear witness to the fact that *Pathelin* is still good theatre. Since the play depends for its success upon excellent characterization, witty dialogue, suspense, a carefully patterned plot, and certain universal foibles of human nature, its reputation as one of our medieval masterpieces seems secure.

LA CONDAMNACION DE BANCQUET

To give some idea of the variety of themes and the differences of treatment in the humorous morality plays, two of the best of them have been chosen for consideration. *La Condamnacion de*

---

[1] Holbrook originally dated Le Roy's print earlier—*c.* 1485 or 1486—but in his 1937 edition of *Pathelin* he seems uncertain. All editions after Levet's, beginning with Beneaut's of 1490, apparently follow his version, and so does the oldest known manuscript of *Pathelin*, dating from the end of the fifteenth century, which is a direct copy of Levet's text.

[2] This *sottie* associates the *divers langaiges* of *Pathelin* with the jargon of Villon. Perhaps the author of the *Vigiles* thought Villon wrote the farce. Villon's thieves' argot, however, is of course very different from the dialectal pastiches of the play. In the latter, although many individual words and certain syntactical tricks can be identified, the author probably attempted merely to give these passages a dialectal flavour. Chevaldin in *Les Jargons de la farce de Pathelin* tried to reconstruct and translate these Breton, Flemish, Norman, and other passages from the varying editions of the farce, but he assumed more exact knowledge of dialects than the author and the printers probably possessed. For characteristic references to the farce in the *sotties* of Droz's *Recueil Trepperel* see the Table there, p. 377.

Bancquet, first printed in 1508, N.S., usually takes highest rank.[1] Its author, Nicolas de la Chesnaye, may have been a physician or lawyer, but has not been certainly identified. At any rate his play combines a sermon on sobriety of diet with a realistic trial for murder and indicates a knowledge of both professions. The characters, Dinner, Supper, and Banquet, each in turn, issue invitations to a number of people, among them the women, Good Company, Greediness, Epicureanism, Custom, and the men, Pastime, I-drink-to-you, and I-pledge-you-in-return. After Dinner's entertainment, though the guests eat and drink well, nothing happens to them. But after Supper's abundant repast, they are attacked by the horribly impersonated ills, Apoplexy, Paralysis, Epilepsy, Quinsy, Pleurisy, Gout, Colic, Dropsy, Gravel, and Jaundice, and when the imprudent and insatiable revellers go on to enjoy Banquet's sumptuous fare, all of them are killed by the various Maladies except Good Company, Custom, and Pastime.

The survivors determine to seek justice from Dame Experience, and the latter half of the play is devoted to a trial of the culprits with various great physicians, Hippocrates, Galen, Avicenna, and Averroës, called in as subordinate judges. Supper is finally judged guilty of assault, Banquet of murder, and, after the latter has confessed his sins, Diet, who has been assisted in guarding the prisoners by Purge, Pill, Blood-letting, Remedy, Sobriety, and Enema, executes the murderer.

The details of this long play obviously regaled the spectators, and many stage-directions indicate how it was performed. At least two levels were required, and in the three great feasts the many mouth-watering viands and beverages described were to be actually displayed or simulated.[2] In the course of the performance the guests dance, instruments are played, and popular songs are sung. Violent action combines with an exciting

---

[1] Ed. by Édouard Fournier, *Théâtre fr. avant la Renaissance*, pp. 216 ff. On the trial scene see Harvey, op. cit., pp. 52 ff. Harvey's statement seems just, i.e. that the 'long, brilliantly farcical scene in which Souper and Bancquet plead their case and are led finally to confess, owes much to the tradition of the *cause grasse* [i.e. burlesque lawsuit] and to the theatre of the Basoche' (p. 64). A modernized version, entitled *La Mort de Souper*, appeared in Paris in 1923.

[2] Cf. the stage-direction regarding the *prunes de Damas* (ed. Fournier, p. 220) which are to be provided, if in season, but, if not, dried ones or wax reproductions, properly coloured, must be used.

spectacle in the attacks of the Maladies, who overturn furniture and fight pitched battles against the revellers. A fool is introduced at various times to provide merriment of divers sorts and some of the incidental scenes have much witty dialogue. The metrical patterns are varied and cleverly contrived with intricate use of an extensive vocabulary and echoic phrases based on words of the same derivation (the so-called 'fraternized rhyme').[1] The characters, despite their abstract nature, have been differentiated in speech and costuming (see, for example, the direction, p. 223, that the Maladies are to take hideous and monstrous forms, to be armed with clubs, and to be dressed so strangely that one can hardly distinguish men from women). But it is the combination of realism and abstraction in the working out of the plot that delights us still both in the festivities pictured and in the trial scene. We could dispense today with the long speeches of the Doctor who from time to time points the moral, and there are other parts that drag, but at its best this morality displays ingenuity and imagination, and in performance its symbolic pageantry, as well as its wit, must have provided excellent entertainment.

LES ENFANTS DE MAINTENANT

Very different from the *Condamnacion de Bancquet* is the morality, *Les Enfants de Maintenant*.[2] The many characters of the former, although individualized by speech and costume, for the most part remain abstractions whereas those of the latter—only thirteen in number—are almost all real individuals who happen to bear abstract names. The one by the grandeur of its spectacles sometimes approaches the religious plays in scope and tone, whereas the other in its earthiness often reminds one of the farces. There is also a diversity of origin: the *Condamnacion*, by a master of law, seems to emanate from the Basoche, the *Enfants*, by a clever student, from the schools.[3]

---

[1] Cf. p. 238: 'Voicy grant curiosité, / Curieuse joyeuseté, / Joyeuse demonstracion . . .' and so on for twenty-four lines.

[2] In Viollet Le Duc, *Ancien théâtre françois*, iii. 5–86.

[3] Harvey's effort to attribute the *Enfants* to a Basochien (pp. 66–67) does not convince me, though of course our author may have been a student of law. However, the end of the play clearly points to a school-piece, probably composed and performed by pupils for their friends and fellows. Also redolent of the schools is the theme and the many citations from the ancients, often in the original Latin.

The moral of the play is that parents should not spoil their children by indulging them but should insist on discipline and a good education. Maintenant and his silly wife, Mignotte, ask Bon Advis what to do about their boys and receive the excellent counsel that they take them to Instruction where the children may be taught a trade or profession. Though Mignotte is afraid of the destructive effects of education, she consents. She tells Instruction she wants her boys to learn everything—all the skills and sciences—but if that is impossible, she would like them to learn how to live without working. Anyway, she says, teach them to read and write and to speak Greek and Latin before Monday morning. Instruction protests that acquiring such subjects will take ten years; they had better learn their father's trade and become bakers. Just don't beat them, begs the mother. Instruction observes that young folk need chastising and that, besides, Mignotte's children are both over-dressed and badly behaved. But to every criticism of her boys the mother merely observes, 'C'est la façon de maintenant.' Nevertheless in the end she leaves them with Instruction.

However, the two boys, Finet (i.e. a sly rogue) and Malduict (i.e. ill-bred), refuse to learn, and eventually they flee school, return to their father, and blackmail him into giving them money and fine clothes. Then they are off to seek an easy life in the service of some great lord. They like the looks of Discipline but she, with her sound advice and heavy scourges, turns out to be as bad as Instruction. At last they meet Jabien (Ne'er-do-well) who promises to make them masters of dice, cards, and all kinds of tricks, if only they will disavow God, practise vice, and, among other things, be haughty to men and gracious to women, and, if the latter do not yield to graciousness, forcibly possess them. The brothers prove to be apt pupils and are especially taken with Jabien's lovely daughter, Luxure. Throughout the play a fool has been furnishing a kind of Greek chorus of comment and at this point he joins the others in singing and dancing. After this interlude of fun, the young men proceed to play various games with Luxure—*glic*, *franc de carreau*, and *merelle*—and lose all they have, including their clothes. Malduict now repents of his evil life and determines to abjure the teachings of Jabien, but Finet continues to sin and goes from bad to worse. He is soon dragged before Honte, who proceeds to make a neat distinction between modesty and shame. She beats and tortures Finet until he is bloody and finally takes him to Despair who condemns him to lose his life on the gibbet of Perdition where he is duly hanged.

The penitent Malduict now reappears, lamenting his sins. Bon Advis counsels him to return to Discipline and Instruction. From Instruction he learns of the joy in heaven over repentant sinners and of how he may lead the good life he has missed. To Discipline, despite her beatings, he listens humbly and hears good advice on avoiding luxury and bad company, on scorning wealth and striving to live temperately. At the end of her harangue she presents him with a simple scholar's robe in token of his new position and then, though he blames his father for having unwisely given him money, he determines to return home and seek pardon. Maintenant forgives his prodigal son and the play ends with apologies for its not being *moralisé*: Malduict says there's an excuse because it is a *jeu d'enfant*; Maintenant adds that the author is still learning; and Discipline tells the audience that anyway the intention was merely 'to introduce the children'.

Whoever the author, he wrote an entertaining, well-constructed play. There are no *longueurs* here as in so many of the moralities; the dialogue moves swiftly; the plot is integrated and even the fool's irrelevancies have been worked into the action (it is he who directs Finet to Jabien and later participates in the entertainment at Jabien's house). The play opens and closes at the home of Maintenant. It reaches a quite terrible climax in the bloody flogging and hanging of the unrepentant sinner and, notwithstanding the apologies at the conclusion, it stresses its moral a second time by the happy ending which contrasts Finet's awful punishment with the rewards awaiting the contrite Malduict. As for the characters, the silly mother and over-indulgent father are exceedingly well drawn. Mignotte's desire to achieve status by making one of her sons a prelate and the other a judge or lawyer obviously mirrors the ambition of many a mother of any time. Universal, too, is the way in which both parents yield to their children's unreasonable requests and suffer the consequences. Much of the humour of the play was obviously designed for a special audience, but educators of all times will appreciate the satiric intention behind some of the speeches of Instruction, who for a consideration will teach anything from the alphabet to civil and canon law. In form the piece betrays careful workmanship, and the author has been particularly adroit in handling a variety of metres and in using the recurring phrase for comic effect. Once the modern distaste for allegory and personified abstractions has been conquered, it will be found that a play like *Les Enfants de Maintenant* is both imaginative and entertaining.

Curiously enough, certain details in this morality resemble those in much earlier and otherwise quite dissimilar plays. For example, the repentance of Malduict, lamenting his sins to Discipline, recalls, even in its rhythms, the famous scene in Rutebeuf's *Miracle de Théophile* where poor Théophile begs the Virgin for forgiveness, and Jabien's advice to the boys is very like the Devil's to Théophile in this same play. Furthermore, the realistic gaming scenes have something of the verve of the tavern episodes in Bodel's *Jeu de S. Nicolas* and the anonymous *Courtois d'Arras*. Like the latter, too, is the return and forgiveness of the prodigal son. But no direct influence of any of the older plays need be posited. Resemblances are mentioned merely to indicate the range of possibilities in the morality plays. Regarded from a historical point of view they may be considered not only as the descendants of a varied lot of ancestors—the serious religious drama on the one hand, the comedies and farces on the other—but also as themselves pointing forward to the theatre of the future.

XXV

Epilogue

THE drama of medieval France was born in the Church of a desire to make Christian doctrine vivid to all worshippers. The role of the Church in the Middle Ages can hardly be exaggerated. It served not only as a devotional centre, but as the focus of social, intellectual, and artistic life. It provided musicians, painters, sculptors, and architects with a potent reason for exercising their talents and in similar fashion it moved writers to employ their dramatic powers in giving form and substance to the history and teachings of Christianity.

At first playwrights who wrote in the vernacular and used biblical material, men like the humble author of *Les Trois Maries*, probably did little more than translate liturgical texts. But they soon discovered the potentialities of their themes, and, from the twelfth-century dramatist who imaginatively conceived the *Mystère d'Adam* to Arnoul Greban who wrote his magnificent *Passion* in the fifteenth century with the originality and artistry of genius, the best of them did not hesitate to create and embellish for themselves. Every detail of the Passion and Resurrection, indeed of the whole story from the Creation to the Last Judgement, could be made to excite and stimulate the multitude. Moreover, within that vast framework innumerable incidents and characters were to be discovered. It is not surprising, therefore, that from the beginning to the end of the medieval period the biblical mystery play enjoyed a position of special eminence.

Early, however, worship of the saints found expression in simpler plays in their honour, miracle plays no less devotional than the mysteries, but more restricted as to treatment. The oldest surviving examples of these in France are certain liturgical texts from the monastery of Fleury preserved in a twelfth-century manuscript, a Latin St. Nicholas play of approximately the same date by the wandering scholar, Hilarius, and the French *Jeu de S. Nicolas* written by Jean Bodel about the year 1200. In the thirteenth and fourteenth centuries the Virgin

Mary, who had appeared in the Easter and Christmas plays of the Church almost from the beginning, began to assume a dominating position in the saint plays, rescuing evil-doers from the consequences of their sins. Narrative accounts of the miracles of Our Lady in Latin and the vernacular had long been popular in France, but, so far as we know, it was Rutebeuf in his *Miracle de Théophile*, written about 1261, who first brought the Virgin upon the stage in her role of intercessor for erring mortals.

Miracle plays remained popular throughout the fourteenth, fifteenth, and sixteenth centuries, often produced by societies that had been founded for various purposes, among them to commemorate Notre Dame or some special saint by giving performances of plays about them on their holy days. In the mediation of the Virgin for those who had committed a great variety of sins, in the diverse stories of men later canonized, in the multiplicity of colourful plots and characters presented by these pieces, audiences saw their own transgressions and need for grace reflected. They could identify themselves with the sinners saved by acts of contrition; the lives and martyrdoms of the saints presented human values they could share. Dramatically considered, these miracle plays made use of an element of suspense lacking in the biblical plays; their action ranged far and wide and in so doing established a new freedom in the choice of persons, scenes, and emotions.

Once the multiform lives of the saints and the many miracles of the Virgin had been dramatized, it was a short step to turning almost any narrative whatsoever into a play by telling it *par personnages*. Thus it came about that well-known stories appeared in dialogued form to be spoken by performers incarnating the characters in these tales. By 1395 spectators could participate in the trials of the patient Griseldis and during the fifteenth century they could witness the raising of the siege of Orléans by Joan of Arc and the exciting history of the destruction of Troy by the Greeks. Yet these plays remain exceptional rather than characteristic and the possibilities of the serious, non-religious theatre represented by them were not fully exploited until a much later period.

Throughout the time that the biblical and saint plays were

being performed, the spirit of comedy was not absent. Sometimes humorous incidents appear in the midst of the mysteries and miracles; much earlier they are dramatized separately. What part the medieval entertainer played in comedy is uncertain, but surely the jongleur responsible for the circulation of all medieval literature often used impersonation and gestures, perhaps even a simple *mise en scène*, in his recitations. And many of these recitations must have been humorous. He might readily have been available as an actor on occasion, but I am inclined to think that his part in the writing of plays has been exaggerated and that the inspiration of the comic and serious dramatists was in origin the same. At any rate the division between serious and non-serious plays is often ill-defined in our earliest texts. For example, Jean Bodel's *Jeu de S. Nicolas* (*c.* 1200) and the anonymous dramatization of the parable about the prodigal son, *Courtois d'Arras* (before 1228), might equally well be placed in either category.

Dating like these from the thirteenth century are the slight, farcical dialogue, *Le Garçon et l'Aveugle*, a few humorous monologues like Rutebeuf's *Dit de l'herberie*, and Adam le Bossu's two plays, *Le Jeu de la Feuillée*, a curious admixture of satire and fantasy, and his *Jeu de Robin et Marion*, a dramatized *pastourelle*. Nothing else in the domain of true comedy remains from this period and the fourteenth century added little, so far as we know, to its repertory: a few humorous touches exist in the *Palatine Passion* and the miracle plays; Deschamps, who lived at the end of the century, wrote two dramatic monologues, one related to farce and the other to the morality play, and in 1398 we hear that 'jeux de personnages par maniere de farces' existed in Paris. It can be confidently assumed that, despite the paucity of our documents and despite the ravages of the Hundred Years War, farces and humorous skits of various sorts were not banished from France during this time, but it seems equally clear that formal comedy as such did not prosper then. In the fifteenth and sixteenth centuries, however, when the playing of comedies was largely in the hands of the Enfants-sans-souci and the Basochiens, we readily recognize new forms and trends. *Sotties*, farces, dramatic monologues, and humorous moralities flourished and a truly comic theatre came into existence.

Throughout most of its early life the swaddling-clothes of its infancy in the Church remain wrapped about the serious medieval drama. The simultaneous stage-setting and the concluding hymn of Matins, the *Te Deum laudamus*, are ever present, and religious themes predominate whether performances take place in cities, towns, or villages, whether indoors or outside, whether on a single platform, a moving float, or on different levels and scaffolds. Presented at first within the church itself, the plays soon moved into the public squares and the halls of societies organized to honour their patron saints. The performers were for the most part non-professionals and in a true sense amateurs. They, like the authors and audiences, responded to the universal appeal of a dominating faith.

The drama of medieval France, whether serious or comic, exhibits certain stylistic devices common to all writing of the Middle Ages designed for oral presentation. It shares with the *chansons de geste* and the romances, for example, the repetitive phrase intended to aid memory and awaken recognition. In the serious plays such recurring words could also be used as drumbeats to heighten emotion, whereas in the farces and *sotties* they served to underscore humorous lines (often in differing contexts) and nudge an audience into cumulative laughter. Since many medieval plays were destined for a single performance and unexacting spectators, infringements of metrical rules appear in them with relatively greater frequency than in most other forms of literature of the time. It is perhaps safe to assume that these could readily be glossed over by clever actors. However, one must not judge our plays by the rigorous standards of a highly perfected technique like that of the troubadour lyrics or that of the professional theatre of a later day.

In the circumstances and notwithstanding the vast anonymity of the Middle Ages, it is remarkable that the names of so many gifted dramatists survive and that so many excellent plays by them and also by persons unknown to us have enjoyed great popularity in subsequent periods, including our own. The anonymous *Mystère d'Adam*, Rutebeuf's *Miracle de Théophile*, several of the *Miracles de Notre Dame*, the Chantilly *Nativité*, and Greban's *Passion* have been successfully performed in Paris and abroad; the musical *pastourelle*, *Le Jeu de Robin et Marion*,

by Adam le Bossu, and the farce, *Maître Pierre Pathelin*, are
perennial favourites; and even morality plays like Nicolas de la
Chesnaye's *Condamnacion de Bancquet* and the English *Everyman*
can be fruitfully transplanted to the modern stage.

The performances at Oberammergau and the elaborate
spectacles of 1951 before the cathedral of Notre Dame in
Paris give some idea of what the great Passion plays of the
Middle Ages were like. Yet to recapture the full impact of the
serious medieval theatre one must remember the spontaneity
and singleness of purpose animating a group of amateur actors
playing in a relatively homogeneous community before a not
too exigent audience. In modern times students' performances
of the less ambitious plays often seem nearer the spirit of the
originals than the finished productions of experts. At all events
the professional theatre, despite its obvious advantages, can
seldom make vivid and real the simplicity of faith that permeates most of the serious drama of the Middle Ages. Accordingly, when reading the old plays today it is well to keep in
mind their origin in the Church and their primary destination,
le menu peuple de Dieu.

No sharp line of demarcation separates the medieval drama
from its successors.[1] The theatre of the Middle Ages did not suddenly die, but in its slow decline bequeathed to its descendants
a stage and various themes capable of fertile new developments.
The simultaneous *mise en scène* lived on into the seventeenth
century and has sometimes been regarded as one of several
causes contributing to the emergence of the unities. In the first
part of that century the Hôtel de Bourgogne represented a
forest, palace, prison, and sea juxtaposed, and many of the
sketches in the *Mémoire de Mahelot* (begun in 1633) indicate settings reminiscent of those of an earlier time. Lebègue, studying the survival of medieval devices, concludes that 'malgré
l'influence de la Renaissance et les dédains des lettrés, la mise

---

[1] On the French theatre in the sixteenth and seventeenth centuries and its
indebtedness to the medieval drama, see Dabney's *French Dramatic Literature
in the Reign of Henri IV* and Lancaster's *A History of French Dramatic Literature in
the Seventeenth Century*, especially Parts I and III, his *French Tragi-Comedy*, and his
edition of the *Mémoire de Mahelot*. Lanson's *Histoire* and *Esquisse d'une histoire de
la tragédie française* are also valuable. On the monologue see Picot, *Le Monologue
dramatique*.

en scène et les jeux de scène du théâtre médiéval ont persisté jusqu'au XVIIe siècle, et parfois au delà'.[1]

The subject-matter of the medieval drama also survived. Even after Parliament's prohibition of 1548 forbidding *mystères sacrés*, the Confrérie de la Passion continued to play them disguised under the newer titles of *tragédies* and *tragi-comédies*, and even after the performance of Jodelle's *Cléopâtre* in 1552, which for Ronsard, if not for modern critics, introduced a revolution in dramatic art, plays of the medieval type continued to please and to exert an influence. Vauquelin, writing his *Art poétique* about 1575 (though it was not published until 1605), expresses his disapproval of pagan divinities as the characters of tragedy and recommends that dramatists turn instead to the Bible and saints' lives. Indeed, at the end of the sixteenth century the old religious mysteries were still being performed in many communities as an annual event, and among the printed texts of this period it is sometimes difficult to distinguish between mysteries and tragedies. Moreover, in the reign of Henri IV (1589–1610) the surviving references to representations of plays indicate a predominance of texts using material from the Bible and saints' lives over the emerging tragedies, pastorals, eclogues, and tragi-comedies based on classical (or pseudo-classical) sources, and often the latter, in order to appeal to spectators accustomed to medieval fare, adopted religious or allegorical subjects.

The moralities continued to be popular and a few plays resembling them were published as late as the seventeenth century. One, *La Goutte*, a *tragédie nouvelle* by Laffemas printed in 1605, indicates the transition to the newer mode by its sub-title and by taking its plot from Lucian, but, as in the older moralities, its protagonist is an allegorical character. However, the type of play most nearly serving as bridge between the medieval drama and the modern *drame libre* was the tragi-comedy, which Lancaster regards as 'the secularized and modernized representation of the medieval drama, from which it inherited its stage, its traditions and its audience'.[2] In themes it harks back to both the religious and secular elements of the *mystères* and

---

[1] 'Quelques survivances de la scène médiévale', in *Mélanges Cohen*, p. 226.
[2] *The French Tragi-Comedy*, p. 1.

miracles and in construction it resembles them rather than the newer tragedies, which replaced action by words, located the climax of the play near its beginning, and adopted a style heavy with classical borrowings, for tragi-comedy ignores the unities and develops its diffuse plots without restraint.

Comedy is practically extinct in the reign of Henri IV except for the persistence of farce and translations or adaptations from the Italian. The farce, however, is the most enduring of all medieval types of dramatic literature, and farces long continued to be played not only in conjunction with the old mystery plays, but also with the newer tragedies, tragi-comedies, and pastorals. In the sixteenth and early seventeenth centuries, texts called 'comedies' are sometimes reworkings of medieval mystery plays like the 'comedy' *Isaac*, sometimes combinations of serious and farcical medieval themes like the *Comédie admirable intitulée La Merveille* (*c.* 1612–14), which manages to merge the idea of selling one's soul to the devil with that of the trickster tricked. But true farces continued to be written and performed, and those of the early seventeenth century, even when fashioned of Alexandrines, often retained the plots, characters, and general tone of their medieval predecessors. The *sermons joyeux* and the dramatic monologues—*les farces à un personnage*—likewise flourished, enjoyed in the provinces when they were banished from Paris, recited by wandering troupes at fairs when other forms of the theatre were prohibited, and still in vogue in 1707 when they too were forbidden. Accordingly, although other types of comedy seem to have played a relatively minor role before the fifteenth century, some form of farce was always popular and continued to exert a potent and enduring influence, achieving its supreme eminence in collaboration with the genius of Molière.

Molière's indebtedness to the farce has long been recognized, whatever disagreement may obtain as to its extent. Lanson writes, 'Molière est parti de la farce', and attributes the national character of the comedies to the fact that the playwright took his material from 'la vieille farce française, création grossière, mais fidèle image du peuple', and again, more categorically, he writes, 'la farce est logiquement comme historiquement la source de toute la comédie de Molière'.[1] Lancaster indicates

---

[1] *Histoire illustrée*, i. 384, 390.

that Lanson went too far in attributing Molière's origins to the
farce, but admits its influence upon him, notably in *Les Pré-
cieuses ridicules* and *Sganarelle*.[1] In any case, though foreign
elements may have contributed to their flowering, Molière's
comedies, deeply rooted in his native soil, continue the tradition of the Old French farce, and his characters, unlike the
artificial literary figures of Larivey with their dependence on
the classics by way of the Italians, have endured as inheritors
of the spirit of *Pathelin*, characters that are at once contemporary and of all time because they are indigenous and have
been accurately observed.

[1] *History*, iii. 854.

List of Books

THE following list does not contain a complete bibliography, but comprises books, articles, and periodicals referred to in the text and footnotes in abbreviated form. Useful bibliographical material on the medieval French drama will be found in the works referred to below s.v. Bossuat, Cabeen–Holmes, and Henshaw, 'Survey'.

AA. Ausgaben und Abhandlungen aus dem Gebiete der romanischen Philologie.
ABDIAS. *De Historia certaminis apostolici.* Early editions and French translations in the Bibliothèque Nationale, Paris. Also in Johann Albert Fabricius, *Codex apocryphus Novi Testamenti.*
Actes des Apôtres. See Girardot, Auguste-Théodore de.
ADAM LE BOSSU. *Le Jeu de la Feuillée.* See Langlois, Ernest.
—— *Le Jeu de Robin et Marion.* See Langlois, Ernest.
AH. Analecta Hymnica Medii Aevi, G. M. Dreves and C. Blume, ed., Leipzig, 1886 ff.
ALBRECHT, OTTO E. *Four Latin Plays of St. Nicholas from the Twelfth Century Fleury Play-book,* Philadelphia, University of Pennsylvania Press, 1935.
ALLEN, P. S. *The Romanesque Lyric,* Chapel Hill, University of North Carolina Press, 1928.
ANDRESEN, HUGO. 'Bruchstück eines altfranzösischen Mystère', *ZRP,* xxvi (1902), 76–100.
ANTS. Anglo-Norman Text Society.
ANZ, H. *Die lateinischen Magierspiele,* Leipzig, 1905.
ARMSTRONG, EDWARD C. *The French Metrical Versions of Barlaam and Josaphat,* Princeton, 1922 (*Elliott Monographs,* x).
ASCHNER, S. 'Zu "Aucassin und Nicolette" ', *ZRP,* xxxv (1911), 741–3.
ATTINGER, GUSTAVE. *L'Esprit de la commedia dell' arte dans le théâtre français,* Paris, 1950.
ATWOOD, E. BAGBY, and VIRGIL K. WHITAKER, ed. *Excidium Troiae,* Cambridge, Mass., Mediaeval Academy, 1944.
Aucassin et Nicolette. See Roques, M.; Suchier, H. and W.
AUERBACH, ERICH. *Mimesis,* Bern [1946].

BAHLSEN, LEOPOLD. 'Adam de la Hale's Dramen und das "Jus du Pelerin" ', *AA,* xxvii (1885).
BARTSCH, KARL. *Romanzen und Pastourellen. Altfranzösische Romanzen und Pastourellen,* Leipzig, 1870.
BASTIN, JULIA, and EDMOND FARAL, ed. *Onze poèmes de Rutebeuf concernant la croisade,* Paris, 1946.
BECKER, CARL. *Die Mysterien 'Le Siège d'Orléans' und 'La Destruction de Troye la grant', eine sprachliche Untersuchung,* Marburg (diss.), 1886.

T

BECKER, PH. AUG. *Die Narrenspiele des neuentdeckten Mischbands von Treppereldrucken*, Leipzig, 1936. (Also in *Berichte über die Verhandlungen der Sächsischen Akademie der Wissenschaften zu Leipzig, Phil.-hist. Klasse*, 87, 2, 1935.)

BÉDIER, JOSEPH. 'Commencements du théâtre comique en France', *Revue des Deux Mondes*, xcix (1890), 869–97.

—— 'Fragment d'un ancien mystère', *Rom.* xxiv (1895), 86–94.

BÉDIER–HAZARD. Joseph Bédier and Paul Hazard, *Histoire de la littérature française*, 2ᵉ éd. rev., Paris, 1948–9.

BELETHUS, JOANNES. *Rationale Divinorum Officiorum* in *PL*, ccii. 119.

BIGONGIARI, DINO. 'Were there Theatres in the Twelfth and Thirteenth Centuries?' *RR*, xxxvii (1946), 201–24.

BODEL, JEAN. *Le Jeu de S. Nicolas*. See Jeanroy, A.; Warne, F. J.

BÖHME, M. *Das lateinische Weihnachtspiel*, Leipzig, 1917.

BONNELL, JOHN K. 'The Easter *Sepulchrum* in its Relation to the Architecture of the High Altar', *PMLA*, xxxi (1916), 664–712.

BOSSUAT, ROBERT. *Manuel bibliographique de la littérature française du moyen âge*, Melun, 1951.

BQS. Bibliothèque du Quinzième Siècle.

BREUER, HERMANN. 'Untersuchungen zum lateinisch-altfranzösischen Adamsspiel', *ZRP*, li (1931), 625–64; lii (1932), 1–66.

BRINKMANN, HENNIG. 'Zum Ursprung des liturgischen Spieles', *Xenia Bonnensia: Festschrift zum fünfundsiebzigjährigen Bestehen des Philologischen Vereins und Bonner Kreises* (Bonn, 1929), pp. 106–43.

BROOKS, N. C. *The Sepulchre of Christ in Art and Liturgy*, Urbana, 1921. (*University of Illinois Studies in Language and Literature*, vii. 2.)

BROWN, CARLETON. 'An Early Mention of a St. Nicholas Play in England', *SP*, xxviii (1931), 594–601.

—— *Essays and Studies in Honor of Carleton Brown*, New York, 1940.

BRUNET, J. C. *Manuel du libraire et de l'amateur de livres*, Paris, 1860–5.

BUJILA, BERNADINE A., ed. Rutebeuf, *La Vie de Ste Marie l'Égyptienne*, Ann Arbor, University of Michigan Press, 1949.

CABEEN–HOLMES. D. C. Cabeen and Urban T. Holmes, ed. *A Critical Bibliography of French Literature*; vol. i, *The Mediaeval Period*, 2nd ed. rev., Syracuse University Press, 1952.

CARGILL, OSCAR. *Drama and Liturgy*, New York, 1930.

CAZALAS, E. 'Où et quand se passe l'action de *Maistre Pierre Pathelin?*' *Rom.* lvii (1931), 573–7.

CFMA. Les Classiques Français du Moyen Âge.

CHAILLEY, JACQUES. *Histoire musicale du moyen âge*, Paris, 1950.

—— 'Nature musicale du "Jeu de Robin et Marion" ', *Mélanges Cohen*, pp. 111–17.

CHAMBERS, E. K. *The Mediaeval Stage*, Oxford, 1903.

CHAMPION, PIERRE. *Histoire poétique du xvᵉ siècle*, Paris, 1923. (*BQS*, xxvii and xxviii.)

CHANTILLY COLLECTION. See Cohen, Gustave, ed. *Mystères et Moralités*.

CHATELAIN, HENRI, ed. *Le Mistere de S. Quentin*, Saint-Quentin, 1908. (Incomplete edition, Paris, 1907.)

—— *Recherches sur le vers français au xvᵉ siècle*, Paris, 1908. (*BQS*, iv.)

CHEVALDIN, L.-E. *Les Jargons de la farce de Pathelin*, Paris, 1903.

CHEVALIER, ULYSSE. *Poésies liturgiques traditionnelles de l'église catholique en occident*, Tournai, 1893.

CHRIST, KARL, ed. 'Das altfranzösische Passionsspiel der Palatina', *ZRP*, xl (1920), 405–89.

CLÉDAT, LÉON. *Rutebeuf*, Paris, 1891, 1902, 1909.

CLOETTA, W. *Beiträge zur Litteraturgeschichte des Mittelalters und der Renaissance*, Halle, 1890–2.

—— ed. 'Le Mystère de l'Époux', *Rom.* xxii (1893), 177–229.

CLOUZOT, HENRI. *L'Ancien Théâtre en Poitou*, Niort, 1901.

COFFMAN, GEORGE R. *Miracle Play*. 'The Miracle Play: Notes and Queries', *PQ*, xx (1941), 205–11.

—— *New Approach*. 'A New Approach to Medieval Latin Drama', *MP*, xxii (1924–5), 239–71.

—— *New Theory*. *A New Theory concerning the Origin of the Miracle Play*, Menasha, 1914.

—— *Nomenclature*. 'The Miracle Play in England—Nomenclature', *PMLA*, xxxi (1916), 448–65.

—— Review of Young, *Drama of the Mediaeval Church* in *Speculum*, ix (1934), 109–17.

COHEN, GUSTAVE. *Adam le Bossu dit de la Halle, Le Jeu de Robin et Marion, suivi du Jeu du Pèlerin. Transposition*, Paris, 1935.

—— *'Comédie' latine*. *La 'Comédie' latine en France au xiiᵉ siècle*, Paris, 1931.

—— *Livre de conduite*. *Le Livre de conduite du régisseur et le compte des dépenses pour le Mystère de la Passion joué à Mons en 1501*, Paris, 1925. (*BQS*, xxx.)

—— *Mise en scène*. *Histoire de la mise en scène dans le théâtre religieux français du moyen âge*, nouv. éd., Paris, 1926, 1951.

—— ed. *Mystères et Moralités*. *Mystères et Moralités du MS. 617 de Chantilly*, Paris, 1920. (*BQS*, xxv.) A second ed., entitled *Nativités et Moralités liégeoises*, Brussels, 1953, appeared after this volume had gone to press.

—— ed. *Recueil*. *Recueil de farces françaises inédites du xvᵉ siècle*, Cambridge, Mass., Mediaeval Academy, 1949.

—— *Rutebeuf, Le Miracle de Théophile. Transposition*, Paris, 1934, éd. rev., 1948.

—— 'La Scène de l'aveugle et de son valet dans le théâtre français du moyen âge', *Rom.* xli (1912), 346–72.

—— 'Le Théâtre à Paris à la fin du xivᵉ siècle', *Rom.* xxxviii (1909), 587–95.

—— *Théâtre*. *Le Théâtre en France au moyen âge*: I, *Le Théâtre religieux*; II, *Le Théâtre profane*. Paris, 1928.

CONS, LOUIS. *L'Auteur de la farce de Pathelin*, Princeton, 1926 (*Elliott Monographs*, xvii).

CORBIN, SOLANGE. 'Le Manuscrit 201 d'Orléans, drames liturgiques dits de Fleury', *Rom.* lxxiv (1953), 1–43.

Courtois d'Arras. See Faral, Edmond.

COUSINS, C. E. 'Deux parties de dés dans le *Jeu de S. Nicolas*', *Rom.* lvii (1931), 436–7.

—— 'Tavern Bills in the *Jeu de S. Nicolas*', *ZRP*, lvi (1936), 85–93.

COUSSEMAKER, EDMOND DE. *Histoire de l'harmonie au moyen âge*, Paris, 1852.

—— ed. *Œuvres complètes du trouvère Adam de la Halle*, Paris, 1872.

CRAIG, BARBARA, ed. *L'Estoire de Griseldis*, Lawrence, University of Kansas Press, 1954.

CRAIG, HARDIN. 'The Origin of the Old Testament Plays', *MP*, x (1913), 473–87.

CRAIG, JOHN DOUGLAS. *Ancient Editions of Terence*, Oxford, 1929.

CRAWFORD, J. P. WICKERSHAM. *Spanish Drama before Lope de Vega*, 2nd ed. rev., Philadelphia, 1937.

CREIZENACH, WILHELM. *Geschichte des neueren Dramas*, vol. i, 2nd ed. rev., Halle, 1911.

CUISSARD, C. 'La Bibliothèque d'Orléans', *Catalogue général des manuscrits des bibliothèques publiques de France*, xii, Paris, 1889.

DABNEY, LANCASTER E. *French Dramatic Literature in the Reign of Henri IV*, Austin, Texas, 1952.

DAVIES, ROBERT. *Extracts from the Municipal Records of the City of York*, London, 1843.

DELBOUILLE, MAURICE. 'De l'intérêt des Nativités hutoises de Chantilly et de Liège', *Mélanges Cohen*, pp. 75–84.

—— 'Essai sur la genèse des Nativités wallonnes de Chantilly et sur leur adaptation française du xviime siècle', *Mélanges Haust*, pp. 97–125.

DENOMY, A. J. 'An Old French Life of St. Barbara', *Mediaeval Studies*, Toronto, i (1939), 148–78.

DESCHAMPS, EUSTACHE. *Œuvres complètes d'Eustache Deschamps*, ed. by Queux de Saint-Hilaire and Gaston Raynaud, Paris, 1878–1903. (*SATF.*)

DESSALLES, L., and P. CHABAILLE, ed. *Mystère de S. Crespin et S. Crespinien*, Paris, 1836.

DE VITO, MARIA SOFIA. 'L'Origine del dramma liturgico', *Biblioteca della 'Rassegna'*, vol. xxi, 1938.

Dialogus Beatae Mariae et Anselmi de Passione Domini in PL, clix. 271–90.

DILL, SAMUEL. *Roman Society in the Last Century of the Western Empire*, London and New York, 1898.

DOUTREPONT, GEORGES. *La Littérature française à la cour des ducs de Bourgogne*, Paris, 1909. (*BQS*, viii.)

DROZ, EUGÉNIE. *Le Recueil Trepperel*, vol. i, *Les Sotties*, Paris, 1935.

DUBECH, L., and others. *Histoire générale illustrée du théâtre*, Paris, 1931–4.

DÜRRE, KONRAD. *Die Mercatorszene im lateinisch-liturgischen, altdeutschen und altfranzösischen religiösen Drama*, Göttingen, 1915.

DUPIRE, NOËL. *Jean Molinet, la vie, les œuvres*, Paris, 1932.

—— 'Le Mystère de la Passion de Valenciennes', *Rom.* xlviii (1922), 571–84.

DURIEZ, GEORGES. *Les Apocryphes dans le drame religieux en Allemagne au moyen âge*, Lille, 1914.
—— *La Théologie dans le drame religieux en Allemagne au moyen âge*, Lille and Paris, 1914.

EETS. Early English Text Society.
ERLER, O. *Das Mystère de S. Denis und seine Quelle*, Marburg (diss.), 1896.
Estoire de Griseldis. See Craig, B.; Glomeau; Groeneveld.
EVANS, JOAN, and P. STUDER. *Saint Joan of Orleans*, Oxford, 1926.

FABER, F. J. *Histoire du théâtre français en Belgique*, vol. i, Brussels and Paris, 1878.
FABRE, JOSEPH. *La Délivrance d'Orléans, Mystère . . . suivi de la reproduction des meilleures pages de l'ancien Mistère du Siège d'Orléans*, Paris, 1913, 1915.
FABRICIUS, JOHANN ALBERT. *Codex apocryphus Novi Testamenti*, Hamburg, 1703, 1719.
FARAL, EDMOND, ed. *Courtois d'Arras*, 2ᵉ éd. rev., Paris, 1922. (*CFMA*, 3.)
—— 'Le Fabliau latin au moyen âge', *Rom.* l (1924), 321–85.
—— *Les Jongleurs en France au moyen âge*, Paris, 1910. (Also in *Bibliothèque de l'École des Hautes Études*, 187.)
—— *La Littérature latine au moyen âge*, Paris, 1925.
—— *Mimes français du xiiiᵉ siècle*, Paris, 1910.
—— 'Quelques remarques sur le *Miracle de Théophile* de Rutebeuf', *Rom.* lxxii (1951), 182–201.
—— *Recherches sur les sources latines des contes et romans courtois du moyen âge*, Paris, 1913.
FAWTIER-JONES, E. C. 'Les Vies de Ste Catherine d'Alexandrie en ancien français', *Rom.* lvi (1930), 80–104.
FORKERT, F. M. *Beiträge zu den Bildern aus dem altfranzösischen Volksleben auf Grund der Miracles de Nostre Dame*; I and II (*Glaubensleben und Kirchliches Leben*), Bonn, 1901.
FOSTER, F. A., ed. *The Northern Passion, French text*, &c., EETS, *Original Series*, vol. 147 (London, 1916), pp. 102–25.
FOULET, L. and C. FOULON. 'Les Scènes de taverne et les comptes du tavernier dans le *Jeu de S. Nicolas* de Jean Bodel', *Rom.* lxviii (1944–5), 422–43.
FOULON, CHARLES. 'La Représentation et les sources du *Jeu de S. Nicolas*', *Mélanges Cohen*, pp. 55–66.
FOURNIER, ÉDOUARD. *Le Théâtre français avant la Renaissance*, Paris [1873].
FRANK, G. 'Authorship of *Le Mystère de Griseldis*', *MLN*, li (1936), 217–22.
—— 'Beginnings of Comedy in France', *MLR*, xxxi (1936), 377–84.
—— 'Cues in *Aucassin et Nicolette*', *MLN*, xlvii (1932), 14–16.
—— 'Genesis and Staging of the *Jeu d'Adam*', *PMLA*, lix (1944), 7–17.
—— 'Introduction to a Study of the Mediaeval French Drama', *Essays and Studies in Honor of Carleton Brown* (New York, 1940), pp. 62–78.

FRANK, G. ed. *Le Livre de la Passion*, Paris, 1930. (*CFMA*, 64.)

—— 'The *Palatine Passion* and the Development of the Passion Play', *PMLA*, xxxv (1920), 464–83.

—— ed. *La Passion d'Autun*, Paris, 1934. (*SATF*.)

—— ed. *La Passion du Palatinus*, Paris, 1922. (*CFMA*, 30.)

—— *Iconography*. 'Popular Iconography of the Passion', *PMLA*, xlvi (1931), 333–40.

—— 'Rutebeuf and Théophile', *RR*, xliii (1952), 161–5.

—— ed. Rutebeuf, *Le Miracle de Théophile*, 2e éd. rev., Paris, 1949. (*CFMA*, 49.*)

—— 'Vernacular Sources and an Old French Passion Play', *MLN*, xxxv (1920), 257–69.

—— 'Wine Reckonings in Bodel's *Jeu de S. Nicolas*', *MLN*, l (1935), 9–13.

FRANK, TENNEY. 'Decline of Roman Tragedy', *Classical Journal*, xii (1916), 177–87.

—— ed. *Economic Survey of Ancient Rome*, Baltimore, 1933–40.

—— 'Status of Actors at Rome', *Classical Philology*, xxvi (1931), 11–20.

Frankfurter Dirigierrole. See Froning, R.

FRIEDLÄNDER, LUDWIG. *Darstellungen aus der Sittengeschichte Roms*, Leipzig, 1921–3.

FROISSART, *Chroniques*. *Œuvres de Froissart*, ed. Kervyn de Lettenhove; *Chroniques*, vol. xv, Brussels, 1871.

FRONING, R., ed. *Frankfurter Dirigierrole* in *Das Drama des Mittelalters*, vol. ii, Stuttgart, 1891.

FULLER, JOHN BERNARD, ed. *Hilarii Versus et Ludi*, New York, 1929.

Garçon et l'Aveugle, Le. See Roques, M.

GÉROLD, TH. *La Musique au moyen âge*, Paris, 1932. (*CFMA*, 73.)

GILL, AUSTIN. 'A Note on the Gamblers' Quarrel Scene in the *Jeu de S. Nicolas*', *MedÆ*, viii (1939), 50–53.

GIRARDOT, AUGUSTE-THÉODORE DE, ed. *Mystère des Actes des Apôtres représenté à Bourges en avril, 1536*, Paris, 1854.

GLOMEAU, M.-A., ed. *Le Mystère de Griselidis*, Paris, 1923.

GOLENISTCHEFF-KOUTOUZOFF, ÉLIE. *L'Histoire de Griseldis en France au xive et au xve siècle*, Paris, 1933.

GRASS, KARL, ed. *Das Adamsspiele. Anglo-normannisches Mysterium des XII. Jahrhunderts*, 3rd ed. rev., Halle, 1928. (*Romanische Bibliothek*, 6.)

GREBAN, ARNOUL. *Le Mystère de la Passion*. See Paris, Gaston, and Gaston Raynaud.

GRENIER, ALBERT. *La Gaule romaine* in T. Frank, *An Economic Survey of Ancient Rome*, iii (1937), 381–644.

GRIFFIN, NATHANIEL EDWARD, ed. Guido de Columnis, *Historia Destructionis Troiae*, Cambridge, Mass., Mediaeval Academy, 1936.

GRIFFITHS, D. D. *The Origin of the Griselda Story*, Seattle, Washington, 1931. (*University of Washington Publications in Language and Literature*, viii. 1.)

GRINGORE. Œuvres complètes, ed. A. de Montaiglon and J. de Rothschild, Paris, 1858–77.

—— Vie de S. Louis in Œuvres complètes, ed. Montaiglon and Rothschild, vol. ii, 1877.

Griseldis. See Estoire de Griseldis.

GRÖBER, GUSTAV. Geschichte der mittelfranzösischen Literatur, bearbeitet von S. Hofer, Berlin, 1933–7.

—— Grundriss der romanischen Philologie, Strassburg, 1902.

GROENEVELD, HINDERK, ed. 'Die älteste Bearbeitung der Griseldissage in Frankreich', AA, lxxix (1888).

GROULT, PIERRE. 'Le Drame biblique dans Courtois d'Arras', Mélanges Cohen, pp. 47–53.

GUESNON, A. 'Adam de la Halle et Le Jeu de la Feuillée', Moyen-Âge, 2ᵉ série, xix (1915–16), 173–233.

—— 'Publications nouvelles sur les trouvères artésiens', Moyen-Âge, 2ᵉ série, xii (1908), 57–86.

GUESSARD, FRANÇOIS, and EUGÈNE DE CERTAIN, ed. Le Mystère du Siège d'Orléans, Paris, 1862.

GUIDO DELLE COLONNE. See Griffin.

GUY, HENRY. Essai sur la vie et les œuvres littéraires du trouvère Adan de le Hale, Paris, 1898.

HÄPKE, GUSTAV. 'Kritische Beiträge zu Jacques Milet's dramatischer Istoire de la destruction de Troye la grant', AA, xcvi (1899).

HANEBUTH, K. Ueber die hauptsächlichsten Jeanne d'Arc-Dichtungen des 15, 16 und 17 Jahrhunderts, Marburg (diss.), 1893.

HARVEY, HOWARD GRAHAM. The Theatre of the Basoche, Cambridge, Mass., 1941. (Harvard Studies in Romance Languages, xvii.)

HENSHAW, MILLETT. 'Attitude of the Church toward the Stage at the End of the Middle Ages', Medievalia et Humanistica, vii (1952), 3–17.

—— 'Survey of Studies in Medieval Drama: 1933–1950', in Progress of Medieval and Renaissance Studies, Bulletin 21, Boulder, Colorado, 1951.

HILARIUS. See Fuller, John Bernard; Young, Drama, ii. 211–19, 276–90, 337–43.

HILDBURGH, W. L. 'English Alabaster Carvings as Records of the Medieval Religious Drama', Archaeologia, xciii (1949), 51–101.

HILKA, ALFONS. 'Das mittelfranzösische Narcissusspiel (L'Istoire de Narcisus et de Echo)', ZRP, lvi (1936), 275–321.

HINKS, ROGER. Carolingian Art, London, 1935.

HIPPE, MAX. Le Mystère du Roy Avennir par Jehan du Prier, dit le Prieur, Greifswald (diss.), 1906.

Hist. litt. Histoire littéraire de la France.

HOEPFFNER, E. 'Date et composition des Jeux dramatiques de Chantilly', Rom. xlviii (1922), 62–92.

—— Review of Cohen, Mystères et Moralités in Rom. xlvii (1921), 607–12.

HOFER, S. See Gröber, G.

HOLBROOK, R. T., ed. *Maistre Pierre Pathelin*, 2e éd. rev., Paris, 1937. (*CFMA*, 35.)

HULUBEI, ALICE. *L'Églogue en France au xvie siècle*, Paris, 1938.

Incarnation et la Nativité, L'. See Le Verdier, Pierre.

JACOBSEN, J.-P. *Essai sur les origines de la comédie en France au moyen âge*, Paris, 1910. (Also in *RPF*, xxiii [1909], 1–22, 81–106, 161–96, and xxiv [1910], 1–17, 81–97.)

JAHN, OTTO. *Ueber die Subscriptionen in den Handschriften römischer Classiker*, Leipzig, 1851. (Also in *Berichte über die Verhandlungen der Königlich Sächsischen Gesellschaft der Wissenschaften zu Leipzig, Philologisch-historische Classe*, vol. iii, 1851.)

JEANROY, ALFRED, ed. Jean Bodel, *Le Jeu de S. Nicolas*, Paris, 1925. (*CFMA*, 48.)

—— 'Le Mystère de la Passion en France', *JS*, N.S., iv (1906), 476–92.

—— 'Notes critiques sur la *Passion de Semur*', *RLR*, xlix (1906), 220–9.

—— 'Sur quelques sources des mystères de la Passion', *Rom.* xxxv (1906), 365–78.

JENKINS, T. A., J. M. MANLY, M. K. POPE, and J. G. WRIGHT, ed. *La Seinte Resureccion, from the Paris and Canterbury MSS.*, Oxford, 1943. (*ANTS*, iv.)

JENNEY, A. M. 'A Further Word as to the Origin of the Old Testament Plays', *MP*, xiii (1915), 59–64.

JENSEN, HANS CARSTENSEN. *Die Miracles de Nostre Dame . . . untersucht in ihrem Verhältniss zu Gautier de Coincy*, Bonn, 1892.

Jeu du Pèlerin. See Langlois, E.

JONES and MOREY. Leslie Webber Jones and C. R. Morey, *The Miniatures of the Manuscripts of Terence*, Princeton, 1930–1.

JONES, WILLIAM POWELL. *The Pastourelle; a Study of the Origins and Tradition of a Lyric Type*, Cambridge, Mass., 1931.

JORDAN, LEO. 'Die Quelle des *Aucassin* und die Methode des Urteils in der Philologie', *ZRP*, xliv (1924), 291–307.

JORGA, N. *Philippe de Mézières*, Paris, 1896. (*Bibliothèque de l'École des Hautes Études*, 110.)

Jour du Jugement, Le. See Roy, Émile.

JS. Journal des Savants.

JUBINAL, ACHILLE, ed. *Mystères inédits du quinzième siècle . . . d'après le MS. unique de la Bibliothèque Ste-Geneviève*, Paris, 1837.

—— ed. *Œuvres complètes de Rutebeuf*, Paris, 1839, 1874.

KELLY, AMY. *Eleanor of Aquitaine and the Four Kings*, Cambridge, Mass., 1950.

KERNODLE, GEORGE R. *From Art to Theatre*, Chicago, 1944.

KNEISEL, ADOLF. *Das Mystère 'La Passion de Jesu-Christ en rime franchoise'*, Greifswald (diss.), 1906.

KNUDSON, CHARLES A. ' "Hasard" et les autres jeux de dés dans le *Jeu de S. Nicolas*', *Rom.* lxiii (1937), 248–53.

KOEPPEN, BERNHARD. *Die beiden Valencienner Passionen in ihrem Verhältnis zu den Quellen*, Greifswald (diss.), 1911.

KRAVTCHENKO-DOBELMANN, SUZANNE. 'L'Esposalizi de Nostra Dona', *Rom.* lxviii (1944–5), 273–315.

KRESSNER, ADOLF, ed. *Rustebeuf's Gedichte*, Wolfenbüttel, 1885.

LÅNGFORS, A. '*Le Miroir de Vie et de Mort* par Robert de L'Omme', *Rom.* xlvii (1921), 511–31, and l (1924), 14–52.

—— 'Notice des manuscrits . . . suivie de cinq poèmes français sur la parabole des *Quatre filles Dieu*', *Notices et extraits des manuscrits de la Bibliothèque nationale et autres bibliothèques*, xlii, 1932.

—— Review of Sennewaldt, *Miracles de Ste Geneviève*, in *Rom.* lxv (1939), 262–5.

LANCASTER, HENRY CARRINGTON. *The French Tragi-Comedy*, Baltimore, 1907.

—— *A History of French Dramatic Literature in the Seventeenth Century*, Part I, vol. i, Baltimore and Paris, 1929.

—— *Le Mémoire de Mahelot, Laurent et d'autres décorateurs de l'Hôtel de Bourgogne et de la Comédie Française au xviiᵉ siècle*, Paris, 1920.

LANGLOIS, ERNEST, ed. Adam le Bossu, *Le Jeu de la Feuillée*, 2ᵉ éd. rev., Paris, 1923. (*CFMA*, 6.)

—— ed. Adam le Bossu, *Le Jeu de Robin et Marion*, suivi du *Jeu du Pèlerin*, Paris, 1924. (*CFMA*, 36.)

—— 'Interpolations du *Jeu de Robin et Marion*', *Rom.* xxiv (1895), 437–46.

—— 'J. Molinet, auteur du *Mystère de S. Quentin*', *Rom.* xxii (1893), 552–3.

LANSON, GUSTAVE. *Esquisse d'une histoire de la tragédie française*, New York, 1920.

—— *Histoire illustrée de la littérature française*, Paris, 1923.

LA PIANA, G. 'The Byzantine Theatre', *Speculum*, xi (1936), 171–211.

LEBÈGUE, RAYMOND. 'Jean Molinet et la *Passion de Valenciennes*', *Rom.* lix (1933), 438–47.

—— *Mystère. Le Mystère des Actes des Apôtres, contribution à l'étude de l'humanisme et du protestantisme français au xviᵉ siècle*, Paris, 1929.

—— 'La *Passion* d'Arnoul Greban', *Rom.* lx (1934), 218–31.

—— 'Quelques survivances de la mise en scène médiévale', *Mélanges Cohen*, pp. 219–26.

—— *La Tragédie religieuse en France; les débuts (1514–73)*, Paris, 1929.

LECOY DE LA MARCHE, A., ed. *Le Mystère de S. Bernard de Menthon*, Paris, 1888. (*SATF*.)

LEGGE, M. DOMINICA. *Anglo-Norman in the Cloisters*, Edinburgh, 1950.

LEMERCIER, P. 'Les Éléments juridiques de *Pathelin* et la localisation de l'œuvre', *Rom.* lxxiii (1952), 200–26.

LENIENT, CHARLES. *La Poésie patriotique en France au moyen âge*, Paris, 1891.

LEO, ULRICH. 'Studien zu Rutebeuf', *Beihefte zur ZRP*, lxvii, 1922.

LE VERDIER, PIERRE, ed. *Mystère de l'Incarnation et Nativité de Notre Seigneur et Rédempteur Jésus-Christ représenté à Rouen en 1474*, Rouen, 1884–6.

LINDNER, ALFRED. *Plainte de la Vierge*, Upsala, 1898. (Also in *Upsala Universitets Årsskrift*, 1898.)

LIUZZI, FERNANDO. 'Drammi musicali dei sec. xi–xiv: 1. Le vergini savie e le vergini folli', *Studi medievali*, N.S., iii (1930), 82–109.

—— 'L'Espressione musicale nel dramma liturgico', ibid. ii (1929), 74–109.

Livre de la Passion, Le. See Frank, G.

LOOMIS, R. S., and G. COHEN. 'Were there Theatres in the Twelfth and Thirteenth Centuries?', *Speculum*, xx (1945), 92–98.

LOZINSKI, G. Review of Sennewaldt, *Miracles de Ste Geneviève*, in *Rom.* lxvi (1940–1), 538–40.

LUCAS, HARRY H., ed. *Les Poésies personnelles de Rutebeuf*, Paris, 1938.

—— ed. *Rutebeuf: Poèmes concernant l'Université de Paris*, Manchester and Paris, 1952.

MACKENZIE, WILLIAM ROY. *The English Moralities from the Point of View of Allegory*, Boston and London, 1914.

MAGNIN, CHARLES. Review of Monmerqué et Michel, *Théâtre français au moyen âge* in *JS*, 1846–7. See especially *JS* (1847), pp. 36–53 and 151–62.

Maître Pierre Pathelin. See Holbrook, R. T.

MÂLE, ÉMILE. *xiie siècle*. *L'Art religieux du xiie siècle en France*, 3e éd., Paris, 1928.

—— *Fin*. *L'Art religieux de la fin du moyen âge en France*, 3e éd., Paris, 1925.

—— *xiiie siècle*. *L'Art religieux du xiiie siècle en France*, 5e éd., Paris, 1923.

MANITIUS, M. *Geschichte der lateinischen Literatur des Mittelalters*, Munich, 1911–31.

MANLY, J. M. 'Literary Forms and the New Theory of the Origin of Species', *MP*, iv (1907), 577–95.

—— *Pre-Shaksperean Drama*. *Specimens of Pre-Shaksperean Drama*, Boston, 1897, 1903.

MARICHAL, ROBERT. 'Les Drames liturgiques du *Livre de la Trésorerie* d'Origny-Sainte-Benoîte', *Mélanges Cohen*, pp. 37–45.

MARSHALL, MARY H. 'Boethius' Definition of *Persona* and Mediaeval Understanding of the Roman Theater', *Speculum*, xxv (1950), 471–82.

—— 'The Dramatic Tradition Established by the Liturgical Play', *PMLA*, lvi (1941), 962–91.

—— 'Theatre in the Middle Ages: Evidence from Dictionaries and Glosses', *Symposium*, iv (1950), 1–39 and 366–89.

MAXWELL, IAN. *French Farce and John Heywood*, Melbourne and London, 1946.

MedÆ. *Medium Ævum*.

Mélanges Cohen. *Mélanges d'histoire du théâtre du moyen âge et de la renaissance offerts à Gustave Cohen*, Paris, 1950.

Mélanges Haust. *Mélanges de linguistique romane offerts à M. Jean Haust*, Liège, 1939.

MERCADÉ. See *Passion d'Arras*.

MERGUET, HUGO. *Lexikon zu den Schriften Cicero's*, Jena, 1877–94.

MEYBRINCK, ERNST. 'Die Auffassung der Antike bei Jacques Milet, Guido de Columna und Benoît de Ste-More', *AA*, liv (1886).

MEYER, ALFRED. *Das Kulturhistorische in 'Le Mystère du Siège d'Orléans'*, Leipzig (diss.), 1906.

MEYER, HELENE. *Die Predigten in den Miracles de Nostre Dame par personnages*, Berlin (diss.), 1911. (Also in *Rom. Forsch.*, xxxi [1912], 706–98.)

MEYER, PAUL. 'Les Trois Maries, mystère liturgique de Reims', *Rom.* xxxiii (1904), 239–45.

MEYER, W. *Frag. Bur.* Fragmenta Burana, Berlin, 1901.

MEYER-LÜBKE, W. 'Aucassin und Nicolette', *ZRP*, xxxiv (1910), 513–22.

MICHA, ALEXANDRE. 'La Femme injustement accusée dans les *Miracles de Notre Dame par personnages*', *Mélanges Cohen*, pp. 85–92.

MICHEL, FRANCISQUE, ed. *Le Mystère de S. Louis*, Roxburghe Club, Westminster, 1871.

MIGNE, *PL.* J. P. Migne, ed. *Patrologiae Cursus Completus: Patrologia Latina*, Paris, 1844–64.

MILET, JACQUES. *L'Istoire de la Destruction de Troye la grant.* See Stengel, E.

MLN. *Modern Language Notes.*

MLR. *Modern Language Review.*

Miracles de Nostre Dame. See Paris, Gaston, and U. Robert.

Miracles de Ste Geneviève. See Sennewaldt, C.

MOKROSS, KARL. *Weitere Studien über das Mystère 'La Passion de Jesu-Christ en rime franchoise'*, Greifswald (diss.), 1908.

MOLINET, JEAN. *Mystère de S. Quentin.* See Chatelain, Henri.

MOMBRITIUS, B. *Sanctuarium seu Vitae Sanctorum*, Paris, 1910.

MONACI, ERNESTO. *Facsimili di documenti per la storia delle lingue e delle letterature romanze*, Rome, 1910.

MONMERQUÉ ET MICHEL. L. J. N. Monmerqué and F. Michel, ed. *Théâtre français au moyen âge*, Paris, 1834, 1842, 1929.

MORAWSKI, T. 'La "Moralité" du cœur et des cinq sens', *RLR*, lxv (1927), 71–85.

MOREY, CHARLES RUFUS. *Mediaeval Art*, New York, 1942.

MORTENSEN, JOHAN. *Le Théâtre français au moyen âge.* Traduit du suédois par E. Philipot, Paris, 1903.

MOSTERT, W., and E. STENGEL, ed. 'L'Ystoyre et la vie de S. Genis', *AA*, xciii (1895).

MP. *Modern Philology.*

MULLER, H. F. 'Pre-history of the Mediaeval Drama: the Antecedents of the Tropes and the Conditions of their Appearance', *ZRP*, xliv (1924), 544–75.

Mystère d'Adam. See Grass, Karl; Studer, Paul.

Mystère de S. Bernard de Menthon. See Lecoy de la Marche.

Mystère de S. Crespin et S. Crespinien. See Dessalles, L., and Chabaille.

Mystère du Siège d'Orléans. See Guessard, F., and Certain.

Mystère du Vieux Testament. See Rothschild, James de.

Mystères et Moralités du MS. 617 de Chantilly. See Cohen, Gustave.

Mystères inédits du quinzième siècle. See Jubinal, Achille.

Nativité et le Geu des trois Roys, La. See Whittredge, R.

Neo. Neophilologus.

NICOLL, ALLARDYCE. *Masks, Mimes and Miracles*, London, 1931.

OLDÖRP, BERNHARD. *Untersuchungen über das Mystère 'La Vengance Nostre-seigneur, Paris, 1491, Anthoine Verard' und sein Verhältnis zu dem 'Mystère de la Vengence de Nostre Seigneur Jhesucrist, etc.' . . .*, Greifswald (diss.), 1907.

OLIVER, THOMAS EDWARD. *Jacques Milet's Drama, 'La Destruction de Troie la grant'; its principal source; its dramatic structure*, Heidelberg (diss.), 1899.

OSTROWSKI, OTTO. *Le Mystère de S. Crespin et S. Crespinien . . .*, Greifswald (diss.), 1909.

OUDIN, JEAN. *Mystère de S. Genis.* See Mostert, W., and Stengel.

PAINTER, SIDNEY. *The Reign of King John*, Baltimore, 1949.

—— *William Marshal, Knight-Errant, Baron and Regent of England*, Baltimore, 1933.

PARFAICT, FRANÇOIS and CLAUDE. *Dictionnaire des théâtres de Paris, contenant toutes les pièces qui ont été représentées jusqu'à présent . . .*, Paris, 1756, 1767.

—— *Histoire du théâtre français depuis son origine jusqu'à présent . . .*, Paris and Amsterdam, 1735–49.

PARIS, GASTON. *Poèmes et légendes du moyen âge*, Paris, 1900.

—— and GASTON RAYNAUD, ed. *Le Mystère de la Passion d'Arnoul Greban*, Paris, 1878.

—— and U. ROBERT, ed. *Miracles de Nostre Dame par personnages*, Paris, 1876–93. (*SATF.*)

PASCAL, R. 'On the Liturgical Drama of the Middle Ages', *MLR*, xxxvi (1941), 369–87.

Passion d'Amboise. See Picot, E., *Fragments inédits.*

Passion d'Arras. See Richard, J.-M.

Passion d'Autun. See Frank, G.

Passion de Semur. See Roy, É.

Passion des Jongleurs. See Foster, F. A.; Pfuhl, Erich; Theben, Hermann.

Passion du Palatinus. See Christ, K.; Frank, G.

Passion provençal du MS. Didot. See Shepard, William P.

PATZER, OTTO. 'The *Miracles de Nostre Dame* and the Fourteenth Century', *MLN*, xx (1905), 44–48.

PAUPHILET, ALBERT. *Le Legs du moyen âge, études de littérature médiévale*, Melun, 1950.

PENN, DOROTHY. *Staging of the 'Miracles de Nostre Dame par personnages'*, New York, 1933.

PETIT DE JULLEVILLE, L. *Comédie. Histoire du théâtre en France. La Comédie et les mœurs en France au moyen âge*, Paris, 1886.

—— *Comédiens. Histoire du théâtre en France. Les Comédiens en France au moyen âge.* Paris, 1885.

—— *Mystères. Histoire du théâtre en France. Les Mystères*, Paris, 1880.

—— *Répertoire. Histoire du théâtre en France. Répertoire du théâtre comique en France au moyen âge*, Paris, 1886.

PFUHL, ERICH, ed. *Die weitere Fassung der altfranzösischen Dichtung . . . über Christi Höllenfahrt und Auferstehung*, Greifswald (diss.), 1909.

PIAGET, ARTHUR. 'Simon Greban et Jacques Milet', *Rom.* xxii (1893), 230–43.

PICOT, ÉMILE, ed. 'Fragments inédits de mystères de la passion : la *Passion d'Amboise*', *Rom.* xix (1890), 264–82.

—— 'Le Monologue dramatique dans l'ancien théâtre français', *Rom.* xv (1886), 358–422, xvi (1887), 438–542, xvii (1888), 207–75.

—— *Recueil général des Sotties*, Paris, 1902, 1904, 1912. (*SATF*.)

PIÉTRESSON DE SAINT-AUBIN, P. 'La Passion de Notre Seigneur Jésus-Christ', *Bibliothèque de l'École des Chartes*, lxxxv (1924), 310–22.

PL. See Migne.

PMLA. Publications of the Modern Language Association of America.

PQ. Philological Quarterly.

QUYNN, D., and H. S. SNELLGROVE. 'Slanderous Comedies at the University of Orléans in 1447', *MLN*, lvii (1942), 185–7.

RABY, F. J. E. *A History of Christian-Latin Poetry from the Beginnings to the Close of the Middle Ages*, Oxford, 1927.

RAUHUT, FRANZ. 'Der *Sponsus*', *Rom. Forsch.*, l (1936), 21–50.

RAYNAUD, GASTON. 'Les *Congés* de Jean Bodel', *Rom.* ix (1880), 216–47.

REESE, GUSTAVE. *Music in the Middle Ages*, New York, 1940.

REICH, H. *Der Mimus*, Berlin, 1903.

REINHARD, JOHN R. 'The Literary Background of the *Chantefable*', *Speculum*, i (1926), 157–69.

Résurrection du Sauveur. See Jenkins *et al.*; Wright, J. G.

RICHARD, J.-M., ed. *Le Mystère de la Passion, texte du manuscrit 697 de la Bibliothèque d'Arras*, Arras, 1891.

RICKERT, EDITH. *Chaucer's World*, New York, 1948.

RILEY, HENRY THOMAS, ed. *Gesta Abbatum Monasterii S. Albani*, vol. i. Rolls Series, London, 1867.

RLR. Revue des langues romanes.

RÖSLER, MARGARETE. 'Die Beziehungen der Puis zu den Gilden', *ZRP*, xlvi (1926), 687–93.

ROHNSTROEM, OTTO. *Étude sur Jehan Bodel*, Upsala, 1900.

ROKSETH, YVONNE. *La Musique d'orgue au xve siècle et au début du xvie*, Paris, 1930.

ROLLAND, JOACHIM. *Théâtre comique en France avant le xve siècle. Essai bibliographique*, Paris, 1926.

Rom. Romania.

Rom. Forsch. Romanische Forschungen.

RONSJÖ, EINAR. *La Vie de S. Nicolas par Wace*, Lund, 1942.

ROQUES, MARIO, ed. *Aucassin et Nicolette*, 2e éd. rev., Paris, 1929. (*CFMA*, 41.)

ROQUES, MARIO. 'D'une application du calcul des probabilités à un problème d'histoire littéraire', *Rom.* lviii (1932), 88–99.

—— ed. *Le Garçon et l'Aveugle*, 2ᵉ éd. rev., Paris, 1921. (*CFMA*, 5.)

—— 'Recueil général des lexiques français du moyen âge', *Bibliothèque de l'École des Hautes Études* (1936), p. 264.

—— Review of Cons, *L'Auteur de la farce de Pathelin*, in *Rom.* liii (1927), 569–87.

ROTHSCHILD, JAMES DE, ed. *Le Mistere du Viel Testament*, Paris, 1878–91. (*SATF*.)

ROY, ÉMILE. *Études. Études sur le théâtre français du xivᵉ et du xvᵉ siècle. La Comédie sans titre . . . et les Miracles de Notre Dame par personnages*, Paris et Dijon, 1901. (*Revue bourguignonne*, xi.)

—— ed. *Le Jour du Jugement, mystère français sur le grand schisme*, Paris, 1902.

—— *Mystère. Le Mystère de la Passion en France du xivᵉ au xviᵉ siècle; étude sur les sources et le classement des mystères de la Passion*, Paris et Dijon, 1903, 1904. (*Revue bourguignonne*, xiii, xiv.)

—— ed. *Passion de Semur* in Roy, *Mystère de la Passion en France*, pp. 73*–123*; 3–203.

RPF. Revue de philologie française et de littérature.

RR. Romanic Review.

RUTEBEUF. *Le Miracle de Théophile.* See Frank, G.; Jubinal; Kressner.

SADRON, PIERRE. 'Notes sur l'organisation des représentations théâtrales en France au moyen âge', *Mélanges Cohen*, pp. 205–18.

SAINTE-BEUVE, C.-A. *Nouveaux Lundis*, vol. iii, Paris, 1870.

SAINTE GENEVIÈVE COLLECTION. See Jubinal, *Mystères inédits*; Sennewaldt; Whittredge.

SALVERDA DE GRAVE, J. J. Review of Cohen, *Mystères et Moralités*, in *Neo.* vi (1921), 274–80.

SATF. Société des Anciens Textes Français.

SAULNIER, V.-L. 'Le Théâtre de Barthélemy Aneau', *Mélanges Cohen*, pp. 147–58.

SCHAAB, OTTO. *Studien über den Teil der beiden Valencienner Passion-Mysterien welcher über die Auferstehung Christi handelt*, Greifswald (diss.), 1909.

SCHELUDKO, D. 'Orientalisches in der altfranzösischen erzählenden Dichtung', *ZFSL*, li (1928), 255–93.

SCHNELL, HERMANN. 'Untersuchungen über die Verfasser der *Miracles de Nostre Dame par personnages*', *AA*, xxxiii (1885).

SCHREINER, HEINRICH. *Weiterer Studien über die erste Valencienner Passion*, Greifswald (diss.), 1907.

SCHÜTTPELZ, O. *Der Wettlauf der Apostel und die Erscheinungen des Peregrinispiels im geistlichen Spiel des Mittelalters*, Breslau, 1930. (*Germanistische Abhandlungen*, 63.)

SEEFELDT, PAUL. *Studien über die verschiedenen mittelalterlichen dramatischen Fassungen der Barbara-legende, nebst Neudruck des ältesten 'Mystère de Ste Barbe en deux journées'*, Greifswald (diss.), 1908.

Seinte Resureccion. See Jenkins *et al.*; Wright, J. G.

SENNEWALDT, CLOTILDE, ed. *Les Miracles de Ste Geneviève*, Frankfurt, 1937. (*Frankfurter Quellen und Forschungen*, 17.)

SEPET, M. *Les Prophètes du Christ*, Paris, 1878.

SEVERS, J. B. *The Literary Relationships of Chaucer's Clerke's Tale*, New Haven, 1942. (*Yale Studies in English*, 96.)

SHEPARD, WILLIAM P., ed. *La Passion provençale du manuscrit Didot*, Paris, 1928. (*SATF.*)

SM. Studi Medievali.

SP. Studies in Philology.

SPANKE, HANS. Review of Fuller, *Hilarii Versus et Ludi*, in ZFSL, lvi (1932), 249–54.

—— 'St. Martial-Studien', ZFSL, liv (1931), 282–317 and 385–422, lvi (1932), 450–78.

Sponsus. See Cloetta, W.; Young, *Drama of the Medieval Church*, ii. 361–9.

STADLER-HONEGGER, MARGUERITE. *Étude sur les Miracles de Notre Dame par personnages*, Paris, 1926.

STENGEL, E., ed. *L'Istoire de la Destruction de Troye la grant*, Marburg and Leipzig, 1883.

—— Review of Roy, *Mystère de la Passion*, in ZFSL, xxix. 2 (1906), 165–90.

STONE, E. N. *Adam . . . a Translation*, Seattle, Washington, 1926. (University of Washington, *Publications in Language and Literature*, iv [1926], 159–93.)

STREBLOW, EMIL. *Le Mystère de Semur. Ergänzende Bemerkungen zu der Ausgabe von Roy*, Borna–Leipzig, 1905. (Greifswald diss.)

STUART, DONALD CLIVE. *Stage Decoration in France in the Middle Ages*, New York, 1910.

STUDER, PAUL. *Le Mystère d'Adam, an Anglo-Norman Drama of the Twelfth Century*, Manchester, 1918, 1928.

STUMPFL, ROBERT. *Kultspiele der Germanen als Ursprung des mittelalterlichen Dramas*, Berlin, 1936.

SUCHIER, HERMANN and WALTHER, ed. *Aucassin und Nicolette*, Paderborn, 1932, 1946. (Latest editions rev. by Walther Suchier.)

SYMONS, DOM THOMAS. 'Sources of the Regularis Concordia', *Downside Review*, lix (1941), 14–36, 143–70, 264–89.

TAYLOR, H. O. *The Mediaeval Mind*, New York, 1919.

THEBEN, HERMANN, ed. *Die altfranzösische Achtsilbnerredaktion der 'Passion'*, Greifswald (diss.), 1909.

THOMAS, ANTOINE. 'Notice biographique sur Eustache Marcadé', *Rom.* xxxv (1906), 583–90.

—— 'Le Théâtre à Paris et aux environs à la fin du xivᵉ siècle', *Rom.* xxi (1892), 606–11.

THOMAS, CATHERINE B. C. 'The Miracle Play at Dunstable', *MLN*, xxxii (1917), 337–44.

THOMAS, LUCIEN-PAUL. 'Les Strophes et la composition du *Sponsus*: textes latin et roman', *Rom.* lv (1929), 45–112.

THOMAS, LUCIEN-PAUL. 'La Versification et les leçons douteuses du *Sponsus*: texte roman', *Rom.* liii (1927), 43–81.

TIVIER, HENRI. *Étude sur le Mystère, du Siège d'Orléans et sur Jacques Milet, auteur présumé de ce mystère*, Paris, 1868.

TOLDO, P. 'Études sur le théâtre français du moyen âge et sur le rôle de la nouvelle dans les farces et dans les comédies', *Studj di Filologia romanza*, ix (1903), 181–369.

TRAVER, HOPE. *The Four Daughters of God, a Study of the Versions of this Allegory with Especial Reference to those in Latin, French and English*, Philadelphia, 1907. (Bryn Mawr diss.)

Trois Maries. See Meyer, P.

TUNISON, J. S. *Dramatic Traditions of the Dark Ages*, Chicago, 1907.

VÄÄNÄNEN, VEIKKO, ed. *D'Une Fame de Laon . . . par Gautier de Coinci*, Helsinki, 1951.

VALOIS, NOËL. 'Étude sur le théâtre français au xive siècle', *JS* (1903), pp. 677–86.

Vie (or *Mystère*) *de S. Louis*. See Michel, Francisque. See also Gringore.

Vieux Testament. See Rothschild, James de.

VIOLLET LE DUC, EUGÈNE. *L'Ancien Théâtre françois*, Paris, 1854–7.

VITO. See De Vito.

WALBERG, E. *Quelques aspects de la littérature anglo-normande*, Paris, 1936.

WALTON, THOMAS. 'Staging *Le Jeu de la Feuillée*', *MLR*, xxxvi (1941), 344–50.

WARNE, F. J., ed. Jean Bodel, *Le Jeu de S. Nicolas*, Oxford, 1951.

WECHSSLER, E. *Die romanischen Marienklagen*, Halle, 1893.

WHITTREDGE, RUTH, ed. *La Nativité et le Geu des Trois Roys*, Bryn Mawr (diss.), 1944.

WILLIAMS, ARNOLD. *The Characterization of Pilate in the Towneley Plays*, East Lansing, Michigan, 1950.

WILMOTTE, MAURICE. *Études critiques sur la tradition littéraire en France*, Paris, 1909.

WRIGHT, EDITH ARMSTRONG. *The Dissemination of the Liturgical Drama in France*, Bryn Mawr (diss.), 1936.

WRIGHT, JEAN GRAY, ed. *La Résurrection du Sauveur*, Paris, 1931. (*CFMA*, 69.)

—— *Study of the Themes of the Resurrection in the Mediaeval French Drama*, Bryn Mawr (diss.), 1935.

YOUNG, KARL. *The Drama of the Medieval Church*, Oxford, 1933.

—— *Origin.* 'Concerning the Origin of the Miracle Play', *Manly Anniversary Studies in Language and Literature* (Chicago, 1923), pp. 254–68.

ZEYDEL, EDWIN H. 'Knowledge of Hrotsvitha's Works prior to 1500', *MLN*, lix (1944), 382–5.

ZFSL. *Zeitschrift für französische Sprache und Literatur.*

ZRP. *Zeitschrift für romanische Philologie.*

INDEX

Abbey of S. Martial, *see* Limoges.
Abdias, 192.
Abelard, 53, 56, 68.
Abregiés, see Mons.
Actes des Apôtres, 168–70, 192–3.
actors: attitude of Church toward, 4;
in late comedies, 244–5, 249–50,
253; in liturgical plays, 69; in ver-
nacular plays, 163–9, 193; lay, in
transitional plays, 75; Roman, 4.
Adam, see Mystère d'Adam.
Adam le Bossu, 85, 96, 168, 225–6;
Jeu de la Feuillée, 211–16, 221, 225–
31, 242, 244, 267; *Robin et Marion*,
211–16, 231–6, 242, 267–8.
Adgar, 123.
Adoratio Crucis, 22–23.
Adso, 132.
Aesopus, 4.
Afranius, 1.
Alcuin, 15.
Alecis, Guillaume, 253 n., 258.
altar, 32–34, 69.
Amiens, 67, 116.
Amis et Amiles, 115, 123, 156.
amphitheatres, 14.
Amphitruo, 12.
Andrieu de la Vigne, 198.
Anglo-Norman, 76, 79, 88.
*Anglo-Norman Resurrection, see Seinte
Resureccion.*
Annunciation, 42.
Anselm, see *Dialogus*.
Antichrist: in *Jour du Jugement*, 132–4;
in play from Tegernsee, 64 n., 70,
132.
Aquinas, St. Thomas, 184.
Archelaus, Herod's son, 36, 38.
Archisynagogus, 42.
Armiger, 36–37.
Arnulfus of Orléans, 16.
Arras, 96–97, 99, 102, 213, 216, 225–
30, 235.
art, influence of plays on, 175.
Aucassin et Nicolette, 237–42.
audiences, *see* spectators.
Augsburg, 75 n.
Aulularia, 12–13.

authors of plays, 173–4, 253. *See also*
under authors' names.
Aveugle et le Boiteux, 198.
Avignon, 64, 70, 71 n.

Babio, 13, 211, 216.
Balaam, 40, 42.
Barlaam and Josaphat, 199.
Basochiens, 249–50, 258, 261, 267.
Baucis et Traso, 13.
Beauvais: *Peregrini*, 28, 66–67; *Daniel*,
55–57, 66–69.
Bede, 7.
Belethus, 24.
Belle Dame sans mercy (by Alain Char-
tier), 252–3.
Benedictines, 67.
Benediktbeuern: Christmas play, 42–
43, 70, 81; Passion plays, 26, 29 n.
Benoît de Sainte-More, 207–8.
bergeries, 232–3.
Berthe au grand pied, 115.
Besançon, 33.
Bibliothèque Ste Geneviève, plays
from, 136–53, 201; see also *Miracles
de Ste Geneviève* and titles of indivi-
dual plays.
Bilsen, 36.
Blasphémateurs du nom de Dieu, 248.
Boccaccio, 156, 159, 200.
Bodel, Jean, 95–98, 168; *Chanson des
Saisnes*, 96; *Congé*, 96–97; *Jeu de S.
Nicolas*, 48, 85, 95–106, 156, 210–16,
242, 264–5, 267.
Boethius, 7, 16 n.
Boileau, 234.
Bonaventura, see *Meditations*.
Bouchet, Jean, 174, 188.
Boulogne, 118 n.
Bourges, see *Actes des Apôtres*.
Boy Bishop, 42, 43 n.
Byzantium, drama in, 3–4.

Caiaphas, 87–88.
Cain and Abel, 77–78, 80, 195.
Calliopius, 8.

PRINTED IN GREAT BRITAIN AT THE UNIVERSITY PRESS, OXFORD
BY VIVIAN RIDLER, PRINTER TO THE UNIVERSITY